Shakespeare Against War

Shakespeare Against War

Pacifist Readings

Robert White

EDINBURGH
University Press

Edinburgh University Press is one of the leading university presses in the UK. We publish academic books and journals in our selected subject areas across the humanities and social sciences, combining cutting-edge scholarship with high editorial and production values to produce academic works of lasting importance. For more information visit our website: edinburghuniversitypress.com

Edinburgh University Press Ltd
13 Infirmary Street
Edinburgh EH1 1LT

Typeset in 11/13pt Sabon LT Pro
by Cheshire Typesetting Ltd, Cuddington, Cheshire, and
printed and bound in Great Britain

A CIP record for this book is available from the British Library

ISBN 978 1 3995 1621 1 (hardback)
ISBN 978 1 3995 1623 5 (webready PDF)
ISBN 978 1 3995 1624 2 (epub)

Contents

Acknowledgements

I have tried not to repeat or presuppose material from my chapter on Shakespeare in a previous book, *Pacifism and English Literature: Minstrels of Peace* (2008), by dealing with different plays and in different ways, though some revised overlaps proved difficult to avoid in sections on *Henry V* and *Hamlet*. Failing to cite these important examples would have left a culpably large hole in the argument. Chapter 3, '"Food for powder": Casualties of War', is a heavily revised version of an invited paper initially delivered to a conference on 'Shakespeare and Mortality' at Shakespeare's Globe in London, organised by Farah Karim-Cooper as part of the quatercentenary proceedings in 2016. Chapter 6 on love and war revises and adds new material to my essay 'Love and War: War Wives and Widows' published in *Literature, Emotions, and Pre-Modern War*, edited by Claire McIlroy and Anne M. Scott (Yorkshire: Arc Humanities Press, 2021), a *festschrift* for Andrew Lynch.

Two recent books, in particular, have encouraged me to think my approach is not so perverse as it may seem to some. These are *Shakespeare at Peace* by John S. Garrison and Kyle Pivetti (2019) and *Shakespeare's Military Spouses and Twenty-First-Century Warfare* by Kelsey Ridge (2021). Both are presentist accounts whereas this book is more historical, though I attempt to draw attention to how processes identified by Shakespeare are still with us. An important new book is *Shakespeare at War: A Material History*, edited by Amy Lidster and Sonia Massai, (2023), which deals with historical appropriations of Shakespeare in times of wars, though without consideration of pacifism.

Another book which complements Ridge's is Alan Warren Friedman's *Shakespeare's Returning Warriors – and Ours* (2021), which unfortunately I found too late for detailed inclusion here. This draws on modern clinical studies of returning soldiers demonstrating Post-Traumatic Stress Disorder and their failure to reintegrate into civilian society, finding unmistakable case studies in earlier literature, such as Homer's Odysseus. Shakespearean examples abound, from the very earliest *Henry VI* plays and their sequel *Richard III* and all the succeeding plays involving war.

While not advancing an overt anti-war thesis, Friedman's summary is as trenchant as Ridge's, and implicitly supports my own theme in Part II of this book:

> *Shakespeare's Returning Warriors – and Ours* addresses a major though underexamined paradigm in Shakespeare's plays: the difficult and usually disastrous return to society of military leaders who have triumphed on the battlefield but then fail to make a successful transition back to the domestic realm. Almost all of them fail so greatly, in fact, that, regardless of their intentions or initial circumstances (which vary greatly), they usually succeed only in causing great harm: destroying those who are closest to them – and themselves – and leaving the social order considerably worse off than it was before they began their botched transition (xiii).

There are too many people to thank who have helped in various ways in the writing of this book, but I single out three late and sorely missed friends who contributed many ideas in conversation and vigorous fellow-feeling, Veronica Brady who was a lifelong and revered pacifist activist, John Willett, and Catherine Belsey. I happily dedicate the book to them and am saddened they cannot read it. Among others, I offer special thanks to Scott Newstok for his uncanny ability to suggest exactly the right reference at the right time, John Goodridge and Stuart Rees (founder of Centre for Peace and Conflict Studies, Sydney University), who both suffered chapters to read, and the two anonymous readers for Edinburgh University Press who commented with generosity and stringency on the whole manuscript. Many others have shared books and ideas, answered queries, inadvertently pointed new directions for my thinking, or provided all-important moral support. These include (among others) Susan Broomhall, Daniel Brown, Dympna Callaghan, Hugh Craig, Emily Crawford, Tanya Dalziell, Daniel Derrin, Kirk Essary, Geoff Gallop, Nigel Gray, Rebecca Huntley, John Kinsella, Michael Levine, Andrew Lynch, Davis McInnis, Sonia Massai, Richard Meek, Katrina O'Loughlin, Bríd Phillips, Kathryn Prince, Ciara Rawnsley, Lawrence Rosenwald, Horst Ruthroff, Peter Underwood (Medical Association for the Prevention of War). Of course, I do not suggest any of these necessarily agrees with my approach, but as the saying goes, we all stand on the shoulders of others, and this is nowhere more true than in the world of scholarship. My professional artist friend Olga Sankey has expertly advised on the cover image. My daughters Marina and Alana continue to practise what I preach, both living lives full of peace, compassion and social conscience.

Quotations from Shakespeare are taken from *The Arden Shakespeare: Complete Works* edited by Richard Proudfoot, Ann Thompson and

David Scott Kastan (London: Thomson Learning, 2001), and occasionally, where convenient, the online Folger Shakespeare Library.

The British Library has kindly given permission for the cover image captioned 'Mayday Scene. Booke of Sir Thomas More' (Harley 7368, f.9). Shakespeare's plea for tolerance towards immigrants in the dramatic manuscript of the collaborative play *Sir Thomas More*, this is the only surviving literary manuscript page in Shakespeare's handwriting. It is discussed in this book on the topic of refugees in Chapter 3.

Part I

Men At War

Chapter 1

'Look upon the hideous god of war': Reading Shakespeare as a Pacifist

When wasteful wars shall statues overturn,
And broils root out the work of masonry,
Not Mars his sword nor war's quick fire shall burn
The living record of your memory.

(Sonnet 55)

Shakespeare in his drama provides eloquent calls to war and heroism when these are appropriate to the action and to the character speaking. However, more often than not these are undercut, balanced against, or outweighed by compelling appeals to peaceful alternatives, conveyed through narrative structure, dramatic context and poetic utterance. Essays in the most recent book on the subject, *Shakespeare at War: A Material History*, edited by Amy Lidster and Sonia Massai, reveals a plurality of possible approaches:

> Views about war, like much else in Shakespeare, are not only multiple and varied across the canon, they are also nuanced through complexity of characterization or dramatic irony within a fictive world.[1]

Changing world events, political circumstances, social attitudes and personal beliefs account for the multiplicity of attitudes towards both war itself and Shakespeare's war narratives in particular. However, by and large the readings have been conducted within some overarching assumptions, that war will always be with us as 'the natural order' and can sometimes be justified, that tales of courage in combat are intrinsically uplifting, and that the existence of disciplined standing armies is necessary in the building of nationhood. Less often considered are the ways in which these

---

1. Amy Lidster and Sonia Massai (eds), *Shakespeare at War: A Material History* (Cambridge University Press, 2023), 1.

assumptions are ethically challenged in Shakespeare's plays, when conscience and the costs in human lives intersect with military imperatives.

Among the many possibilities of different views, one avenue has rarely been systematically explored, that Shakespeare shows through his plays a deep scepticism about war and a temperamental inclination towards peaceful resolution to conflict. Samuel Johnson described Shakespearean comedy as 'a mode of thinking congenial to his nature', and I believe much the same can be said on behalf of peace in his dramatic forays into war and peace.[2] Given the undiminishing cultural authority accorded to Shakespeare on behalf of a range of different causes for over four centuries, it seems important at least to pursue an argument that he was at heart anti-war and proto-pacifist. The pen – or in his case the quill – is mightier than the sword.

The dramatist gives enough evidence to locate his human sympathies as centred on exercising sympathetic imagination and a core of values that include anti-war sentiments and peaceful resolutions, though the latter do not always eventuate without ominous qualification pointing to potential future conflict. In this way idealism is tempered with realism. More generally, it also emerges that his plays trace underlying processes of causes and human consequences of war which have repeatedly been played out through history down to the present day. Some also reveal Shakespeare's apparently lifelong curiosity about what makes the senior military trained mind tick, with portrayals of commanding officers finding themselves out of their depth in love relationships. In imagery and themes, war infiltrates love, with problematical consequences.

Shakespeare's knowledge of war was immense and detailed, as established by the critical pioneers in the field, C. G. Cruickshank in *Elizabeth's Army* and Paul A. Jorgensen in *Shakespeare's Military World*,[3] followed by many others who have analysed particular aspects. But in the critical heritage of Shakespearean studies there is not much discussion of peace. Remarkably, even in the volume covering the Renaissance in the recent six-volume *A Cultural History of Peace*, Shakespeare rates barely a mention,[4] and there is no entry on 'Peace' in Charles Edelman's encyclopaedic *Shakespeare's Military Language*.[5] *The Oxford Companion to Shakespeare* also has no such entry, but in the very short summary

2. 'Preface to Shakespeare', *Dr Johnson on Shakespeare*, ed. W. K Wimsatt (Harmondsworth: Penguin Shakespeare Library, 1960), 64.
3. C. G. Cruickshank, *Elizabeth's Army* (London, 1946), and Paul A. Jorgensen, *Shakespeare's Military World* (Los Angeles: California University Press, 1956).
4. Isabella Lazzarini, *A Cultural History of Peace in the Renaissance* (London: Bloomsbury, 2020).
5. Charles Edelman, *Shakespeare's Military Language* (London: Athlone Press, 2000).

under 'War' in that volume, Martin Wiggins concludes by circumspectly acknowledging at least the anti-war content: 'Shakespeare typically evokes both sides of the question: there is undoubtedly patriotism in the treatment of the French campaigns of *1 Henry VI* and *Henry V*, but the plays also never lose sight of the bloody, destructive realities of battle'.[6] Other critics, reluctant to concede even this much, are positively scathing in pre-empting a peace-centred approach to Shakespeare as a 'hopeless' and 'utopian' cause. One places it as reminiscent of 'various earnest, radical, sometimes violent attempts in the 1960s and 1970s to reshape society into a kind of secular paradise'.[7] The bias is not confined to Shakespearean criticism. Recent academic studies in the Social Sciences (for example, Psychology and Sociology) reflect a related imbalance of coverage when dealing with armed combat. A thorough statistical study has found that 'The academic literature in the social sciences focuses more on violence and aggression than nonviolence and pacifism',[8] and this by a large margin.

A couple of essays stand out as initial clarion calls for a scholarly mission. One brief and modest precursor was published in 1918, significant as the final year of the exhausting and demoralising First World War which had dulled popular enthusiasm for war and sharpened minds to the appeal of peace. It was also a year significant for the cause of suffragettes, with the passing of the *Representation of the People Act* giving the vote to qualified women, and also the *Parliament (Qualification of Women) Act* giving the right to women of election to parliament. In an article titled 'War and Peace in Shakespeare', Zabelle C. Boyajian, writing in *The Contemporary Review*, challenged the prevailing view of Shakespeare's glorification of war and 'military virtues', asserting instead the author's 'gentleness'. The word 'gentle' is used twice to describe the author of the plays in the First Folio, in the introductory material to that momentous publication. 'The main point', Boyajian argues, is that 'Shakespeare's most attractive women are all peace-lovers – they do not believe in bloodshed or violence', citing as evidence the views of Rosalind, Viola, Virgilia, Lady Percy, Portia wife of Brutus (who commits suicide) and Cressida.[9] Moreover, she writes, 'There is no serious

6. Martin Wiggins, 'War' in *The Oxford Companion to Shakespeare*. Michael Dobson, Stanley Wells, Will Sharpe, Erin Sullivan (eds), Second ed. online version (Oxford University Press, 2015), 155.
7. Patrick Gray, 'Shakespeare and War', *Critical Survey* 30 (2018), 1–25, 3.
8. Daniel M. Mayton II, *Nonviolence and Peace Psychology* (New York: Springer, 2009), Section 1.1.
9. Zabelle C. Boyajian, 'War and Peace in Shakespeare', *The Contemporary Review* 114 (1918), 569–77, 569.

attempt in Shakespeare to justify any war morally' (570), concluding that 'he thoroughly understood the philosophy of pacifism' (576). Boyajian is now forgotten but at the time was a celebrated painter living in London, and respected author of books and essays on writers.

Writing almost seventy years later in 1995 and apparently unaware of Boyajian's article, the Quaker poet-academic Laurence Lerner took a similar tack, also drawing on the example of Shakespeare's women, whose fortunes by then had become a respected academic pursuit. He invoked the analogy of the late-century consolidation in academic writing and teaching of women's studies, a discipline whose perspective has now become an essential approach in all branches of the humanities, social sciences, law, and beyond. It is unlikely that nowadays any university teacher of literature would – or could – entirely ignore women writers in any period, or the material condition of women in history. More generally, gender studies have become embedded as compulsory studies in literary theory courses. Lerner's intention was to advocate on behalf of an equally ambitious project for literary scholars and teachers signalled in his title, 'Peace Studies. A Proposal'. The 'Proposal' is that the study of literature can contribute to a wider educational, social, and political 'peace movement'.[10] Lerner argues that the diverse range of methodologies forged by feminism can potentially apply also in peace studies:

> Just as women's studies concerns itself with asking how far all experience is conceptually gendered, so peace studies can ask how far militarism informs our conceptualizing of other experience. (648)

A comparably double-pronged methodology can apply by first looking at positive representations in literature of peace / women, and secondly providing resistant and 'against the grain' readings of militaristic / misogynistic attitudes in texts. Lerner offers a brief, exemplary analysis of *Henry V* along these lines:

> A pacifist reading of *Henry V* will search for two things. First, for those moments when the text complicates the simple heroism which it appears to glorify; and second, those occasions when we resist the text, by measuring it against criteria which, as readers committed to a contrary ideology, we bring to bear on it. Naturally we do not use these criteria to perform a simple act of rejection; we rather ask them to operate as a palinode, rejecting the text while not abolishing it, leaving it to interact with its own contradiction. (647)

10. Laurence Lerner, 'Peace Studies: A Proposal', *New Literary History*, 26 (1995), 641–65.

In other words, if we interpret 'as readers committed to a contrary ideology', the plays can be enriched by acknowledging a plurality of sometimes conflicting points of view, which may include pacifism.

My own previous contribution, *Pacifism and English Literature: Minstrels of Peace*,[11] was more general in scope than this book, containing just one chapter on Shakespeare in an attempt to historicise his works within the anti-war tradition of Renaissance humanism, and showing that Shakespeare was far from alone amongst his predecessors and contemporaries. My earlier account left much more to be said on Shakespeare's plays as individual works. For example, I dealt with some comedies in which war is a backdrop, but not the equally relevant *All's Well That Ends Well*; with the Graeco-Roman *Troilus and Cressida* and *Coriolanus* but not *Antony and Cleopatra*; with *Hamlet* and *Macbeth* but not *Othello* and *King Lear*. The book mentioned briefly the History plays in general in which war is a constant subject, but without fully exploring the distinction between civil and international wars, nor the paradoxical attitudes represented, for example, in Falstaff's situationally located and often self-contradictory words and roles. A primary aim then was to show that anti-war viewpoints did not emerge only in the second Henriad, as some scholars maintain, following the lead of Steven Marx in his pioneering essay 'Shakespeare's Pacifism',[12] let alone as late as the openly anti-war *Troilus and Cressida* (1601) as others have assumed. Following Marx's lead focused mainly on 'just war theory' in *Henry V*, John Gittings offers a measured and qualified version of the 'late starter' view. After conceding that Shakespeare 'never glorified war unambiguously', he goes on to say that he 'shifted in his later years towards a more distinctly pacific outlook':

> As with Homer, Shakespeare is too great an artist, and his genius is too finely tuned to the human predicament, for us to attach either pro- or anti-labels to his work, but our understanding is enriched by the breadth of his view.[13]

It is difficult to disagree with such a balanced conclusion, especially from the author of a timely historical study entitled *The Glorious Art of*

11. R. S. White, *Pacifism and English Literature: Minstrels of Peace* (London: Palgrave, 2008).
12. Steven Marx, 'Shakespeare's Pacifism', *Renaissance Quarterly*, 45 (1992), 49–95. For my own views on the article, see R. S. White, 'Pacifist Voices in Shakespeare', *Parergon: Journal of the Australian and New Zealand Association for Medieval and Early Modern Studies*. 17 (1999), 135–62.
13. John Gittings, *The Glorious Art of Peace: From the Iliad to Iraq* (Oxford University Press, 2012).

Peace, except to counter that a 'distinctly pacific outlook' can be found throughout Shakespeare's writing if we look beneath the surface.

Some have acknowledged the contemporary urgency of the debate in the light of the weapons constantly being developed as more and more catastrophically destructive killing machines. At the Shakespeare Association of America conference in 2006 (in the depths of invasions of Afghanistan and Iraq), a roundtable panel discussion on 'The Military Theater' organized by Scott Newstok included an abstract by Steven Marx titled 'Shakespeare Against Militarism'. This begins by boldly stating, 'I believe Shakespeare's role in regard to the contemporary military should be to help expose and oppose the plague of militarism that infects American society'. More recently in 2019, we find a forthright, statement in *Shakespeare at Peace* by John S. Garrison and Kyle Pivetti:

> Shakespeare thought a great deal about the causes of war. But we want to pursue another option – that Shakespeare has a great deal more to say about the causes of peace. That he was a pacifist is still worth hearing.[14]

Shakespeare at Peace is a lively, presentist study, reading Shakespeare in the light of modern attitudes such as 1960s' 'flower power', Bob Dylan's protest lyrics, Barack Obama's surprising (prematurely awarded?) Nobel Peace Prize in 2009, Donald Trump's aggressively racially exclusionist verbiage, and related contemporary cultural and political topics. The phrase 'still worth hearing', however, gives pause for thought, since very few writers have ever argued that Shakespeare 'was a pacifist'.

War studies

Lerner's 'Proposal' may have failed to ignite a movement analogous to feminism in widespread acceptance, but since the 1990s scholarly studies on war itself have proliferated in Shakespeare studies, at least showing the breadth and continuing importance of the subject. These are certainly not pro-war in orientation, but for the most part they are factually based, widening our respect for Shakespeare's detailed knowledge of warfare but with the effect of imputing to him a neutrality on the moral issues it raises. In a survey article on the field, Andrew Hiscock notes that such interest stems from Jorgensen's *Shakespeare's Military World*, and adds:

---

14. John S. Garrison and Kyle Pivetti, *Shakespeare at Peace* (London: Routledge, 2019), 3.

Jorgensen lamented that analyses lacked adequate historicization, choosing rather to foreground thematic or psychological interests than an engagement with Tudor military culture.[15]

Accordingly, as Hiscock documents, war has become a happy hunting ground for new historicists, many of whom see the drama as necessarily complicit with state justifications of war, given the dangers of non-compliance with public policy, as Patricia Cahill explains: 'what links such works to discourses of modernity are their ideological investments in narratives of national identity and their strategies for charting the terrain of otherness'.[16] This set of assumptions more or less preclude anti-war attitudes, as being too liable to state disapproval. Nina Taunton in *1590s Drama and Militarism: Portrayals of War in Marlowe, Chapman, and Shakespeare's Henry V*, scours archives of military Early Modern manuals, treatises and correspondence, asking questions about 'stratagems of war' and how the chain of command operates. Her considerations once again do not extend to objections to the existence of military force itself.[17]

Simon Barker's *War and Nation in the Theatre of Shakespeare and his Contemporaries* does harshly interrogate the value systems underlying military life.[18] Historical accounts of Elizabethan military experience reveal a systemic culture and profession whose overarching *raison d'étre* is war, where training seeks to instil uniformity of outlook based on discipline, obedience, and following orders in the service of violence usually waged in organised fashion. All these conditions, I hope to show, are present in Shakespeare's plays.

Some scholars approach the subject of war in Shakespeare's plays from a dramaturgical point of view, bypassing questions about concepts of war and peace. For example, Charles Edelman in *Brawl Ridiculous: Swordfighting in Shakespeare's Plays* (1992) is concerned with the weapons used and how such scenes were staged, with an eye to Elizabethan performance conditions and conventions.[19] Kate McLoughlin's

15. Andrew Hiscock, '"More warlike than politique": Shakespeare and the theatre of war – a critical survey', *Shakespeare*, 7 (2011), 221–247, 228.
16. Patricia Cahill, *Unto the Breach: Martial Formations, Historical Trauma, and the Early Modern Stage* (Oxford University Press, 2008), 3.
17. Nina Taunton, *1590s Drama and Militarism: Portrayals of War in Marlowe, Chapman and Shakespeare's 'Henry V'* (Aldershot: Ashgate, 2001).
18. John S. Garrison and Kyle Pivetti, *Shakespeare at Peace*; Kelsey Ridge, *Shakespeare's Military Spouses and Twenty-First-Century Warfare* (New York: Routledge 2021); Simon Barker, *War and Nation in the Theatre of Shakespeare and his Contemporaries* (Edinburgh University Press, 2021).
19. Charles Edelman, *Brawl Ridiculous: Swordfighting in Shakespeare's Plays* (Manchester University Press, Revels Plays Companion Library, 1992).

Authoring War: The Literary Representation of War from the 'Iliad' to Iraq (2011), generously scattered with Shakespearean allusions, examines more specific issues than war itself, again in terms of staging necessities. Since battle-scenes with whole troops could not possibly be enacted on stage, Shakespeare conveys 'news' of action to both the characters and audiences, making his accounts analogous to modern *reportage*.[20] Like journalists, Shakespeare's 'reporters' as anxious eye-witnesses could be trustworthy, or unreliably peddling propaganda and false rumours. The figure himself appears as 'RUMOUR painted full of tongues' in the opening to *2 Henry IV*:

> Upon my tongues continual slanders ride,
> The which in every language I pronounce,
> Stuffing the ears of men with false reports.
>
> (Induction, 6–8)

Shakespeare clearly understood that in uncertainties of the battlefield the adage by Sun Tzu, the classic Chinese military strategist applies, 'all warfare is based on deception'. McLoughlin's analysis is not presented from a viewpoint which is either sympathetic to, nor critical of war as an issue, but dwells instead on how war has been 'represented' through reports in dramatic, poetic and fictive terms. Another historical study is by Susan Harlan, *Memories of War in Early Modern England: Armour and Militant Nostalgia in Marlowe, Sidney and Shakespeare*, in which the trope of arming and disarming enacts a struggle between male bodies harking back to Medieval chivalry, outmoded in Shakespeare's time but perhaps viewed nostalgically.[21]

If there is a prevailing orthodoxy among critics, it is probably that Shakespeare presents sympathetically 'just wars' but not 'unjust' ones such as the Trojan War in *Troilus and Cressida*. Paola Pugliatti takes up the theme in *Shakespeare and the Just War Tradition*, drawing mainly on the many military manuals of the day.[22] Essays in Patrick Gray's *Shakespeare and the Ethics of War*, tend to follow the editor's introductory preference in steering an intended Aristotelian medium line based on just war theory.[23] But at least tacitly this overlooks the many wars that

20. Kate McLoughlin's *Authoring War: The Literary Representation of War from the 'Iliad' to Iraq* (Cambridge University Press, 2011), 39–42.
21. Susan Harlan, *Memories of War in Early Modern England: Armour and Militant Nostalgia in Marlowe, Sidney and Shakespeare* (London: Palgrave, 2016).
22. Paola Pugliatti, *Shakespeare and the Just War Tradition* (Burlington: Ashgate, 2010).
23. Patrick Gray (ed.), *Shakespeare and the Ethics of War* (New York: Berghahn Books, 2019).

defy such a neat binarism, especially the civil wars in the History plays in which it is rarely possible to discriminate between right and wrong. In reality, almost always *both* sides to a conflict claim to be engaged in a 'just war', which is a barely logical rhetorical vacuity invariably claimed by all aggressors. Shakespeare regularly reflects the moral complexity of such conflicts waged in an ethical grey area.

'Just war' theorists rarely address the fundamentalist argument that the phrase is a contradiction in terms, and that the objective of killing people can never be just. The rejection of military force as inherently unjust was a view available in the Early Modern period and usually couched in Christian terms with reference to the Gospels in particular. Desiderius Erasmus in the early 1500s was the main spokesman:

> As to the usual arguments and means of justifying war ... [if] you look narrowly into the case, you will find that they are chiefly the private, sinister, and selfish motives of princes, which operate as the real causes of all war.[24]

'The real causes of all war' is categorical in refuting the 'usual arguments and means of justifying war'. It could be applied especially to civil wars, as a description of the familial, internecine struggles by rival claimants to the English throne in Shakespeare's chronicle plays, despite the antagonists' high-minded 'arguments' and dynastic justifications. The only sitting king who resists the fray is the outrightly pacifist Henry VI, who pays dearly for his misfortune in being the holder by birth of the office coveted by princes holding 'private, sinister, and selfish motives'. In my next chapter, I hope to show that the notion of 'just war' is not unreservedly endorsed in the multivocal and dialectic medium of Shakespearean dramatic action, and that Erasmus's view is, more often than not, represented in the plays.

Another widely expressed approach appeals to Medieval and Early Modern codes of 'honour' as justifying violence in war. This too seems not to be the case without severe qualification in the plays. The jurist Theodor Meron in *Bloody Constraint: War and Chivalry in Shakespeare* concludes that the plays in general,

> deride the claim that war is necessary for the sake of honour or to save face. They bring into relief the unmitigated horrors of war. Finally, they demonstrate the inescapable futility of war'.[25]

---

24. Desiderius Erasmus, *Complaint of Peace*, English edition 1795; quoted from first American edition, (Boston and New Jersey: Charles Williams and D. Allinson, 1813), 132.
25. Meron, *Bloody Constraint: War and Chivalry in Shakespeare*, (Oxford University Press, 1998), 22.

I hope in Chapter 3 to illustrate Shakespeare's regular habit of contextually undercutting notions of honour. Another counter to positive views of war lies in emphasising the social degradations caused by it in the Early Modern period, an Erasmian theme reflected also in the plays. Curtis Breight in *Surveillance, Militarism and Drama in the Elizabethan Era* robustly challenges the new historicist argument that dramatists of necessity fell into line behind state policy, asserting instead that poverty and land enclosures created a whole sub-class which mainly bore the brunt of the dreadful suffering caused by war, under an exploitative state policy of social control, and that writers were well aware of this.[26] Nick de Somogyi in *Shakespeare's Theatre of War* emphasises the unpleasant realities of Early Modern war – especially siege warfare – and its deadly consequences for individuals and society.[27] He deals with casualties of war, showing that theatre, given its metaphorical use in the phrase 'theatre of war', was a medium in which views opposed to war could be played out. There are then, some critical studies which incrementally advance Lerner's project.

Shakespearean soldiers

Wars and soldiers are ubiquitous in the plays. Among the forty works (including collaborations), at least twenty-five are actually set in a time of war, usually historically specified. It is remarkable also how much detailed and specialised military terminology occurs in every single play, as though metaphors of war percolate into all aspects of society.[28] The 'Index of Shakespeare's Works' appended to Edelman's *Shakespeare's Military Language* shows that military vocabulary occurs in every play from first to last, even in the most unlikely. In the chronicle History plays and most tragedies some form of national or international conflict is overt and central to the plots, but it is also just below the surface and indirectly present in other plays. A point about *Hamlet* in particular made by Pugliatti can be applied to a string of other plays. She describes *Hamlet* as,

> the play in which war, although absent as staged event, is most insistently present both as topic of discussion and as metaphor . . . Although war is

26. Curtis Breight, *Surveillance, Militarism and Drama in the Elizabethan Era* (Basingstoke: Macmillan 1996).
27. Nick de Somogyi, *Shakespeare's Theatre of War* (Aldershot: Ashgate, 1998).
28. Edelman, *Shakespeare's Military Language*, 413.

visually absent from the action, the pressure of the threat of war does not relent throughout the whole play.[29]

In qualified terms, something similar can be said about *Much Ado About Nothing*, *All's Well That Ends Well*, and *Cymbeline*. Even in *The Comedy of Errors* the emotional backdrop is an international trade war between Ephesus and Syracuse. Transgressing merchants face punishments including death, turning them into civilian casualties of an international conflict. In the other play involving twins, *Twelfth Night*, the survivors of shipwreck are forced to remain *incognito* and disguised since their ship's involvement in piracy related to an unspecified international maritime conflict that makes them liable to death if identified. We are reminded that in the 1590s a naval 'cold war' was being waged between England and Spain, both employing piracy as a secretive, state sanctioned weapon. In these plays the issue of war, though 'visually absent', is a constant 'threat' driving the plots, and this will be a part of my subject here.

My second theme in this book, relating to war and love in Shakespeare's plays, deals with his psychologically penetrating insights into a surprisingly frequent number of high-ranking military officers who become emotionally compromised or 'perplexed in the extreme'. Among others, these include Titus Andronicus, Harry Hotspur, Henry V (in his courtship behaviour), Othello, Iago and Cassio, Macbeth, Hector, Agamemnon and Achilles, Mark Antony and Enobarbus, and Coriolanus. Even Sir John Falstaff, in some of his various roles as soldier, recruiting officer, and clown is another complex figure in this over-represented professional class. Bertram in *All's Well that Ends Well* and Posthumus in *Cymbeline* are mercenaries rather than commissioned officers, but they too are placed in intimate situations for which they are emotionally unprepared. Most if not all of the many Shakespearean military officers are cast in an ambiguous and critically distanced light, and their professional training contributes to an ambivalence which prevents unequivocal audience sympathy. They provide case studies in what Jorgenson describes as Shakespeare's 'special interest in the qualifications, problems and psychology of army officers',[30] especially, we might add, when the soldier is forced into more unaccustomed circumstances of a love relationship. I have no biographical theory to offer about what drew Shakespeare to return so often to exposing the emotional inadequacies of this military

---

29. Paola Pugliatti, *Shakespeare and the Just War Tradition* (Farnham: Ashgate, 2010), 139.
30. Jorgensen, *Shakespeare's Military World*, 65.

type, but it is an issue which certainly intrigued him and at least invites closer analysis. I shall be drawing on a book which draws parallels with the modern equivalent, *Shakespeare's Military Spouses and Twenty-First-Century Warfare*, written by Kelsey Ridge, who has special knowledge of the experiences of 'army wives' in the modern American military industry.[31] Ridge interprets the various fates of Shakespeare's 'military spouses' in the light of such factors as the profession's cultural insularity, the effect of war on gender relations in a prevailing context of 'toxic masculinity', the stresses uniquely affecting marriage in the armed forces, and mental illness afflicting combat veterans, such as post-traumatic stress disorder, their suffering adversely affecting their partners as well.

Looking beyond the major protagonists, it is remarkable how many and particularised army personnel there are among the plays' *dramatis personae*. We find subordinate officers sometimes presented sympathetically and sometimes satirically, such as 'Corporals' Nym and Bardolph (the latter promoted to 'Lieutenant' in *Henry V*, before being executed for looting a church), the Welsh patriot Captain Fluellen who is an expert on the laws of war, alongside the Irish Captain Macmorris and Captain Jamy from Scotland, each mocked for their regional accents. The choleric, emotionally explosive ensign Pistol ('Captain Peesel') is representative of an apparent Elizabethan infiltration of underqualified and degraded men into a previously respectable army class. He is ridiculed by Doll Tearsheet in *2 Henry IV*, in a speech delivered in a way that suggests the dramatist expected it to strike a chord of recognition from his audience:

> Captain! thou abominable damned cheater, art thou not ashamed to be called captain? And captains were of my mind, they would truncheon you out, for taking their names upon you before you have earned them. You a captain? You slave! For what? For tearing a poor whore's ruff in a bawdy-house? He a captain? Hang him, rogue, he lives upon mouldy stewed prunes and dried cakes. A captain? God's light, these villains will make the word as odious as the word 'occupy'; which was an excellent good word before it was ill sorted: therefore captains had need look to 't.
>
> (*2 Henry IV*, 2.4.137–47)

Even when violence is not in issue, Shakespeare often represents the profession of soldier as one to be comically portrayed, as in Jaques' satirically unsympathetic description of the egotistical and splenetic state of

---

31. Kelsey Ridge, *Shakespeare's Military Spouses and Twenty-First-Century Warfare*.

> a soldier,
> Full of strange oaths, and bearded like the pard,
> Jealous in honour, sudden, and quick in quarrel,
> Seeking the bubble reputation
> Even in the cannon's mouth.
>
> (*As You Like It*, 2.7.149–53)

The comic Don Armado in *Love's Labour's Lost* is 'a soldier, a man of travel' (5.1.100), greeted by Holofernes as 'most military sir' (5.1.34). He regards it as 'base for a soldier to love' (1.2.57) and would prefer to draw his sword 'against the humour of affection' (1.2.58–9), but when unmasked for hypocrisy by falling in love, he reverts to his professional ethic, vowing, 'I will right myself like a soldier' (5.2.721), as though his profession is an ingrained guide to ethics.

Contrasting with the array of satirically drawn, lowly officers stand some non-officers who are wholly sympathetic, army 'privates' such as Michael Williams, John Bates, and the Boy in *Henry V*, who all display true courage in confronting their fears in battle. More lowly still are motley groups of reluctant and infirm Gloucestershire conscripts chosen by Falstaff in *2 Henry IV* in a mockery of army recruitment. Mouldy objects because of the domestic problems that service will cause in his family: 'My old dame will be undone now for one to do her husbandry and her drudgery. You need not to have pricked me, there are other men fitter to go out than I' (3.2.115). Touchingly, Feeble is more 'courageous' and 'as valiant as the wrathful dove or most magnanimous dove' in accepting likely death: 'I will do my good will, sir; you can have no more' (3.2.156). Shakespeare shows detailed knowledge of the reputations and psychologies of all ranks, reserving special and critical attention for those who have most responsibility as leaders.

Beyond the circle of men in war settings are completely innocent civilians who become 'collateral damage' of war. Caught up in military circumstances are women such as Desdemona and Emilia, wives neglected by their husbands such as Harry Hotspur's wife Kate, Anne Neville the emotionally ravaged wife of Richard III, Cressida, Coriolanus's Virgilia, and Brutus's Portia. Lady Macduff is the most shocking example, abandoned (as she sees it) by her husband, and massacred with her children by Macbeth's secret police, simply because they are related to Macduff. Cinna the Poet in *Julius Caesar* is an almost symbolic casualty representing writers in civil war, killed by insurrectionists for no reason other than that his name coincidentally matches that of a conspirator. Although the scene verges on a grotesquely comic tone, it has a deadly import in showing the indiscriminate and dehumanising consequences of war:

3 PLEBIAN
Your name, sir, truly.
CINNA
Truly, my name is Cinna.
1 PLEBIAN
Tear him to pieces, He's a conspirator.
CINNA
I am Cinna the poet! I am Cinna the poet.
4 PLEBIAN
Tear him for his bad verses, tear him for his bad verses.
CINNA
I am not Cinna the conspirator.
4 PLEBIAN
It is no matter, his name's Cinna. Pluck but his name out of his heart and turn him going.
3 PLEBIAN
Tear him, Tear him!

(3.3.26–35)

The chilling episode suggests that the profession of writing itself was hazardous during civil war. As a writer in an age of political unrest, when contentious words could be punished with cutting off a hand or a tongue, the playwright must have felt an acutely personal investment in the fate of the poet Cinna. Likewise, a hapless scrivener in *Richard III* speaks for writers who understand why witnesses to corruption are too frightened to expose lies or to act as whistle blowers to power:

Here's a good world the while! Who is so gross
That cannot see this palpable device?
Yet who's so bold but says he sees it not?
Bad is the world, and all will come to naught
When such ill-dealing must be seen in thought.

(3.6.10–14)

Spoken directly to the audience in soliloquy, he anticipates Seamus Heaney's line written in time of war, 'Whatever you say, say nothing'. In Shakespeare, when war rages, nobody is exempt from danger.

Anti-war Shakespeare

There are plenty of anti-war invectives in Shakespeare's epigrammatic phrases sprinkled through the whole canon, some spoken by critics of war and others by apologists whose words inadvertently reveal its true horror: 'This churlish knot of all abhorred war' (*1 Henry IV*, V.i.16), 'the stern tyrant war', 'the hideous god of war' and 'O, war thou son of hell', all from *2 Henry IV* (Induction 14; 2.3.35; 5.2.33). On occasions when 'Doth dogged war bristle his angry crest / And snarleth in the gentle eyes of peace' (*King John*, 4.2.149–50), the result is 'vast confusion' (*King John* 4.3.152). Antony 's provocation in *Julius Caesar* to 'let slip the dogs of war' (3.1.273) draws on the same bestial imagery. Soldiers in war are licensed in cruelly taking 'our goodly agèd men by th'beards', and committing sexual violence in 'Giving our holy virgins to the stain / Of contumelious, beastly, mad-brained war' (*Timon of Athens*, 5.1.172–4). War is 'fierce and bloody' (*King John*, 1.1.17) and 'cruel' (*Timon of Athens*, 4.3.60). Its symbols are 'famine, sword, and fire' (*Henry V*, Prologue 7), the phrase repeated to describe the destructiveness of 'blood and sword and fire' (*Henry V*, 1.2.131). The behaviour of Macbeth in war is praised by his King but reported in terms that reflect repulsively on the bloody activity itself, as he 'unseamed' his adversary 'from the naves to th'chops / And fixed his head upon our battlements' (*Macbeth* 1.2.24–5), the fate that awaits the protagonist himself. Civil war is 'civil butchery' (*1 Henry IV*, 1.1.13), condemned for its unnatural, intra-family slayings. 'The ugly form of base and bloody insurrection' is described as 'damned commotion' coming 'in base and abject routs, led on by bloody youth, guarded with rags, / And countenanced by boys and beggary' (*2 Henry IV*, 4.1.32–3).

Counterpointing the anti-war refrains are emotionally and morally compelling appeals to peace, for example Henry VI's meditation, sitting on a 'molehill' overlooking the field of battle below him (see Chapter 2), and the Duke of Burgundy at the end of *Henry V*. The opposite of civil war is 'civil peace', 'Whose white investments figure innocence, / The dove and very blessed spirit of peace' (*2 Henry IV*, 4.1.45–46 *passim*). In Shakespeare's last single-authored play *The Tempest*, Gonzalo envisages an ideal society without war:

> All things in common nature should produce
> Without sweat or endeavour, treason, felony,
> Sword, pike, knife, gun, or need of any engine
> Would I not have. But nature should bring forth
> Of its own kind, all foison, all abundance,
> To feed my innocent people.
>
> (*The Tempest*, 2.1.160–5)

In addition, some version of peaceful harmony is built into the structure and closure of each of Shakespeare's plays through poetic justice, although in some the loss after violence significantly outweighs the achieved peace (the death of Cordelia), as though to emphasise that those lost through war cannot be retrieved.

Speaking more generally, it is a perennial refrain that pacifists are ineffectual 'idealists', while those who believe that war is ineradicable and can genuinely solve problems, are 'realists'. Shakespeare shows that it is a false antithesis, and that it is by being brutally realistic about the nature of war that we can recognise the necessity of contemplating ideals. It is a short step to claim that pacifism is a more rational, open-eyed and 'realistic' mode of thinking, than militarism predicated on dreams of victory and myths of heroism that perpetuate appalling destruction of lives and livelihoods. Another way of describing the difference is to ask whether the anti-war poetry of Wilfred Owen and Siegfried Sassoon is more other-worldly and 'idealistic' than that of their more pro-war, patriotic contemporaries such as Rupert Brooke or Laurence Binyon; or whether Alexander Baxter's searingly honest descriptions of a conscientious objector's experiences in war are less 'realistic' than rationalisations of military involvement;[32] or whether Henri Dunant would ever have conceived and effected the ideals of the Red Cross without having witnessed and documented with unremitting medical clarity thousands of pointless atrocities of the Battle of Solferino.[33] Similarly, a deep pessimism (proven by history to be well-founded) may be a catalyst for defiant hope for change. There is no necessary incompatibility between recognising that Shakespeare was steeped in knowledge of military language, war rhetoric and practices on the one hand, and on the other holding a strong preference for peace. Indeed, it is likely that the one leads to the other.

Early pacifism

Another fallacy to be addressed alongside the false dichotomy between 'peace as idealism' and 'war as realism', is that it is anachronistic to read into Shakespeare's works an anti-war philosophy that could not have existed three hundred years before the word 'pacifism' was introduced into English (in 1905), and long before there was an identifiable, organised 'peace movement', inaugurated in the 1790s, with 'The Friends of

---

32. Archibald Baxter, *We Will Not Cease: The Autobiography of a Conscientious Objector* (Christchurch, New Zealand: The Caxton Press, 1939).

33. J. Henri Dunant, *A Memory of Solferino* (Geneva: Imprémerie Jules-Guillaume Fick, 1862).

Peace' who found a voice through the Correspondence Societies.[34] This is negated, however, in the light of the range of supporting sources available in Shakespeare's time and long before, showing that pacifism was espoused by influential writers through time. In classical antiquity there had been major writers concerned with the iniquities of war and who praised the goddess of peace, Eirene. Among Greeks we find passages from Homer and the historian Thucydides, and whole works by the comic dramatist Aristophanes (*The Acharnians*, *Peace* and *Lysistrata*), and tragedians Euripides, Aeschylus and Sophocles (*Trojan Women* and others).[35] It is sometimes claimed that these Greek dramatists represented a golden age of anti-war plays.[36] It is not misleading then, to say that the origins of a 'peace movement' were laid by the most memorable ancient writers 'reborn' in the Western Renaissance, Admittedly, pagan writers were also called upon in Early Modern Europe to justify war. Susan Harlan mentions that Sir Philip Sidney in his *Defence of Poetry* 'writes of the battlefield as a space where militant values are transmitted by way of older texts: he claims that "poetry is the companion of camps" and reminds his reader that Alexander left his tutor Aristotle behind, but took "dead Homer" into battle with him'.[37] However, a careful reading of works by that 'dead Homer' reveals qualifying poetic expressions of anti-war sentiments. *The Iliad* is by no means consistently in favour of battle, and instead often emphasises through powerful, elegiac imagery the way even a great war hero, of necessity, destroys age-old human livelihoods, habitats, and monuments:[38]

> Such was the mighty conflict . . . [Diomedes] stormed over the plain like a raging winter torrent that sweeps away the dykes in its swift flood. Close-built embankments and the walls of fertile vineyards fail to hold stay its onset driven by Zeus' storm and before it the proud works of men all tumble to ruin.[39]

Soldiers are reduced to the status of rampaging animals 'wreaking carnage': 'As a lion launches itself on a herd grazing some wooded pasture,

34. J. E. Cookson, *The Friends of Peace; Anti-war liberation in England 1793–1815* (Cambridge University Press, 1982).
35. See Gittings, *The Glorious Art of Peace*, 53–64.
36. The claim is made and justified in a comparative study by Donald David Deagon, *Pacifism in Greek and Modern Drama* (unpub. PhD Tulane University: ProQuest Dissertations Publishing, 1969, 7006391).
37. Susan Harlan, *Memories of War*, 3.
38. See Lawrence Rosenwald, 'Sketch of a Pacifist Critic', *Raritan* 39 (2019), 1–20, esp. 4–5, 15.
39. Homer, *Iliad*, trans. A. S. Kline (Rijksmuseum online, 2009), 97.

and breaks the neck of a heifer or two, so Diomedes dragged those men roughly from their chariot' (5.166). The charioteers lie dead on the ground, 'to the vultures' joy and their own wives' sorrow' (11.162). The most forceful statement of 'the note of incurable bitterness that continually makes itself heard' in the *Iliad* is that of Simone Weil, writing in anguish on the fall of Paris in 1939–40: 'the cold brutality of the deeds of war is left undisguised':

> The wantonness of the conqueror that knows no respect for any creature or thing that is at its mercy or is imagined to be so, the despair of the soldier that drives him on to destruction, the obliteration of the slave or the conquered man, the wholesale slaughter – all these elements combine in the Iliad to make a picture of uniform horror, of which force is the sole hero.[40]

Weil writes, 'the lives you destroy are like toys broken by a child, and quite as incapable of feeling; heroism is but a theatrical gesture and smirched with boastfulness'. It is this kind of reading of the *Iliad* that I believe Shakespeare also responded to in his version of the events in the Iliad, *Troilus and Cressida*, and in *Coriolanus* and the History plays.

The same attention to war's destructiveness can be found in Virgil's *Aeneid*. It is often hailed as a work in praise of heroism, but in the poem war, as witnessed by humble onlookers like shepherds, is several times linked with metaphors of impersonal desecration of the human and natural world, made clear in Dryden's translation:

> Now peals of shouts come thund'ring from afar,
> Cries, threats, and loud laments, and mingled war:
>
>   . . .
>
> And hearken what the frightful sounds convey.
> Thus, when a flood of fire by wind is borne,
> Crackling it rolls, and mows the standing corn;
> Or deluges, descending on the plains,
> Sweep o'er the yellow ear, destroy the pains
> Of lab'ring oxen and the peasant's gains;
> Unroot the forest oaks, and bear away
> Flocks, folds, and trees, and undistinguish'd prey:
> The shepherd climbs the cliff, and sees from far
> The wasteful ravage of the wat'ry war.[41]

The episode in which Dido is left grieving on the shore as Aeneas continues on his military mission was seen by later writers as an iconic

40. Simone Weil, transl. Mary McCarthy, 'The Iliad, or the Poem of Force', *Chicago Review*, 18 (1965).
41. Virgil, *Aeneid*, Book 2, 298–318, trans. John Dryden.

representation of a woman's love blighted by the exclusively masculine commitment to a warlike destiny, an image of the emotionally abandoned wives in Shakespeare. The example of Dido is sometimes cited as a distant echo in *Othello*.[42]

An anti-war intellectual tradition in Europe stretched back to Medieval times, as Ben Lowe has shown in detail in his book *Imagining Peace: A History of English Pacifist Ideas*.[43] Among these are Chaucer's *Tale of Melibeus* and works by Gower, Lydgate and Langland, who strongly and repeatedly assert the moral primacy of peace over war in the Christian tradition.[44] Gower writes that God 'Forbids that horrid sin to us / — Murder most foul and villainous' and links this commandment by adding that God sent his son,

> Whose song of peace the shepherds heard:
> 'Peace upon earth' (this was their word)
> Among all people of good will.
> And so, upon this question still
> If charity be held in awe,
> Then deadly wars offend its law [. . .]
> Such wars make war on Nature too:
> Peace is the end her laws pursue —
> Peace, the chief gem in Adam's wealth.[45]

Dante has been referenced by a critic who argues that 'A body of anti-war and pacifist writings had . . . been accumulating from ancient times and during the medieval and early modern periods':

> Dante reserved a special circle of 'nether' hell, described by his Virgil as a place of punishments for militarists destined to suffer the sufferings they have inflicted on others in life: 'But fix thine eyes below, for the river of blood draws in which are boiling those that by violence do injury to others . . . centaurs in line armed with arrows . . . the margin of the red boiling [moat], in which the boiled made piercing shrieks'.[46]

42. Richard Meek, 'Othello's Sympathies: Emotion, Agency and Identification', *Shakespeare Survey* 74 (2022), 194–207, 198.
43. Ben Lowe, *Imagining Peace: Imagining Peace: A History of English Pacifist Ideas* (Pennsylvania University Press, 1997).
44. See R. F. Yeager, 'Pax Poetica: On the Pacifism of Chaucer and Gower', Studies in the Age of Chaucer 9 (1987), 97–121, and Lowe, *Imagining Peace*.
45. John Gower, *Confessio Amantis*, trans. Terence Tiller (Harmondsworth: Penguin Books 1963), 145.
46. Dante Alighieri, *The Divine Comedy*, 'Inferno', trans. John D. Sinclair (Oxford University Press, 1948), Canto XII.

Patrick Whalen argues that this description is an instance of 'dystopic *déjà vu*' in which Dante is recalling the 'combat trauma' he suffered in a battle he had himself participated in as a cavalry soldier twenty years earlier in 1269. Pointing to 'the dominant military idiom' of the passage, Whalen concludes, 'that Dante's hell is a massive militarized zone is clear'.[47]

All religious sacred texts in both east and west prioritise peace over war as a fundamental ethical stance. Christ's many statements and actions of forgiving enemies by 'turning the other cheek' make a case for his being a pacifist *avant la lettre*,[48] and in post-Reformation Europe, there were religious groups such as Mennonites, Quakers and others, which consistently opposed war in all forms as part of their creed. 'Practical Christianity' was advanced by a range of humanist thinkers during the Renaissance. These writers saw war as the main impediment to their educational project of social renewal, and as Andrew Hiscock has asserted, they were 'unremittingly passionate in their demonization of war . . .'. Erasmus, who is often cited as a source for Shakespeare and can be claimed as the patron saint of pacifism, repeated through many works and letters that 'the whole philosophy of Christ argues against war'.[49] He was the most exemplary and influential humanist who espoused pacifism explicitly and frequently. The pamphlet *The Complaint of Peace* (1521) was his most sustained statement on the subject, and it seems to have been written either from his own harrowing eye-witness observation of the horrors of war, or as a feat of empathetic imagination which he encourages the reader to exercise:

> Imagine now that you see barbarous cohorts that inspire terror by their very faces and the sound of their voices. On both sides iron-clad battle lines, the fearful clash and glitter of arms, the hateful roar of a great multitude, the threatening looks, harsh bugles, the terrifying blare of trumpets, the thunder of barbadons [cannons], no less frightening than real thunder but more harmful, the mad uproar, the furious clash of battle,

47. Patrick Whalen, 'A Hell of One's Own': Combat Trauma in Dante's *Inferno*', *War, Literature and the Arts*, 31 (2019), 1–10.
48. See White, *Pacifism and English Literature*, ch. 3, 'Sacred Texts'.
49. Andrew Hiscock, '"Man is a Battlefield Within himself": Arms and the Affections in the Counsel of More, Erasmus, Vives and their Circle', in Stephanie Downes, Andrew Lynch and Katrina O'Loughlin *Emotions and War: Medieval to Romantic Literature* (London: Palgrave, 2015), 152–68, 162, 160. Quotation from Erasmus from *The Collected Works of Erasmus: Literary and Educational Writings* in sundry volumes (Toronto University Press, 1986), vol 5, 284.

the monstrous butchery, the merciless fate of the slain and those who kill, the slaughtered lying in heaps, the field running with gore.[50]

Montaigne shows ambivalence on the subject. Sometimes he praises military life, as in his essay 'Of Experience': 'no occupation is as pleasant as soldiering . . .', offering some rather unconvincing reasons for this opinion.[51] However, such an attitude is far outweighed by his many biting attacks on war itself, based on his close-up personal observations during the Wars of Religion.[52] In one example the sentence swerves from ironically misleading approval of war as 'the most grandiose and glorious of human activities', to a tone of trenchant and withering sarcasm. He is arguing that 'Animals obey the rules of Nature better than we do . . .':

> As for war – the most grandiose and glorious of human activities – I would like to know whether we want to use it to prove our superiority or, on the contrary, to prove our weakness and imperfection. We know how to defeat and kill each other, to undermine and destroy our own species: not much there, it seems, to make [animals] want to learn from us.[53]

By the time we get to the end of the paragraph, its opening has been heavily ironized and replaced by open cynicism. Many times in his essays Montaigne expresses a characteristic scepticism and distaste for the violence and cruelty of war, often likening it to the ignoble torturing of animals in hunting. He regularly expressed sympathy for the victims, while to victors of battles in his own troubled times he advocated that they employ clemency and mercy, advising the vanquished against an urge to revenge, and urging instead the yielding exercise of forgiveness as a state of virtue.[54] 'Conversation' in his essay of this title is presented as a mode of settling disputes diplomatically before they become violent.

Among Shakespeare's English contemporaries there were writers who extolled peace and denigrated war. There would surely have been more, but for the restrictions placed on literary women in terms of 'approved'

50. *Complete Works of Erasmus*, 35:403–4, quoted Robert Apelbaum, *The Renaissance Discovery of Violence* (Bristol University Press, 2021), 112.
51. Michel de Montaigne, 'Of Experience', *The Complete Essays*, transl. M. A. Screech (London: Penguin Books, 1987), 1244.
52. Mark Greenslade, 'Montaigne and the Wars of Religion' in Philippe Desan (ed.), *The Oxford Handbook of Montaigne* (Oxford University Press, 2016), 138–57.
53. Michel de Montaigne, 'An Apology for Raymond Sebond', *The Complete Essays*, 527. For more examples, see Alfredo Bonadeo, 'Montaigne on War', *Journal of the History of Ideas*, 46 (1985), 417–426.
54. David Quint, *Montaigne and the Quality of Mercy: Ethical and Political Themes in the 'Essais'* (Princeton University Press, 1998).

genres. In at least the biblical translations of Mary Herbert (Sidney), a priority is given to Psalms, a Biblical work in which peace is extolled. She translates 'And still in peace, maintain that peaceful place' (Psalm 51) and:

> Too long, alas, too long have I dwelled here
> With friendly peace's furious enemies:
> Who when to peace I seek to call them,
> Faster I find to the war they arm them.
>
> (Psalm 120)

Spenser in *The Faerie Queene* acknowledges that in the many allegorical conflicts between good and evil 'just war' is usually unavoidable, yet he consistently praises peace as the higher state.[55] A 'holy aged man' advises his knightly charge, '. . . wash thy hands from guilt of bloudy field: / For bloud can nought but sin, & wars but sorrowes yield' (Book 1, Canto X, Verse 60). It is a lesson that other knights must learn:

> O fly from wrath, fly, O my liefest Lord:
> Sad be the sights, and bitter fruits of warre,
>
> . . .
>
> But louely concord, and most sacred peace
> Doth nourish vertue, and fast friendship breeds.
>
> (Book 2, Canto 3, Verse 30)

Thomas Lodge espouses the positive virtues of peace and the irrationality of war:

> Peace doth depend on reason, warre on force,
> The one is humane, honest and upright:
> The other brutish, fostered by despight.[56]

John Donne preached several sermons which take up an anti-war stance: 'For the first temporal blessing of peace we may consider the loveliness the amiableness of that, if we look upon the horror and ghastliness of war'.[57] In arguing powerfully for universal peace, Donne lists

---

55. See Michael West, 'Spenser's Art of War: Chivalric Allegory, Military Technology, and the Elizabethan Mock-Heroic Sensibility', *Renaissance Quarterly*, 41 (1988), 654–704, and Jessica Wolfe, 'Spenser, Homer, and the Mythography of Strife', *Renaissance Quarterly*, 58 (2005), 1220–1288.
56. Thomas Lodge, *A Fig for Momus* (London: 1595), Eclogue 4.
57. Donne, Sermon preached at Whitehall, 30 April, 1620. *No Man is an Island: A Selection from the prose of John Donne*, ed. Rivers Scott (London: The Folio Society 1997), 117.

the destructive social, environmental and familial consequences of war, quoting Isaiah to evoke a devastated, post-battle landscape:

> As peace is of all goodness, so war is an emblem, a hieroglyphic, of all misery . . . It is but a little way that the poet hath got in the description of war, . . . that now that place is ploughed, where the great city stood . . . [W]hen the prophet Isaiah comes to the devastation, to the extermination of a war, he expresses it first thus; *Where there were a thousand vineyards at a cheap rate, all the land become briars and thorns*: that is much; but there is more, *the earth shall be removed out of her place; that land, that nation, shall no more be called that nation, nor that land*: but, yet more than that too; not only, not that people, but no other shall ever inhabit it. *It shall never be inhabited from generation to generation, neither shall shepherds be there; not only no merchant, nor husbandmen* . . . In a word, the horror of war is best discerned in the company he keeps, in his associates. And when the prophet Gad brought war into the presence of David, there came with him *famine* and *pestilence* . . . Let her *warfare* be at an end, they read, *Finita malitia ejus*, Let her *misery* be at an end; war and misery is all one thing . . .[58]

Donne was no armchair critic of war, since he had served under Essex in a military expedition in 1597 during which he witnessed violent action. In his verse-letter titled 'The Calm', the poetic persona draws on the poet's experience, summarising the diverse personal motivations of men who engage in war whether by choice or coercion. The speaker, becalmed at sea after a near-fatal skirmish with the Spanish navy, describes the fatal vicious circle facing such implicated individuals:

> Whether a rotten state, and hope of gain,
> Or to disuse me from the queasy pain
> Of being beloved and loving, or the thirst
> Of honour, or fair death, out pushed me first,
> I lose my end; for here as well as I,
> A desperate may live, and a coward die.[59]

The siren call of armed forces for recruits has always been based on enticing young men in 'hope of gain' in a secure and glamorous job, especially at times of high unemployment. It is a perennial pattern based on making military service sound appealing, familiar from Farquhar's

58. Donne, Sermon XII preached at Whitehall, (1621), March 8. Online accessed 28 July 2021. https://www.biblestudytools.com/classics/the-works-of-john-donne-vol-1/sermon-xii.html
59. *John Donne: The Complete English Poems* ed. A. J. Smith (Harmondsworth: Penguin English Poets, rev. edn. 1977), 200.

satirical comedy *The Recruiting Officer* (1706) to Ken Loach's more critically sombre movie, *Looks and Smiles* (1981, dramatised from the novel by Barry Hines). It seems baffling that the reality of a deadly occupation awaiting those driven by 'the thirst / Of honour, or fair death' is so often unforeseen or recklessly ignored – 'for here, as well as I, / A desperate may live, and a coward die'. Returning soldiers often wrote memoirs detailing their own experiences, to the extent that they initiated a sub-genre.[60] London was full of veterans no doubt ready to share their experiences, risking charges of treason by countering official discourses on war.

Donne was by no means alone among Shakespeare's literary near-forebears and contemporaries in England. Renaissance humanists inveighed against both war and the hunting of animals (as did Shakespeare in *As You Like It* and *Love's Labour's Lost*). Among them were John Colet, Thomas More (holding some reservations on war as sometimes inevitable to defend territory from invasion), Samuel Daniel, and others, through to John Milton who often condemned war.[61] Gascoigne in *A Hundred Sundry Flowers* acknowledges Erasmus by name and includes a mouthpiece for anti-war invective when speaking autobiographically of his own mental distress suffered in the wars of the Low Countries.[62] Sir Walter Raleigh in *A Discourse of the Original and Fundamental Cause of Natural, Arbitrary, Necessary, and Unnatural War* (1615? pub. 1650) initially defines war as 'the exercise of violence under sovereign command against withstanders', employing 'the sword, the arrow, the gun, with many terrible engines of death'. 'Among human actions [war] is the most lawless', he writes, citing especially cases of war motivated by rulers' ambition or revenge which can be 'avoided' by enlightened princes. Of civil war, Raleigh writes:

> What deluded then have a great part of mankind been, who have either yielded themselves to be slain in causes which if truly known their heart would abhor, or have been the bloody executioners of other men's ambition! It is a hard fate to be slain for what a man should never willingly fight.[63]

60. See Paul Scannell, *Conflict and Soldiers' Literature in Early Modern Europe*.
61. Steven Marx writes on Milton's turn to pacifism under the influence of George Fox and the Quakers in 'The Prophet Disarmed: Milton and the Quakers', *Studies in English Literature 1500–1800* (Winter, 1992), 1–26.
62. Apelbaum, *The Renaissance Discovery of Violence*, 128. For more detailed analysis, see Elizabeth Heale, '"The Fruits of War": The Voice of the Soldier in Gascoigne, Rich and Churchyard', *Early Modern Literary Studies*, 14 (2008), 1–39.
63. Sir Walter Raleigh, *A Discourse of the Original and Fundamental Cause of Natural, Arbitrary, Necessary, and Unnatural War*, *The Complete Works of Sir Walter*

As a modern commentator sums up, 'Because violence was senseless, Raleigh felt that warriors would incur God's wrath'.[64] He writes with sympathy of refugees driven from their land by invasion: 'the miseries accompanying this kind of war are most extreme', describing them as facing 'the calamities of such forcible transplantations'. Robert Allott in his anthology *England's Parnassus* (1600) includes Shakespearean passages among 'the choycest flowers of our English Poets' writing on themes of 'concord', 'peace' and 'war'. Although, as Simon Barker has shown, in public discourse 'the concept of the just war . . . pushed to the margins any residual notions of pacifism',[65] yet it endured and persisted even in repudiation, to the extent that it was reviled as a dangerous threat to national pride.

There have always been different kinds of peace. At one end of a spectrum is the *Pax Romana* as a peace based on military conquest and occupation, calculated to maintain state security, defend against 'pagan' threats, and expand empire.[66] It is not true peace, but docility imposed through military defeat, inviting eventual rebellion. In mid-spectrum are a peace which is merely an interlude between a never-ending sequence of retaliatory wars, usually a ceasefire, truce or armistice – as in a battle described by Spenser: 'He maketh warre, he maketh peace again / And yet his peace is but continuall iarre' (*The Faerie Queene*, Book 2). In this spirit, the Tribunes in *Coriolanus* comment upon how peaceful Rome is without its unruly military hero, before his return bent on revenge to besiege Rome with the Volscian army under Aufidius. One of the common and misleading justifications given for waging war is that it will bring 'peace', still glibly summed up in an adage deriving from ancient Rome, 'if you want peace, prepare for war' (*si vis pacem, para bellum*). A more apocalyptically disastrous version of 'peace' as the end (in both senses, as closure and purpose) of war, is when – as in Jacobean revenge tragedies – all major protagonists perish.

Even if there was no 'peace movement' in the modern sense, yet there were enough published forebears and contemporaries of Shakespeare to claim as exemplars in a pacifist tradition. John Gittings in *The Glorious Art of Peace* gives many documented anti-war accounts, ranging comprehensively across centuries, cultures, and nations, from the time of Homer to the invasion of Iraq in 2003. The tradition extended into the

Raleigh, 8 vols (Oxford University Press, 1829), reproducing original text, London: 1650, vol 8, 253–99.

64. Bonadeo, 'Montaigne on War', 426, quoting Raleigh's *Discourse of War* (London: 1650), *Works*, vol. 8, 284.
65. Barker, *War and Nation*, 70.
66. See Gittings, *The Glorious Art of Peace*, 80.

eighteenth century. Later in this book I shall draw attention to a lasting state of peace analysed by Immanuel Kant in his pamphlet, *Towards Perpetual Peace* (1795). He based his radical view of peace as dependent on eliminating the possible causes for war, such as giving no motive for revenge in peace terms, and dismantling military forces and the arms industry. He prophetically pointed out that a war of mutual 'extermination' will indeed create peace, but it is the silence prevailing 'in the great graveyard of the human race'.

For a second answer to the charge of anachronism in 'reading Shakespeare as a pacifist', we need look no further than his own plays and their critical legacy to realise that concepts could exist before specific words are coined to name them. Modern readings and performances of his works amply demonstrate that even before the naming of racism, environmentalism, ecology and climate change, democracy, disability, communism and socialism, the ideas behind these abstractions have enough precedents to fill books titled *Shakespeare and . . . .*[67]

Finally, the choice of opposing war, especially through choosing conscientious objection, is always an individual decision, which in wartime has always carried personal dangers of being condemned as cowardice or treachery and leading to incarceration. Whether or not an organised 'peace movement' or even democratic political representation exists, does not remove this jeopardy. The conditions of conscription into the Elizabethan military shown in operation in the *Henry IV* plays allowed no safe opportunity for such individual resistance except through bribery, as we shall see in Chapter 3.

Even without the unrecorded voices of fearful and reluctant soldiers, mothers, wives, widows, orphans and observant scriveners, there is ample likelihood that those opposing war have existed ever since war began, and that their permanent recorders were writers in different genres. There is surely a sense in which pacifist thought, far from being anachronistically imposed on past times, has always existed in the minds of all but those who intend to benefit from armed aggression. Shakespeare draws upon various traditions of thought from the religious

---

67. As a very small sample of such titles, see Alwin Thaler, *Shakespeare and Democracy* (Knoxville: The University of Tennessee Press, 1941); Sonya Freeman Loftis, *Shakespeare and Disability Studies* (Oxford University Press, 2021); Lynne Bruckner and Dan Brayton (eds), *Ecocritical Shakespeare* (Burlington VT: Ashgate, 2011); Randall Martin, *Shakespeare and Ecology* (Oxford University Press, 2015); Irena K. Materyk and Joseph G. Price, *Shakespeare in the World of Communism and Socialism* (University of Toronto Press 2006). More generally, see James O'Rourke, *Re-Authorizing Shakespeare Through Presentist Readings* (London: Routledge, 2012), and the *Oxford Shakespeare Topics* series.

to the secular in his presentations of war. The ventriloquized responses are context-bound and depending on the motivations of characters in their dramatic situations, but there are enough of them to make a case for a general authorial attitude. From time to time they include visceral repulsion from violence, grief at the waste of human lives and livelihoods, and doubts about the ethical impropriety and emotional failure in military officers, however heroic may be their reputations.

Definitions

Pacifism as a philosophical stance is often derided as lacking in precise definition and as hopelessly utopian in aims, not to mention being equated with cowardice, 'appeasement' and treason during wartime. However, the dictionary definition of pacifists as those who 'believe that war and violence are unjustifiable and that all disputes should be settled by peaceful means'[68] is clear and serviceable enough as a starting point, and does not self-evidently seem an irrational stance or unachievable in practice. More comprehensive analysis reveals that within its range there are shades of difference from conditional 'pacificism' (objecting to a particular war) through to absolute and uncompromising pacifism, in all circumstances. A Mennonite theologian, J. H. Yoder, has discriminated between many different types, from the arguable case of 'just-war pacifism' at one end of a spectrum, to principled absolutism under all conditions based on conscience at the other end; from religious conviction to secular rationalism; from opposition to a specifically military activity to a more general belief in nonviolence as an agent for social change (Gandhi, Martin Luther King), and rejection of all activities supporting armed conflict.[69] Whatever narrow precision might be lost in such a wide coverage is compensated for by near-universal applicability of the concept to the range of human experience throughout the ages.

On a general point, in this book I do not address with any precision the much-disputed definitions of 'war' itself, a subject which is broached to some extent in most books on military history. Likewise, I give the much-disputed word 'war'[70] its widest ambit, to cover any situation

68. David S. Patterson, 'Pacifism' in *1914–1918 Online International Encyclopedia of the First World War* (2014), accessed 18 January 2023, https://encyclopedia.1914-1918-online.net/article/pacifism
69. J. H. Yoder, *Nevertheless: Varieties of Religious Pacifism* (Scottsdale, PA: Herald Press, 1992).
70. For a convenient summary of views and a very short bibliography see Hew Strachan, 'The idea of war', ch. 1 in *The Cambridge Companion to War*, ed. Kate McLoughlin

where *de facto* armed militia are engaged in conflict with the intent to commit violent acts to achieve their ends (whatever these may be), internationally between states or intranationally in civil war, in conflicts waged on land, sea – or nowadays more often air, cyberspace, and (soon) extra-terrestrial space. This fits within the World Health Organization's definition of violence as,

> The intentional use of physical force or power, threatened or actual, against oneself, another person, or against a group or community, that either results in or has a high likelihood of resulting in injury, death, psychological harm, maldevelopment or deprivation.[71]

The only qualification is that 'violence' becomes war when it is collective, intentional and in some way organised, rather than personal or unpremeditated. Such inclusiveness was the guiding spirit behind the Geneva Conventions in 1949, deliberately made binding upon even parties which are not signatories. In practice, these and other intended protections, inhibitions and protocols are regularly flouted with impunity in armed conflict, which is often made to sound innocuous in metaphors such as 'the heat of battle', 'the fog of war', and other such poeticisms designed to cloak violations like 'murder of all kinds, mutilation, cruel treatment and torture', the taking of hostages, and 'outrages upon personal dignity, in particular humiliating and degrading treatment'.[72] Also proscribed are destruction and looting of sites of cultural and historic significance, hospitals and schools, and state censorship of arts and literature. In any other context these acts would by definition be considered as intentional and serious criminal acts, but in war they are routinely excused and normalized as inevitable 'accidents'. To the pacifist, they are not so much 'breaches' of conventions as definitional and intrinsic to the nature of war, and provide sufficient argument for the banning of war itself as criminal by its nature. As we shall see, Shakespeare provides examples of these wider definitions of war and pacifist stances. Each armed conflict and act of resistance is specific to its play, though there are enough running similarities to draw links between them and argue for a consistent, underlying set of attitudes.

(Cambridge University Press, 2009), 7–14. For more detail see works by Emily Crawford, arguing for a similarly inclusive definition: *The Treatment of Combatants and Insurgents under the Law of Armed Conflict* (Oxford University Press, 2010) and *Identifying the Enemy: Civilian Participation in Hostilities* (Oxford University Press, 2015).
71. Quoted Mayton, *Nonviolence and Peace Psychology*, Section. 1.3.
72. Emily Crawford, *The Treatment of Combatants*, 22.

Bearing in mind Lerner's lead, it is time (in John Lennon's words) to 'give peace a chance'. Given Shakespeare's status as the world's most-quoted, most-performed and most studied writer, it is reasonable to ask: what does he tell us of war and its alternative? Gonzalo's vision would surely be far preferable to all people on earth, than the bleak actuality in which we live, described in Matthew Arnold's 'Dover Beach', a desolate, spectral landscape as pervasive now as then:

> And we are here as on a darkling plain
> Swept with confused alarms of struggle and flight,
> Where ignorant armies clash by night.

Chapter 2

'Bloody-hunting slaughtermen': War Crimes and Unjust War in the History Plays

Judging from the many times a handful of speeches in *Henry V* have been quoted approvingly by politicians and media, Shakespeare has a lot to answer for in the waging of wars over the centuries. From the Napoleonic wars ending at Waterloo in 1815 through to the twenty-first century, Henry's rousing patriotic calls to arms, 'Once more unto the breach . . .' and the 'St Crispin's Day' speeches, rang out many times in England. During World War One they were recited in Edwardian schools, and the play has always been Shakespeare's most popular when war breaks out.[1] Even the fact that Shakespeare's Englishmen were invading France was overlooked by the adversarial nations on the modern occasion when the countries were joined in the same 'Entente'. As Tom Honselaars discovered, 'it is allusions to *Henry V* that abound in the Anglo-French space of the Great War'.[2] For example, he writes, the Chancellor of the University of Nancy took Henry's lines as expressions of fraternal endeavour in which Shakespeare 'celebrates the glory of all those who, fighting for the good cause, become "brothers" and are "ennobled"'. Shakespeare seems to have anticipated this incongruity, because in the performance some adroit structural changes and textual juxtapositions were used to underwrite the impression of 'rapprochement and entente between the enemy nations'.[3] Ironically, such creative adaptations to suit the times open the door to claiming that Shakespeare's plays are not irredeemably patriotic but offer skillful analyses of war itself, irrespective of the forces involved.

The Chorus's lines have also been used to support war efforts in modern times, and assumed by many to be tacit endorsement of authorial

1. *Henry V*, ed. Andrew Gurr, New Cambridge Shakespeare, (Cambridge Univerity Press, 1992) 46.
2. Tom Honselaars, 'Great War Shakespeare: Somewhere in France, 1914–19', *Actes des congrès de la Société française Shakespeare*, 33 (2015), consulted 5 September 2020, paras. 7, 27.
3. Honselaars, para. 22

approval in the play as a whole. However, as Steven Marx has pointed out, the Chorus is not a reliable narrator but a highly partisan propagandist for Henry and his English troops, underwriting and exaggerating the rhetoric of enthusiastic jingoism.[4] Adam McKeown has drawn attention to the Chorus's one-sidedness as a patriotic reporter. In discussing the ambiguity of the phrase 'English Mercuries' (2.0.7), alluding as it does to the idea of soldiers as not only messengers but also liars and thieves, McKeown argues for the play's wider ambivalence marking the Chorus's deceptiveness. This reading mirrors a divided perception of ordinary soldiers of war in Early Modern writers who, like Donne,

> ask their readers to see war as both a testing ground for personal and national valor and a destructive force that ravages human pride and renders whole countries bare, peace both an Eden on earth and a state of gnawing restlessness and internal anxiety.[5]

The sentimentalist's uncritical reading of Shakespeare's Henry V descanting on war is seen as far from the complete story.

World War Two also produced enthusiastic appropriations of *Henry V* to support pro-war fervour in Britain, fanned by government propaganda. The play was enlisted and financially subsidised in 1944–5 on behalf of Allied forces in Laurence Olivier's movie. With an eye to visually symbolic 'brand recognition', a volley of arrows from long bows (the newly invented, controversial weapons of mass destruction in Henry's day), metamorphoses mid-flight into a phalanx of RAF bombers heading from green fields of England towards Germany. Olivier also contributed stirring recitations to patriotic documentaries directed by Humphrey Jennings.[6] These included 'This royal throne of kings, this sceptr'd isle' extolled by John of Gaunt in *Richard II* (2.1.40), conveniently forgetting that the threat of war feared by John of Gaunt lies not in potential invaders, but English antagonists in civil war. Such appropriations were encouraged and funded by the state, in ways described by theatre historian, Laurence Raw:

> The creation of CEMA (Council for the Encouragement of Music and Arts) in 1940 offered government support to drama companies and music

---

4. Steven Marx, 'Holy War in *Henry Fifth*', *Shakespeare Survey*, 48 (1995), 85–99. See also Joel B. Altman, '"Vile Participation": The Amplification of Violence in the Theater of *Henry V*', *Shakespeare Quarterly*, 42 (1991), 1–32.

5. Adam N. McKeown, *English Mercuries: Soldier Poets in the Age of Shakespeare*, (Vanderbilt University Press, 2009), 19.

6. These have been reissued on DVD in *Listen to Britain and other Films by Humphrey Jennings* (2002).

societies who found it difficult to sustain their activities during the war in an attempt to boost morale through the politics of art. CEMA became associated with leading companies and stars: both the Sadlers' Wells Ballet and the Old Vic Company toured Britain in an effort to 'remind people what the country was fighting for' (Heinrich 'Theatre' 63).[7]

With such financial blandishments there was little or no incentive for theatre companies to foreground any subversive or anti-war sentiments in the Shakespearean texts, nor to suggest there were other possible readings. Audiences, however, may sometimes have drawn their own conclusions from the contemporary circumstances of performances, when 'even during an air-raid, most of them stayed in the auditorium while the performance continued'.[8] Responses may possibly have included a swelling lift in national spirits, but just as likely they would have been a reminder of heightened anxiety among those who had sons, brothers and nephews in the front-line facing assault. This will be relevant when we look at *King Lear* in Chapter 5. It is possible also that some directors failed to attract funding from CEMA because their productions could be seen as uncomfortably reflecting the realities of war or undermining 'the war effort'. In other words, the choice to use Shakespeare as ready-made propagandist for war need not necessarily be inherent in the plays themselves, but attributable to a selectively favoured need during wartime, by emphasising some parts and downplaying others. Such dramatic appropriations were attributable to the historical circumstances of the 1940s, and not necessarily true to the texts.

More recently still, in a lecture entitled 'The West Must Prevail' delivered to the Margaret Thatcher Foundation in 2002 and leading up to the invasion of Iraq, US Vice-President Cheney displayed a cultural literacy which seems unexpected in George W. Bush's administration, this time using Shakespeare's *King John*. In praising his British hosts at a time when there were mass demonstrations in London against war, Cheney sought to trigger the spirit of the Falklands conflict: 'Whenever I think of Margaret Thatcher, I can't help but recall the final lines from Shakespeare's *King John*, "Naught shall make us rue if England to itself do rest but true"'.[9] To think of Cheney not being able to 'help but recall' a quotation from such a little known play stretches credulity and it seems more likely that it occurred to his speech-writer, perhaps a poorly paid literature graduate There is also plenty wrong with Cheney's

7. Laurence Raw, 'People's Theatre and Shakespeare in Wartime: Donald Wolfit's *King Lear* in London and Leeds, 1944–45', *Shakespeare*, 12 (2016), 55–66, 55.

8. Raw, 'People's Theatre', 56.

9. https://www.margaretthatcher.org/document/110687 (accessed 15 September 2020).

intended use of the passage. He may not have trusted himself to recite more iambic pentameters, let alone to read the play as a whole, since he ignores an ensuing, conditional phrase, warning that England is not 'true' to itself when sabotaged by its own revolting lords who throw in their lot with England's enemy, like the demonstrators then chanting outside Cheney's venue. The sting is in the last line:

> O, let us pay the time but needful woe,
> Since it hath been beforehand with our griefs.
> This England never did, nor never shall,
> Lie at the proud foot of a conqueror,
> But when it first did help to wound itself.
>
> (5.7.110–18)

Cheney also ignores the dramatic context. The speech is the last in the play, uttered by the Englishman Philip the Bastard at a 'rueful' moment when the English have actually been defeated by the French (though they are persuaded not to press their advantage), and the King has been poisoned. Far from celebrating a famous victory it expresses 'needful woe', and the character is vowing 'revenge' (5.7.71), which ominously threatens yet another war if the rebellious courtiers do not unite:

> Now these her princes are come home again
> Come the three corners of the world in arms
> And we shall shock them! Nought shall make us rue
> If England to itself do rest but true.
>
> (5.7.110–13)

King John has been described by Simon Barker as a play in which 'war weakens the state more than strengthens it',[10] belying the call for English unity in defying foreign invasion. Politicians who use *Henry V* in support of the dubious enterprise of a foreign invasion based on 'false intelligence' are on equally thin ice. Cheney's boss, President George W. Bush, who led a 'coalition of the willing' to invade Afghanistan and Iraq, confessed that this play was his favourite literary work.[11] He seems to have shaped himself as a latter-day military leader in the same mould as

---

10. Simon Barker, *War and Nation*, 133.
11. For reflections on the fondness for this play more generally amongst US Republicans, see Scott Newstrom (Newstok), 'Right Pitches Dubya as Henry V', *AlterNet*, May 29, 2003. Newstrom refers to 'the preposterous use of Shakespeare by those who have read the play (badly), bullying an audience unfamiliar with *Henry V* into conceding the connection. It is no small irony that this audience likely includes the president himself.

Henry, and his infamous and premature 'mission accomplished' speech on May 1, 2003 seems to have been intended to emulate his hero's rousing speeches. Once again, context is forgotten.

In other words, passages from Shakespeare's plays have routinely been yanked from their dramatic contexts and selectively reframed to support the latest war effort. Similarly, even phrases like Mark Antony's unsettling 'Cry havoc and let slip the dogs of war' in *Julius Caesar* (3.1.273), thrillingly intoned by Marlon Brando in Mankiewicz's film during the Cold War (1953), can be recontextualised to suit any war, though in the Shakespearean context it is a calculated incitement to violent civil war. Shakespeare can be a comforting, heritage presence in war to 'remind people what the country is fighting for'. As Graham Holderness observes, the plays themselves as unified wholes are deeply ambiguous and 'make themselves available for reactionary or progressive reproductions', depicting alternately calls for liberty and 'forces of oppression'.[12] What Andrew Lynch says of Medieval texts is as true of Renaissance ones, and particularly Shakespeare's, in which there are always qualifying subtexts: 'Close reading of many Medieval texts uncovers resistance in them to ideas of "glorious" or "holy" war, forming a basis for our proper scholarly resistance to their modern instrumentalization in those terms'.[13] The historian Peter Lake confirms this observation from an Elizabethan perspective. In the case of *Henry V*, for example, he reminds us that it would have been politically dangerous if Shakespeare had steered audiences towards unambiguous pro- or anti-war positions, since controversial and partisan tracts and pamphlets were being circulated for or against war, depending on factional divisions at court and diverse class interests of onlookers. Lake's subtle reading of *Henry V* as a whole represents a studious attempt to leave it up to auditors as individuals to choose whatever interpretation appeals to their political interests in unpredictable and changing national situations:

> it was inevitable that members of the audience, which was after all, composed of persons of very different opinions, presuppositions and religious identities, would resolve the questions posed to them by the play very differently'.[14]

---

12. Graham Holderness, *Shakespeare Recycled: The Making of Historical Drama* (Brighton: Harvester Wheatsheaf, 1992), 89–90.
13. Andrew Lynch, 'Preface', *Literature, Emotions, and Pre-Modern War*, Claire McIlroy and Anne M. Scott, eds., (Yorkshire: Arc Humanities Press, 2021), vii–xiv, xiv.
14. Peter Lake, *How Shakespeare Put Politics on the Stage: Power and Succession in the History Plays* (New Haven, Yale University Press 2016), 572.

This is as true now as it was in Shakespeare's day. Lake shows that throughout his canon, Shakespeare shows himself warily leaving open the most sensitive political material, to pre-empt their application to future events that might embarrass or reverse judgements expressed in his plays. In those based on English chronicles, he was, after all, presenting crucial episodes from Tudor history, peopled by ancestors of current courtly families with varying allegiances and Queen Elizabeth herself. Even when being ultra-cautious, Shakespeare's plays could arouse controversy, as when the deposition scene in *Richard II* was censored, and subsequently appropriated by dissidents supporting the Earl of Essex. He was more free to speak his mind when dealing with ancient stories from Graeco-Roman times, which may partly explain why *Troilus and Cressida* allows no such ambiguity and is accepted as by far his most outspoken anti-war play. Even in this case, however, its apparently dangerous, veiled reference to the Earl of Essex's rebellion may have led to its being banned and never performed at the time. In the play the prophetess speaks with conviction against the Trojan war:

CASSANDRA
Virgins and boys, mid-age and wrinkled old,
Soft infancy, that nothing canst but cry,
Add to my clamour! let us pay betimes
A moiety of that mass of moan to come.
Cry, Trojans, cry! Practise your eyes with tears!
Troy must not be, nor goodly Ilium stand;
Our firebrand brother Paris burns us all.
Cry, Trojans, cry! A Helen and a woe!
Cry, cry! Troy burns, or else let Helen go.

(2.2.104–12)

Her prophecy comes tragically true, and her words are just as applicable as Henry V's when any war comes into sight, though less often quoted.

Like history itself, Shakespeare's plays leave answers open to determination and reinterpretation in the light of future events, while initiating and inviting discussion on multiple, sometimes contradictory readings. This pluralistic recognition is shared by many critics and performers. At least since the politically inflected, theatre-based *aperçus* of Hazlitt (on *Henry V*), Brecht (on *Coriolanus*), and the critically formulated commentaries of A. P. Rossiter (on *Richard II*) and Norman Rabkin (again on *Henry V*), it has been accepted as axiomatic that Shakespeare's dramatic works incorporate paradoxes, where mutually exclusive positions co-exist as equal opposites, inviting audiences to choose a preference or leave the decision in abeyance.[15]

Endless wars

It is clear that Shakespeare acquired a deep knowledge of army vocabulary, battle strategies and tactics, gleaned from his sources, from memoirs of returning soldiers either published or orally transmitted, and from widely available military manuals (of which some 200 were printed in the sixteenth and seventeenth centuries, forty titles in 1578–1600 alone, including new editions and translations).[16] Historian David Lawrence notes that 'There is now a growing consensus that late Tudor and early Stuart society was in fact highly militarized, with elites actively participating in the country's military culture and an English citizenry quite knowledgeable of military affairs'.[17] Shakespeare certainly belonged in the latter group. He learned about military tactics, and about how the mind of a professional officer works especially when faced with emotional problems. His imagination could feelingly comprehend the sufferings of victims of war. Given the heterogeneous materials and shifting points of view among characters, it is perilous to claim with confidence that he unequivocally endorsed any particular war that he dramatized.

Even when the dramatist provides ostensibly peaceful endings to his plays, these are not necessarily imbued with faith that triumph will last, showing instead a realistic awareness of human capacities for perpetuating violence even against their own interests. Nowhere is this more obvious than in the plays based on chronicle history, which were tailor-made for serialisation. Each ends by leaving ominously open the grounds for yet another war of succession, offering an ideal opportunity for a sequel, immanent in a fragile moment of temporary stability in the kingdom. *Henry VI Part 2* may have been his first play based on chronicle sources, and it ends on a jubilant note, celebrating apparent peace after military victory by the House of York:

---

15. A. P. Rossiter, *Angel With Horns* (London: Longman, 1961), Norman Rabkin, *Shakespeare and the Common Understanding* (New York: Free Press, 1967).
16. P. Robinson, *Military Honour and the Conduct of War* (London: Routledge, 2006); Pugliatti, *Shakespeare and the Just War Tradition*, 92; Nina Taunton, *1590s Drama and Militarism*.
17. David R. Lawrence, 'Reappraising the Elizabethan and Early Stuart Soldier: Recent Historiography on Early Modern English Military Culture', *History Compass* 9 (2011), 16–33, 17.

'twas a glorious day.
Saint Albans' battle won by famous York
Shall be eternized in all age to come.

(5.3.30–1)

But as its successor shows, such a peace achieved through civil war has
not ended war and is not 'eternized in all age to come' – the Wars of
the Roses are far from done. Similarly, when Shakespeare later came to
write *Henry V*, his audience would already be aware from the earlier
Henry VI cycle that the apparently glorious victory of the English over
the French would be swiftly reversed, and shown to be as futile as the
oscillating fortunes in the civil wars, when Henry himself is dead. So
much is conveyed by the Chorus in the final lines of *Henry V* itself, when
the word 'bleed' is a pithy reminder of the human wastefulness of wars
past and present: '. . . they lost France and made his England bleed, /
Which oft our stage hath shown . . .' (Epilogue, 12–13). We recall that
even the decisive battle of Agincourt in 1415 was only one skirmish in a
so-called 'hundred years war' lasting until the English defeat at Orléans
in 1429, and that there followed oscillating civil wars in England from
1455 to 1487. *Henry VI Part 3* ends with the murder of that King by
the Duke of Gloucester, whose snarling and vengeful soliloquy in the
final scene forebodes more slayings to come in *Richard III*. The opening lines of *Richard III* circle back to the description of 'Saint Alban's
battle' as a York victory – 'Now is the winter of our discontent / Made
glorious summer by this sun of York' (1.1.1–2), but the sunny claims
do not last. Since King Richard was not in the Tudor line leading to
Elizabeth the First, Shakespeare could safely portray him as a serial
killer, 'murderous' and 'determined to prove a villain' (1.1.30), but even
his death does not end the disputes over the crown. Grievances that
lead to future revenge in an ever more destructive sequence of wars run
right through the History plays, except for the one that hails the birth of
Elizabeth, *Henry VIII*. The kind of providential and optimistic readings
of Shakespeare's Histories by early critics are given the lie by the inherently pessimistic structure of the plays.

Throughout the early trilogy, Henry VI himself, first ruling in minority
and thereafter powerless to influence events, is spokesman for pacifism
as an alternative to endless wars. In *Part 1* he pleads 'Civil dissension
is a viperous worm / That gnaws the bowels of the Commonwealth'
(*1 Henry VI*, 3.1.73–4), and in *Part 2*, he quotes Christ's authoritative
Sermon on the Mount: 'I prithee peace, . . . / For blessed are the peacemakers on earth' (3.1.32–4). He appeals to conscience, virtue and justice
as the basis of peace. He grieves in the knowledge that it is his own status

as monarch and his family's deadly divisions that cause needless tragedy for so many personal fatalities and community disruptions. Henry is also the only courtly character who empathises with the sufferings of hapless citizens caught up in war. He comments at length and pityingly on the casualties, on witnessing '*a Father that has killed his son, bringing in the body*' and '*a Son that has killed his father, dragging in the dead body*':

> Woe above woe! grief more than common grief!
> O that my death would stay these ruthful deeds!
> O pity, pity, gentle heaven, pity!
>
> (*3 Henry VI*, 2.5)

The remorseful father's own reflection is an indictment of civil war itself:

> O, pity, God, this miserable age!
> What stratagems, how fell, how butcherly,
> Erroneous, mutinous and unnatural,
> This deadly quarrel daily doth beget!
>
> (*3 Henry VI*, 2.5.88–92)

Arguably more effective on the stage than the page, the scene in which Henry overlooks the battlefield is visually powerful, its pastoral setting and stasis counterpointing the petty squabbles and feverish political machinations at court, turning attention instead to the tragic consequences of 'civil butchery' for ordinary people. From his vantage point on a 'molehill', most likely the playhouse balcony overlooking the battle, Henry is speaking from high ground both geographically and morally, observing the tragic fates of his subjects. Simon Barker provides detailed analysis of the scene, drawing out the dramatic and social complexity of the 'poignant and reflective' scene with its 'overarching sense of pity'.[18] Although many critics, echoing his onstage detractors, reproach the King for his weakness and ineptitude (he was, after all, a minor when he gained power – 'Henry the Sixth, in infant bands crowned King' [*Henry V*, Epilogue]), yet in the theatre the scene acts as a powerful counterpoint to the war. It has credence as an authorial intrusion encouraging the audience to recognise the overt subversion of military glory, and condemnation of civil war as an intrinsically immoral way of pursuing power. The leading protagonists and their descendants were to continue killing their own relatives through seven plays. Shakespeare is condemning civil war as a particularly poignant waste of English lives, but as dramatic spectacle it is equally possible to conclude that he is generalizing the issues to incorporate war itself.

18. Simon Barker, *War and Nation*, 122–4.

By way of summary, Andrew Hiscock casts light upon the costs of these wars to commoners, whether civilians or conscripted soldiers, who are invariably the principal casualties:

> With specific reference to their theatres of war, the Henry VI plays unmask the terrifyingly indiscriminate manner in which violence pollutes the everyday lives and selves of those contained within their dramatic worlds, and the ways in which butchery and slaughter (the politics of control *in extremis*) come to monopolize wholly the imaginative lives and emotional intelligence of anyone wishing to claim the power of command in such an environment.[19]

It is a theme emphasised also in the later *Henry IV* plays and *Henry V*. As we shall see in the next chapter, the chameleon character of Sir John Falstaff acts as a dramatic catalyst for a range of observations 'from below', in his multiple, conflicting roles as soldier, recruiting officer, 'coward' and proto-pacifist.

Shakespeare does not confine such moralizing for English victims of civil war in the *Henry VI* cycle. In *Part 1* he places a similar sentiment in an international war, in the utterance of England's antagonist, Joan of Arc. The historical figure is usually seen as an example of transgression against the assumption that women are peacemakers while men drive war.[20] Yet at a moment in the play Shakespeare extends dramatic sympathy to her, through her elegiac description of the sufferings of her own countryfolk, melting the heart even of her impatient, warmongering countryman who supports the English:

JOAN LA PUCELLE
Look on thy country, look on fertile France,
And see the cities and the towns defaced
By wasting ruin of the cruel foe.
As looks the mother on her lowly babe
When death doth close his tender dying eyes,
See, see the pining malady of France;
Behold the wounds, the most unnatural wounds,
Which thou thyself hast given her woeful breast.
O, turn thy edged sword another way.
. . .
Return thee therefore with a flood of tears,
And wash away thy country's stained spots.

19. Andrew Hiscock, '"More warlike than politique"', 230–1.
20. Ronald Edsforth, 'General Editor's Preface' in *A Cultural History of Peace*, 6 vols. (London: Bloomsbury, 2020), 13.

BURGUNDY
Either she hath bewitched me with her words,
Or nature makes me suddenly relent.

(1 Henry VI 3.7.44–59)

What is striking about these Shakespearean expressions of sympathy for commoners who suffer in war is first, that they are unnecessary in terms of plot, unusual in other plays of the time (Marlowe showed no taste for them in his narrative-driven plays), and that they are presented as direct appeals to audience pity, and invested with an affective, poetic power largely absent from self-seeking speeches of politicians who advocate violence. They are speeches penned by one whose writing skill lies in empathy, and whose touchstone of human dealings is peace.

'Henry V' and Just War Theory

Putting to one side the opportunistic appropriations by modern politicians of bellicose speeches in Shakespeare's plays, if there is a critical consensus on Shakespeare's attitude to war it is probably along the lines that he favoured 'just' wars and opposed unjust ones (especially civil wars).[21] Paola Pugliatti in *Shakespeare and the Just War Tradition* claims to propose an 'even-handed' orthodoxy, arguing that Shakespeare adheres to Augustinian 'just war theory' (*ius ad bellum*).[22] If not pacifism, this is intended at least as a more morally attuned alternative to outright militarism, Franziska Quabeck offers 'nuanced' mediation between the rival points of view: 'As an approach to war in Shakespeare, just war theory breaks down the "either/or" dilemma, offering a perspective that is neither militarist nor pacifist', instead offering a kind of debate between the two. However, even when appealing to this *via media*, Quabeck finds only two unequivocal 'just wars' in Shakespeare's plays (*Richard III* and *Macbeth*), a scant finding:

> Rather than rejecting violence altogether, the plays posit carefully-limited conditions for a just war. In the representation of warfare, unethical behaviour is the norm; almost all of the wars the plays depict are unjust, violating one prescribed principle of just war theory or another, with the notable exceptions of Richmond's war against Richard, as well as Malcolm's war against Macbeth. The two more radical extremes of pac-

---

21. See for example John Mark Mattox, 'Henry V: Shakespeare's Just Warrior', *War, Literature, and the Arts*, 12 (2000), 30–54.
22. Paola Pugliatti, *Shakespeare and the Just War Tradition*.

ifism and militarism are not adequately complex to capture this more nuanced ethics of war.[23]

The stark dichotomy – 'just or unjust' – is admittedly too simplistic, but why, one asks, is pacifism, a belief that all human problems can be negotiated without violence, deemed just as 'radical' and 'extreme' as militarism? Even an argument claiming Shakespeare's preoccupation with 'just war' that can find only two unambiguous examples raises questions.

Both plays show armed conflict as resistance against regicides who have proved themselves unabashed murderers and tyrants in power. They turn more properly not on the issue of 'just war' but on the principle of Aquinian Natural Law, that a tyrant who has gained power through murder can legitimately be overthrown in order to restore peace to the body politic. The 'civil butchery' and acts of assassination and torture are initiated by acts of regicide followed by tyrannical rule. However, even in these examples of manifestly 'just wars', there was a strong alternative line of thought, for example explicated in the important text, *The Mirror for Magistrates*, several times expanded between 1559 and 1574. The Christian adage 'Vengeance is mine, saith the Lord' states unequivocally that it is up to God or history to dislodge tyrants (even if He uses future human agents), since impetuous vengeance breeds future revenge. Even in the two exceptional plays, Shakespeare appears to be carefully aware of this reasoning and to take steps not to preclude it. Macduff's killing of Macbeth is heavily dependent on quasi-supernatural conditions (the prophecies of the Witches, Birnam Wood's apparent movement, and Macduff's caesarean birth) amounting to a preordained historical destiny unravelling to remove the tyrant. In *Richard III* 'shallow Richmond' appears only in the fifth Act, without personal characterisation or motivation, and depicted more like an agent of divine intervention than an individual human being. An alternative 'moral' might be proposed, that it is symbolically not civil war that establishes peace but the warning of the sequence of ghosts he has assassinated that visit Richard before battle – the repeated, haunted keenings, 'Despair and die' (5.1). Mortality, the inevitability of death, is the nemesis of tyrants, whether it is in battle or in their beds. Dictators throughout history, for all their paranoid attempts to protect themselves, refuse to discard their illusions of immortality:

RICHARD
By the apostle Paul, shadows tonight
Have struck more terror to the soul of Richard

23. Franzisa Quabeck, 'Shakespeare's Unjust Wars', *Critical Survey*, 30 (2018), 67–80, 68, 78. The article is a follow-up to Quabeck's book, *Just and Unjust Wars in Shakespeare* (Berlin: de Gruyter, 2013).

Than can the substance of ten thousand soldiers
Armed in proof and led by shallow Richmond.

(5.1.229–33)

Just war theory can be challenged on several grounds, first along the lines proposed by Saint Paul: 'Dearly beloved, avenge not yourselves, but rather give place unto wrath, for it is written: Vengeance is mine; I will repay, saith the Lord' (KJV, Romans 12:19–20). In secular as well as Christian terms, this leaves the correction of injustices up to providence and historical events rather than hands of human individuals, a process that can take generations to effect. Interpreted strictly, this rules out just wars. Augustine, however, felt it imperative to codify conditions favouring a just war, but his classic formulation is paradoxical, if not a contradiction: '*Peace is the instinctive aim of all creatures, and is even the ultimate purpose of war*'.[24] The first phrase builds upon the fundamental precept of Natural Law that all creatures instinctively seek the preservation of life, but it implodes under the second – not that peace is opposed to war but that it justifies war. Upon such shaky foundations has been built the concept of just war. John Gittings, editor of the *Oxford International Encyclopedia of Peace*, summarises in his book *The Glorious Art of Peace: From the Iliad to Iraq*, the conditions under which war can be justified:

> (i) there must be a just cause (in self-defence or to punish aggression), (ii) war must be undertaken with the right intention (not for revenge), (iii) it may only be undertaken by a competent authority (the state), (iv) it should only be undertaken as a last resort, and (v) peace is the ultimate objective (the warrior should be a peacemaker).[25]

Damaging critiques can be made of all these conditions, such as their imprecision and subjectivity, and the knowledge that they are invariably politically constructed and claimed by self-interested bodies along partisan lines. It would be unprecedented for any national leader to claim seriously that his war is unjustified, though in reality history is of course littered with trumped up cases. In this sense the conditions act not as constraints on violence, but just as often provoke self-vindicating fabrications and camouflaging of intentions. The first two conditions and the fourth are malleable to individual interpretation and rationalisation, rather than objective proof. The third condition has always been con-

---

24. Augustine, *Concerning the City of God against the Pagans* transl. Henry Bettinson (Harmondsworth: Penguin Books,1972), Book XIX Chapter 12, 866.
25. Gittings, *The Glorious Art of Peace*, 81.

troversial since 'the state', even in democracies, is personified in a single 'commander-in-chief' who may claim a mandate from an electoral system even when his policy lacks public support. In Elizabethan times the dubiousness was repeatedly questioned by some, such as Samuel Daniel, whose poetical history *The Civil Wars* (1595) was read by Shakespeare:

> See how these great men clothe their private hate
> In those fair colours of the public good;
> And to effect their ends pretend the State,
> As if the State by their affections stood.[26]

'Affections' stand for self-interested whims. Daniel provides epigrammatical lines to post the 'wiser' course of not trusting 'great men' but 'wise': 'Wise men ever have preferréd far / Th'unjustest peace before the justest war'. He cryptically summarises the English civil wars as conflicts in which 'two Crowns did sway / The work of slaughter, two Kings' Causes wrought / Destruction to one People',[27] a view which is mirrored in Shakespeare's *Henry VI* plays. The fifth condition ('peace is the ultimate objective') gives the game away completely, with what looks like a blatant contradiction, a pious platitude or loophole. Alcibiades in *Timon of Athens* exercises the logic in 'let war breed peace' (5.4.83). The 'warrior' is licensed to be 'peacemaker' solely on his own terms as victor, and the peacemaking comes only after inflicting a mortally damaging and humiliating defeat of a vanquished 'enemy' that lays the seeds for future revenge. Such 'peace terms' seem less like a 'just' negotiation over the root cause of the conflict than an unchallenged assertion of superior force.

By common consent *Troilus and Cressida* presents the Trojan war as manifestly unjust, based as it is on the personal abduction of Helen by Paris.[28] It is also, as one critic describes, 'a war whose cost is egregiously disproportionate to its cause'.[29] What is less often remarked upon is that in comparison with all its sources the play is also more comprehensively and trenchantly anti-war in tone than they are, meaning that it is Shakespeare's own considered choice, arguably reflecting a general

26. Samuel Daniel, *The Civil Wars of England between the two Houses of Lancaster and York*, in *The Complete Works of Samuel Daniel*, ed. Alexander Grosart (London: Spenser Society, 1885), vol 2, 39.
27. Daniel, *Complete Works*, vol. 2, 299, spelling modernised.
28. See White, *Pacifism and English Literature*, 168–73 and *passim*; Gittings, *The Glorious Art of Peace*, 109–22; Franziska Quabeck, 'Shakespeare's Unjust Wars', *Critical Survey*, 30 (2018), 67–80, 68, 78.
29. Franziska Quabeck, 'Shakespeare's Unjust Wars' in Gray, *Ethics of War*, 68–82, 76.

distaste for war itself. It illustrates the jaundiced opinion of Erasmus already quoted, 'they are chiefly the private, sinister, and selfish motives of princes, which operate as the real causes of all war', since in this case the cause is Paris's abduction of Helen. Shakespeare's Thersites is the reductive spokesman: 'After this, the vengeance on the whole camp! Or rather, the Neapolitan bone-ache! For that, methinks, is the curse dependent on those that war for a placket' (2.3.216–18).

By common critical consent the war in *Troilus and Cressida* is unjust, but on the other hand the play which is most often discussed in relation to just war theory is *Henry V*. For some, the play is a *locus classicus* for maintaining Shakespeare's belief in just war theory, and that Henry is Shakespeare's version of an 'ideal' king, taking at face value Henry's care in constructing a case for invading France. But others have seen it as an example of Shakespeare's stance of studied ambivalence, and resistant readings have been offered ever since Hazlitt's excoriating attack on the cynical expediency of *Henry V*'s eponymous king.[30] On this reading, Henry's initial dialogue with the Archbishop of Canterbury is a less than wholehearted acceptance of responsibility, from a leader looking for an excuse, however tenuous, to wage war, and seeking the blessing of the clergy to do so:

> For God doth know how many now in health
> Shall drop their blood in approbation
> Of what your reverence shall incite us to.
> Therefore take heed how you impawn our person,
> How you awake our sleeping sword of war.
>
> (1.2.18–22)

The King pointedly distinguishes between 'you' (the clergy) and 'we' as royal plural in 'our person' and 'our sleeping sword of war'. The phrase 'what your reverence shall *incite* us to' (my italics) places full responsibility for causing future casualties squarely on the shoulders of the Archbishop and his retinue. It is the first example of Henry evading personal responsibility by pre-emptively shifting the blame in the event of things going wrong, a personal habit which comes to characterise him. War against France gives him a handy, cynical opportunity to employ his father's advised stratagem of distracting the populace from civil problems:

---

30. See Hazlitt's chapter on *Henry V* in *Hazlitt's Criticism of Shakespeare: A Selection*, ed. R. S. White, (Lampeter: Edwin Mellen Press, 1996).

> Therefore, my Harry,
> Be it thy course to busy giddy minds
> With foreign quarrels, that action, hence borne out
> May waste the memory of the former days.
>
> (*2 Henry IV*, 4.5.12–15)

It is a startlingly frank observation on a perennial political strategy by governments of manipulating public opinion away from civil unrest and internal challenges. In the Roman empire it was explicitly endorsed by Scipio in particular.[31] Henry's main anxiety, as he reveals later in the play speaking in soliloquy and addressing God, is to 'waste the memory of the former days' when his father had deposed Richard II which threatens his own legitimacy.

Shakespeare had to be extremely careful in his handling of the Salic Law, a notoriously ambiguous legal fiction respecting claims through female lineage. Not only did Elizabeth look increasingly likely to die without issue, nor to nominate a successor, but also she listed herself as 'Queen of France' among her titles.[32] So sensitive were the issues that it seemed Shakespeare took exceptional care in structuring the narrative. He is threading a diplomatic needle, by not openly criticising Henry's actual decision to invade while indirectly leaving open questions about the process of making the decision. In a nutshell, he encourages 'misinformation' from the clergy which allows him to pay lip service to his war being just.

The scene in which Henry interrogates the Archbishop of Canterbury can be staged in radically different ways that either do, or do not whitewash the King. Olivier cut the scene in half and directed the clergymen as comically verbose, digressive and dithery, as though they are simply not on top of their brief as they drop their notes. The lengthy speech is made virtually incomprehensible to either audience or reader. But there is a more politically motivated explanation for the clergy's nervousness. They are worried that the case for invading France is not especially strong, but they must contrive to give the King the answer he wants to hear, since behind Henry's own solicitation lies a direct, Machiavellian threat. We have already learned in the very first scene that if the clergy do not please the King he will legislate that they forfeit to the crown half their lands and considerable financial assets – in modern terms, a policy of savage 'sanctions'. This reading, unsympathetic to Henry, is pursued in detail by historian Peter Lake in *How Shakespeare Put Politics on the*

31. Bonadeo, 'Montaigne on War', 418.
32. See Introduction *King Edward III*, ed. Richard Proudfoot and Nicola Bennett, Arden ed. Third Series (London: Bloomsbury, 2017), 12, 19–22.

Stage,[33] while John Sutherland is another who regards Henry's resumption of English entitlement to France as thin and probably spurious.[34] Nicholas Hytner in his National Theatre production (2003) used as prop the famously false 'dossier' of non-existent 'evidence' used to justify the invasion of Iraq in the same year,[35] against the written advice of many eminent international lawyers, including James Crawford, later to be the first Australian jurist appointed to the International Court of Justice.

Morally, financially and politically speaking, the clergy are the 'oligarchs' of their day. Their pre-arranged tactics are to present Henry with an apparently plausible (though logically strained, sophistical, and evasively circumlocutory) dynastic claim to seize part of France, because they realise this is the conclusion he wishes to hear. In performance, Henry's brisk intervention can be played as less convincing than merely an efficient chairman's attempt to close longwinded discussion: 'May I with right and conscience make this claim?' (1.2.96). Writing this in 2022, my memory is fresh of an uncannily similar occasion when President Putin was filmed, impatiently drumming his fingers on the desk, asking each of his 'courtiers' in turn whether they agree to support a policy of denying sovereignty and independence to Ukraine, paving the way for Russian invasion. One adviser who clearly has reservations is brutally humiliated as Putin barks 'Speak plainly'.[36] Performances of the play in coming days will surely draw attention to the menacing parallels.

Shakespeare shows that the possibility of an unjust 'cause' for his war has percolated down the army ranks, and he has the commoner Williams vocalise the disturbing charges 'if the cause be not good':

> But if the cause be not good, the King himself hath a heavy reckoning to make when all those legs and arms and heads chopped off in a battle shall join together at the latter day and cry all, 'We died at such a place', some swearing, some crying for a surgeon, some upon their wives left poor behind them, some upon the debts they owe, some upon their children rawly left. I am afeard there are few die well that die in a battle, for how can they charitably dispose of anything when blood is their argument?
>
> (4.1.132–41)

33. Lake, *How Shakespeare Put Politics on the Stage*, 364–71.
34. *Henry V, War Criminal? & Other Shakespeare Puzzles* John Sutherland and Cedric Watts. Oxford University Press (2000).
35. See Amy Lidster and Sonia Massai (eds), *Shakespeare at War*, ch. 22.
36. '"Speak Plainly": Putin has tense exchange with his spy chief – video', *The Guardian*, 22 February 2022: https://www.theguardian.com/world/video/2022/feb/22/speak-plainly-putin-tense-exchange-spy-chief-ukraine-video.

These are not questions the disguised king wishes to answer, and he throws personal responsibility back onto victims to answer for themselves when their own day of judgement comes. In his understanding, victory in battle will absolve at least himself.

Even a single writer can illustrate some vacillation over 'just war theory' in *Henry V*, by paying attention to the historical context in which the King is judged. Theodor Meron, a highly distinguished international humanitarian lawyer specialising in war crimes, provided a 'lawyer's commentary' on aspects of policy in Shakespeare's time, and his two books have rather different emphases and conclusions. In *Henry's Wars and Shakespeare's Laws: Perspectives on the Law of War in the Later Middle Ages*, Meron examines how Shakespeare's Henry V paid lip service to the law of nations of his own day.[37] He concludes that, with a few lapses, Shakespeare's Henry in important respects does act in accordance with Medieval legal norms and justice and the code of chivalry, and that his war against France is not waged with illegitimate motives or actions. In that book Meron addresses 'The Siege of Harfleur and Treatment of Occupied Territory', and puts 'the best possible light' on Henry's order to kill prisoners, as a decision based on grounds of military necessity at a dangerous moment for the King's own limited forces. In that book, Meron concedes that in some aspects the code of chivalry itself was a romantic veneer veiling a brutal enterprise, as previous generations of historians like Maurice Keen had claimed,[38] but his conclusion is 'that chivalry performed an important social function based on upholding justice and protecting the weak'. A large qualification, in Meron's terms, is that 'on the battlefield, rules of chivalry protected only members of the knightly class', and did not routinely extend rights or obligations to commoners amongst warring men.

However, in Meron's later book (1998), *Bloody Constraint: War and Chivalry in Shakespeare*, a different set of conclusions emerges, with the emphasis now placed on changing attitudes to chivalry in Shakespeare's 1590s rather than Medieval times.[39] Meron concludes here that in the context of Elizabethan England in which chivalry had declined, it is possible to detect in Shakespeare's practice a recognition that, 'perhaps Shakespeare wanted to discourage war that, without the veneer of chivalric rules, appeared to be entirely barbaric'. Even the decision made by directors and readers about the historical setting to choose – 1415,

---

37. Theodor Meron, *Henry's Wars and Shakespeare's Laws: Perspectives on the Law of War in the Later Middle Ages* (Oxford: Clarendon Press, 1993).
38. Maurice Keen, *Chivalry* (New Haven: Yale University Press, 1984).
39. Theodor Meron, *Bloody Constraint.*

1599, 1918, 1945, or the 2020s – is dramatically consequential. Meron promises to 'return to Shakespeare's pacifism in the conclusions of this chapter' (22). He goes on to state more trenchantly that in Shakespeare's view, generally 'wars are not only tragic and bloody, but also futile' (pp. 7, 8). 'Characters challenge war through a combination of legal and literary means . . .' (22), and 'Shakespeare's protagonists attack the futility of war' throughout the canon (38). He quotes a string of 'allusions to the negative aspects of war' in a variety of plays: 'If speaking of the horrors of war discourages war, then Shakespeare does so most effectively, filling his text with moving references to the brutality and bloodiness of war' (41). In his promised 'conclusions of this chapter', Meron asserts that 'the evidence largely supports a pacifist preference' and he now rejects the idea of 'just war' in *Henry V*:

> Consider also the debunking of the war's justification in *Henry V* (1599), that play's demonstration of the war's cruelty and bloodshed, the sarcastic, greed-based description of the quarter for ransom transaction (Pistol), and the showing of the war's eventual futility. *Troilus and Cressida* (1602–1603), a decidedly anti-war play, coincided with the accession to the throne of the pacifist James Stuart. Undoubtedly, the humanist pacifism of Erasmus and More must also have played a role. In *Troilus*, war was reduced from the epic to the satiric, and from chivalric to the simply bloody and chaotic. In *Troilus*, war was no longer a corrective for an imperfect peace. It was a senseless slaughter destined for an annihilation of Troy.

Meron returned again to 'the question of whether Shakespeare was a pacifist' twenty years later in a more stage- and film-centred article entitled 'Shakespeare: A Dove, a Hawk, or simply a Humanist?'.[40] Evidently still uneasy about unqualified either-or opinions, he concludes cautiously that there is not enough evidence to claim Shakespeare as a consistent pacifist from the texts alone, but that in practice performances are invariably slanted or edited in ways which direct, coerce, or pre-empt our independent judgement towards one conclusion or the other. He still asserts, however, that in general the dramatist shows 'a profound uneasiness with war and violence', often demonstrating 'the inescapable futility of war' (956), and concluding that Shakespeare is pre-eminently a 'humanist'. He now acknowledges that as literary readers and theatre audiences we cannot ignore the multiple issues of historical and dramatic context, the emotive power of imaginative language when pitted

---

40. Theodor Meron, 'Shakespeare: a dove, a hawk, or simply a humanist?', *American Journal of International Law*, 111 (2017), 936–56.

against arid legal abstractions, topical circumstances, and most importantly assumptions made in performances in different periods, over how
to stage the play and what to omit. However, in summary Meron goes so
far as to use the phrase 'Shakespeare's pacifist tendencies', arguing that
'his leanings were primarily pro-peace in nature' (939–40), with which
obviously I would not disagree.

Henry's clearly premeditated intention to go to war sees him seeking
excuses, since it is hardly a compelling reason to invade a country on
the pretext of a perceived insult, when jokingly gifted tennis balls by
the French Dauphin. The gesture is intended as condescendingly lighthearted but it elicits the first of Henry's threatening tirades as he blames
an enemy for provoking violence, and in doing so claims for himself
heavenly authority:

> And tell the pleasant Prince this mock of his
> Hath turned his balls to gun-stones, and his soul
> Shall stand sore charged for the wasteful vengeance
> That shall fly with them: for many a thousand widows
> Shall this his mock mock out of their dear husbands,
> Mock mothers from their sons, mock castles down,
> And some are yet ungotten and unborn
> That shall have cause to curse the Dauphin's scorn.

He makes it brutally clear who he claims will be blamed for the slaughter
to come:

> So get you hence in peace. And tell the Dauphin
> His jest will savour but of shallow wit
> When thousands weep more than did laugh at it.
>
> (1.2.282–97)

Whether interpreted as patriotic indignation or confected anger, this
looks like Henry seizing the opportunity to reinforce his already determined decision to invade France. The second characteristic revealed in
the speech is Henry's pious invocation of 'the will of God / To whom
do I appeal', which he is to repeat several times. In this, he is not being
modestly self-effacing, but grandiosely inviting his subjects to equate his
own success with God's power. He later disingenuously uses the trope to
write his own victory as God's will, a *post facto* vindication of his own
belligerent decisions. There is nothing unusual in victors claiming that
might is right, and Christian audiences would have deemed it appropriate, but to more secular audiences it can be played as calculated rhetoric.
In his private quasi-prayer on the night before Agincourt, he bargains
directly and transactionally with God to overlook his father's illegitimate

acquisition of the crown (though decidedly not doubting his own right to it). Shakespeare had dramatised the usurpation in *Richard II*, though his deposition scene fell foul of the Master of the Revels and was omitted from performance.[41]

To traits revealed in the early scenes – bullying, threatening, and shifting blame and responsibility – we can add Henry's later tendency to lie and mislead, no more in evidence than in his disguised impersonation of a commoner, 'Harry le Roi', luring the soldier Williams into unwitting self-incrimination by expressing scepticism about the integrity of kings and questioning the legitimacy of their cause (4.1). Even more audacious is Williams' lack of repentance when the king's disguise is revealed, more or less accusing the King of being an *agent provocateur* and offering begrudging recrimination and only a dutiful request for 'pardon':

> Your majesty came not like your self: you appeared to me but as a common man – witness the night, your garments, your lowliness, and what your highness suffered under that shape. I beseech you take it for your own fault and not mine, for had you been as I took you for, I made no offence; therefore I beseech your highness, pardon me. [*kneels*] (4.8.50–6)

Is it, I wonder, significant that the dramatist lends his own name to this invented character (as he did to the schoolboy being put through his Latin lessons in *The Merry Wives of Windsor*). Did he personally even play Williams on the stage, as a man who speaks with such integrity on behalf of commoners, against wagers of war in general?

By foregrounding so clearly the issue of the responsibility of leaders which, as Williams and Bates persist in arguing, cannot be evaded or shifted, Shakespeare carefully distinguishes the moral position of the foot-soldiers, whose fears, doubts, undoubted courage, loyalty, and (perhaps) misguided gullibility in a war of dubious legality are fully demonstrated. Bates risks treason in wishing the king 'to be ransomed, and many a poor men's lives saved' (4.1.120). Shakespeare here is tapping into a classical 'axiom' quoted (from Valerius Maximus) by his contemporary Montaigne in an essay describing war as a 'monstrosity', 'that soldiers should go more in fear of their captain than the enemy'.[42] Whether or not we judge Henry's conduct in waging war as exemplary or disingenuous, at the very least he and the dramatist both acknowledge that some legal justification is required to legitimise a 'foreign quarrel'

41. Peter Lake, *How Shakespeare Put Politics on the Stage*, 356. See Lake's whole chapter 15 '*Henry V* and the Fruits of Legitimacy', 349–97 for the most thorough discussion on the related subjects of legitimacy and just war in the play.
42. Michel de Montaigne, 'On Physiognomy', *The Complete Essays*, 1180, 1178.

and turn it into a just war. No such scruple had impeded or fretted the mind of Marlowe's all-conquering Tamburlaine in his wars of aggression.

War crimes

Henry commits at least one blatant war-crime when he orders the slaughter of prisoners of war, in order to free up his own limited troops for battle rather than guarding the prisoners:

KING HENRY V
The French have reinforced their scatter'd men.
Then every soldier kill his prisoners!
Give the word through.

(4.6.36–8)

In justifying this abuse of law, protocol and military convention, he seems already to have lied to his officers that the order is in retaliation for French crimes. Captain Gower willingly supports this royal sleight of hand, even as his words reveal an unintended irony which an informed audience can spot: '. . . the King most worthily hath caused every soldier to cut his prisoner's throat. O, 'tis a gallant king!' (4.7.5–10). Further emphasising the contradictions, Shakespeare's cameo scene in which the English boy is found to have been killed – itself a French act also 'expressly against the laws of war' according to the military expert Fluellen – comes some fifty lines *later* in the scene. It is seized upon by Henry to cement his own deflectionary 'spin': 'I was not angry since I came to France / Until this instant' (4.7.54–5).[43] Some critics point out the practical impossibility of the vastly outnumbered English forces killing so many prisoners without meeting resistance from them, even if they are bound and unarmed.[44] This seems cancelled out, however, by the fact that according to laws of chivalry Henry was bound to grant freedom to the prisoners as 'parolees', so long as they gave their 'word' (*parole*) not to resume hostilities.[45] Even given this honourable course, Shakespeare's Henry does not take it. Other critics and directors try to remove the tarnish from Henry's reputation by reversing the sequence to

43. Peter Lake, *How Shakespeare Put Politics on the Stage*, 360.
44. Charles Edelman gives a detailed analysis of the issues in relation to the play's confused sources in '"Then Every Soldier Kill His Prisoners": Shakespeare at the Battle of Agincourt', *Parergon*, n.s. 16 (1998), 31–45.
45. Raine Liivoja, 'Chivalry without a Horse', 78.

establish that the killing of the boy is the cause for retaliation. Olivier in his movie (reputedly at the request of Churchill), chronologically reversed the speeches, since otherwise Henry emerges as less than the ideal military leader the film sought to portray. In a similar act of white-washing, he omits Pistol's crude order to '*couper la gorge*'.[46] Branagh simply omits the references to the massacre of prisoners, perhaps to avoid the textual problem. Simon Barker, however, points out that there is no equivalent episode in Holinshed, so since it was Shakespeare's invention and choice of presentation there seems no compelling textual reason to assume it is a mistake.[47] J. C. Maxwell argued persuasively that this is one of several points in the play where Henry is fully aware of what he is doing, exploiting an occasion and using 'angry' rhetoric to create self-consciously a narrative which absolves himself by blaming the French.[48] John Sutherland remained agnostic, musing that Henry's repeated command to kill the prisoners was not in fact carried out. But if it was, Sutherland seems to suggest that it points to Henry's callous-ness, that in the King's eyes it was only the 'unqualitied' and expenda-ble commoners rather than 'gentles' (officers and aristocrats) who were slaughtered: 'there are prisoners and prisoners . . . As well shed tears for the dead horses festering in Agincourt's fields'.[49]

Less commented upon and equally damaging, the very presence of a boy in Henry's army is also 'expressly against the laws of war'. There is more than one minor on the English side, since the Boy, speaking of the camp luggage, fears that 'The French might have a good prey of us, if he knew of it, for there is none to guard it but boys' (4.4.76–7). His fears are realised when later Gower and Fluellen disapprovingly discuss the slaughter of all the boys (4.7.1–10), a manifest war crime by the French this time, since guarding luggage in war was deemed in Medieval law to be a safe zone. Shakespeare's overall point seems to be that war is itself a license for crimes, a conclusion most evident in Henry's address to the citizens of Harfleur.

Presiding over a posthumous moot indictment of the overall record of Henry V's war of invasion held in Washington in 2010, Supreme Court justices unanimously found Shakespeare's King guilty of war crimes. A generation of critics before, between, and during the two World Wars would have pursed their lips in disapproval at such irreverent treatment

46. These and other missions from the movies are traced by Meron, 'Shakespeare: a dove, a hawk, or simply a humanist?'.
47. Simon Barker, *War and Nationalism*, 137.
48. J. C. Maxwell, 'Simple or Complex? Some Problems in the Interpretation of Shakespeare', *Durham University Journal*, xlvi (1954), 112–15.
49. Sutherland, *Henry V, War Criminal?*, 113–15.

of the hero of a play they had enthusiastically supported as 'a patriotic work, written in time of colonial war to justify the expansionism and xenophobia of a nation consolidating an empire'.[50]

The siege of Harfleur

As well as (at least arguably) committing war crimes, Henry is certainly capable of imagining them. When his war rhetoric is in yeasty flight he lets slip the violence which underlies his conception of heroic action. The aggression is often expressed in sexual terms, a preoccupation which Joshua S. Goldstein, a Professor of International Relations, claims is all but universal in army parlance, especially 'in a community of men ... deprived of usual social and emotional outlets'.[51] C. L. Barber and Richard Wheeler as psychoanalytical readers note that even the 'Once more unto the breach, dear friends' speech 'is set up retrospectively as an invitation to gang rape', full of 'sex-war imagery': '... This phallic imagery, deliberately ruthless, is not only fearful in the sense of inspiring fear, but also inspired *by* fear'. They see 'moral cruelty, and sexual cruelty, as elements of his character ... We are either with him or against him, depending on whether or not *we* supply the dissenting or qualifying perspective'.[52] The 'qualifying perspective' comes at certain points in the play, such as the parody of Henry's 'breach' speech by seedy 'slackers and cowards and criminal camp-followers in Bardolph, Nym and Pistol'.[53]

Instilling fear is Henry's main weapon, along with verbal threats of future brutality which come fluently to his lips. Reading as a pacifist makes it possible to see his address to the besieged citizens of Harfleur as inadvertently one of the most repulsive indictments in literature of the military mind in operation, and again unprecedented in Shakespeare's source. Magnanimously offering the civilians his 'best mercy' is not an ethical option seriously considered by Henry, since his alternative to their surrender – open threats to practise genocide and mass torture of civilians – is a heinous set of war-crimes, the shocking extent of which requires full quotation.

50. David J. Baker, '"Wildehirissheman": Colonialist Representation in Shakespeare's *Henry V*' in R. J. C. Watt, *Shakespeare's History Plays* (London: Longman and Pearson Education, 2002), 193–203.
51. Joshua S. Goldstein, *War and Gender* (Cambridge University Press, 2001), 333 and ch.6 in general, 'Conquests: sex, rape, and exploitation in wartime'.
52. C. L. Barber and Richard Wheeler, *The Whole Journey: Shakespeare's Power of Development* (Berkeley: University of California Press, 1986), 220–1.
53. Barber and Wheeler, *The Whole Journey*, 220–3.

How yet resolves the Governor of the town?
This is the latest parle we will admit.
Therefore to our best mercy give yourselves,
Or like to men proud of destruction
Defy us to our worst: for, as I am a soldier,
A name that in my thoughts becomes me best,
If I begin the battery once again,
I will not leave the half-achieved Harfleur
Till in her ashes she lie buried.
The gates of mercy shall be all shut up,
And the fleshed soldier, rough and hard of heart,
In liberty of bloody hand shall range
With conscience wide as hell, mowing like grass
Your fresh-fair virgins and your flowering infants.
What is it then to me if impious war,
Arrayed in flames like to the prince of fiends,
Do with his smirched complexion all fell feats
Enlinked to waste and desolation?
What is't to me, when you yourselves are cause,
If your pure maidens fall into the hand
Of hot and forcing violation?
What rein can hold licentious wickedness
When down the hill he holds his fierce career?
We may as bootless spend our vain command
Upon th'enraged soldiers in their spoil
As send precepts to the leviathan
To come ashore. Therefore, you men of Harfleur,
Take pity of your town and of your people
Whiles yet my soldiers are in my command,
Whiles yet the cool and temperate wind of grace
O'erblows the filthy and contagious clouds
Of heady murder, spoil and villainy.
If not, why, in a moment look to see
The blind and bloody soldier with foul hand
Defile the locks of your shrill-shrieking daughters,
Your fathers taken by the silver beards,
And their most reverend heads dashed to the walls,
Your naked infants spitted upon pikes,
Whiles the mad mothers with their howls confused
Do break the clouds, as did the wives of Jewry
At Herod's bloody-hunting slaughtermen.
What say you? will you yield, and this avoid?
Or, guilty in defence, be thus destroyed?

(3.3.1–43)

It is a truly shocking speech. If only in intention at this stage, Henry baldly states that he is prepared to licence his troops to commit multiple atrocities. The phrase 'Herod's bloody-hunting slaughtermen' alludes to the notorious biblical genocide of male children under two years of age. The violent momentum of Henry's lines may sound inspirational in battle, but the effect is vastly different in this context. It amounts to an incitement to his own troops to commit acts of brutality against civilians. If he orders, 'The flesh'd soldier, rough and hard of heart' 'In liberty of bloody hand shall range / With conscience wide as hell', itemising as victims 'naked infants spitted upon pikes', violation of 'shrill-shrieking daughters', and 'reverend heads dash'd to the walls'. In particular, licence to rape is obsessively on Henry's mind since he repeats it three times, with what seems dangerously close to vicarious relish. As Jordi Coral points out, the threat comes notwithstanding the fact that rape was officially outlawed in the code of chivalric conduct and explicitly proscribed by the historical Henry V himself.[54] Coral also points out the parallel echoes of rape imagery in the tavern scene, especially surrounding Pistol's lust, and in the Dauphin's fears that French women will be raped by the English soldiers: 'the play is fraught with explicit allusions to rape as a predictable consequence of armed conflict, so much so that the most outrageous threat is uttered by the king himself' (410). The specific choice of rape imagery in the Harfleur speech goes further than revealing the character, since it also sheds light upon the activity in which Henry is engaged. (Once again, it is a Shakespearean emphasis, since according to the historical record Henry used the equally brutal tactic of firing twelve cannons to force the town to surrender.)[55] Modern feminists have persistently drawn links between war and violent misogyny:

> If symbolic and actual rape encode domination, then misogyny serves as an important motor of male aggression in war. Rape is 'the ultimate metaphor for the war system,' according to Betty Reardon. As a symbolic form of rape, armed violence genders the victor as male and the vanquished as female.[56]

54. See Jordi Coral, '"Maiden Walls That War Hath Never Entered": Rape and Post-Chivalric Military Culture in Shakespeare's *Henry V*', *College Literature*, 44 (2017), 404–435. Coral points out the parallel echoes of rape imagery in the tavern scene, especially associated with Pistol.
55. Kelly DeVries and Robert Douglas Smith, *Medieval Military Technology*, 2nd ed. (Toronto: University of Toronto Press, 2012), 165–67.
56. Joshua S. Goldstein, *War and Gender*, 371. See more generally ch. 6, 'Conquests: sex, rape, and exploitation in wartime.

Today scholars who study gender and war have coined a new word, 'gendercide', to describe the practice of using rape as a deliberate tactic of war.[57] A chapter by Joshua S. Goldstein covers among other things the time-honoured visual representation of weapons of war as phallic objects, often pictured moving rapidly away from the spectator-position of the camera and leading to an explosion simulating orgasm. The writer documents research on the subject in general which indirectly points to another rhetorical effect implicit in Henry's speech. In context, it is not addressed solely to the citizens of the beleaguered town but also to his own soldiers, sharpening the link between male desire, voyeurism and military endeavour, as he offers the soldiers license for sexual 'spoils'.[58] Despite the self-evidently abhorrent subtext linking war and sexual violence, evidence suggests that some attitudes are implicitly the product of the *raison d'étre* of war itself.

Such consequences, Henry warns, will be the fault of the innocent people of Harfleur as punishment for refusing to surrender. In modern military legalese in international law, the question is whether he is criminally evading his 'command responsibility'. Although even nowadays there is a grey area between intentionally encouraging, or failing to investigate lawless acts by subordinates, Henry seems as close as one could imagine to 'constructive' incitement,[59] and indifference to legal and moral constraints. Henry is following a famous military precedent, since Montaigne notes that Julius Caesar 'did not show much of a conscience . . . After a victory he would often allow [his soldiers] unbridled licence; he would even free them from the rules of military discipline'.[60] Among other things, Henry is sabotaging his own argument, delivered later to Williams and Bates, that the king cannot be held responsible for the individual sins of his subjects even in war, since here he shows himself willing to release his men to act without conscientious restraint and against canons of chivalry, war, and law.

Voices from afar – including those of Homer, Chaucer, Gower, Erasmus and Colet[61] – had lamented that such threats to women, chil-

---

57. For example, see Adam Jones (ed.), *Gendercide and Genocide* (Nashville Vanderbilt University Press, 2004).

58. Goldstein, *War and Gender*, 355–6.

59. For an illuminating and detailed account of the modern legal understanding, see Aaron Fellmeth and Emily Crawford, '"Reason to know" in the international law of command responsibility', *International Review of the Red Cross*, 184 (2022), 1223–1266.

60. Montaigne, 'Observations on Julius Caesar's methods of waging war', *The Complete Essays*, 834.

61. For Erasmus and Colet's 'quasi-Christian' pacifism see Barker, *War and Nation*, ch. 2.

dren and the elderly, as well as tragic separations of families, lost live-lihoods and despoiled subsistence farms, are in the context of war not aberrations but inevitable consequences. In Derek Cohen's pithy sum-mation, 'In *Henry V*, finally, violence has become the handmaiden of absolutist monarchy'.[62]

In a variety of ways, Henry's speech threatening Harfleur, far from confirming his status as a charismatic and 'ideal' leader, constructs him-self as a personification of the allegorical figure of war described by Shakespeare's contemporary Thomas Sackville:

> Lastly stood War in glittering arms yclad,
> With visage grim, stern looks, and blackly hued;
> In his right hand a naked sword he had,
> That to the hilts was all with blood imbrued;
> And in his left (that kings and kingdoms rued)
> Famine and fire he held, and therewithal
> He razed towns, and threw down towers and all.
>
> Cities he sack'd and realms (that whilom flower'd
> In honour, glory, and rule above the best),
> He overwhelm'd, and all their fame devour'd,
> Consum'd destroy'd wasted, and never ceased.[63]

Sackville's description recalls another Shakespearean quintessential, machine-like man of war, Coriolanus, a living forerunner of the arms industry which owes no 'patriotic' or sentimental attachment to a single nation but is promiscuously open to changing sides: 'When he walks he moves like an engine, and the ground shrinks before his treading' (5.4.18).[64]

The example of Coriolanus opens a line of enquiry into another accusation of a specific war crime arguably committed by Henry in his speech before Harfleur. Coriolanus's vow to besiege Rome in a spirit of personal revenge violates the international humanitarian law against what is now referred to as 'collective punishment' of an innocent popu-lation, and Henry's threats amount at the very least to an incitement of his troops to do likewise. To those who argue that the law is a modern one (codified in the Geneva Conventions of 1949, Article 33), there are two answers. First, it is an enactment in words of a centuries' old moral

62. Derek Cohen, *Shakespeare's Culture of Violence* (London: Palgrave, 1993), 62.
63. Thomas Sackville, Earl of Dorset, *The Induction* in *The Works of Thomas Sackville*, ed. Reginald Sackville-West (London: J. R. Smith, 1859), 115–16.
64. For an extended analysis of this play see White, *Pacifism and English Literature*, 158–68.

condemnation which was certainly culturally available to Renaissance writers. Secondly, Shakespeare's frequently performed plays are akin to new works in the historical contexts of each performance, drawing and commenting on topical events, debates and norms prevailing outside the theatre at the time. In this sense, they are living documents and always open to contemporary interpretations.

As often occurs, an inspired or controversial production may reveal starkly a latent potential in the text, as did the radical director Michael Bogdanov in his Brechtian 'Wars of the Roses' for the English Shakespeare Company (1987–90). I recall vividly that stage performance, which brought out the underlying tawdriness of wars and the shabby intentions behind their waging, by making topical reference to wars in the 1980s. David Fuller reviewed it sympathetically, contrasting the 'patriotic jingoism' of many versions with their 'almost inevitable glorification of war':

> Like the mixture of accents, the costumes too mark a contrast with Olivier's cinematic historical realism: they include contemporary dress (especially battle fatigues, reminders of Vietnam, Northern Ireland, or the Falklands . . .). In *Henry V* the army recruits use the Union flag to suggest the xenophobic nationalism associated in the 1980s with English football hooliganism. In *Henry IV* Pistol, and in *Henry VI* Cade and his followers, use the Union flag, associating it with the violence of the contemporary far right National Front. A notorious popular press (*Sun*) headline, 'Gotcha' (on the sinking of the Argentinean battleship 'General Belgrano' during the 1983 Falklands war), makes an appearance before Agincourt, as does a banner reading, 'Fuck the Frogs.'[65]

Reviewers also pointed out that Henry's high-toned speech delivered to the band of 'noblest Englishmen' was immediately visually undercut on stage by parody, with the entrance of the dishevelled and tiring conscripts hollowly parroting Henry:

BARDOLPH
On, on, on, on, on! to the breach, to the breach!
NYM
Pray thee, Corporal, stay; the knocks are too hot, and for mine own part I have not a case of lives. The humour of it is too hot, that is the very plain-song of it.

Pistol follows Bardolph's parody with platitudinous doggerel from a popular song: 'Knocks come and go . . . / And sword and shield / In bloody

65. David Fuller, 'The Bogdanov Version: The English Shakespeare Company "Wars of the Roses"', *Literature/Film Quarterly*, 33 (2005), 118–141, 119.

field / Doth win immortal fame'. But Nym's 'the knocks are too hot' and the Boy's honest confession of homesickness and fear are more heartfelt: 'Would I were in an alehouse in London! I would give all my fame for a pot of ale and safety' (3.2.1–13). The 'fame' was promised by the King, but the Boy does not live to experience it. He drives home the point with a lengthy soliloquy delivered to the audience, contemptuously shredding the reputations of 'these three swashers' for their hypocrisy and dishonesty, resolving to leave their company (3.2.29–55). The dramatist forges a link between the boy and the audience with this direct address from him which comes as prelude to his reported death, a moment which, no matter how the play is ideologically inflected in performance, is a universally moving moment, alongside the reported death of Falstaff, in his bed rather than at war. In Bogdanov's case, the genius of juxtaposing the heroic and its direct parody was not the director's inspiration but the playwright's considered choice. Empathy for Nym's palpable fear of death and the Boy's plaintive homesickness as a child darkens the tone. Even the royalist-inclined Prologue draws attention to how the glamourising of war is unavoidably contrasted with its circumstantial tawdriness:

> And so our scene must to the battle fly
> Where – O for pity! – we shall much disgrace
> With four or five most vile and ragged foils
> Right ill-disposed in brawl ridiculous
> The name of Agincourt.
>
> (4.PROLOGUE. 48–52)

The contrast of heroic rhetoric and debasing satire in the theatre is close in effect to Wilfred Owen's ironic words on 'the old Lie': *Dulce et decorum est / Pro patria mori*.

Henry's warnings to the people of Harfleur may take an infamous place in the history of modern siege warfare. Apart from the sheer scale of victims caused by bombardment from the air, the episode anticipates the more recent, deliberate intimidation of civilians into submission. Morally repugnant as it seems, one of the regular justifications made for aerial warfare, from the examples of Dresden and Hiroshima through to Baghdad, Gaza and Ukrainian cities, has been a calculated policy of bombarding cities. The assumption is that threats of destruction will persuade civilian populations to beg their own leaders to admit defeat in order to avoid a massacre of the innocent population. It has rarely worked as intended in practice, and even Winston Churchill in World War One expressed reservations about its moral legitimacy.[66] In 1996 Harlan K.

---

66. See White, *Pacifism and English Literature*, 241–7.

Ullman and James P. Wade (approvingly) coined the phrase 'shock and awe' to dignify this so-called 'Mission Capability Package' (MCP)' to the US military establishment. A central plank of the theory was that a 'doctrine of rapid dominance' would demoralise civilian populations in a way calculated to prevent further carnage and bring peace'.[67] Using different means to the same end, historical precedents for the theory can found in Marlowe's Tamburlaine and Shakespeare's Henry V at Harfleur.

The Chorus's epilogue abruptly suggests also the historical pointlessness of the victory achieved by this 'star of England', since it is to provoke retaliation and soon to be reversed:

> Henry the Sixth, in infant bands crown'd King
> Of France and England, did this king succeed;
> Whose state so many had the managing,
> That they lost France and made his England bleed:
> Which oft our stage hath shown; and, for their sake,
> In your fair minds let this acceptance take.
> *Exit*

(Epilogue)

The playwright is deftly reminding his audiences that he had already dramatized these 'future' events. He is perhaps touting publicity for a stage revival of *1 Henry VI* on the following afternoon. Its opening lines lament the death of the young Henry V, and the sequence of plays shows England losing France and itself rapidly falling into civil war. The underlying logic is that a country which relies on armed force and military heroes to subjugate others will find its power unlikely to outlast the individual who promoted and promulgated such conquests.

John Keegan observed in *The Face of Battle*, his classic historical study of combat across five centuries that 'What battles have in common is human':

> the behaviour of men struggling to reconcile their instinct for self-preservation, their sense of honour and the achievement of some aim over which other men are ready to kill them. The study of battle is therefore always a study of fear and usually of courage; always of leadership, usually of obedience; always of compulsion, sometimes of insubordination; always of anxiety, sometimes of elation or catharsis; always of uncertainty and doubt, misinformation and misapprehension, usually also of faith and sometimes of vision; always of violence, sometimes also of cruelty, self-sacrifice, compassion; above all, it is always a study of solidarity

67. Harlan K. Ullman and James P. Wade, *Shock and Awe: Achieving Rapid Dominance* (Washington: National Defense University, 1996).

and usually also of disintegration – for it is toward the disintegration of human groups that battle is directed.[68]

Without referring to Shakespeare, Keegan manages here to include the extraordinarily wide range of 'human' responses to war depicted in the History plays. Through witnessing first-hand media coverage of conflicts pursued in the name of 'just wars', twenty-first century audiences as rarely before have questioned the causes of armed interventions from within or without. Just as importantly, the conduct and consequences of wars have been scrutinised. All have led to trials for war crimes, civilian casualties, torture, persecution of ethnic groups, family displacements, millions of fleeing refugees, traumatisation, mental illness and suicides amongst soldiers, and marital problems in the families of combatants and veterans. The rest of this book will examine more closely 'the disintegration of human groups [towards which] battle is directed'.

68. John Keegan, *The Face of Battle* (New York: Viking Press, 1976), 83.

Chapter 3

'Food for powder': Casualties Of War

Orson Welles in an interview unexpectedly claimed his own 'favourite picture' to be not *Citizen Kane* but *Chimes at Midnight* (1965, named in Europe *Falstaff*): 'If I wanted to get into heaven on the basis of one movie, that's the one I would offer up'. The movie traces the raffish knight's progress through the sequence of plays in which he appears. The guiding conception of Welles, ever the underminer of conventions himself, is that Shakespeare, with typical subversion, planted within the plays named for English kings a more mischievous 'history from below' perspective. Welles described his idea of the battle scene as 'terrible . . . it's supposed to show the end of the chivalric idea. It's supposed to show the way it's [war's] going to be from now on'.[1] The scene has proven to be one of the most memorable and admired sequences in the film. What war is 'going to be' after the decline of chivalry is a spectacle of brutal atrocity. It is an intrinsically anti-war visualisation, a sentiment repeated by Welles himself in interviews, and demonstrated by the camera's eye and the tempo of the action. The pre-battle preparations are presented with chivalric panoply, flags fluttering gaily, spear-tips glinting in sunlight, and all rapid action. Soldiers, anonymously regimented like machines in their heavy armour, are winched up onto gallows-like erections and lowered onto their horses, a sequence finding its comic climax when the corpulent Falstaff is dropped unceremoniously. Mist rises as the rival armies thunder on horses towards each other, and music trumpets the anticipation of a sporting event. But as conflict is joined, the scenes steadily deteriorate into an ever-slower succession of hacking and bashing, a grotesque blood-bath as much as mud-bath, filmed mostly at ground level to draw in the audience affectively and reinforce the 'from beneath' social and political perspective of the film. Horses

1. 'Arena – The Orson Welles Story', Part 2, 19:23, accessed 10.01.24. https://www.youtube.com/watch?v=brVah-r65pI

stumble, fall, and die, with possible visual cues to the open-mouthed horse's protest against outrageous human violence in Picasso's anti-war artwork, *Guernica* (1937). The effect is graphically described by film critic Peter Cowie:

> Welles uses low-angle shots to emphasise the speed and urgency of the early fighting, and soldiers hurtle in agony across the glaring sky. Mist and smoke confuse the issue, and the battle becomes a series of personal clashes. There is a palpable force behind each wild swing of a ball and chain: men grunt with the sheer effort of surviving. Heads smack fatally against the ground. But the sweeping cavalry charges degenerate by degrees into a heavy violence as men and horses tire and the battlefield becomes a quagmire. Figures writhe and scrabble in a Flanders mudbath, their limbs jerking like Harryhausen's prehistoric monsters. They seem to be claimed by the mud – to belong to it.[2]

According to the historical record, rain upon water-retaining clay at Agincourt caused a quagmire.[3] There are also many unmistakable visual recollections of trench warfare in World War One, still within living memory for soldiers, including the kind of helmets worn. In armour, all the soldiers on both sides look alike in the mud, calling into question the pretence that they represent differing political claims, and the engagements sound like a myriad of tin cans being banged together in a dehumanising cacophony. The screams of dying men curdle the air and the music changes register, interweaving wailing chants of dismay with doom-laden percussion and shrieking trumpets. A significant part of the scene's filmic power lies in its sheer, agonising length, becoming ever more laboured and murderous, until the mud virtually swallows the amorphously unidentifiable figures, grappling in slow motion.

Welles's choices in depicting the battle scene provide a salutary reminder that staged productions of Shakespeare's plays can foreground visual images that strongly guide audience responses to a play as a whole. Given the text's silence on the conditions at the battle of Agincourt, directors have a wide latitude, and the choice can be ideologically guided. It would have been possible for Welles to sanitise it, as stage productions often do, by having noble knights in shining armour sword-fighting one-to-one, taking a cue from the Chorus's pleas for the

---

2. Peter Cowie, *The Cinema of Orson Welles* (New York: Da Capo Press, 1983), 191–2.
3. Review by Lori A. Davis Perry of Juliet Barker, *Henry V and the Battle that Made England: Agincourt* in *War, Literature and the Arts*, 18 (2006), 329: online, accessed 26 July 2001.

audience's imaginative cooperation to compensate for the staging limitations (Prologue 11–18). With the resources of the cinema-maker to shoot scenes outdoors with a large cast, Welles could more graphically depict action than on stage and amplify Shakespeare's paucity of actors. So does Olivier (1945), though driven by a patriotic, pro-war agenda his choices differ radically. Welles emphasises that the Medieval battle would have been a particularly brutal affair in every way. Historically, before the war even began Henry's army had been decimated by a third, dying not in battle but from dysentery. 'We few, we happy few, we band of brothers' were diminished further by inclement conditions, as the French Constable describes: 'his numbers are so few, / His soldiers sick and famished in their march' (3.5.60). The terrible aftermath of Agincourt has been graphically described by historians:

> the tremendous rolls of the dead, the thousands of naked and mutilated corpses, and later, the power vacuums created by the slaughter of so many political and military professionals. . . . Armored knights were well armed against blows to their bodies. But the necessity for visors created a single weakness in their armor that combatants on both sides ferociously exploited. Thus, most of the knights killed on the battlefield were left with mutilated faces. All of their identifying personal effects—armor, shields, clothing—were stripped from the bodies by neighbourhood foragers soon after the battle. As a result, bodies were soon impossible to identify, and families waited in agonized suspense for weeks or months without verifiable information. In many cases this meant that transfers of estates, property, titles, or even legal authority were left in limbo for months or years.[4]

Undoubtedly the episode in *Chimes at Midnight* can be claimed as anti-war in its refusal to glamourise armed warfare, and in its placement of the visual emphasis upon its dehumanizing nature. In particular, Welles is concerned throughout to highlight the suffering of ordinary soldiers rather than the anxieties of the chilly royal family.

The Elizabethan soldier's lot

Throughout history, combatants who are incapacitated or die in battle have been praised in literature for fighting and dying as heroes. This is only right and proper for men who exhibit such personal courage, often demonstrated by those whose lowly status in the armed forces requires

4. Perry, review of *Henry V and the Battle that Made England*, 329.

them to follow rather than issue commands. However, it is more debatable whether the causes for which they have fought are always just and noble, or whether they should have been exposed to such mortal danger by their politician masters and commanding officers.

Before and throughout Elizabeth's reign, the nation had been preparing and involved in war of some kind though, despite conflicts at sea culminating in the defeat of the Spanish Armada, military engagement did not reach its shores. The belligerent language directed at Spain and historical fears of Scottish marauders and Irish rebels created a prevailing expectancy of potential invasion, and English men were conscripted into the army. Others chose to join foreign service in the ongoing European conflicts between Catholic and Protestant nations.[5] There was widespread suspicion of such mercenaries since their militias were notoriously brutal and not under public control as were national armies. In truth the soldiers were desperate for meagre financial reward.[6] Above them were 'gentlemen volunteers' seeking fame and glory, officers serving abroad whose position provided Shakespeare with the prototype for Bertram and Parolles in *All's Well That Ends Well*. They were regarded (or saw themselves) as motivated by neo-chivalric principles, religious and patriotic zeal, and desire for a reputation of personal honour commonly assumed to be the entitlement of more aristocratic gentlemen volunteers.[7] Historically, as Paul Robinson has documented, military honour had from classical times been bifold in nature, incorporating dread of shame and aspiration to glory.[8] Elizabethan warriors typically may have embarked with hopes of glory but often returned disillusioned.

5. For critical discussion of distinctions such as those between 'gentlemen volunteers', 'professionals' and 'mercenaries' among British soldiers fighting abroad, see Paul Scannell, *Conflict and Soldiers' Literature in Early Modern Europe: The Reality of War* (Bloomsbury, 2015). A survey of historical scholarship from 2000 to 2010 is provided by David R. Lawrence, 'Reappraising the Elizabethan and Early Stuart Soldier (2011). Mark Charles Fissel's in *English Warfare 1511–1642* (London: Routledge 2001) provides information about the nitty-gritty details of soldier's lives, such as how they were levied, how they were paid, and how they were fed. A much earlier, pioneering study of the field as a whole is L. Boynton, *The Elizabethan Militia 1558–1638* (London: Routledge & Kegan Paul, 1967).

6. See S. J. Stearns, 'Military Disorder and Martial Law in Early Stuart England', in B. Sharp and M. C. Fissel (eds.), *Law and Authority in Early Modern England: Essays Presented to Thomas Garden Barnes* (Newark: University of Delaware Press, 2007), 106–35.

7. See especially David Trim, (ed.), *The Chivalric Ethos and the Development of Military Professionalism* (Leiden: Brill, 2003), and R. B. Manning, *Swordsmen: The Martial Ethos in the Three Kingdoms* (Oxford University Press, 2003).

8. Paul Robinson, *Military Honour and the Conduct of War* (London: Routledge, 2006).

These veterans were returning home in a continual stream, retailing eyewitness tales of battlefield violence, bearing all-too-visible wounds and physical disablements which condemned many to lives of beggary. They were often undeservedly perceived as mutinous ex-soldiers who posed threats of unruliness to law and order on their return to civilian society:

> soldiers returning maimed from Continental wars found themselves adrift when their services were no longer required. The consequences were an increase, real or perceived, in rates of crime and civil disorder . . .[9]

Gamini Salgado wrote in his account of the Elizabethan underworld that 'the vast majority of sturdy beggars may (as Marx believed) have been recruited from the ranks of discharged serving-men and ex soldiers',[10] many of them no doubt mentally afflicted in ways that made them alarming to the domestic populace. This form of prejudice may account for the rumour (probably incorrect, since fomented by Edmund) in *King Lear* that Edgar, before disguising as Poor Tom the (very 'sturdy') Bedlam beggar marked by 'roguish madness' (3.7.103), had been 'companion to the riotous knights', Lear's now discharged retinue of soldiers (2.1.94–5). The fictional history Edgar invents for his impersonation of a beggar includes having had 'horse to ride, and weapon to bear' (3.4.134) implying a military position. Such alarming individuals and groups were conspicuous enough to find their way into plays, such as the work nowadays attributed to Dekker, *A Larum for London, or the siege of Antwerp: with the virtuous acts and valorous deeds of the lame Soldier* (1602). The 'lame Soldier' is lieutenant Stump, who does not let the handicap diminish his frenetic fighting spirit:

> *Enter a Soldier*
> *Soldier.* Arm you my Lord, and to the fight again,
> A crew of straggling Soldiers (lately vanquished)
> Have gathered head, and in the heat of rage,
> Give fresh assault: the leader to the rest,
> Is a lame fellow that doth want a leg,
> Who lays about him like a devil of hell.
>   . . .

9. *Broadview Anthology of Sixteenth Century Poetry and Prose*, ed. Marie Loughlin, Sandra Bell, Patricia Brace (Ontario: Broadview, 2012), 377, referring to Paul Griffiths, *Lost Londons: Change, Crime, and Control in the Capital City, 1550–1660* (Cambridge University Press, 2008).
10. Gamini Salgado (ed.), *Cony-Catchers and Bawdy Baskets* (Harmondsworth, Penguin Books, 1972), 11.

It is impossible to passe the streets,
They are so pestered with this brainsick crew.

(1054–1060; 1066–7)[11]

Compassionate voices were raised against the lack of adequate aid for returned, stigmatised soldiers who had left to 'fight for *Antwerp's* liberty' against the Spanish on behalf of Protestantism:

A sweaty Cobbler, whose best industry,
Is but to clout a Shoe, shall have his fee;
But let a Soldier, that hath spent his blood,
Is lam'd, diseas'd, or any way distres'd,
Appeal for succour, then you look askance
As if you knew him not; respecting more
An Ostler, or some drudge that rakes your kennels,
Than one that fighteth for the common wealth.

(609–616)

The sight of soldiers returning from various conflicts without a leg or an arm was common enough to be figured in stage plays in characters like Ralph in Dekker's *The Shoemaker's Holiday*, Captain Bowyer in *The Trial of Chivalry*, and the representative figure evoked by Boult in Shakespeare's *Pericles*:

What would you have me do? go to the wars, would you, where a man may serve seven years for the loss of a leg, and have not money enough in the end to buy him a wooden one?

(19.195–9)

In one of several curious loose ends in *Twelfth Night*, Orsino is reminded that his 'young nephew Titus lost his leg' on a naval vessel called the Tiger (5.1.58). The plight of such figures described or shown on stage reminded audiences of casualties visible outside the playhouse walls, and of the pitifully inadequate welfare made available to disabled veterans by successive Acts of parliament.[12] By highlighting different kinds of 'wound narratives', we can see a vulnerable underside of a soldier's life, which at least qualifies any fictional emphasis on military exploits and prowess, and undermines outright glorification of war.

Some soldiers returned with less visible scars. Patricia Cahill, in *Unto the Breach: Martial Formations, Historical Trauma, and the Early*

---

11. Dekker, *A larum for London*, ed. W. W. Greg (Malone Society Reprints, Oxford University Press, 1913), language modernised here.
12. de Somogyi, *Shakespeare's Theatre of War*, 8, 11ff, 31–42.

Modern Stage, scrutinises contemporary materials through the trauma scars less visible to the eye: '. . . English culture became increasingly "possessed" by the wounds of war'.[13] There are those suffering from what we would call post-traumatic stress disorder, amongst whom could be Pistol in *2 Henry IV*. He appears to be clinically and literally shell-shocked,[14] exhibiting anti-social violence and suicidal impulses ('Then death rock me asleep, abridge my doleful days' [2.4.194]). Jonathan Bate has suggested that his speeches are 'a reminder of the heaven-ringing Tamburlainean verse' of Marlowe's warrior,[15] and Maurice Charney had earlier suggested Pistol's verbiage is Shakespeare's debunking parody of Marlowe.[16] Such rhetoric in this context is mocked and diminished by Shakespeare to signs of dangerous megalomania. Pistol enters the tavern offering to 'discharge' his gun indiscriminately, and recklessly unhinged 'choler', which Mistress Quickly malapropistically begs him to 'aggravate', threatens a brawl. Falstaff drives him out with his sword, restoring a tenuous peace which allows a touching version of courtship to be played out between himself and Doll Tearsheet, to be overshadowed and interrupted by the rude awakening of a call to arms.

The fate of heroes: *Sic transit gloria mundi*

As we have seen in the previous chapter, Shakespeare's words have been appropriated over the last four hundred years to underwrite pro-war attitudes and praise heroism, but contextualised inspection suggests that just as often he debunks or undermines the notion of heroic death in war as a misguided myth. Some of his war casualties die unlamented, in causes that are discredited, futile, or egotistically motivated by self-aggrandizing and vengeful leaders. Even some of the nobility are provided with merely grudging and perfunctory eulogies that call into question the notion of heroism. Michael Neill in his magisterial *Issues of Death* draws attention to Troilus's metaphorical observation that death

---

13. Patricia Cahill, *Unto the Breach*, 139–40.
14. The suggestion is made by de Somogyi, *Shakespeare's Theatre of War*, 170–4. More generally, see his first chapter on 'Casualties of War', and also Geoffrey L. Hudson, 'Disabled Veterans and the State in Early Modern England' in David Gerber (ed.), *Disabled Veterans in History* (Ann Arbor: University of Michigan Press, 2000).
15. Jonathan Bate, *The Genius of Shakespeare* (London: Picador, 1997), 125.
16. Maurice Charney, 'The Voice of Marlowe's Tamburlaine in Early Shakespeare', *Comparative Drama*, 31 (1997), 213–223, 220.

in battle is always 'a contemptuous stripping of "distinction" among "heaps" of anonymous bodies':[17]

> and I do fear besides
> That I shall lose distinction in my joys,
> As doth a battle, when they charge on heaps
> The enemy flying.
>
> (*Troilus and Cressida*, 3.2.23–6)

Even for those who do not die, fame achieved in war is transitory. Montaigne sometimes wrote of courage with admiration,[18] but at other times with undisguised and scathing contempt for the false bravery of aggressors destroying the weak:

> Valour in war is a fraud . . . Valour has really nothing to do with virtue, it is merely an exercise in violence. A man of valour is not necessarily 'a *valuable man* or a *worthy man*'.[19]

Shakespeare as dramatist sometimes drives home the humiliation of war heroes by stripping them of any claims to 'distinction', honour, or even dignity, by his portrayal of their deaths on the battlefield. Hector in *Troilus and Cressida* is dragged to his death by horses in 'shameful' circumstances: 'He's dead, and at the murderer's horse's tail, / In beastly sort, dragged through the shameful field . . .' (5.11.3–4). Among Troilus's final words is a cryptic phrase which is hardly the memorial of a hero: 'But march away. / Hector is dead. There is no more to say' (5.11.23). His death is greeted as little more than a cause for future war: 'Hope of revenge shall hide our inward woe' (5.11.31). Hector himself had initially voiced reluctance about pursuing the unjust 'pelting war', and he acknowledges Cassandra's prophecy that many innocents will die. But he suddenly allows himself to be persuaded to support the war by hot-headed youths proclaiming a mantra of 'honour'. Ulysses reports that Achilles is stirred from his lethargy to arm against Hector as a result of public shaming and by the sight of his wounded lover Patroclus with 'his mangled Myrmidons, / That noseless, handless, hacked and chipped, come to him' (5.5.33–4). Thersites, acting as chorus, derisively scorns 'those that war for a placket', linking war with violent masculine sexuality and abduction – 'war and lechery confound all' (2.3.80).

17. Michael Neill, *Issues of Death: Mortality and Identity in Renaissance Tragedy* (Oxford: Clarendon Press, 1997), 27.
18. See Sam McChesney, 'The Meaning of Courage in Montaigne's *Essays*', *The European Legacy*, 26 (2020), 141–48.
19. Quoted Bonadeo, 'Montaigne and War', 423.

Coriolanus is hacked to death by baying Volscians, and his end is even more ignominious than Hector's:

ALL PEOPLE
Tear him to pieces! Do it presently! He killed my son! My daughter! He killed my cousin Marcus! He killed my father!

. . .

AUFIDIUS
                              Insolent villain!

ALL CONSPIRATORS
Kill, kill, kill, kill, kill him!

(5.6.120–9)

Only two onlookers resist the mob's hatred. The First Lord appeals for calm, 'Peace ho! No outrage, peace!', and the Second Lord, is at least respectful if only in offering a grudging and qualified encomium:

1 LORD
                    Bear from hence his body,
And mourn you for him. Let him be regarded
As the most noble corse that ever herald
Did follow to his urn.
2 LORD
                        His own impatience
Takes from Aufidius a great part of blame.
Let's make the best of it.

(5.6.141–6)

The Second Lord is saying that since Coriolanus culpably brought on his own fate by his 'impatience', this partly exonerates Aufidius from blame for the plan to besiege Rome. Phrases like 'the most noble corse' and 'Let's make the best of it', on top of reproof for his 'impatience' strike brutally dismissive notes, far from a heroic eulogy. It is ironic that the body of the man who would not show his wounds publicly is now regarded as no more than a bloodstained corpse. In some ways Coriolanus is an exemplary figure in this context, since apart from being a disastrous failure as a politician, his sole function is as a dehumanised military being. His only recognition of 'honour' is as victory in war. He acts in a spirit of vengeful resentment, undistracted by appeals to ideals such as patriotism or defending the community which has nurtured him and benefited from his congenital taste for violence. It is only when his literal mother equates herself with 'the mother country' for which he fought, that he shows compassion for his intended victims. The brutal legacy of his single-handed, vindictive insurrection of Rome on behalf of the enemy Volscians is said to be that of a man who already 'Hath widow'd and unchilded many a one' (5.6.150–1) in the Volscian city of Actium, and one who threatens to do the same in Rome in retaliation for no more than a personal grudge against its citizens. In Judith Butler's suggestive phrase, these military leaders lack 'grievability', unlike many humbler soldiers.[20] No flights of angels sing them to their rest since they are perfunctorily dismissed, and the creed of military heroism by which they have lived is cast into doubt. The more emotionally complicated circumstances in which Othello and Antony die will be reserved for later chapters, but suffice it to say here that their wounds are self-inflicted in a spirit of shame, and far from confirming anything like military prowess.

One character persistently identified with military 'honour' who comes to an unlamented end, this time in civil war, is Harry Hotspur in *1 Henry IV*. His very name denotes the impetuous cavalryman, but his single-minded dedication to battle is mocked in a spirit of parody by his opposite, Prince Hal:

> I am not yet of Percy's mind, the Hotspur of the north he that kills me some six or seven dozen of Scots at a breakfast, washes his hands, and says to his wife, 'Fie upon this quiet life. I want work'. 'O my sweet Harry,' says she, 'how many hast thou killed to-day?' 'Give my roan horse a drench,' says he, and answers, 'Some fourteen', an hour after, 'a trifle, a trifle'.

> (2.4.100–17)

As Daniel Derrin argues, Shakespeare here mingles images of horror with laughter in the Aristotelian sense of 'laughable deformities', ridiculing devotion to war *sine dolore* without evoking the actual pain of battle.[21] Although a man of action rather than intellect, Hotspur is given a moment of introspection at the point of death, finally acknowledging the hollowness of his mission:

> But thoughts, the slaves of life, and life, time's fool,
> And time, that takes survey of all the world,
> Must have a stop. O, I could prophesy,
> But that the earthy and cold hand of death
> Lies on my tongue: no, Percy, thou art dust
> And food for –

> (*1 Henry IV*, 5.4.80–5)

---

20. Judith Butler, *The Force of Nonviolence: An Ethico-Political Bind* (London: Verso, 2020).

21. Daniel Derrin, '*Sine Dolore*: Relative Painlessness in Shakespeare's Laughter at War', *Critical Survey*, 30 (2018), 81–97.

Prince Henry, his nemesis, looking on the 'mangled face', finishes the sentence; 'For worms, brave Percy'. He refers to Hotspur's 'ill-weaved ambition' and 'ignominy' even as he alone delivers 'fair rites of tenderness' in a brotherly, soldier-to-soldier epitaph. Others fight for honour and are praised. Four noblemen die in battle in *Henry V* but 'None else of name; and of all other men / But five and twenty'; the ten thousand French dead are likewise reported as mere numbers, with specific and ranked listing reserved for individual 'princes', 'nobles' and 'knights' (4.8.79–111). In *Macbeth* the elder Siward's only compensation for the loss of his son is that 'he had his hurts . . . on the front' 5.8.12) rather than in retreat, making him 'God's soldier': 'They say he parted well, and paid his score'. He is emblematic of those disregarded in the official annals of 'honourable' deaths in war, and who end up as food for worms. As Auden concludes his anti-war poem 'The Shield of Achilles': 'the strong / Iron-hearted man slaying Achilles / Who would not live long'.

Two Shakespearean kings who die showing bravery in battle prove in a rather perverse way the Shakespearean rules that death in war does not confer fame, and that bravery is not equated with honour. They too, like Coriolanus and Hector but for different reasons, are not accorded ennoblement for heroism. Richard III, though not a professional soldier but primarily a politician, tries to be as eloquent in morale-boosting rhetoric as Henry V in an '*oration to his army*' (5.3.250), though he is considerably less expansive or successful in rallying his troops. He is praised, at least by a partisan, for courage in fighting alone on foot after being deserted by others:

CATESBY
The King enacts more wonders than a man,
Daring an opposite to every danger:
His horse is slain, and all on foot he fights,
Seeking for Richmond in the throat of death.

(5.4.2–5)

He dies famously calling for 'A horse! A horse! My kingdom for a horse' (5.5.7), in a desperate and solitary attempt to defend his own right to rule the kingdom. Out of context his actions could be regarded as conventional heroism, but any semblance of heroic status is clearly denied him by his history of crimes. Despite the character's mercurial energy, wit, and seductive appeals to the audience in soliloquies, little redeems him morally as more than 'a bloody tyrant and homicide' (5.5.200) including infanticide, whose royal status is criminally ill-gotten. Richard III's death is reported without verbiage in a stage direction – '*Alarum. Enter KING*

RICHARD III and RICHMOND; they fight. KING RICHARD III is slain' (5.5.1), followed by a brutally derogatory phrase, 'the bloody dog is dead' (5.5.2). Simon Barker notes how frequently in the mid-twentieth century, from Brecht's *Arturo Ui* and Olivier's stage and screen performances to the Loncraine / McKellen's film version, *Richard III* was appropriated to act as 'anti-fascist resistance' in modern history, and as condemnation of militarism that forcibly props up unpleasant political regimes.[22]

Macbeth, though endowed with more capacity for conscience than Richard, similarly forfeits any regal rights by the galvanizing act of regicide which brought him the crown. Initially hailed and promoted by King Duncan as a courageous military hero for his record on the battlefield, he ends the play still fighting, now against the odds and for his life: 'They have tied me to a stake. I cannot fly, / But bear-like, I must fight the course' (5.7.1–2). His career in the play suggests that success as a soldier is not of itself an appropriate or desirable qualification for a king, nor an automatic badge of 'honour' in other circumstances. On the contrary, bloody feats on the battlefield may be reframed as a repulsive normalising of murder. Assassinating Duncan in his own house, which immediately brings suspicion on him, is the impetuous act of a soldier 'gone rogue', rather than a politician's circumspect strategy. He had considered the possibility that 'Chance may crown me, / Without my stir' (1.3.143–4), but had instead overridden his conscience and proceeded with the reckless bravado associated at the outset with his profession as soldier. In the play, indiscriminate bloodthirstiness is built into the fabric of its blood-soaked imagery. Glorification of war as test of 'honour', a word used several times in *Macbeth* in paying lip service to the connection between military carnage and heroic values, is rapidly juxtaposed with the first of many bloody images. The Witches seem to be spirited up as battlefield scavengers, and one in effect parodies the battlefield when she says that she has been 'Killing swine' (1.3.2), just as the soldiers have been reported as killing each other. In household economies, 'swine' were hung up to 'bleed' before they finally died. In *Macbeth* the reference is placed with gruesome precision, defining the nature of the raging battle in which soldiers hack each other as though carving meat. 'Brave Macbeth' is reported to have taken on an adversary and violently 'unseam'd him from the nave to the chops, / And fix'd his head upon

---

22. Simon Barker, *War and Nation* (Edinburgh University Press, 2021), 111–16. See also Wilheim Hortman, 'Shakespeare on the Political Stage in the Twentieth Century', in Stanley Wells and Sarah Stanton (eds), *The Cambridge Companion to Shakespeare on Stage* (Cambridge University Press, 2002), 212– 29.

our battlements' (1.2.22–3), again evocative of a butcher's precision, mirroring the ending in which Macbeth's own head is severed from his body and he is reviled as a 'dead butcher' (5.9.36). 'All they that take the sword shall perish with the sword', said Jesus in the Gospels (*Matthew* 26, 52), a fate exemplified by Richard and Macbeth.

One of the few exceptions, a military commander who arguably is not subjected to sustained moral critique or ridicule, is the rarely analysed Alcibiades in *Timon of Athens*. Wilson Knight offered an idealised opinion that this soldier is 'youth and strength armed against old age, dotage, greed . . . effacing a worn out and effete civilization, bringing retribution for its crimes, restoring harmony and health'.[23] However, Alcibiades is more ambiguous than this suggests, and his role in the narrative seems not fully assimilated and left uneasily hanging as though Shakespeare is uncertain of his status. On one hand, he is presented as a loyal friend of Timon, supporting him through financial ruin and desertion of fair-weather friends. Alcibiades offers to lead his army, Coriolanus-like, in revenge against the ungenerous and ungrateful populace's rejection of Timon. Also like Coriolanus, he is driven by his own personal vendetta against civic authorities in Athens, as the senators have rejected his plea for mercy on behalf of one of his soldiers who has killed a man in a fit of rage. Puzzlingly, Alcibiades is accompanied by two mistresses, Phrynia and Timandra, who are addressed as prostitutes by Timon. In linking them with the army, Timon's curse resembles that of Thersites in *Troilus and Cressida*, invoking venereal disease and a link between sexuality and the army: 'Be a whore still, they love thee not that use thee; / Give them diseases, leaving with thee their lust' (4.3.83–4). Adding to the ambiguity of Alcibiades's place in the play, he is, unlike Coriolanus this time, magnanimous when the senators capitulate and offer him rehabilitation into Athens. But still, however, Shakespeare seems unable to leave the character morally unscathed, since his offer, however generous, is phrased in troubling terms that define peace only in terms of war:

> Bring me into your city,
> And I will use the olive with my sword,
> Make war breed peace, make peace stint war, make each
> Prescribe to other, as each other's leech.
> Let our drums strike.

> (5.5.77–81)

Alcibiades' speech in context is a less than veiled warning to the senators of dire consequences if they do not keep their side of the bargain.

---

23. G. Wilson Knight, *The Wheel of Fire: Interpretations of Shakespearian Tragedy* (Oxford University Press, 1930), 237.

His medical imagery of war and peace ('stint', 'prescribe' and applying leeches) is curiously unreassuring, verging on a threat of military control rather than ensuring 'mutual sustenance'. At this final stage of the play Athens is more or less a city under martial law, and the military figure Alcibiades a dubious guarantor of peace.[24] In a different time and place he could represent the kind of menacing military *junta* capable of bringing dictators to power.

The ambiguous nature of heroism in war concerned Shakespeare throughout his writing career. Apparently mentored by Marlowe, the master of bellicose rhetoric in the *Tamburlaine* plays,[25] Shakespeare at the outset wrote plays depicting war, but with a less glorifying sensibility than his contemporary.

Demise of chivalry

Talbot in *1 Henry VI* is one Shakespearean figure who does prove his heroism in international conflict, and he is a character who dies honourably, wholeheartedly supporting his country's enterprise. In the Medieval context he is a paragon of chivalry, but in the 1590s as chivalry itself had waned, his conduct is old-fashioned and his lonely death ultimately pointless. Talbot is the English scourge of the French until they capture him, but as the cunning Countess of Auvergne learns to her cost, he is up to the challenge. She taunts him as 'a child, a silly dwarf . . . this weak and writhled shrimp' (*1 Henry VI*, 2.3.22–3), mocking his disempowered status as a prisoner of war. But with a timely trumpet call he summons to his aid the might of the English army. Whether his explanation is interpreted as modesty or audacity, he presents himself as 'but shadow of himself' (2.3.61) while his 'substance, sinews, arms, and strength' lie in the national troops as a body, which he threatens will destroy France. It is in fact the author who is boasting of his power here. The stage implications of the famous scene, where troops are 'shadows' played in turn by actors, provides a metatheatrical moment, drawing attention not to individual heroism but to the power of the dramatic medium in its incorporation of functions between writer, actors and audiences to produce a collective response. It is a frequent Shakespearean trope, which he repeated from Puck's 'if we shadows have offended' through

24. See the editorial note in *Timon of Athens*, ed. Anthony B. Dawson and Gretchen E. Minton (London: Arden Shakespeare Third Series, Cengage Learning, 2008), 340.
25. See Alan Shepard, *Marlowe's Soldiers: Rhetorics of Masculinity in the Age of the Armada* (Aldershot and Burlington, VT: Ashgate, 2002).

to Prospero's rueful observation that when 'revels' end, the actors as 'spirits' are released from their theatrical roles, they vanish and 'leave not a rack behind'. Like Hotspur, Talbot's claim to lasting, heroic fame and glory is undermined after his death, even when endlessly replayed in each new performance. The playwright, in the case of Shakespeare, is the one whose fame has endured. The subtext runs that without the trumpeting echo chamber of his living actors – his 'shadows' – heroism would die with the demise of each representative historical figure portrayed.

Talbot maintains his herculean efforts in war in France, though in a manifestly losing cause which leads to the destruction of the English army. Regarded as an 'ornament of knighthood' (4.1.29), he uses the occasion of stripping Falstaff of the garter to assert his own allegiance to old-style chivalric values in their 'good old days':

> When first this order was ordained, my lords,
> Knights of the Garter were of noble birth,
> Valiant and virtuous, full of haughty courage,
> Such as were grown to credit by the wars.
>
> (4.1.33–6)

He reproves and shames the plotting politicians, who are becoming less interested in the international conflict than in pursuing their internecine squabbles. It is he who reminds others again of the former feats in war of Henry V, who defeated France with the same odds against him. However, despite his principled valour, Talbot's own death in battle is neither witnessed nor lamented by other characters, and causes his status to change from hero to victim. His own son mimics Talbot's brave but self-destructive values, by choosing not to flee but to die as 'sealed the son of chivalry' (4.6.29). The son is caught in a logical quandary created by his commitment to chivalry, and it makes his death as unavoidable as his father's. Talbot tells young John to flee so that he can live to avenge his father's death, but the reply is that he would not be his father's son if he retreated. Given his father's ethic, he chooses immediate death, and they die together, a dramatic replication of the tragic and unnecessary deaths of fathers and sons bemoaned by the King in *1 Henry VI*. Cradling his son's body, Talbot addresses death as an inescapable adversary – 'Thou antic death, which laugh'st us here to scorn' (4.7.130) – before dying himself. The French sweep in to gloat over their illustrious spoils. The Bastard of Orleans bays 'Hew them to pieces. Hack their bones asunder' (4.7.159). He is restrained only by Charles the Dauphin's minimal respect now they are dead. In terms of Shakespeare's generally negative representation of heroism, then, Talbot and his son die with honourable valour but to no worldly avail. Sir William Lucy rhetorically begins to intone Talbot's full military honours, only to be cut off by the reductive contempt of Joan la Pucelle: 'Here's a silly stately style indeed . . . /Him that thou magnifiest with all these titles / Stinking and fly-blown lies here at our feet. (4.7.84–8). They are as much food for worms as Hotspur. Joan tells the grieving Lucy he can have the corpses which otherwise 'would but stink, and putrefy the air' (4.7.202), and Charles agrees – 'So we be rid of them, do with them what thou wilt' (4.7.206). It may be the final and most telling indignity to Talbot that, although he is one of very few military heroes in Shakespeare who dies unequivocally with honour in international rather than in ignoble factional war, even generations of critics, including those like Kirby Farrell who have written on heroism in Shakespeare,[26] have largely ignored him. The few who do consider the Talbots' heroic chivalry, such as James Bulman in *The Heroic Idiom of Shakespearean Tragedy*, find that his allegiance to a culpably rigid code is little more effective in battle than a rhetorical gesture, as Joan cruelly highlights. Such outdated chivalry holds no capacity for adaptation as a way of living, and as Bulman puts it, the Talbots, like other soldiers, may die with epic resolve and courage, 'but die nevertheless'.[27] Not for them the glorious afterlife promised in military manuals. Talbot's death is often treated as an example of Shakespeare's nostalgia for chivalric values which seem to die with this figure, but what seems more obvious is a realistic recognition of chivalry's futility and irrelevance in a different world. Eric Mallin, in *Inscribing the Time: Shakespeare and the End of Elizabethan England*, suggests that a revival of Medieval chivalry in the 1590s was generated by the expectation of courtly fealty paid to Elizabeth,[28] and therefore became cosmetic pageantry not transferable to the battlefield. Talbot and his son are seen, in Robert B. Pierce's phrase, as 'abstract patterns of English heroism' designed to contrast with the degenerate world around them.[29] In a military sense, they are ineffectual and their deaths tragic but pointless, casting doubt on whether their devotion to honour holds even a 'nostalgic' appeal to the dramatist. As Welles said, 'it's the way war is going to be from now on'.

Michael Murrin dates the turning point towards modern warfare with persuasive precision to the invention and increasing deployment

26. Kirby Farrell, *Play, Death and Heroism in Shakespeare* (Chapel Hill: University of South Carolina Press, 1989).
27. James Bulman in *Heroic Idiom of Shakespearean Tragedy* (University of Delaware Press, 2003), 32.
28. Eric Mallin, *Inscribing the Time: Shakespeare and the End of Elizabethan England* (Berkeley, Los Angeles: University of California Press, 1995).
29. Robert B. Pierce, *Shakespeare's History Plays: The Family and the State* (Ohio State University Press, 1971), 45–6.

of gunpowder in European warfare during the fifteenth century, and Nina Taunton draws attention to the contemporary debate between the longbow and firearms as effective killing machines.[30] Paul Robinson in *Military Honour and the Conduct of War* makes a similar point, that hand-to-hand conflict was becoming increasingly less the norm in the waging of war in Elizabethan times with the development of explosive devices.[31] It was clear which weaponry would prove superior. As a result, notions of honour were changing. What emerges is that lip service paid to customary chivalry exercised little more than a mollifying and restraining influence on the conduct of war through the appeal to mercy. The somewhat pessimistic aim was to place a civilising restraint upon an uncivilised practice.[32] The code of chivalric honour called for such things as humane treatment of prisoners, protection of women, children, non-combatants and peaceful civilians, and it has been claimed as a forerunner of modern institutions and conventions created to limit the indiscriminate destructiveness of war.[33] However, there was no way of enforcing compliance or punishing breaches, especially those of leaders. Little has changed, since today in our 'civilised' times, articles in the Geneva Conference are blithely ignored by those determined to go to war, and the United Nations is regularly either politically exploited to offer a fig-leaf of legitimacy for invasion, while its decisions are vetoed and bypassed, or simply treated with disdain.

Commoners and 'collateral damage': 'None else of name'

Bates and Williams in *Henry V* darkly surmise that this is the king's war, not theirs, and they fear 'honour' in battle may be dubiously misplaced in an unjust and unworthy cause. They worry less about their own death as about the severing of their social and family fabrics, and the disastrous

30. Michael Murrin, *History and Warfare in Renaissance Epic* (University of Chicago Press, 1997); Nina Taunton, *Drama and Militarism*, 132–3.
31. Paul Robinson, *Military Honour and the Conduct of War* (London: Routledge, 2006).
32. Most modern accounts of chivalry along these lines build upon Johan Huizinga, *The Waning of the Middle Ages* (London: Edward Arnold, 1924). Chapter 1 is titled 'The Violent Tenor of Life' which sets the theme.
33. Raine Liivoja, 'Chivalry without a Horse: Military Honour and the Modern Law of Armed Conflict' in Rain Liivoja, Andres Saumets (eds), *The Law of Armed Conflict: Historical and Contemporary Perspectives* (Tartu, Estonia: Tartu University Press, 2012, 75–100.

economic consequences for surviving families, as Williams says: '. . . I am afeard there are few die well that die in a battle for how can they charitably dispose of anything when blood is their argument? (4.1.131–42). Some Medieval writers and Renaissance humanists pointed to exactly these long-term consequences as the likely price of war to commoners and to conscripts who die as cannon fodder. Helen Cooper, in an essay entitled 'Speaking for the Victim', deals with fifteenth-century *pastourelles* as a mode of complaint for the suffering of the rural peasantry faced with marauding soldiers under 'the long shadow cast by the trauma of war over its victims'. She premises that 'real peasants, the suffering common man and woman, can speak a political wisdom that does not always get a voice elsewhere', and that such honesty is rarely addressed to 'the prince in question'.[34] In this sense Williams and Bates are unusual in their forthright truth-telling to the monarch, disguised as a commoner himself and speaking as an *agent provocateur*. Similarly for Shakespeare's company hoping to please Elizabeth I with their play, it would have taken some derring-do to include in a play such defiant sentiments, addressed to an ancestor of a living 'prince in question' who gave this promise to her people in addressing the army at Tilbury:

> I know I have the body but of a weak and feeble woman, but I have the heart and stomach of a king, and of a king of England too . . . rather than any dishonour shall grow by me, I myself will take up arms, I myself will be your general, judge, and rewarder of every one of your virtues in the field . . .[35]

As Welles conceived in *Chimes at Midnight*, the main vehicle for Shakespeare's 'history from below' is Falstaff. In his contradictory and changing guises in different contexts, this chameleon character incorporates shifting perspectives. He represents nobility as the knight 'Sir John', then a draconian recruiting officer, and then as mouthpiece for commoners' complaints. His first appearance in *1 Henry VI* is as a disreputable noble who deserts having 'played the coward' (4.1.131), but at least his desertion allowed him to escape with his life, unlike many others. In this play he is perhaps unfairly singled out as personal scapegoat for a defeat at the Battle of Patay which seemed inevitable, given the historical outnumbering of soldiers to the tune of 23,000 French

---

34. Helen Cooper, 'Speaking for the Victim', in *Writing War: Medieval Responses to Warfare*, ed. Corinne Saunders, Francoise le Saux and Neil Thomas (Cambridge: D. S. Brewer, 2004), 213–31, 229, 215.
35. 'Speech at Tilbury Camp', *Queen Elizabeth I: Selected Works*, ed. Steven W. May (New York: Washington Square Press, 2004), 77.

to 6,000 undermanned and malnourished English troops under Talbot's command, but he must live with the dramatic stigma. No wonder Lord Cobham ('Sir John Oldcastle') as the living descendant of the Protestant martyr was indignant enough to force the change of name from Oldcastle to 'Fastolfe' in the Folio text, a near-anagram of 'Fat-self', later to become the equally allegorical 'Fall-staff'.[36] It seems to have given Shakespeare a peculiar satisfaction in depicting the character's irrepressible future, when in *Henry IV Part 1* he is resurrected as the low-life companion to the future king. His outrageous lies include taking credit for killing Hotspur and his part in the Gadshill ambush planned by Poins but endangering Falstaff. The critical heritage seems to indicate the bemusing fact that the dishonorable Sir John Falstaff's after-fame has been far more fondly regarded than his illustrious monarch's, a contrast ironically established in the cruel 'rejection' scene and the touching eulogies in *Henry V* by his true admirers who believe that the King has broken his heart. Welles's movie is testament to the corpulent figure's popularity with audiences, contrasting with the less-than-sympathetic King's identification with dictates of power and *realpolitik*. His ability to 'rise up' from apparent death (in fact sleep) on the field of battle is a key to his slippery, shape-changing legacy, which has continued to make people laugh as he predicted – 'I am not only witty in myself, but the cause that wit is in other men' (*2 Henry IV*, 1.2.10). It is this capacity which links him with the dramatist himself with the ability to express a multitude of conflicting points of view. Both license us to laugh *in* war and *at* law alike.

In his famous set-piece on war in *1 Henry IV*, Falstaff vocalises in soliloquy a coherent rebuke to claims of 'lineal honour' for which men fight wars and die degrading deaths:

FALSTAFF
I would 'twere bed-time, Hal, and all well.
PRINCE HENRY
Why, thou owest God a death.
Exit PRINCE HENRY
FALSTAFF
'Tis not due yet, I would be loath to pay him before his day – what need I be so forward with him that calls not on me? Well, 'tis no matter, honour pricks me on. Yea, but how if honour prick me off when I come on, how then? Can honour set to a leg? No. Or an arm? No. Or take away the grief of a wound? No. Honour hath no skill in surgery, then? No. What

---

36. See Peter Corbin and Douglas Sedge (eds.), *The Oldcastle Controversy* (Manchester University Press, 1991).

is honour? A word. What is in that word honour? What is that honour?
Air. A trim reckoning! Who hath it?
    He that died a-Wednesday. Doth he feel it? No. Doth he hear it? No.
'Tis insensible, then? Yea, to the dead. But will it not live with the living?
No. Why? Detraction will not suffer it. Therefore I'll none of it. Honour
is a mere scutcheon – and so ends my catechism.
Exit

(1 Henry IV, 5.1.124–140)

His insistent list of 'No's serves to demolish any positive value in the
'airy word' honour epitomised in Hotspur, when pitted against 'the grief
of a wound', loss of limbs, and the inevitable oblivion of death on the
battlefield. To dismiss the 'catechism' as simple cowardice is to neglect
its internal logic, its power as a direct address to the audience, and the
implicit reflection on the circumstances of Hotspur's later death alone.
Its category is pacifism, and its tone authorial. Welles evidently agreed.
Falstaff, of course, is far from a consistent pacifist – nor is he consistent
in anything for that matter – and it is part of his evasive adaptability
that makes him a vehicle for myriad causes and subject positions that
make him a range of characters, not just one, but this is a strong and self-
consistent statement that reverberates. After debunking military honour
in this scene, he later lies when he claims false credit for killing Hotspur,
and his *credo* marks him rather as duplicitous than as a consistent pros-
elytiser against war. However, his expression of the sentiment itself is the
choice of remaining alive that underlies pacifism at its most common-
sense: 'The better part of valour is discretion, in the which better part I
have saved my life' (*1 Henry IV*, 5.4.118).[37] He poses an unanswerable
counter to militarism, that the hollow abstraction of 'honour' in war
does not compensate for the violation of human dignity in death: 'Tis
insensible, then. Yea, to the dead'. Here Falstaff speaks on behalf of
Shakespeare's anxious commoners and helpless conscripts, yet Falstaff
himself later recruits these very types in Mouldy, Shadow, Wart, Feeble,
who see themselves and their families as potentially the true victims of
war. It is hard to regard them with anything but respect and pity, despite
Falstaff's own supercilious attitude in this different context.
    There had even been an unobtrusive but telling 'prequel' to Falstaff's
speech, suggesting its sentiment had been on Shakespeare's mind from

---

37. All discussions of Falstaff's 'cowardice' must begin with the important essay by
Maurice Morgann, *An Essay on the Dramatic Character of Sir John Falstaff* (London:
T. Boys, Ludgate Hill, 1777). Michael Goldman, 'Falstaff Asleep' in *Shakespeare and
the Energies of Drama* (Princeton, New Jersey: Princeton University Press 1972),
45–57.

the start of his career in writing plays about war. An anonymous Watchman in *3 Henry VI* is told that King Edward is camping 'in the cold field' while other lords 'lodge in towns', for the reason that it is 'the more honour because more dangerous' (4.3.14–17). The Watchman sagely replies, 'Ay, but give me worship and quietness / I like it better than a dangerous honour',[38] a cryptic encapsulation of Falstaff's later, extended deflation of honour. The sentiment echoes the central assumption of classical Natural Law, that survival is the preeminent moral law, held instinctively by every species, implicitly refuting the blandishments of heightened rhetoric to gain glory by risking violent death in war. To be back in a tavern with 'a pot of ale and safety' (3.2.14) seems a more sensible course.

Not long before Falstaff's alignment with the cause of common people, the 'endlessly inventive' persona,[39] is shown in an antithetical capacity of 'knight', corruptly and cynically exploiting his job as recruitment officer to line his own purse. In doing so, however, he reveals more of the plight of commoners as victims in war. He admits to himself, 'I have misused the King's press damnably' in making 'three hundred and odd pounds' through bribery. He is not so much 'ashamed' of this fact as embarrassed by the sight of the pitifully inadequate men he now has at his disposal, refusing to let them parade publicly at Coventry (*1 Henry IV*, 4.2.11–47 *passim*). His description, however superficially amusing, is also Shakespeare's sombre, documentary observations on the ugly side of Elizabethan military practice of 'pressing' conscripts, which would have been recognizable to his audience as an ever-present threat, even in and around the theatre itself. Many of Falstaff's enlistments are the dregs left over after 'a commodity of warm slaves' of yeomen's sons 'have bought out their services', leaving only a pool of the less wealthy, starved and ill paupers, ex-prisoners and thieves. His lengthy description of them hovers between revulsion and pity:

> and now my whole charge consists of ancients, corporals, lieutenants, gentlemen of companies – slaves as ragged as Lazarus in the painted cloth, where the glutton's dogs licked his sores: and such as indeed were never soldiers, but discarded unjust servingmen, younger sons to younger brothers, revolted tapsters, and ostlers trade-fallen, the cankers of a calm world and a long peace, ten times more dishonourable-ragged than an old fazed ancient; and such have I to fill up the rooms of them as have bought out their services, that you would think that I had a hundred and fifty tattered prodigals lately come from swine-keeping, from eating

38. Quoted by Pugliatti, *Shakespeare and the Just War Tradition*, 117.
39. Goldman, 'Falstaff Asleep', 57.

draff and husks. A mad fellow met me on the way, and told me I had unloaded all the gibbets and pressed the dead bodies. No eye hath seen such scarecrows. I'll not march through Coventry with them, that's flat: nay, and the villains march wide betwixt the legs as if they had gyves on, for indeed I had the most of them out of prison. There's not a shirt and a half in all my company, and the half shirt is two napkins tacked together and thrown over the shoulders like an herald's coat without sleeves; and the shirt to say the truth stolen from my host at Saint Albans, or the red-nose innkeeper of Daventry. But that's all one, they'll find linen enough on every hedge.

(*1 Henry IV*, 4.2.23–8)

The disturbing passage is often abbreviated or cut in performance since in the modern theatre it seems overlong (and insufficiently amusing), but it is crucial evidence of Shakespeare's dark, eye-witness account of the sordid realities of Elizabeth's army. Later Falstaff realises in the heat of battle that the risk of death has become as real to him as to his now decimated band of 'ragamuffins', whose three survivors (out of a hundred and fifty) face a bleak future as beggars:

Though I could scape shot-free at London, I fear the shot here, here's no scoring but upon the pate . . . God keep lead out of me, I need no more weight than mine own bowels. I have led my ragamuffins where they are peppered; there's not three of my hundred and fifty left alive, and they are for the town's end, to beg during life.

(*1 Henry IV*, 5.3.30–8)

We see in action Falstaff's shameless treatment of the poor in his job as recruiting officer, but when faced with death himself he finds common cause with his charges: 'God keep lead out of me'. Through Falstaff's many changes, what remains consistent is the dramatist's unsparing depiction of victims of war.

Intriguingly, Shakespeare's own father, as an alderman and 'high bailiff' (mayor in modern terms), would have been responsible for recruiting in Stratford in 1569. The duties may have been occasional and infrequent, but that particular year was significant because of the 'Northern Rising', a failed attempt to place Mary Queen of Scots on the throne. Although now largely forgotten, this Catholic rebellion was regarded by Elizabeth as a serious threat to her position. It was the only domestic armed challenge to her reign and she responded ruthlessly. Three thousand rebels were killed after it was defeated, many more were rendered destitute, and whole villages and castles were burned down as punishment. In addition, threats of war from France and a Catholic alliance with Spain at the time persuaded the Queen to order musters of able-bodied men throughout England.[40] Coventry, mentioned by Falstaff, was one such traditional muster point in Warwickshire, the closest to Stratford-upon-Avon, in which there was also reported a small uprising of recusants. Could the circumstances have remained in Shakespeare's retentive memory from when, as an inquisitive and observant five-year-old, he witnessed such a muster? His father was involved in the widespread preparations for war and he no doubt boasted for years about his role.

Falstaff is the quintessential figure embodying 'humour' in the word's various senses, and although he is not located in a comedy, the comic vision he lives by and advocates has implications for comedy as a genre. John Morreall, in defining 'humour' does not mention Falstaff's speech about honour but he captures its spirit: 'As the Irish saying goes, you're only a coward for a moment, but you're dead for the rest of your life'. In amplifying, Morreall sees this philosophy of self-preservation as pointing to the larger contrast between tragedy and comedy. Both, he suggests, are based on an inherent incongruity, but they differ in respectively expressing contrasting responses to circumstances:

> Tragedy valorizes serious, emotional engagement with life's problems, even struggle to the death. Along with epic, it is part of the Western heroic tradition that extols ideals, the willingness to fight for them, and honor. The tragic ethos is linked to patriarchy and militarism – many of its heroes are kings and conquerors – and it valorizes what Conrad Hyers (1996) calls Warrior Virtues – blind obedience, the willingness to kill or die on command, unquestioning loyalty, single-mindedness, resoluteness of purpose, and pride.[41]

Comedy, in contrast, embodies an anti-heroic, pragmatic attitude towards life's incongruities. From Aristophanes' *Lysistrata* to Charlie Chaplin's *The Great Dictator*, Heller's *Catch 22*, comedy has mocked the irrationality of military discipline and blind respect for authority. Comedy's own methods of handling conflict include Falstaff's congenital trickery, running away, and outright mockery. Replacing 'Warrior Virtues', it extols critical thinking, cleverness, adaptability, and an appreciation of physical pleasures like eating, drinking, and sex – the qualities

---

40. Still cited as one of the only accounts of the local implications of the Rising is R. R. Reid, 'The Rebellion of the Earls', *Transactions of the Royal Historical Society*, New Series, 20 (1906), 171–203.

41. John Morreall, 'Philosophy of Humour', *Stanford Encyclopedia of Philosophy*, 6 Comedy (2016). https://plato.stanford.edu/entries/humor/

most associated with Falstaff. His speech on honour can be generalised as encapsulating the essence of comedy itself in the larger sense, as a corrective of human follies. The speech also distinguishes between mindless death and mindful life, or war and peace.

The History plays maintain a double perspective of 'king's history' and Wellesian 'history from below'. The final words of noblemen proclaiming faith to the king and 'our chivalry', are belied by an almost culinary image of bloody corpses 'Larding the plain' (*Henry V*, 4.6.8). Eulogies for dead noblemen are hollow verbiage, while for 'poor men' disregarded as 'none else of name' eulogies are unavailable. Falstaff's contemptuous terms when recruiting prophesy their heralded deaths: 'Tut, tut; good enough to toss; food for powder, food for powder; they'll fill a pit as well as better: tush, man, mortal men, mortal men' (*1 Henry IV*, 4.2.64–6). In Shakespeare's theatre, we can imagine a shudder running through those who filled the stage 'pit' below and in front of the actors on hearing these chilling words, no doubt sensing recruiters among them at the time.

So many times does Shakespeare stir pity for victims of violence that it might be claimed as his own dramatic *forte*. It is evidenced in most – perhaps all – of his single-author plays and there is some evidence that his occasional collaborators recognised this as his special skill. In the play co-authored with Fletcher, *The Two Noble Kinsmen*, Shakespeare chose – or was delegated by his collaborator – to contribute the parts of the three war-widowed Queens and the Jailer's Daughter. Their speeches are powerfully affective expressions of 'victim mentality'.

A consensus has emerged among scholars that *King Edward III* (printed 1596) represents a collaboration between authors, one of whom was Shakespeare, and it is now published in several series of his works. Computer metrics seem to confirm that at least Scenes 2 and 3 depicting love involving the Countess, and Scene 12 are his. Given Shakespeare's track record in the creation of strong female roles and the complexities of love, this would make sense. The later 'war' scenes are not usually attributed to him, at least on statistical grounds, even though they are reminiscent of *Henry V*.[42] However, as the latest Arden editors suggest, Shakespeare may also have been 'the originator of further piecemeal revisions',[43] and it would also seem certain that collaborators would discuss

---

42. Timothy Irish Watt, 'The authorship of *The Raigne of Edward III*', in Hugh Craig and Arthur F. Kinney (eds), *Shakespeare, Computers, and the Mystery of Authorship* (Cambridge University Press, 2009), 116–33.
43. Arden ed., 80. This view was proposed by R. L. Armstrong in *Anglistica*, 14 (1965), and accepted by the editor of the New Cambridge edition of *Edward III*.

the different parts. In this spirit, I would like at least to draw attention to one speech in the short Scene 5, which, whether or not written by Shakespeare himself, arguably reflects his influence or advice about writing parts for victims of war. (A small, overlooked piece of evidence is that the main source in both the Countess scenes and also Scene 5 was not the generally more favoured Holinshed's chronicles, but the French chronicle by Froissart, as though this was in front of a single playwright when composing these Francophile scenes.) Scene 5 begins with a stage direction indicating a pronounced dramatic shift of emphasis away from English military triumphalism towards the feelings of the French victims. The opening stage direction redirects attention away from kings and soldiers to an image of common humanity facing defeat in a ferocious war: '*Enter two Frenchmen, a Woman, and two little children [with baggage]; meet them another Citizen*'. The very short scene is initially undistinguished in versification and could have been written by one of many contemporary playwrights, until we reach the more striking final speech, conveying 'what it feels like' to be 'poor inhabitants' facing imminent and undeserved annihilation in war, even among the 'enemy' population:

3 FRENCHMAN
Fly, countrymen and citizens of France!
Sweet-flowering peace, the root of happy life,
Is quite abandoned and expulsed the land,
Instead of whom, ransack, constraining war
Sits like to ravens upon your houses' tops.
Slaughter and mischief walk within your streets
And unrestrained make havoc as they pass,
The form whereof even now myself beheld
Upon this fair mountain whence I came:
For so far off as I directed mine eyes,
I might perceive five cities all on fire,
Cornfields and vineyards burning like an oven,
And as the leaking vapour in the wind
Turned but aside. I likewise might discern
The poor inhabitants, escaped the flame,
Fall numberless upon the soldiers' pikes.
Three ways these dreadful ministers of wrath
Do tread the measures of their tragic march:
Upon the right hand comes the conquering King,
Upon the left his hot, unbridled son,
And in the midst their nation's glittering host;
All which, though distant yet conspire in one
To leave a desolation where they come.
Fly, therefore, citizens if you be wise,

Seek out some habitation further off.
Here if you stay your wives will be abused,
Your treasure shared before your weeping eyes.
Shelter yourselves, for now the storm doth rise.
[*Drum afar off*]
Away, away! Methinks I hear their drums!
Ah, wretched France, I greatly fear thy fall,
Thy glory shaketh like a tottering wall.
Exeunt.

(Scene 5, 46–68)

Putting a brake on the play's narrative flow towards inexorable English victory, the speech focuses sympathetically on the terror of the vanquished. We might recall Joan la Pucelle's plea on behalf of besieged French townspeople who 'see the cities and the towns defaced' (*1 Henry VI*, 3.7.44–59). It momentarily undercuts the dominant English aristocratic parochialism by expanding our gaze to a more general condemnation of the suffering inflicted by war itself on ordinary citizens, whatever their nationality. These include the mute woman and her children fleeing. In substance it could well have been the 'report back' to the citizens of Harfleur by their governor in *Henry V*, so closely are the threats echoed in this scene. In general terms, whether or not the passage was actually written by Shakespeare himself, its dramatic placement, point of view, and emotional empathy for enemy victims are all consistent with his sensibility and aversion to violent 'abuses' in war demonstrated elsewhere. Later in *Edward III* in another 'siege' scene, this time spoken by a woman, the English Queen Philippa speaks on behalf of French 'Citizens' in begging 'mercy' of the English King to 'take pity on this town'. Her emotive appeal in the last scene succeeds in bringing final peace:

QUEEN
Ah, be more mild unto these yielding men.
It is a glorious thing to stablish peace,
And kings approach the nearest unto God
By giving life and safety unto men.

. . .

KING EDWARD
Although experience teach us this is true –
That peaceful quietness brings most delight
When most of all abuses are controlled –
Yet, insomuch it shall be known that we
As well can master our affections
As conquer other by the dint of sword,
Philippe, prevail, we yield to thy request.

(Scene 18, 39–53)

Given Shakespeare's unrivalled pre-eminence – almost his dramatic signature – in adopting the emotive points of view of victims, it seems implausible that he would not at least have been consulted in a play which he undoubtedly co-wrote.

It is one of the more inconveniently overlooked attitudes bequeathed by Shakespeare, that death in battle is not a way to leave life garlanded with fame and poetic eulogy, since heroism rarely outlives its practitioner once he has become 'food for worms'. Simone Weil again: 'No comforting fiction intervenes; no consoling prospect of immortality' for combatants. Far more deserving of compassion are the diverse, innocent victims of warfare: "I am afeard there are few die well that die in a battle'. These are melancholy conclusions which the world, in its remorseless commitment to war as a preferred way of solving international problems, chooses persistently to ignore.[44]

Refugees

Most tellingly perhaps, the sole speech apparently written and revised in Shakespeare's own handwriting ('Hand D') in the unpublished, collaborative, and apparently never staged *Sir Thomas More*, is the humanist More's eloquent plea to anti-immigration rioters to extend sympathy to Lombard refugees who faced persecution in 1517. It was a topical issue in London in 1593 with the influx of Huguenots fleeing persecution in France.[45] The startlingly fresh relevance for our own times, with millions being inhumanely turned away from safe asylum with slogans like 'stop the boats', was brought to modern attention by Ian McKellen's

44. See Robert Fisk, 'Shakespeare and War', *Counterpunch*, 1 April 2007: http://www .counterpunch.org/2007/04/01/shakespeare-and-war/ accessed 1 September 2023.
45. For attribution, see MacDonald P. Jackson, 'The Date and Authorship of Hand D's Contribution to Sir Thomas More: Evidence from "Literature Online"', *Shakespeare Survey*, 59 (2006), 69–78. E. A. J. Honigmann, writing as a former asylum seeker himself, argues that no one other than Shakespeare could have written the speech: 'Shakespeare, Sir Thomas More and Asylum Seekers', *Shakespeare Survey*, 57 (2007), 225–35. Honigmann also writes on Huguenot immigrants associated with Shakespeare in 'Shakespeare and London's Immigrant Community circa 1600' in *Elizabethan and Modern Studies*, ed. J. P. Vander Motten (Ghent: Seminarie voor Engelse en Amerikaanse Literatuur, R.U.G., 1985), 143–53. I have argued elsewhere that such scenes may represent a cultural memory as aftermath of the St Bartholomew's Day massacre in Paris: 'The Cultural Impact of the Massacre of St Bartholomew's Day', in *Early Modern Civil Discourses*, ed. Jennifer Richards (London: Palgrave Macmillan, 2003).

moving and celebrated rendition in the Royal Shakespeare Company's 'Shakespeare Live' celebration (2016):

> Imagine that you see the wretched strangers,
> Their babies at their backs, and their poor luggage,
> Plodding to th' ports and coasts for transportation,
> And that you sit as kings in your desires,
> Authority quite silent by your brawl
> And you in ruff of your opinions clothed:
> What had you got? I'll tell you. You had taught
> How insolence and strong hand should prevail,
> How order should be quelled – and by this pattern
> Not one of you should live an aged man,
> For other ruffians, as their fancies wrought
> With selfsame hand, self reasons, and self right,
> Would shark on you, and men like ravenous fishes
> Would feed on one another.
> DOLL WILLIAMSON
> Before God, that's as true as the Gospel.
> 　　　　　. . .
> MORE
> Would you be pleased
> To find a nation of such barbarous temper
> That breaking out in hideous violence
> Would not afford you an abode on earth,
> 　　　. . . what would you think
> To be thus used? This is the strangers' case,
> And this your mountainish inhumanity.
> 　　　　　　(2.4.81–94; 1420–52 *passim*)

Beginning with Shakespeare's frequent injunction for his audience to 'Imagine', and drawing attention to his reminders of Christ's Sermon on the Mount ('as true as the Gospel'), the extract ends with reproof of the 'mountainish inhumanity' of those comfortable in their 'ruffs' genuflecting to figures of 'authority' who preach that might is right – 'How insolence and strong hand should prevail'. The value system driving the empathy and eloquence could not be clearer.

Chapter 4

Revenge and Mutually Assured Destruction: Reflections on *Hamlet* and Kant

Shakespeare and revenge

At first glance the apparently insatiable Elizabethan taste for revenge drama or 'tragedy of blood' (referring to kinship as much as gore), seems intriguingly antiquated.[1] The genre included some of the most popular plays of the period, such as Kyd's *The Spanish Tragedy*, Shakespeare's *Titus Andronicus* and *Hamlet* (possibly building on a mysterious lost ancestor, the so-called *Ur-Hamlet*). Other examples still performed are Middleton's *The Revenger's Tragedy* in which the central protagonist

---

1. The genre has attracted voluminous critical studies much of it focused on *Hamlet*, but less since the 1990s. Here is a representative list. A. H. Thorndike, 'The Relations of Hamlet to the Contemporary Revenge Play', *Publications of the Modern Language Association*, 17 (1902), 125–220; Lily B. Campbell, 'Theories of Revenge in Renaissance England', *Modern Philology* 38 (1931), 281–96; Fredson Bowers, *Elizabethan Revenge Tragedy* (Princeton, 1940); Irving Ribner, *Patterns in Shakespearean Tragedy* (London, 1960); Ernst de Chickera, 'Divine Justice and Private Revenge in *The Spanish Tragedy*' 38–58, *Modern Language Review*, 57 (1962), 228–32; Eleanor Prosser, *Hamlet and Revenge*, 2nd ed. (Stanford, 1971); Ronald Broude, 'Revenge and Revenge Tragedy in Renaissance England', *Renaissance Quarterly* 28 (1975); Charles A. Hallett and Elaine S. Hallett, *The Revenger's Madness: A Study of Revenge Tragedy Motifs* (Lincoln, Nebraska: University of Nebraska Press, 1980); Harry Keyishian, *The Shapes of Revenge: Victimization, Vengeance, and Vindictiveness In Shakespeare* (New Jersey: Humanities Press, 1995); John Kerrigan, *Revenge Tragedy: Aeschylus to Armageddon* (Oxford University Press, 1996); Michael Neill, 'English Revenge Tragedy' in *A Companion to Tragedy*, ed. Rebecca Bushnell (Oxford: Blackwell, 2005), 328–50; Tanya Pollard, 'Tragedy and Revenge', in *The Cambridge Companion to English Renaissance Tragedy*, ed. Emma Smith and Garrett A. Sullivan (Cambridge University Press, 2010), 58–72; Linda Woodbridge, *English Revenge Drama: Money, Resistance, Equality* (Cambridge University Press, 2010); George Oppitz-Trotman, *The Origins of English Revenge Tragedy* (Edinburgh University Press, 2019). Some others are cited elsewhere in this chapter.

is named Vindice, Marston's *Antonio's Revenge*, Webster's *The White Devil* and others. In *The Spanish Tragedy* and *Hamlet*, a person discovers the murder of a close relative, and having no recourse to public justice, takes the law into his own hands by embarking on a path of retaliation leading to murder. He often simulates or suffers madness, and ends up violently slaughtered alongside other implicated protagonists in a final bloodbath. The pattern is played out in family terms, but this can be a metaphor for all-engulfing disputes between warring nation-states, or factional dynasties within a nation in civil war. In this sense, it is far from obsolete.

In Shakespeare's practice, revenge is not a discrete genre but a motivation. Linda Anderson in *A Wild Kind of Justice: Revenge in Shakespeare's Comedies* shows that even in unlikely plays dealing comically with romantic love, revenge motives are prominent, despite the theme's negative connotations and presumed historical links with Senecan tragedy.[2] Anderson shows that in *The Two Gentlemen of Verona, Twelfth Night, Much Ado About Nothing, The Merchant of Venice, Measure for Measure, The Merry Wives of Windsor, The Tempest,* and even *Love's Labour's Lost* and *A Midsummer Night's Dream* (especially in Oberon's case), the plots turn centrally on an individual's grievance over some perceived wrong which threatens and sometimes does lead to acts of revenge. The most obvious example of a 'revenge comedy' is *The Merry Wives of Windsor*, since the plot turns on the come-uppances perpetrated by Mistresses Ford and Page against Falstaff for his attempted seductions, and against Ford for his jealousy in refusing to trust his wife. Anderson writes, 'So permeated with revenge is *The Merry Wives* that even the slightest characters express vengeful feelings ...'.[3] Romantic comedy as a genre dictates that this impulse needs to be defused or transcended in order to attain social cohesion and harmony, sometimes only precariously achieved but at least socially managed (Malvolio, Shylock, and Caliban). Underlying this logic is a clear weighting towards finding peaceful solutions to problems, by obviating or containing the possibility of future revenge. Malvolio's menacing last words, 'I'll be revenged on the whole pack of you' (*Twelfth Night*, 5.1.401), is left hanging in the air, while the previous line by Feste indicates that in comedy conflicts can be resolved by time rather than human agency, gesturing to a deferred peace in this case: 'And thus, the whirligig of time brings in his revenges' (5.1.400).

2. Linda Anderson, *A Kind of Wild Justice: Revenge in Shakespeare's Comedies* (Newark: University of Delaware Press, 1987).
3. Anderson, *A Kind of Wild Justice*, 77.

Revenge was a preoccupation for Shakespeare right from the start of his career in *Titus Andronicus* and the *Henry VI* trilogy, and it is ubiquitous and unceasing in all the chronicle plays. While these plays exploit the theatrical sensationalism of the theme, the dramatist gives full weight to the realisation that revenge is morally problematical, and potentially leads to endless murders, like dominoes falling. Theodor Meron in *Bloody Constraint* puts this forcefully in his analysis of the early play *3 Henry VI*:

> While Rutland exemplifies individual innocence, Clifford invokes a claim to intergenerational revenge. The dialogue between Clifford and Rutland does not leave any doubt as to where Shakespeare's sympathy lies with regard to vendettas. Shakespeare shows how the cycle of violence spreads: Clifford kills Rutland in revenge for his father's death at the hands of York, Rutland's father. Although King Edward had just enunciated the chivalric principle of mercy towards the vanquished (*3 Henry VI*, II.vi. 44–45), Richard and Warwick are then allowed to kill Clifford in revenge for his murder of York and Rutland. As Warwick claims, 'measure for measure must be answered' (*3 Henry VI*, II.vi.55).[4]

In all the Shakespearean History plays and most of his tragedies, revenge becomes closely connected with war waged between nations or factions, based on rival dynastic claims to the throne. In these plays war *is* revenge, and the life-and-death stakes are high. Peter Lake in a section titled 'When honour becomes revenge' sees the pattern running through all the History plays and history itself:

> Once the war has started and people have been killed, factional rivalry and dynastic competition become blood feud. Now the issue is not who should be king but rather how quickly and effectively one side can revenge itself upon the other.[5]

Revenge also runs through the power struggles depicted in the Graeco-Roman plays including *Julius Caesar*, since they too present international wars and civil wars of succession as sequences of revenge and counter-revenge.[6] *Troilus and Cressida* turns on the thoroughly disgraceful abduction of Helen, provoking Trojan revenge and a historically iconic conflict. Coriolanus threatens revenge against the Roman populace for what he sees as his public humiliation in not being awarded

4. Theodor Meron, *Bloody Constraint*, 201
5. Peter Lake, *How Shakespeare Put Politics on the Stage: Power and Succession in the History Plays* (New Haven: Yale University Press, 2016), 114–19, 114.
6. Keyishian, *The Shapes of Revenge*, ch. 4 and 6.

the consulship, joining forces with the state's enemy the Volscians to make war. It is made clear that in both professional and personal senses his presence is synonymous with war. He is used within the state as a willing tool of aristocratic hoarders of grain led by Menenius, whose eloquently expressed but devious 'trickle down' economic theory is designed to quell civil obedience. Significantly, Erasmus had identified economic inequality as a prime cause of war. If eliminated, he argues, so would be war: '. . . war, envy, fraud would immediately depart from life once and for all; in short a whole army of evils would march out of our lives once for all'.[7] Meanwhile, the soldier's overt militarism and preference for violence has mouthpieces among the 'serving classes'. The reasons given are dubiously contradictory, contemptuously praising war as a masculine institution preferable to peace:

SECOND SERVINGMAN
Why, then we shall have a stirring world again. This peace is nothing but to rust iron, increase tailors, and breed ballad-makers.
FIRST SERVINGMAN
Let me have war, say I. It exceeds peace as far as day does night: it's spritely walking audible, and full of vent. Peace is a very apoplexy, lethargy; mulled, deaf, sleepy, insensible; a getter of more bastard children than war's a destroyer of men.
SECOND SERVINGMAN
'Tis so, and as wars, in some sort, may be said to be a ravisher, so it cannot be denied but peace is a great maker of cuckolds.
FIRST SERVINGMAN
Ay, and it makes men hate one another.
THIRD SERVINGMAN
Reason; because they then less need one another. The wars for my money. I hope to see Romans as cheap as Volscians.

(4.5.225–40)

Quite apart from the unpleasantly male-centred assumptions behind the images ('ravisher . . . cuckolders'), these seem to be expressions of what Karl Marx came to identify as false consciousness, reasoning against the servingmen's own class interests. 'I hope to see Romans as cheap as Volscians' is like an inadvertently suicidal sentiment bringing destruction on their own families. Shakespeare identifies the servingmen in this critical light, by immediately following their exchange with that between the Tribunes, who give a glimpse of the rare and brief time of peace when the aggrieved military hero is absent:

---

7. 'Adage 1', *Complete Works of Erasmus*, 30: 29–30.

SICINIUS
We hear not of him, neither need we fear him.
His remedies are tame i'th' present peace
And quietness of the people, which before
Were in wild hurry. Here do we make his friends
Blush that the world goes well; who rather had,
Though they themselves did suffer by't, behold
Dissentious numbers pest'ring streets, than see
Our tradesmen singing in their shops and going
About their functions friendly.

(4.6.1–9)

The Tribunes are often performed and critically analysed as machiavellian conspirators who invite Rome's defeat by provoking Coriolanus, a view based on the assumption that audiences are predisposed to sympathise with the lone protagonist (played by a star actor) in righteous conflict against 'the masses'. This view depends mainly on uncritically accepting Menenius's condescending rationalisation of class divisions. It was not necessarily an opinion shared by Elizabethan commoners, who were themselves active in food riots against aristocratic hoarding of grain in 1607–9 which had led to steep price rises.[8] Bertolt Brecht, in his dialectical approach when he adapted the play (left unfinished), draws what strikes him as the 'clear' message, stated by the First Citizen in the opening moments, that 'Caius Marcius [later Coriolanus] is the chief enemy of the people' (1.1.4), as one who rages against elected representatives of the citizens and thus against the interests of the republic itself.[9] Central to the Tribunes' expression of civil interests is a reasonable assumption that peace is preferable to the constant war personified in Coriolanus, as he pursues singlemindedly the priorities of his own violent profession, self-styled heroic individual driven by anger (*furor*) to revenge.[10]

8. Annabel Patterson, *Shakespeare and the Popular Voice*, (Oxford: Basil Blackwell, 1989), 137. See also an essay which summarises the historical background and critical approaches by Elyssa Y. Cheng, 'Moral Economy and the Politics of Food Riots in *Coriolanus*', *Concentric: Literature and Cultural Studies*, 36 (2010), 17–31: *http://www.concentric-literature.url.tw/issues/M/2.pdf*

9. See 'Study of the First Scene of Shakespeare's "Coriolanus"' transcribed in John Willett (ed. and trans.), *Brecht on Theatre: The Development of an Aesthetic* (New York: Hill and Wang, 1964), 252–65. For an account of the differences between the versions by Shakespeare and Brecht see Martin Scofield, 'Drama, Politics, and the Hero: "Coriolanus", Brecht, and Grass', *Comparative Drama*, 24 (1990–91), 322–341.

10. See Gordon Braden, *Renaissance Tragedy and the Senecan Tradition: An Anger's Privilege* (New Haven: Yale University Press, 1985).

More typically, however, the revenger in Elizabethan drama, although undoubtedly lonely in his mission, acts on behalf of his family interests in a 'blood feud'. If allowed to follow its course, revenge may leave entire families dead at the end of a play, and the only resolution possible comes when nobody is left alive to pursue the revenge. In one version of *Gorboduc* (1561–1570), an early Elizabethan play which fuses revenge, morality and history, subjects are warned, 'Much less in blood by sword to work revenge / No more than may the hand cut off the head'.[11] The pattern is almost literally enacted in *Titus Andronicus*, where the unrelenting sequence of wars of revenge and counter-revenge between Tamora and the Andronici leaves both families annihilated, half of them grotesquely eaten in a pie. In the cases of Hieronimo in *The Spanish Tragedy* and Shakespeare's *Titus Andronicus* and *Hamlet*, the protagonist acts on behalf of a family member who has been murdered. In these cases, revenge leaves entire families dead at the end of a play, and the only resolution possible is a vacuum leaving nobody alive. In Marston's *Antonio's Revenge*, the climax is reached when 'all' disputants die:

ANTONIO
This for my father's blood. [*He stabs Piero*]
PANDULPHO
This for my son.
ALBERTO
This for them all.

(5.5.80)

There are personal vendettas in *Othello* (Iago and Cassio, Iago and Othello) and in a sense *Timon of Athens*,[12] and these are played out within a context which includes war. The sub-plot involving Gloucester's sons, Edgar and Edmund in *King Lear* is a straightforward revenge which could stand on its own as an example of the orthodox tradition in revenge tragedy. The soliloquy of Edmund the bastard very clearly states his grievances against both his father and brother stemming from his illegitimacy and virtual disinheritance, and his actions are driven by revenge. These precipitate a counter-revenge leading to his own death, effected in a formal duel by the 'legitimate' Edgar, disguised as a chivalric knight 'whose name is lost', claiming to avenge Edmund's father and brother against a 'traitor'. Edmund accepts the challenge: 'By rule

---

11. Quoted Irving Ribner, *The English History Play in the Age of Shakespeare* (London: Routledge, 1965), 41.
12. See Richard D. Fly, 'The Ending of *Timon of Athens*', *Criticism*, 15 (1973), 242–52. https://www.jstor.org/stable/23099656?seq=11#metadata_info_tab_contents

of knighthood, I disdain and spurn / Back do I toss these treasons to thy head' (5.3.143–4). Neither negotiation nor hope for forgiveness is offered, and death of at least one party will be the sole outcome.

By often placing the action in the historical past, and in countries outside England like Spain and Italy, Protestant English dramatists could avoid attracting official accusations of inciting illegal duels and public violence, by implying instead that such events happened only in uncivilised and usually popish environments. The playing out of primitive drives for revenge could be experienced as theatrical spectacle, but at a safe distance and with a free conscience. Ironically, the same could be said in a temporal sense of revenge plays revived on the modern stage, since the taste for revenge drama evidently persists.

What no doubt attracted dramatists to the motif is that in essence it problematises a retributive justice which applies with ambivalent relevance to the fates of both agents and victims of violent crimes.[13] There is evidence in the plays themselves and in other sources that revenge motives, even at the time, were ambivalently regarded in society, and that such ethical uncertainty was part of the fascination. Characteristic revenge plots hinge upon the spirit of the Old Testament's 'an eye for an eye and a tooth for a tooth' (Exodus 21:23–7, and Leviticus 24:19–21), but in the New Testament Gospels, Christ in the 'Sermon on the Mount' and elsewhere rejects this philosophy in favour of forgiveness and turning the other cheek. In Elizabethan England, private revenge was unlawful, and acknowledged to be opposed to Christian teaching. Prohibitions on revenge were steadily extended also by secular concerns for social law and order, with laws which proscribed private duels and lynch mobs. Francis Bacon famously wrote that 'Revenge is a kind of wild justice', and he encapsulates the moral paradox of a form of justice that is outside law:[14]

> REVENGE is a kind of wild justice; which the more man's nature runs to, the more ought law to weed it out. For as for the first wrong, it doth but offend the law; but the revenge of that wrong putteth the law out of office.

Deriving from the Roman *lex talionis*, it evinces an apparently mathematical reciprocity of justice, especially in cases where public justice is tainted or unavailable. Derek Dunne quotes the line 'Oh . . .Millions of deaths', spoken by the Duke as he expires in Middleton's *The Revenger's*

13. See especially Janet Clare, *Revenge Tragedies of the Renaissance* (Liverpool University Press, 2003).
14. Francis Bacon, *Essays* (London: 1625), 'On Revenge'.

Tragedy (3.5.186), thus fulfilling Vindice's fantasy of 'constant venge-ance' (3.5.109).[15] The pattern has some conceptual validity when we consider that the fictional avenger is driven primarily by a burning passion for righting a wrong, especially if the lawmaker himself (Lorenzo in *The Spanish Tragedy* and King Claudius in *Hamlet*) has committed the first wrong, thus rendering official justice untrustworthy or impossible. Furthermore, the Lord might take His time to 'repay', and does not always seem to deliver promptly. The revenger is then placed in the position of a victim pitted against an all-powerful tyrant, since no other mechanism for justice is available.[16] G. K. Hunter argued that the avenger is aware of his ineffectuality but still proceeds on a solitary path towards martyrdom: '[Titus Andronicus] is the martyr of a world from which the true strain of justice has vanished . . . Much of his madness turns on the search for justice'.[17] Much the same could be said of Hamlet's predicament. On the other hand, even if revenge has some vestiges of justice, it is at best a 'wild' form and outside the law, since it often involves murder, and invariably the revenger is or becomes a wrongdoer himself, in turn inviting further retaliation. As Keyishian shows, the revenger, if not congenitally vindictive or ruled by habitual anger or envy, is often placed in the role of a victim and his vengeance, intended as a matter of justice and equity, is paradoxically as criminal an act as the initial wrong committed against him.[18]

Although the revenge plot is usually located in a family and the revenger is a lonely individual, it more broadly models the course of war, in its competitive and ultimately destructive spiralling towards annihilation of whole populations. The underlying pattern of a simmering family affair can be writ large in political grievances between nations, leading to war and mutual destruction. The motivation towards revenge is a cause of war, and as it follows its course it is microcosm of war. As Montaigne

---

15. See Derek Dunne, '"Superfluous Death" and the Mathematics of Revenge', *Journal of the Northern Renaissance*, 6 (2014) online (accessed 1 September 2023): http://www.northernrenaissance.org/superfluous-death-and-the-mathematics-of-revenge/para.1.

16. The popularity of revenge tragedy in the Jacobean age has sometimes been explained historically as modelling the ongoing dispute between James I and Parliament: see for example Eileen Allman, *Jacobean Revenge Tragedy and the Politics of Virtue* (Newark: University of Delaware Press, 1999). This study also detects in some plays such as Webster's *The Duchess of Malfi* a gendered struggle against patriarchy by an androgynous hero, waged over woman as victim.

17. G. K Hunter, 'Seneca and English Tragedy', *Dramatic Identities and Cultural Tradition: Studies in Shakespeare and his Contemporaries* (Liverpool University Press, 1978), 186.

18. Harry Keyishian, *The Shapes of Revenge*, 101.

observes in an essay dealing with war in history, '. . . if the revenging individual happens to have at his disposal a large enemy, the result is likely to be wholesale massacre of both warring armies'. Of Alexander waging war against Thebes, he writes, 'a day was not long enough to slake the vengeance of Alexander: this carnage lasted until the very last drop of blood remained to be spilt . . .' in an ethnic cleansing.[19] Even Seneca, widely credited as the main classical source for revenge drama (wrongly, according to G. K. Hunter), whose plays had been translated in the 1560s by Jasper Heywood, confessed in his own private capacity in a letter, that the results would be alarming should the pattern be replicated in disputes which are not individual but national:

> We are mad, not only individuals but nations also. We restrain man-slaughter and isolated murders, but what of war and the so-called glory of killing whole peoples? . . . The same deeds which would be punished by death if committed in secret are applauded when done openly by soldiers in uniform. Man, the gentlest of animals, is not ashamed to glory in blood-shedding and to wage war when even the beasts are living in peace together.[20]

History has shown that his misgivings were justified.

Modern performances of *Macbeth*, especially filmed versions, detect in the play's ending that even if Macduff is an agent for divine retribution against the tyrant, yet his personal motive for revenge means that the pattern will recur. The movies routinely hint at repetition of future violence to overthrow Malcolm, by characters who may harbour a grudge or potential motive, such as Fleance, Donalbein, the mysterious Ross who is another powerful thane and cousin of the Macduffs, or another. Malcolm's own nightmarish revery of how his own future regime may resemble Macbeth's (4.1), and his generally weak presence, do not bode well for lasting peace. Welles makes explicit the never-ending revenge-provokes-revenge pattern, by shifting from the beginning to the end the Witches' line, 'Peace, the charm's wound up' (1.1.38). Likewise, contrary to critical accounts giving the impression that the issue of civil war begins only after the assassination of Duncan and ends with the death of Macbeth, whereas Shakespeare graphically insists the war is raging from the beginning, and Macbeth is identified as only one violent soldier among others.

19. Montaigne, *The Complete Essays*, 6.
20. Seneca, *Letters* XCV, trans. Arthur Stanley (ed.), quoted in *The Stars of Peace* (London: J. N. Dent & Sons, 1940), 15.

Hamlet

Hamlet is built upon the ambivalent moral status of revenge, as well as positing rational alternatives in cautious circumspection and diplomacy. The motif of revenge recurs at all levels of the play, even down to apparently tangential details such as the old play 'The Murder of Gonzago' recalled fondly by Hamlet and the Players, which seems to be a revenge drama whose protagonist is driven by 'aroused vengeance' (2.2.489). Hamlet himself ponders the vicious moral circle he faces when contemplating revenge, recognising Bacon's dilemma that two wrongs cannot make a right, and more usually the sequence leads to third and fourth wrongs, until few major characters remain. For an audience in a Christian society aware that 'the Everlasting' had 'fix'd his canon' not only against 'self slaughter' but also murder (1.2.131), the prince's internal vacillations and circumspection would have been understood. Surprisingly, Hamlet's moral scruples were often castigated by twentieth-century critics and actors who said he 'delayed' too long, and Laurence Olivier intoned as a prologue to his movie in 1948 that the philosophy student of Wittenberg was a man 'who could not make up his mind'. René Girard mused sardonically during the period of the Cold War and fears of nuclear war, that presumably such commentators would more readily take the word of a ghost claiming to be from purgatory and demanding retribution for his murder, and would leap to instant retaliation:[21]

> Should our enormous critical literature on *Hamlet* fall some day into the hands of people otherwise ignorant of our mores, they could not fail to conclude that our academic tribe must have been a savage breed indeed. After four centuries of controversies, Hamlet's temporary reluctance to commit murder still looks so outlandish to us that more and more books are being written in an unsuccessful effort to solve that mystery. The only way to account for this curious body of literature is to suppose that, back in the twentieth century no more was needed than some ghost to ask for it, and the average professor of literature would massacre his entire household without batting an eyelash . . . Let us imagine a contemporary Hamlet with his finger on a nuclear button. After forty years of procrastination he has not yet found the courage to push that button. The critics around him are becoming impatient. The psychoanalysts have volunteered their services and have come up with the usual answer. Hamlet is a sick man . . .[22]

21. René Girard, 'Hamlet's Dull Revenge', in *Literary Theory / Renaissance Texts*, edited by Patricia Parker and David Quint (Baltimore: John Hopkins University Press, 1986), 280–302.
22. Girard, 'Hamlet's Dull Revenge', 299–300.

Simply to state it in such bald and mocking terms draws out the absurdity of such reasoning, and helps to justify Hamlet's own conscientious scruples to test the Ghost's veracity before acting. Another critic who traces revenge into issues of nuclear deterrence and the reporting of modern wars is John Kerrigan, in his polymathic book, *Revenge Tragedy: Aeschylus to Armageddon*. His very broad definition of revenge as 'A offends B, B retaliates against A' captures virtually all reactive human behaviour rather than just those end-stopped in murder, highlighting the ubiquity of revenge.[23] Using this foundation, Kerrigan traces the pattern of revenge through to the 'Armageddon' of modern warfare. Nowadays it is alarming to contemplate the scenarios implicit in a handful of unpredictable individuals bearing grudges having access to the nuclear code, especially since the theory of 'nuclear deterrence' itself turns on the threat of retaliative revenge.

Hamlet himself does not leap to such hasty conclusions as his critical detractors. He is warned by Horatio that the apparition might be tempting him to 'the dreadful summit of the cliff', there to adopt 'some other horrible form' and lure him to his death (2.1.72). The same thought occurs to Hamlet as late as the end of the second Act:

> The spirit that I have seen
> May be a de'il, and the de'il hath power
> T'assume a pleasing shape. Yea, and perhaps
> Out of my weakness and my melancholy,
> As he is very potent with such spirits,
> Abuses me to damn me! I'll have grounds
> More relative than this. The play's the thing
> Wherein I'll catch the conscience of the King.
>
> (2.2.533–40)

The 'grounds more relative than this' come later in his playlet which he nicknames 'the mousetrap'. But even at the performance of the play-within-a-play, Claudius's response is not conclusive proof of guilt, but only inferred from the King's verbally non-committal but evidently affronted behaviour. The audience knows the truth of the Ghost's report before Hamlet does, having been privy to Claudius's confessional soliloquy ('O, my offence is rank: it smells to heaven' [3.3.36–72]), which may account for the impatience of some critics to get the job done. If anything, the dramatist is at pains to show his protagonist not culpably 'delaying' but acting circumspectly within the limits of evidence available, and exercising his own conscience. The fact that the Prince of

23. Kerrigan, *Revenge Tragedy: Aeschylus to Armageddon*, 298–9.

Denmark is a student of philosophy from Wittenberg University who, Derrida-like, muses openly that 'there is nothing either good or bad, but thinking makes it so' (2.2.251), allows him to ponder acutely on the ethical quandary he faces.

There are other plots in *Hamlet* involving a son avenging his father. Laertes is motivated by his father's death and his sister's madness and death, both inadvertently attributable to Hamlet. There is also a third which is less often recognised, and it directly links up the logic of revenge with war. It is initially – misleadingly – set up as the primary reason for the appearance of the Ghost, suggesting that war will be the major theme of the play. Horatio describes the Ghost as bearing 'that fair and warlike form / In which the majesty of buried Denmark / Did sometimes march' (1.1.46–8) and 'Armed at point, exactly, cap-à-pie' (1.2.199). In discussion with Marcellus, Horatio further emphasises the military apparel of the Ghost:

Such was the very armour he had on
When he the ambitious Norway combated,
So frowned he once, when in an angry parle
He smote the sledded Polacks on the ice.

(1.1.59–62)

Marcellus says he walks 'With martial stealth' (1.1.65), connecting the apparition with the mysterious war preparations in Denmark, as workmen labour around the clock to produce 'such daily cast of brazen cannon /And foreign mart for implements of war' (1.1.71–3). Horatio explains that these events are linked with a suspected, imminent, retaliatory war by Norway against Denmark, caused by King Hamlet's slaughter of the old 'ambitious Norway', King Fortinbras in battle. Young Fortinbras, as military leader, is presumed to be approaching to avenge his own father's murder at the hand of old Hamlet – exactly comparable to the revenges undergone by both Hamlet and Laertes. The difference is that Fortinbras's uncle dissuades his nephew from attacking Denmark. It is a point to the credit of Claudius that he has headed off this likely military invasion by dispatching high-ranking ambassadors, Cornelius and Voltemand, to the King of Norway, to persuade him to restrain Fortinbras.[24] He has effectively nipped in the bud the danger of continuing warfare between the two nations. Timothy Hampton describes this

24. Timothy Hampton, *Fictions of Embassy: Literature and Diplomacy in Early Modern Europe* (New York: Cornell University Press, 2011), ch. 6, 'Hamlet's Diplomacy: State-Building, Dispatch, and Revenge', 138–62, 145–7. Hampton uses this to argue that Claudius is more 'modern' and sophisticated than old Hamlet, using diplomacy

as 'one of the few successful gestures of diplomatic dispatch and negotiation in Early Modern literature . . . conflict is diverted through diplomacy' (145–6). In this sense, Claudius has utilised the problem-solving
strategy of diplomacy advocated by Shakespeare's Touchstone in *As You
Like It*, to be examined in my final chapter. However, here Claudius has
not been entirely successful in averting another war, since Fortinbras
is still bent on a course of revenge to regain land lost in war. He now
aims to take a strip of Polish land after recruiting 'a list of lawless resolutes' of mercenaries from rural Norway. As the entry on 'Poland' in
the *Oxford Companion to Shakespeare* notes, Shakespeare's reference
to the country itself is 'confused and confusing', but the main point is
that Fortinbras needs permission to cross Denmark in order to reach
and reclaim Poland, which is his new, more limited mission.[25] Claudius
agrees, in return for Fortinbras's promise not to invade Denmark itself.
None the less, despite the success of the embassy, the Danish military
preparations continue in secrecy, indicating some mistrust of the hot-
headed young prince of Norway's real intentions. It is ironic that permission to do so is granted by Polonius, whose name semantically appears
to link him with the Latin for Poland.[26] The relevance of the subplot is
often overlooked (and the role of Fortinbras cut in many productions,
especially since he does not appear in the sources of *Hamlet*), because
it seems to lead nowhere in the main plot, except to explain the arrival
of Fortinbras at Claudius's court at the end. But it does also lead to
Hamlet's most clearly pacifist sentiments, revealing his temperamental
leanings against war and, I suggest, Shakespeare's.

To return to the complicated historical terms of a thirty-year-old armistice, Horatio explains how lands of the former 'Fortinbras of Norway',
including Poland, fell to 'old' King Hamlet, though he is evidently unaware of the terms of agreement more recently negotiated by Claudius.
The situation is as complex as the one described in *Love's Labour's Lost*
over Aquitaine. Horatio assumes the approaching army is hostile to
Denmark and bent on revenge:

instead of force to solve the problem. However, Hampton does not explain why
military preparations continue, perhaps through mistrust.

25. Jerzy Limon, 'Poland'. *The Oxford Companion to Shakespeare*. Michael Dobson,
Stanley Wells, Will Sharpe, Erin Sullivan (eds), Second ed. online version (Oxford
University Press, 2015), 117.

26. See Krystyna Courtney Kujawińska and Katarzna Kwapisz Williams, '"The Polish
Prince": Studies in Cultural Appropriation of Shakespeare's *Hamlet* in Poland'
(University of Łódz, Poland: 2001), 1–15. http://triggs.djvu.org/global-language
.com/ENFOLDED/BIBL/___HamPol.htm

At least the whisper goes so. Our last King,
Whose image even but now appeared to us,
Was, as you know, by Fortinbras of Norway –
Thereto pricked on by a most emulate pride –
Dared to the combat, in which our valiant Hamlet
(For so this side of our known world esteemed him)
Did slay this Fortinbras, who by a sealed compact
Well ratified by law and heraldry
Did forfeit, with his life all these his lands
Which he stood seized of to the conqueror:
Against the which, a moiety competent
Was gaged by our King; which had return
To the inheritance of Fortinbras
Had he been vanquisher, as, by the same co-mart,
And carriage of the article design,
His fell to Hamlet. Now, sir, young Fortinbras,
Of unimproved mettle, hot and full,
Hath in the skirts of Norway here and there
Sharked up a list of lawless resolutes
For food and diet to some enterprise
That hath a stomach in't, which is no other,
As it doth well appear unto our state,
But to recover of us by strong hand
And terms compulsatory, those foresaid lands
So by his father lost. And this, I take it,
Is the main motive of our preparations,
The source of this our watch, and the chief head
Of this post-haste and rummage in the land.

(1.1.79–106)

Bernardo agrees that this situation is the likely reason 'that this porten-tous figure / Comes armed through our watch so like the King / That was and is the question of these wars' (1.1.108–10). It turns out that both are wrong, since the Ghost is more personally concerned with avenging his own death at his brother's hand, but the shadow of poten-tial war remains a continuing dramatic context throughout the play. It becomes significant in the final lines when the dying young Hamlet, now King, nominates Fortinbras his successor, thus effectively acceding to a peaceful invasion, and allowing Fortinbras to avenge his father's death at the hand of Hamlet's father. His gesture, somewhat unexpectedly, is another major concession through an act of diplomacy which avoids war by yielding to a bloodless coup. Eerily, the description matches not only the reason offered for the armed build-up to Russia's invasion in 2022 to 'reclaim' lost territory of the previous USSR country, Ukraine.

Although the geography has changed over the centuries, the same countries, Denmark Norway and Poland, are all directly involved, as millions of refugees flee to these countries which also fear the same future fate. Even though Horatio's theory will turn out to be only indirectly and accidentally true, yet young Prince Hamlet is persuaded of it, and asks pointedly for confirmation from the eye-witnesses of the Ghost's military bearing – 'Armed, say you? . . . From top to toe' – and Marcellus replies with conviction, 'Armed, my lord. / My lord, from head to foot . . . he wore his beaver up' (1.2.224–28). Left alone on stage, Prince Hamlet draws his own conclusion that the appearance of the ghost is connected with an impending war: 'My father's spirit – in arms! All is not well; / I doubt some foul play. Would the night were come!' (1.2.253–5). There is no reason for Hamlet to know of Claudius's negotiations, and for all we know he goes to his grave assuming Fortinbras is invading Denmark. Just as in *Othello* and *Antony and Cleopatra*, the opening is misleading and deflectionary from the main plot, even to the extent of allowing the audience to expect that the dead King will be the titular protagonist in a revenge for wartime defeat. Instead, the son is charged to avenge the 'murder most foul' (1.5.26) of the father, rather than to fight re-ignited old battles, which leads to the play as we have it.

When Hamlet meets Fortinbras's military leader in 4.4 (a scene that does not appear in full in the Folio version and is often deleted in performance), the tone is mutually cordial and diplomatic, as the Captain explains that the immediate target is Polish land, which will require a military solution:

> CAPTAIN
> Truly to speak, and with no addition,
> We go to gain a little patch of ground
> That hath in it no profit but the name.
> To pay five ducats, five, I would not farm it;
> Nor will it yield to Norway or the Pole
> A ranker rate, should it be sold in fee.
> HAMLET
> Why, then, the Polack never will defend it.
> CAPTAIN
> Yes, it is already garrisoned.
>
> (4.4.18–25)

In soliloquy, Hamlet confides more generally on this war of conquest:

> HAMLET
> Two thousand souls and twenty thousand ducats
> Will not debate the question of this straw!

> . . .
> Witness this army of such mass and charge,
> Led by a delicate and tender prince,
> Whose spirit with divine ambition puffed,
> Makes mouths at the invisible event,
> Exposing what is mortal and unsure
> To all that fortune, death, and danger dare,
> Even for an egg-shell.
> . . .
>   I see
> The imminent death of twenty thousand men
> That for a fantasy and trick of fame,
> Go to their graves like beds, fight for a plot
> Whereon the numbers cannot try the cause,
> Which is not tomb enough and continent
> To hide the slain . . .

>   (4.4.26–65 *passim*)

Hamlet regards the strip of land as hardly worth fighting over, and in doing so he casts more general doubt on war itself as a means of arbitrating territorial disagreements. Given the intimacy of address between character and audience of a soliloquy which carries a presumption of sincerity, it seems clear that the 'sweet prince' and his dramatic creator prefer peace to war, at least with respect to this apparently futile war that threatens the lives of 'twenty thousand men'.

Hamlet is a play in which the audience, like its protagonist, is constantly faced with the need to 'by indirections find directions out' (2.1.63). By connecting secretive preparations for war with motive for private murder, the dramatist draws attention to the parallel in each – revenge. The family conflict is analogous to the wider, international war in which nation is pitched against nation, since both turn on the logic of violent retaliation. It is a rarely noticed irony that the play ends with the son capitulating in a national humiliation to the son of his father's foe, as Hamlet hands power over Denmark to young Fortinbras ('strong-arm', making semantic sense of Horatio's phrase 'strong in hand'). He anoints as his successor the latest military invader who has entered to the tune of a 'warlike volley' (V.ii.357), a warrior who had originally intended to avenge his own father's fate. Fortinbras's accession is at most an uneasy and temporary resolution, holding ominous signs for future strife in the sovereign state of Denmark. Fortinbras may be surprised but also delighted by the fortuitous turn of events handing him kingship on a plate. He did not intend to invade Denmark but takes the outcome in his stride, as a bloodless revenge for his father's death, by usurping the son of the slayer.

Hamlet's meditation on the wastefulness of the war involving Poland, Norway and Denmark suggests more generally that soldiers relinquish their precious lives in a futile cause. In his view, as well as losing their own lives they endanger their families' futures causelessly, in following leaders who seek 'greatly to find quarrel in a straw / When honour's at the stake' (4.4.55–6). 'Honour' here bears the note of heavy sarcasm we have noted in the History plays. Judged in this light, it is a profound irony that such a proto-pacifist prince with his dying breath declares as his successor his temperamental opposite, the military invader of his country whom he had described as 'puff'd' with 'divine ambition'. Fortinbras, reflecting his own military values, praises and buries Hamlet as a soldier, which seems the most incongruous cachet:

> Let four captains
> Bear Hamlet like a soldier to the stage,
> For he was likely, had he been put on,
> To have prov'd most royal; and for his passage,
> The soldiers' music and the rite of war
> Speak loudly for him. . . .
> Go, bid the soldiers shoot.
>
> (5.2.403–8)

Misunderstood to the end and now borne to his grave as 'like a soldier', it is a sad end for a professed pacifist. Ironically, Hamlet in seeing Fortinbras before he has met him as 'a delicate and tender prince' seems to be as wrong as Fortinbras in judging him.[27]

Since 'the rest is silence' in the play, we are given no grounds to surmise what will happen in the future. Some twentieth-century Polish productions, politically slanted towards suspicion of corrupt totalitarian rule in a police state, have drawn on the historical record, that Fortinbras's rule was to prove cruel and grim.[28] But the lesson of history and the logic of the play's events point towards counter-insurgency from Danish loyalists determined to avenge their young King Hamlet's usurpation in a *de facto* invasion by 'the ambitious Norway', and to restore their nation's sovereignty. There are available 'liegemen to the Dane' (1.1.16) such as Marcellus, Francisco, Bernardo and Horatio, as loyal supporters of the 'old' regime of the Hamlet line. The bleak message of the play is that in matters of fraternal murder the sequence of revenge can be ended only

---

27. For one of the very few critical considerations of the various problems raised here, see Simon Barker, *'Like a soldier to the stage': Field Commander Hamlet and the Ends of Tragedy* (Cheltenham: Cyder Press, University of Gloucestershire, 2009).
28. See Krystyna Courtney Kujawińska, 'The Polish Prince'.

when an entire ruling family is destroyed, and that analogously at the level of war between nations, the conflict will be endlessly repeated in mindless commitment to an antiquated and barbaric model of justice visited upon the living by the dead. In political and military terms the play in a sense ends exactly where it started, with the ground laid for a looming constitutional and military crisis, leading to generational cycles of potentially never-ending national revenge and counter-revenge. It is Shakespeare's prophetic insight into the future fates of many countries invaded up to the present day, in which thousands of combatants will 'go to their graves like beds' on land destined to become scorched earth and useless for any civilised purpose, destroyed in the name of 'honour'. Unbeknown to Putin, his 'special operation' (a phrase honed to perfection by successive military incursions into Palestine by the Israeli state's military) in Ukraine leads back to *Hamlet*.

Revenge in the modern world

Shakespeare's plays might seem far removed from contemporary realities, yet they show basic processes at work, which seem to stretch from ancient times in his sources into an indeterminate future. As in Elizabethan times so today, popular culture tacitly confirms that a philosophy of revenge is not only central to the perpetuation of wars, but it also drives mass entertainment. Judging from television ratings of dramas like *Peaky Blinders* in the UK (set in the immediate aftermath of World War One) and *Underbelly* in Australia, many viewers are glued to watching drama that appears to be a straightforward modern survival of revenge tragedy in the context of gangland murders. The mafia ethic of alternating revenge killings fuelled *The Godfather* and its two sequels, along with a host of other movies along the same formulaic lines. In the third of the *Godfather* sequence (1990), the director Francis Ford Coppola claimed he wanted to make audiences think of *King Lear*. The playwright is referenced directly in the line 'All bastards are lions. Shakespeare wrote poems about them'. In this movie, the 'godfather' Michael Corleone (Al Pacino) intends his ill-gotten fortune to found and fund a benevolent Foundation, envisaged partly as a father's gift to create a safe future for his children, and thus, as King Lear had hoped, 'that future strife / May be prevented now' (1.1.33–4) in the interests of family unity. In both cases things go badly wrong since in some mobsters' views the spiral of violence cannot with honour be terminated without more deaths, given the mafia tradition of vendetta, and because different revenges causally proliferate in turn. In the movie one 'bastard' nephew refuses to lay down arms and quell his resentment, and it takes only this one to keep the fire of hatred burning. Michael Corleone is sadly aware of the disastrous dynamic ensuring that whole families can be wiped out by systematic mutual retaliation, forecasting the agonizing climax when his beloved daughter, Cordelia-like, is murdered in a failed attempt to assassinate him: 'When they come, they come for one you love'. He himself is wounded but not killed, uttering a single sustained 'howl' standing for Lear's five as he cradles his dead daughter. It is an unmistakable allusion to the ending of *King Lear*. Coppola kept Corleone alive with a view to a mooted remake billed as *The Godfather, Coda*, in which the aged godfather lives on in a state comparable to the 'purgatorial' mental torture of old King Hamlet, or of Lear's 'I am bound / Upon a wheel of fire that mine own tears / Do scald like molten lead' (4.7.46–8).[29] The conventions underlying the multiplication of 'mafia movies' and video games called by names such as 'Mafia Revenge' mirror the Elizabethan exemplars and derive from them. More generally, 'warplay' computer games aimed at children and adolescents can reflect innovations in weaponry to enhance the sense of novelty.[30] Revenge tragedy, even in its apparently antiquated examples, has entered today's cultural psyche in ways that makes it apparently ineradicable.

More worrying still, and beyond the world of media and fiction, it seems impossible not to conclude that foreign policies of a majority of non-neutral nations in the world casually ignore international laws, treaties and edicts, and routinely threaten and carry out cold-blooded retaliation against nations defined as 'enemies'. The routine is depressingly familiar: choose a nation with a different political system, a different religion, and its own long history of unique culture, and by manipulating media, persuade the public that this 'enemy' is an existential threat to 'national security'. The rash of inverted commas around phrases in this paragraph indicates the prevalence of euphemistic jargon and pure fiction in reporting and documenting the progression towards war. Shakespeare was certainly no stranger to this use of language, his most famous example being Brutus's words before the bloody assassination of Caesar: 'Let's be sacrificers but not butchers, Caius . . . Let's carve him as a dish fit for the gods' (*Julius Caesar*, 2.1.165, 172). At the more harmless initiation of the spectrum, we see the almost amus-

29. See '"My daughter took the bullet for me": Why Francis Ford Coppola is restoring *The Godfather Part III*', *Independent* 13 December, 2020 (accessed 1 September 2023): https://www.independent.co.uk/arts-entertainment/francis-coppola-godfather-part-three-coda-b1767375.html
30. See Goldstein, *War and Gender*, 293–8.

ing retaliation of a pageant-like, tit-for-tat expulsion of ambassadors, always in precisely symmetrical numbers. They are routinely accused of spying, a practice also universal in the sixteenth century diplomatic world, in England under spymaster Lord Walthamstow, prototype for Shakespeare's Polonius. The diplomatic pirouetting acts signal that a negotiated solution to the problems will no longer even be discussed, and it is also perversely self-defeating in eliminating the channel of communication through which the warring sides could mediate. The next stage consists of bellicose rhetoric and belligerent displays of military might, with one 'side' (as though it is a sports team) sending fighter jets and warships on 'exercises' to patrol artificially contested boundaries, a provocation inviting the same from the opponents. 'Virtual war games' are simulated in the safety of offices, continents away from potential battlegrounds. When conflict escalates and eventually breaks out either by design, miscalculation, or mischance, there is a fiction of 'proportional response', once again modelled on revenge. First come 'conventional' bombs lobbed ostensibly at an army target, answered swiftly by a 'contained and proportionate' retaliatory attack, in theory calculated to kill equal numbers of combatants but in fact spraying in aimless destructiveness over cities. Thence follows 'limited escalation' on both sides with 'surgical strikes', a deliberately disingenuous phrase which is a shocking insult to the medical profession, given the non-surgical propensity of bombs to cause a 'collateral' mess in populated cities. The phrase, 'saturation bombing', is at least more graphically candid. Armed forces no longer 'retreat' but practise 'tactical realignment'. Unmanned 'drones' – another deliberate verbal obfuscation like 'friendly fire' – take over, to unnerve and intimidate civilians without risking military casualties. By this stage there is no looking back, as the revenge pattern re-duplicates. International opinion and disapproving motions from supra-national bodies like the United Nations are vetoed or ignored, casualties mount, now mainly innocent civilians and fleeing refugees. How else can we describe the 'logic' behind such events, including the wilful threat of nuclear weapons, than as being based on revenge and retaliation? The spiralling escalation is defined pithily by Milton: 'For what can war but endless war still breed?'.[31] Repeated official declarations that 'a nuclear war cannot be won and must never be fought', and that such weapons are merely for 'deterrence', are less than reassuring, especially when uttered by leaders of the very nations possessing such weapons, whose leaders have no intention of voluntarily relinquishing them. Behind their platitudes lies King Lear's ill-concealed threat towards his daughters: "–

31. Milton, Sonnet 15, 'To Fairfax'.

I will do such things – / What they are, yet I know not: but they shall be / The terrors of the earth'. (2.2.437–41).

Hypothetically, the modern endgame sketched above is the same as in Shakespeare's depiction of the Wars of the Roses, from the ceremonial exchange of white and red roses, to mounting corpses in which neither side can avoid counter-revenge, and the decimation of rival dynasties. Once the inexorable routine has begun, it has its own self-perpetuating momentum which must be played out to the bitter end. Shakespeare generalises the perverse logic in a way analogous to the theme of Erasmus's *Praise of Folly*:

> But man, proud man,
> Dress'd in a little brief authority,
> Most ignorant of what he's most assur'd –
> His glassy essence – like an angry ape
> Plays such fantastic tricks before high heaven
> As make the angels weep; who, with our spleens,
> Would all themselves laugh mortal.
> (*Measure for Measure*, 2.2.118–24)

'War *is* revenge' is a phrase that can at least be seriously debated. At the apparent termination of every war (except those that exterminate a whole population in a sustained policy of genocide masked as 'ethnic cleansing'), the terms laid down by the victors invariably do not bring lasting peace, but simply plant new grievances in the humiliated and angry 'losers' of the war, laying the groundwork for the next war to be waged in counter-revenge. The intention behind the Treaty of Versailles in 1919 was that World War One should be the 'war to end all wars', but its effect was to lead, in a single generation, straight to the growth of German nationalism in the 1930s, rearmament, World War Two, and the so-called Cold War, down to the invasion of Ukraine. When politicians reframe defeat into a need for national revenge and reprisals, the telling factor is the ease with which whole populations can be persuaded, confirming how deeply embedded is the revenge narrative in popular consciousness. Public policy on the international stage mirrors staged revenge plays from four centuries ago. Caught in the crossfire between warring families or nations, we may hear the muffled sounds of Mercutio's anguished curse: 'A plague o' both your houses' (*Romeo and Juliet*, 3.1.92, 107).

Ending revenge: Kant's 'Perpetual Peace'

The philosopher Immanuel Kant became familiar with Shakespeare's works through his contact with Johann Gottfried Herder. Herder occasionally quoted from them and he contributed himself to the prevailing Romantic humanism which was driving critical interpretations of Shakespeare. He was amongst the first generation who rebelled against eighteenth-century, neoclassical rewritings of the plays and went back to the unrevised texts, taken to exemplify the playwright's unique 'genius', a loaded and much debated word amongst philosophers of the time.[32] While only once did Kant quote from *Hamlet*, he has been described by one critic as showing in his philosophical approach a special 'affinity' with the character.[33] Another, who was heavily influenced by Kant, was Coleridge, who claimed 'I have a smack of Hamlet myself, if I may say so'.[34] Hamlet in conversation with fellow students Rosencrantz and Guildenstern, swings between positive optimism and negative pessimism:

> I have of late, but wherefore I know not, lost all my mirth, forgone all custom of exercises; and, indeed, it goes so heavily with my disposition that this goodly frame, the earth, seems to me a sterile promontory, this most excellent canopy, the air, look you, this brave o'erhanging firmament, this majestical roof fretted with golden fire, why, it appeareth nothing to me but a foul and pestilent congregation of vapours.
>
> (2.2.297–305)

Kant envisaged an 'affinity' between the opposed states of idealism and disgust, writing in the *Critique of Practical Reason*, 'Two things fill my mind with ever new and increasing admiration and reverence . . .: *the starry heavens above me and the moral law within me*'. In the earlier *Critique of Judgment* (1790) he had viewed human existence as a 'splendid misery' (paragraph 83), but proposed that the ultimate abolition of violence and oppression requires a paradigm shift in human thinking, depending on a universally agreed 'civil morality' and application of an

---

32. See especially Andrew Cutrofellow, 'Kant's Debate with Herder About the Significance of the Genius of Shakespeare', *Philosophy Compass*, 3 (2008), 66–82; Patrick Swinden, 'Coleridge and Kant' in *Literature and the Philosophy of Intention* (London: Palgrave Macmillan, 1999). More generally on Kant, see the multiple references to his influence in *A Cultural History of Peace in the Age of Enlightenment*, ed. Stella Ghervas and David Armitage (London: Bloomsbury, 2020), esp. 30ff.
33. Andrew Cutrofellow, *All for Nothing: Hamlet's Negativity* (Cambridge MA: MIT Press, 2014), 43.
34. Coleridge, *Table Talk*.

'expanded horizon' (paragraph 40).[35] These are consolidated by habits of taking the opinions of others into consideration in all our judgements, thus undermining the kind of narrow-minded nationalism which leads to war. In this spirit he wrote *Perpetual Peace* as a reconciliation between views. Without claiming an explicit link between Kant and *Hamlet*, I offer here what amounts to a closeness of viewpoint between the philosopher and the dramatist on the related subjects of revenge, war, and peace.

In the incisive clarity of his widely influential pamphlet *Perpetual Peace: A Philosophical Sketch* (English translation published in 1795), Kant argued that the precondition for a 'perpetual peace' is the removal of any possible justification for revenge at the end of a war. Only then can peace be not just a cessation of hostilities but a permanent condition. Kant was open-eyed in recognising the almost insuperable stumbling blocks in the way of achieving perpetual peace. He begins by contrasting 'the rulers of states in particular, who are insatiable of war' and 'the philosophers who dream this sweet dream [of peace]'. He addresses the charge of impotent idealism routinely levelled against pacifists by 'the practical politician' who,

> assumes the attitude of looking down with great self-satisfaction on the political theorist as a pedant whose empty ideas in no way threaten the security of the state, inasmuch as the state must proceed on empirical principles.

His six 'Preliminary Articles' all pertain to eliminating the emotive driving force of revenge with its consequential, perceived need for retaliation. The first Article reads, '*No Treaty of Peace Shall Be Held Valid in Which There Is Tacitly Reserved Matter for a Future War*'. To this is added, 'Otherwise a treaty would be only a truce, a suspension of hostilities but not peace, which means the end of all hostilities'. The second is '*No Independent States, Large or Small, Shall Come under the Dominion of Another State by Inheritance, Exchange, Purchase, or Donation*'; the fourth is '*National Debts Shall Not Be Contracted with a View to the External Friction of States*, and sixth, '*No State Shall, during War, Permit Such Acts of Hostility Which Would Make Mutual Confidence in the Subsequent Peace Impossible*'. To these, Kant appends an explanation which today would be expanded to include things like surveillance by secret agents, cyber intrusion, espionage, covert planning for 'regime change', and destabilisation by spreading propaganda:

35. Immanuel Kant, *Critique of Judgment* (1790), trans. J. H. Bernard (New York: Hafner Publishing, 1951).

'*Such Are the Employment of Assassins (percussores), Poisoners (vene-fici), Breach of Capitulation, and Incitement to Treason (perduellio) in the Opposing State'.*[36] This shades into the fifth Article covering state sovereignty: *'No State Shall by Force Interfere with the Constitution or Government of Another State'.* All these Conditions seek not merely to prevent revenge but to eradicate any probable reason for it.

Kant's remaining Article is even more fundamental as a condition for ending war: *'Standing Armies (miles perpetuus) Shall in Time Be Totally Abolished'.* Japan's post-war Constitution passed in November 1946 encapsulated this essential basis for lasting peace:

> Aspiring sincerely to an international peace based on justice and order, the Japanese people forever renounce war as a sovereign right of the nation and the threat or use of force as means of settling international disputes. In order to accomplish the aim of the preceding paragraph, land, sea, and air forces, as well as other war potential, will never be maintained. The right of belligerency of the state will not be recognized. (Constitution, Article 9)

This, ironically, was imposed as a 'punishment' for Japan after World War Two, but nonetheless was welcomed by the population, and it stands as one attempt to implement 'perpetual peace'. However, the United States, now an ally rather than enemy, from the 1950s onwards encouraged and even pressured Japan incrementally to 'reinterpret' (effectively to circumvent) this exemplary and apparently unambiguously pacifist Article into virtually its diametric opposite by a semantic sleight of vowing to relinquish only 'belligerent' wars of aggression. Japanese governments accordingly began to re-arm precipitously in the name of 'defence' (including pre-emptive strikes) of alliances, becoming in time one of the world's most powerful and modern armed forces and in the process vastly profiting the American arms industry.[37] Judging from polls, the Japanese people themselves preferred the unadulterated, pacifist intention, even if their leaders did not. Interpreted cynically, it had suited American foreign policy to disarm Japan after the War in humiliating fashion under US occupation, but this became an annoying hindrance during and after the Cold War when anti-communism became the ruling Western obsession. The relevance of Japan's Article 9 to Shakespeare has been intimated in an account of a Japanese production of *Romeo*

36. Immanuel Kant, *Perpetual Peace: A Philosophical Essay* (1795).
37. For a thorough historical and legal analysis, see Jeffrey P. Richter, 'Japan's "Reinterpretation" of Article 9: A Pyrrhic Victory for American Foreign Policy?', *Iowa Law Review* 101 (2016), 1223–62.

and Juliet by Hirohisa Igarashi, 'The Impossibility of Turning Rancour to Love: The Post-war Controversy over the Pacifist Constitution and Yukio Ninagawa's Construing of *Romeo and Juliet*'.[38]

Kant's essay on peace had far-reaching influence, for example in contributing to the establishment of the United Nations and recognition of refugee rights. But events down to the present day continue tragically to highlight how far away we still are from dismantling policies based on primitive revenge and instead implementing conditions for perpetual peace. My final chapter will argue that Shakespeare's underlying attitudes, expressed in pre-Enlightenment terms, are comparable with Kant's.

38. Hirohisa Igarashi, 'The Impossibility of Turning Rancour to Love: The Post-war Controversy over the Pacifist Constitution and Yukio Ninagawa's Construing of *Romeo and Juliet*', *Shakespeare* 17 (2001), 230–41.

Chapter 5

'Bind fast his corky arms':
Torture in *King Lear*

One of the most celebrated series of productions of *King Lear* was that of Donald Wolfit which played in London and toured provincial Britain to great acclaim during and after World War Two from 1943 to 1953. In its British context it is often cited as a 'definitive' staging of *King Lear*. Its power seems to have been connected with the immediacy of British wartime experiences felt during the War and extending into the rationed post-war cultural environment.[1] By contrast, seasons in New York in 1943 and again in 1953 were unsuccessful. The apparent indifference of American audiences to Wolfit's production may be connected with their having avoided the earliest years of a War which never impinged on their safely distant shores, thus sparing them from the harrowing European experiences of being bombed on their own soil and losing millions of close relatives in combat.

Laurence Raw has described the performances and changing audience responses, in a chapter whose title, 'Shakespeare on the Home Front', places it in the context of the War in Britain.[2] He argues that Wolfit's production 'had a direct bearing on the wartime audience's daily struggles in its representation of a harsh, unforgiving world dominated by tyrants' (59). Several times, Raw links the claps of thunder as the storm approaches with Lear's stormy state of mind, a critical commonplace. But he surprisingly does not mention the more topical point, that to audiences in Britain the more visceral response to the deafening thunder machine in the theatre must have been related to the terrifyingly

1. Jay L. Halio, *The Tragedy of King Lear*, The New Cambridge Shakespeare (Cambridge University Press, 1992), 49.
2. Laurence Raw, *Theatre of the People: Donald Wolfit's Shakespearean Productions 1937–1953* (Lanham, Maryland: Rowman and Littlefield, 2015), ch. 4. For case studies of two performances in particular, see also Laurence Raw, 'People's Theatre and Shakespeare in Wartime: Donald Wolfit's *King Lear* in London and Leeds, 1944–45', *Shakespeare*, 12.1 (2016), 55–66.

unpredictable, night-time bombing of cities. There were also visible reminders of the times. Raw writes that the London season was attended by uniformed soldiers including some American servicemen, and '[the London] Scala Theatre season played to packed houses until Wolfit was forced to move out, as the theatre was commandeered by the US Army'. Raw draws a distinction between Wolfit's *Lear* as a prime example of what he terms 'Shakespeare in wartime', distinguished from 'wartime Shakespeare'. The latter were productions that 'consciously memorialize violent histories and events taking place in a country's past', referring presumably to the History plays.[3] Wolfit's dedication to touring meant that audiences in different parts of Britain were exposed to the play, which 'proved an effective means of forging a sense of community during a period of strife'. During the war itself the production evoked,

> a sense of shared endeavour ... Both performers and audience par-
> ticipated in a collective ritual, proving that the British way of life – as
> expressed through Lear – would survive, despite the Luftwaffe's best
> attempts to disrupt it' (66).

There was a paradoxical awareness of daily casualties contrasting with more hopeful 'alternative ways of living', represented by Kent's loyalty and the poignant reunion of Lear with his daughter after the battles. The production depicted 'a hostile, unforgiving world in which human beings seemed largely insignificant', but was leavened with affecting moments revealing community values of compassion for social victims, for example in Lear's 'Poor naked wretches' soliloquy (3.4.28–36). Even the changes in production made after the War, raising different audience responses and reacting to changing times, hit a different but equally topical note of 'bitterness and loss of identity', in a population wondering whether wartime sacrifices had been worthwhile, given the continuing food shortages, the steady dismantling of empire, and emergence of Cold War tensions that portended an even more terrifying war in the making.

Some critics in the 1940s reflected similarly sombre and fearful preoccupations centring on experiences in World War Two, as did writers during subsequent wars, like Vietnam.[4] On the stage, Samuel Beckett's

---

3. Raw, 'People's Theatre', 62.
4. It does not surprise me that the pioneering, neglected book by the pacifist poet Edwin Muir, *The Politics of King Lear* (Glasgow: Jackson, 1947) was a lecture delivered in 1945 as the Seventh W. P. Ker Memorial Lecture at Glasgow University and published in 1947 when the minds of Muir and others were sharpened by the recent experience of war. Similarly, Stanley Cavell was writing during – and about – the Vietnam War in 'The avoidance of love: A reading of *King Lear*' in *Must We Mean*

bleak plays *Waiting for Godot* (1948) and *Endgame* (1957) were written in the wake of the War, as were works in the 'theatre of cruelty'
linked with Artaud, Grotowski and Genon in the 1960s. Jan Kott,
his critical analyses primed and sharpened by post-war experiences in
Eastern Europe, drew attention to the pervading influence of *King Lear*
on Beckett's plays.[5] Kott inspired Peter Brook's celebrated production
in 1962, which was infused with the spirit then prevailing in Britain, of
exhausted austerity and post-war *ennui*. There was a gathering nuclear
anxiety (a medical condition named 'nucleomituphobia'), following the
detonations at Hiroshima and Nagasaki and the build-up of an increasingly alarming arms race. As Raw concludes, 'Wolfit's Lear proved
beyond question that directors of Shakespeare in wartime – both past
and present – do not need to update the plays in order to affect their
audiences' (65) – change the context of reception, and the play changes.
In the decades since that period when war was on the European 'home
front', *King Lear* was steadily displaced in the bulk of critical discourse
by *Hamlet* with its psychological anxieties and more cerebral concerns.[6]
None the less, the subject of war itself in *King Lear* still invites reflection. This chapter will centre on just one war crime, the use of torture in
interrogating Gloucester as a prisoner of war. But brief discussion of the
place of war in the play is necessary first.

King Lear is rarely analysed as a play centrally concerned with the
causes, progress, and consequences of war, but even its stage directions
indicate as much with the visibility of armies: '*Enter with drum and colours Cordelia, Gentleman, [officer] and soldiers*' (4.4.1), and '*Alarum
within. Enter with drum and colours LEAR, CORDELIA and soldiers . . .*' (5.2.1). However, the exact status of the war precipitated by
Lear's rash 'division of the kingdom' (1.1.1–4) between his daughters
(or just as pertinently, his sons-in-law) and his enraged disinheritance

What We Say? (Cambridge University Press, 1976), 278–353. More recent works
that are relevant to this essay are R. A. Foakes, *Hamlet versus Lear* (Cambridge
University Press, 1993), Maynard Mack, *King Lear in Our Time* (London: Methuen,
1966), Jonathan Dollimore, '*King Lear*: A Materialist Reading' in *Radical Tragedy*
(Hemel Hempstead: The Harvester Press, 1984), 195–201, and Kiernan Ryan, '*King
Lear*: 'men / Are as the time is' in *Shakespeare: Harvester New Readings* (Hemel
Hempstead: Harvester Wheatsheaf, 1989), 66–73 and *passim*; and Philippa Kelly,
The King and I (London: Continuum, 2011) and *King Lear: The Bell Shakespeare*
(Sydney: Halstead Press, 2002).

5. Jan Kott, *Shakespeare Our Contemporary* (London, Methuen, 1965), 100–33.
6. See R. A. Foakes, *Hamlet versus Lear*, 1993). Though Foakes agrees that World
War Two ushered 'a new awareness of the atrocities of war' and led to the critical
supremacy of *Lear* in the Cold War of the 1950s and '60s, his argument was first
published in the 1980s, before the tide had turned decisively back towards *Hamlet*.

of Cordelia, is problematical. This is partly because of textual differences between the Quarto and Folio versions of the play which are too technical to broach in detail here,[7] but more importantly because of differing perspectives held by characters. Briefly, it is in the interests of the new rulers Cornwall, Goneril and Regan to claim that the conflict is an international invasion by the King of France and his wife Cordelia, and for patriotic reasons a French army must be repelled by English forces. This view is self-interestedly advanced by Goneril and Regan, and confirmed by Cornwall's 'the army of France is landed' (3.7.2–3), and also accepted by Albany in the Quarto but not in the Folio, 'France invades our lands' (5.1.25). Goneril is adamant that it is not a civil war: 'domestic and particular broils / Are not the question here' (5.1.30–1). She and Regan had joined forces to pre-empt the possibility of civil war, by disbanding Lear's hundred-strong retinue as a potential standing army in an insurrection, using the excuse of their domestic unruliness. On the other hand, Cordelia, Kent and their forces regard the conflict as a justified civil uprising to reinstate 'the old kind King' (3.1.28) by rallying to overthrow a tyrannical regime. Cordelia is told the 'news' that 'the British powers are marching hitherward', and she asserts that they have been incited to arms to restore her 'aged father's right' (4.4.21–9). She sees it, then, as a civil war to reinstate Lear as King. It is widely accepted that the play was written as a veiled warning to King James I of Great Britain, VI of Scotland, known for his pacifist tendencies and in the process of devising the Act of Union, not to create disunity by dividing the kingdom. In this context it was seen as imperative not to risk dividing the fragile unity of the United Kingdom, nor to allow a consolidation of Scotland's traditional alliance with France, England's historical adversary, or allow Catholic Ireland to become a pathway for invaders.[8] Both foreign invasion and civil war were Jacobean scenarios if the British

7. Varying arguments have been mounted on the textual problem: see Foakes's Arden 'Appendix 1' with references to others, esp. 140–3 and 396–7 and 401–2. See also Gary Taylor, 'Monopolies, Show Trials, Disaster, and Invasion: *King Lear* and Censorship' in Gary Taylor and Michael Warren (eds), *The Division of the Kingdoms: Shakespeare's Two Versions of 'King Lear'* (Oxford: Clarendon Press, 1983) 80–81, arguing against topical Jacobean sensitivity to the possibility of France invading England. Taylor had already addressed the question in 'The War in *King Lear*', *Shakespeare Survey* 33 (1980), 27–34. The most thorough discussion is by Richard Knowles in 'Revision Awry in Folio *Lear* 3.1', *Shakespeare Quarterly*, 46 (1995), 32–46.
8. For summaries of the different views on the historical topicality of *King Lear* see James Shapiro, *1606: Shakespeare and the Year of Lear* (London: Faber and Faber, 2015), 44–5 and elsewhere. See also Annabel Patterson, *Shakespeare and the Popular Voice*, 106–7.

Union was threatened, so the play seems to cover both bases at the risk of creating its own internal dramatic tensions and textual discrepancies.

Kent and Cordelia's understanding, however appealing and obviously authorially endorsed, itself raises other problems, even beyond the axiomatic legal fact that Lear has abdicated and has no 'right' to rule. Secondly, at the end of the play, the deaths of the restored King and also his only surviving blood-relative Cordelia leave radically uncertain the question of succession.[9] The legitimate Albany immediately abdicates, arguably repeating Lear's disastrous misjudgement. Kent and Edgar as the senior courtiers are offered a 'power-sharing' role, which also seems to mirror the doomed arrangement between Goneril and Regan and their husbands. Kent refuses and instead departs on a 'journey' to meet his 'master', most likely to suicide. Finally Edgar is left, and although Lear's godson, he has no clear dynastic claim to the bloodline of the royal family, and he does not respond to the offer.[10] Like many critics, Russell Peck admits Edgar's accession is 'disputable' but takes it 'at face value',[11] though this is somewhat undermined by recognition of Edgar's many flaws and inadequacies that would seem to disqualify him as a king with moral authority – his gullibility that makes him easy prey for Edmund, 'foolish honesty' (1.2.188), naïveté, questionable deception of his father in not disclosing his identity and trickery at the non-existent cliff-edge, his barely necessary incoherent, mad persona as 'Poor Tom', and more. The last four lines of the play do not address the question of succession at all, and most mysteriously they are differently attributed, to Albany in the Quarto and Edgar in the Folio.

This leaves open but unspoken the suggestion that the (absent) King of France now rules, as the only heir through marriage. This implies a conclusion which was no doubt unpalatable to Elizabethan English audiences, that French royalty has a claim through marriage to rule England.[12] In a play which sceptically interrogates notions of authority

---

9. I have elsewhere discussed the problems of succession and attitudes to authority in general in *King Lear*: R. S. White, '*King Lear* and Philosophical Anarchism', *English*, xxxvii (1988), 181–200.

10. Few critics indicate that there is even a question to be discussed about Edgar's claim, for example most recently Sandra Logan, 'Cordelia, Foreign Queenship, and the Commonweal' in *The Palgrave Handbook of Shakespeare's Queens*, ed. Kavita Mudan Finn and Valerie Schutte (London: Palgrave Macmillan, 2018), 69–86, 80.

11. Russell Peck, 'Edgar's Pilgrimage: High Comedy in *King Lear*', *Studies in English Literature 1500–1900*, 7 (1967), 219–37, 220 fn.

12. Although neither makes this particular point, for summaries of the different views on the historical topicality of *King Lear* see James Shapiro, *1606*, 44–5; and Patterson, *Shakespeare and the Popular Voice*, 106–7.

throughout, the apparently deliberately unresolved issue of who holds authority in Britain at the end of the play is significant, especially since Shakespeare could easily have avoided problems by simply following all his sources. These left Lear and Cordelia alive, thus conveniently moving the King of France out of the equation, although in the sources some years later Lear dies, Cordelia is usurped and commits suicide. In recognition of the problems, Nahum Tate's rewriting (1681) also left out the King of France altogether by marrying Cordelia and Edgar in a reassuringly patriotic and happy ending. His version was staged in preference to Shakespeare's through to the early nineteenth century, which may also account for the modern critical preference to anoint Edgar as King. Regardless of the unresolved ambiguities, what is certain is that war, whether civil or international or both, is in the foreground of *King Lear*, and that by the end there are just as many problems left as in the beginning.

Torture

In modern times torture used in war is banned under international law, and (almost, with the conspicuous exception of US Vice-president Cheney) universally condemned as barbaric and inhumane, at least in non-authoritarian states. More generally than in the context of war alone, the right not to be tortured, whether inflicted as punishment or provocation, is absolute and cannot be abrogated under any circumstances. The Universal Declaration of Human Rights states that 'No one shall be subjected to torture or to cruel, inhuman or degrading treatment or punishment' (Article 5). It is regarded as employing overt terror to replace justice under the rule of law. However, like other atrocities, there are many exceptions, even among self-professed 'humane' countries professing to obey the rule of war, for example those perpetrated at Abu Ghraib prison in Iraq and others revealed by whistle-blowers. In earlier times, with a black irony, 'justice' itself could include torture (*peine dure et forte*) as the test of guilt, as in cases of witchcraft or as punishment for treason and recusancy. But even in such cases torture was generally 'greatly abhorred' in Elizabethan and Jacobean England. In 1628, judges in a case ruled that torture on the rack was not available, for 'no such punishment is known or allowed by our law'.[13] Not completely banned, its use was limited to approval through the monarch's personal warrant,

13. Ernest G. Black, 'Torture Under English Law', *University of Pennsylvania Law Review*, 75 (1927), 344–8, 344.

in other words it existed as an instrument of state wielded by the ruling authority and not within common law, mainly applicable in political cases of treason. When Cornwall orders Kent to be placed in the stocks it is as punishment for speaking treason to authority, prompting the outraged demand 'Who stocked my man?' by Lear, who still regards himself as having regal powers. In practice, torture has been (and still is) used more commonly as a means of extracting information from prisoners of war than being regarded as a punishment for a crime.

Only unflinching dramatists would be willing to portray such spectacles on stage. Marlowe had done so in portraying the torture of Edward II: 'LIGHTBORN So, lay the table down, and stamp on it, / But not too hard, lest that you bruise his body' (5.5.114–15).[14] In Kyd's *The Spanish Tragedy* the King threatens to torture Hieronimo, who in response tears out his tongue so that he cannot reveal information.[15] *The Taming of the Shrew* portrays sustained physical and mental torture, though not in a military context, but the main Shakespearean example occurs in *King Lear*, in what Samuel Johnson declared 'an act too horrid to be endured in dramatic exhibition'.[16] He supplies a moral framework that dramatically demonstrates the cruel inhumanity by following the event with strongly contrasting vignettes of exemplary human kindness, and with a later, revealing dialogue between Albany and his wife.

The blinding of Gloucester functions as a reflection of the barbarity of war itself that instigates such atrocities, since he is interrogated as a prisoner of war withholding vital information about Lear's whereabouts and plans. In a formal sense, torture here is claimed by the perpetrators as an instrument of state against treason (that is, according to the prevailing law in Early Modern England), since Cornwall, Regan and Goneril are monarchs mandating torture to extract information in time of war from a 'filthy traitor'. Cornwall emphasises his own 'legitimate' authority:

> Go seek the traitor Gloucester;
> Pinion him like a thief, bring him before us.
> [*Servants leave*]
> Though well we may not pass upon his life

14. Christopher Marlowe, *The Complete Plays*, ed. J. B. Steane (London: Penguin Classics, 1969).
15. For lengthier treatment of torture on the Elizabethan stage, see Timothy Adrian Turner, *Torture and the Drama of Emergency: Kyd, Marlowe, Shakespeare*, PhD Dissertation, The University of Texas at Austin, 2010; partially republished as articles.
16. *Samuel Johnson on Shakespeare*, ed. W. K. Wimsatt, (New York, 1960), 97.

Without the form of justice, yet our power
Shall do a courtesy to our wrath, which men
May blame but not control. Who's there? the traitor?

(3.7.23–7)

Similar premonitions of ancient and modern dictators, avoiding account-
ability by proclaiming not that they are *above* the law but that they *are*
the law, are voiced in Goneril's retort when Albany threatens to pros-
ecute Edmund for treason: '. . . the law is mine, not thine. / Who can
arraign me for it?' (5.3.156–7). In his madness Lear himself, even when
he is no longer the King, voices an absolutist belief that rulers are above
the law: 'No, they cannot touch me for coining. I am the king himself' (4.6.83). But in his state of disarmed powerlessness and new-found
moral lucidity, he comes to recognise caustically the difference between
the person and the office of a ruler: 'There thou might'st behold the great
image of authority: a dog's obeyed in office' (4.6.155).

Cornwall and Regan bind Gloucester and question him specifically
on his part in the military situation which they claim to be a war waged
from France, led by Cordelia with forces loyal to Lear:

CORNWALL
Come, sir, what letters had you late from France?
REGAN
Be simple answered for we know the truth.
CORNWALL
And what confederacy have you with the traitors,
Late footed in the kingdom?
REGAN
                              To whose hands
You have sent the lunatic King? Speak.
GLOUCESTER
I have a letter guessingly set down,
Which came from one that's of a neutral heart,
And not from one opposed.
CORNWALL
                    Cunning.
REGAN
                              And false.
CORNWALL
Where hast thou sent the king?
GLOUCESTER
To Dover.
REGAN
Wherefore to Dover? Wast thou not charged at peril –

CORNWALL
Wherefore to Dover? Let him first answer that.
GLOUCESTER
I am tied to the stake, and I must stand the course.

(3.7.42–53)

Dover is the seaport where the loyalist forces from France are expected.

The torture enacted on stage is shockingly graphic. Cornwall, encouraged by Regan, stamps on one of Gloucester's eyes and then gouges out the other. Cornwall bases his justification, such as it is, on no more than a ghoulish metaphor generated from a suspicion that Gloucester is a spy for the former king, and that half-blinded he should not be allowed to 'see more' (spy) with his other eye. The morally guiding signal to the audience comes with the courageous intervention of Cornwall's nameless Servant:

1 SERVANT
                    Hold your hand, my lord.
I have served you ever since I was a child,
But better service have I never done you
Than now to bid you hold.
REGAN
                    How now, you dog?
1 SERVANT
If you did wear a beard upon your chin,
I'd shake it on this quarrel. What do you mean?
CORNWALL
My villein!
[*They*] *draw and fight*
1 SERVANT
Nay then, come on, and take the chance of anger.
[*He wounds Cornwall.*]
REGAN [*To Another Servant*]
Give me thy sword. A peasant stand up thus?
[*She takes a sword, and runs at him behind. Kills him.*]
1 SERVANT
O, I am slain. My lord, you have one eye left
To see some mischief on him. O!
[*He dies.*]
CORNWALL
Lest it see more, prevent it. Out, vile jelly.
Where is thy lustre now?

(3.7.66–83)

The Servant does not verbalise an intent to kill his own master, but intervenes to prevent the torture. If it had happened on the battlefield, he would be court-martialled for mutiny, but it would also signify the kind of ethical conundrum often faced by soldiers when command hierarchy clashes with conscience on witnessing or being implicated in a war crime by a superior officer. His own violence in this case is committed in a spirit of unpremeditated, righteous spontaneity, defending Gloucester as victim of a war crime. His phrase 'The chance of anger' recalls Kent's 'anger hath a privilege' (2.2.72). The Elizabethan theorist of emotions, Thomas Wright, affirmed that irascible passions need not always be extinguished (as the Stoics insisted), but could be 'moved & stirred up for the service of vertue', as operates here.[17] The Servant's corpse is unceremoniously thrown on a dunghill, but he has mortally wounded Cornwall. The horrifying scene, cannot be staged as anything but irredeemably abhorrent to audiences. The Servant's role in *King Lear* might be seen first as that of an agent of poetic justice visited upon Cornwall, and also as a moral guide to the audience's judgement of the incident, leaving no doubt in an audience's mind of the playwright's stance.

As if to leave no ambiguity, the longer *Quarto* version adds an aftermath functioning in the fashion of a morality play. The scene ends with two other servants offering a choric judgement on what the audience has just witnessed, significantly anticipating Albany's word to describe the perpetrators as 'monsters':

> *Exeunt [CORNWALL and REGAN]*
> 2 SERVANT
> I'll never care what wickedness I do
> If this man come to good.
> 3 SERVANT
>   If she live long
> And in the end meet the old course of death,
> Women will all turn monsters.
>   . . .
> 3 SERVANT
> Go thou: I'll fetch some flax and whites of eggs
> To apply to his bleeding face. Now heaven help him!
>
>   (3.7.98–106)

Their gesture is one of several moments when acts of cruelty give way to compassion, in a play offering 'kindness' and 'pity' as natural, human and humane qualities. These signs, as Toria Johnson demonstrates, however ineffectual they are in the 'unstable and unreliable' wider world

---

17. Thomas Wright, *The Passions of the Mind in General* (London, 1604).

of *King Lear* act as moral touchstones.[18] Why the exchange does not appear in the Folio is open to speculation. If (as seems likely) the Folio is a streamlined revision for a stage performance, the dramatist may have thought the scene speaks for itself to a shocked audience to take the moral. But alternatively (and somewhat in conflict) the omission could reinforce the feeling that the Folio is altogether bleaker and more pessimistic than the Quarto, and that the forces of evil are in ascendancy over humane values. (If the Quarto is the revised text, the same reasoning can be reversed, that the audience's point of view requires a staged statement, or that the playwright is consciously writing adding more hopeful material.)

Such moments offer in cameo statements of an altruistic ethic that might be a model constituting instinctual behaviour, summed up by a philosopher of nonviolence Judith Butler as the need 'to preserve the life of the other',[19] and in Renaissance terminology termed sympathy and compassion.[20] Bruce Smith has noted that 'Beginning in the early 1640s and continuing throughout the years of the Commonwealth (1649–1660) the number of religious and political books with the word 'compassion' and 'compassionate' in their titles increased exponentially'.[21] Unlike the heartless courtiers, the servants in *Lear* express and practise a range of responses which are communitarian, humane, and medically healing, leaving it to 'heaven' to judge the deserts of evil. Another exemplar in the next scene is the unnamed 'Old Man' who has been tenant for Gloucester and his father for eighty years, and who now leads his blind master to Edgar impersonating 'poor Tom', the 'bedlam' beggar who is even lower on the social scale. The shadowy presence in the play of a whole underclass of 'houseless' beggars, was memorably visualised in the extraordinary, wordless opening to Kozintsev's social realism movie (1970). The old man insists on offering 'comforts' to Gloucester even though it endangers his life, and he also promises clothing for the near-naked

18. Toria Johnson, '"To feel what wretches feel": Reformation and the Re-naming of English Compassion' in Kristine Steenberg and Katherine Ibbett (eds.), *Compassion in Early Modern Literature and Culture* (Cambridge University Press, 2021).
19. Judith Butler, *The Force of Nonviolence*, ch. 2 heading.
20. Amongst the growing number of studies associated with the Australian Research Council Centre of Excellence for the History of Emotions (2011–18), see especially essays in Steenberg and Ibbett (eds.), *Compassion in Early Modern Literature and Culture*, and Richard Meek and Erin Sullivan (eds), *The Renaissance of Emotion: Understanding Affect in Shakespeare and his Contemporaries* (Manchester University Press, 2015); and Richard Meek, *Sympathy in Early Modern Literature and Culture 1580–1640* (Cambridge University Press, 2023).
21. Bruce Smith, 'The Ethics of Compassion' in Steenberg and Ibbett (eds.), *Compassion in Early Modern Literature and Culture*, 25–43.

'beggar-man': 'I'll bring him the best 'parrel that I have, / Come on't what will' (4.1.14–53). Such acts of kindness are in stark contrast to the conduct of the prevailing 'ruling class', while between the two lies a group of those discarded from authority and marked by empathy and compassion – Lear in his newly enlightened consciousness, Gloucester, Edgar, Kent and Cordelia, as well as the politically impotent but 'moral' Albany. The later scene in prison, in which Lear is reconciled with Cordelia weeping tactile 'wet' tears (4.7.71), is where forgiveness, the alternative to cruelty reaches its apotheosis, to be examined in the final chapter.

Must humanity perforce prey on itself?

The torture of Gloucester most starkly exemplifies an underlying debate traced by Shakespeare through *King Lear*, the inhumanity unleashed in war. The play raises questions as to whether evil consequences of war can be considered as products of any essentialist and innately predatory 'human nature'. The Duke of Albany raises the fundamental concern about the self-destructiveness of human violence:

> If that the heavens do not their visible spirits
> Send quickly down to tame these vile offences,
> It will come:
> Humanity must perforce prey on itself,
> Like monsters of the deep.
>
> (4.2.47–50)

His wife admonishes him, suggesting that his stance is cowardly, and warning that he should turn his attention to the immediate military situation in Britain, which she asserts is under threat of imminent French invasion:

> GONERIL
>   Milk-livered man,
> That bear'st a cheek for blows, a head for wrongs,
>   . . .   Where's thy drum?
> France spreads his banners in our noiseless land;
> With plumed helm thy state begins to threat,
> Whilst thou, a moral fool, sits still and cries,
> 'Alack, why does he so?'.
>
> (4.2.51–8)

Speaking at a time when events call for urgent military preparation and retaliation, she derides her 'milk-liver'd' husband as the image of a pacifist. The phrase 'That bear'st a cheek for blows' blasphemously ridicules Christ's 'turn the other cheek', while the sarcastic 'a head for wrongs' and 'a moral fool' positions him as one standing up for justice. Albany responds by calling her a 'devil' and 'fiend'. But his ringing statement, can be turned into an anguished question, '*Must* humanity perforce prey on itself, / Like monsters of the deep'? Lear himself echoes this, in a way that establishes it as central to the play's vision: 'Is there any cause in nature that makes these hard hearts?' (3.6.74). Although uttering this in complaint, he himself in his rage vows dreadful revenges on his 'thankless' daughters (1.4.816).

The answer offered by the play is a conditional 'no', that cruelty is not a norm of human dealings, but an aberration to which authority figures are especially prone. One such recognition of this must be the power of community and gestures of kindness in appalling times, represented by Gloucester's Servants and the Old Man. To these mouthpieces for different shades of benevolence can be added the poignant presence of beggarly outcasts and helpless fringe-dwellers, who exist as social victims of the courtly power struggles. Lear himself, exposed to the stormy elements on the heath which is their daily habitation, comes to a position of empathy for their 'houseless poverty', even though his perception is useless, as Toria Johnson points out: 'if this is the moment in which Lear recognises the importance of pity, of acting in the interest of men, then it comes too late to be of any use'.[22] This may be true to the dramatic moment, yet the bleak realisation may be overly pessimistic, since another interpretation is possible. Lear's tardy realisation can activate the same benevolent ethic in audiences facing human casualties of war, poverty, and injustice:

Poor naked wretches, whereso'er you are,
That bide the pelting of this pitiless storm,
How shall your houseless heads and unfed sides,
Your looped and windowed raggedness, defend you
From seasons such as these? O, I have ta'en
Too little care of this. Take physic, pomp,
Expose thyself to feel what wretches feel,
That thou mayst shake the superflux to them,
And show the heavens more just.

(3.4.27–36)

The final line seems like a non-sequitur, as an anomalous Christian reference in a pagan setting in which human agency rather than divine

22. Toria Johnson, '"To feel what wretches feel"', 227–8.

intervention has relentlessly driven the action.[23] It is secular, regal 'pomp' on earth which is in need of health-giving 'physic', and which can effect equitable redistribution of 'the superflux' from wealthy rulers, to redress the unjust plight of the homeless and hungry – 'houseless heads and unfed sides'. The conclusion which Lear is groping for seems clear enough, that things can and should be 'shown' or replicated on earth as they are decreed in the moral law of some concept of heaven. Humanity need not 'perforce prey upon itself', since the predatory and unjust actions are the product of choices made by incorrigible individuals whose actions cannot be controlled.

King Lear raises fundamental issues about war. It probes causes of armed conflict, such as victors in war drawing arbitrary borders like Lear's rewriting of the map in his 'division of the kingdom'. (Consider how many wars have been caused, complicated, or inflamed by imperial partitioning over centuries of the India subcontinent, Africa, and Europe.) Revenge and counter-revenge are generated in waves during the progress of war. The torture of Gloucester in particular shows that war creates the worst in human behaviour. All these lead to more fundamental questions still, raised by Albany's shocked exclamation. Is violence 'natural', as William Golding's post-war novel *Lord of the Flies* (1954) seems to intimate? Among the sciences, anthropologists from Darwin and Kropotkin to Margaret Mead, and psychologists like Jung and Freud, have pondered the problem. To end this chapter on a hopeful note, here is another answer from a group of scientists that offers a decisive answer for our own times. An important but now neglected result of World War Two was a document initiated in 1986 and adopted by UNESCO in 1989, known as the Seville Statement. A group of international scientists from different fields of study issued a 'Statement on Violence' addressing the prevailing 'biological pessimism'. It begins:

> Believing that it is our responsibility to address from our particular disciplines the most dangerous and destructive activities of our species, violence and war; recognising that science is a human cultural product which cannot be definitive or all encompassing . . . we, the undersigned scholars from around the world and from relevant sciences, have met and arrived at the following Statement on Violence. In it we challenge a number of alleged biological findings that have been used, even by some in our disciplines, to justify violence and war. Because the alleged findings

23. J. C. Maxwell's pithy formulation was that '*King Lear* is a Christian play about a pagan world', in 'The Technique of Invocation in King Lear', *Modern Language Review*, 45 (1950), 142. See also William Elton, *King Lear and the Gods* (San Marino: Huntington Library, 1966).

have contributed to an atmosphere of pessimism in our time, we submit that the open, considered rejection of these mis-statements can contribute significantly to the International Year of Peace.

Misuse of scientific theories and data to justify violence and war is not new but has been made since the advent of modern science. For example, the theory of evolution has been used to justify not only war, but also genocide, colonialism, and suppression of the weak.[24]

Five Propositions are listed, each opening with the words 'IT IS SCIENTIFICALLY INCORRECT', namely: (1) 'to say that we have inherited a tendency to make war from our animal ancestors . . . Warfare is a peculiarly human phenomenon and does not occur in other animals'; (2) to say that war or any other violent behaviour is genetically programmed in our human nature'; (3) 'to say that in the course of human evolution there has been selection for aggressive behaviour more than for other kinds of behaviour . . . "Dominance" involves social bondings and affiliations; it is not simply a matter of possession and use of superior physical power . . .'; (4) 'to say that humans have a "violent brain" . . . There is nothing in our neurophysiology that compels us to react violently'; and (5) 'to say that war is caused by "instinct" or any single motivation . . . The technology of modern war has exaggerated traits associated with violence both in the training of actual combatants, and in the preparation of support for war in the general population. As a result of this exaggeration, such traits are often mistaken to be the causes rather than consequences of the process'. In a brief Conclusion drawing on developments in social sciences, the signatories resoundingly state that,

> Just as 'wars begin in the minds of men' so peace also begins in our minds. The same species who invented war is capable of inventing peace. The responsibility lies with each of us.

Unfortunately, the wise words were quickly forgotten, but they can be reignited by *King Lear*. We can now only imagine the *frisson* which must have struck audiences at Wolfit's performances in London, when sirens began to wail outside and blasts deafened the lines, 'Poor naked wretches, whereso'er you are, / That bide the pelting of this pitiless storm', while 'houseless beggars' huddled in makeshift shelters and train tunnels. In such a wartime extremity the play's questions must have posed something urgently existential: 'Is this the promised end? / Or image of that horror?' (5.3.261–2).

---

24. The text of the Statement can be found on the UNESCO website.

Part II

Love and War

Chapter 6

Love in Times of War

War in Shakespeare's works is usually treated in the light of military manuals as a technical subject which is 'men's work', and questions are rarely raised concerning what happens to women and to love in times of war. In discussions of the comedies the existence of war is either ignored altogether or diminished to the level of 'background noise',[1] while in History plays the equation is reversed, in that war is kept firmly in the foreground and love provides moments of insignificant contrast. In tragedies the loss of love is generally regarded as part of the individual male protagonist's fate, otherwise unrelated to war as milieu or his profession as soldier. However, with the renewed critical interest in emotions, an interpenetrating nexus between war and love emerges, as though the one becomes internalised in the other. The modern tendency has been to 'hierarchise' the structure of earlier drama, distinguishing between major plot and sub-plots, whereas Elizabethan audiences were clearly expected to keep various dramatic strands in operation in polymathic fashion, as in a madrigal where all parts contribute to the whole.

   In this chapter we look first at some examples from each genre, showing how a woman's position is jeopardised in different ways by war, to be followed in the next by a more detailed reading of *All's Well that Ends Well*. In this 'problematic' romantic comedy, the potentially disturbing setting of military conflict is integral to the action. Next, *Othello* and *Antony and Cleopatra* can be seen as plays which also present experiences of women caught in the crossfire of male-dominated issues of war. This experience of women caught up in war begins at the very start of Shakespeare's writing career. In *Titus Andronicus* the first of many victims of revenge and counter-revenges is the completely innocent

---

1. Among exceptions which analyse war in the comedies are the chapters by Helen Wilcox and Ruth Morse (cited below) in eds. Ros King and Paul J. C. M. Franssen, *Shakespeare and War* (Basingstoke: Palgrave Macmillan, 2008).

Lavinia, raped, mutilated and silenced. In even *The Comedy of Errors*, however farcical its tone, the emotionally harmful effects of the trade war between Syracuse and Ephesus disrupt the certainties of married life and women's place more generally. It persists through to one of the last plays, *Cymbeline*, in which the war between Britain and Rome looms as a complication for the love plot between Imogen and Posthumus.[2]

An apparently effervescent comedy with indeterminate closure, *Love's Labour's Lost* is full of military imagery. The men describe themselves as 'affection's men-at-arms' (4.3.286) in their amatory pursuit of the women:

KING
Saint Cupid, then! And, soldiers, to the field!
BEROWNE
Advance your standards, and upon them, lords!
Pell-mell, down with them! But be first advised
In conflict that you get the sun of them.

(4.3.340–3)

As Carolyn E. Brown notes, the women in the play are warned of the skirmish by Boyet as their 'scout' (another military term):

BOYET   Prepare, madam, prepare.
Arm, wenches, arm. Encounters mounted are
Against your peace. Love doth approach, disguised,
Armèd in arguments. You'll be surprised.
Muster your wits, stand in your own defence,
Or hide your heads like cowards, and fly hence.

(5.2.86–92)

The military imagery persists, in which the weapons are 'wits' and 'arguments' rather than physical implements: 'the pervasive martial connotations throughout the play establish a military ambiance . . .'.[3] Brown also suggests that the Princess's wounding of the deer (4.2.) foreshadows her 'military action' in a form of 'siege', though this seems less convincing in the light of her humanist objections to hunting. All this might be explained as a stock trope of Petrarchan love conventions, but more surprisingly Shakespeare also provides many explicit and puzzling ref-

2. See Pivetti and Garrison's *Shakespeare at Peace*, 132–6.
3. Carolyn E. Brown, 'The Princess's Political Mission in *Love's Labour's Lost*: The Embassy to get Aquitaine and "All that is" Navarre's', in *The Palgrave Handbook of Shakespeare's Queens*, ed. Kavita Mudan Finn and Valerie Schutte (London: Palgrave Macmillan, 2018), 313–29, 319.

erences to the French religious wars, with historically referenced names like Navarre, Longueville and Moth associated with the event so culturally traumatic in England and among Protestant nations, the persecution of Huguenots culminating in the Massacre of St Bartholomew's Day in 1572.[4] More recently Aurélie Griffin and Carolyn Brown have uncovered other intriguing allusions to the Massacre in *Love's Labour's Lost*. These allusions seem in such a lighthearted comedy to point to something deeper, suggesting that a matter of diplomatic negotiations in which the parties will 'arbitrate' (5.2.737) the right of France to repossess Aquitaine, could have led to the violence of war as an extension of political dispute. The serious debate is never fully addressed in the play, first because of the men's frivolous deflection of attention from it, and then the sobering news of the death of the Princess's father enforcing her rapid 'dispatch' under a 'cloud of sorrow' (5.2.742). At the very least, in this play love is shadowed by diplomatic uncertainties and potential looming international conflict, so that the two become conceptually intertwined, with crucial significance for the unexpected ending.

The complicated and unresolved issue of surrendering Aquitaine from Navarre to France depends upon payment of unpaid reparations as a result of past 'wars' (2.1.131). The Princess asserts that the payment has been made by France, but Navarre flatly refutes this, saying that only half has been paid. The issue is postponed until 'acquittances' can be produced as evidence, but the sudden death of King Charles reported at the end of the play leaves the dispute unresolved. The deferment of the expected marriages emerges as more meaningful in the light of the suspended political conflict. Showing the centrality to the play of this dispute between nations, Shakespeare devotes fifty lines to explicating the problems, couched in polite but frosty terms (2.1.127–77). But whenever Shakespeare provides lengthy and (to modern eyes) digressive information (as in the Archbishop's speech on Salic law in *Henry* V), it is always worth asking why. In this case, the whole point is lost if these lines are shortened in performance in an effort to maintain audience attention on the love-plot, making the play less intellectually substantial than it can be. To avert resumption of conflict requires at least diplomacy so the stakes are high. Aquitaine, situated between Spain and France, had been contested by different nations and principalities from Roman times to

---

4. See R. S. White, 'The Cultural Impact of the Massacre of St Bartholomew's Day' in *Early Modern Civil Discourses*, edited by Jennifer Richards (Palgrave, 2003), 183–99; Aurélie Griffin, 'The Princess of France: Difference and Diff(é)rance in *Love's Labour's Lost*' in *The Palgrave Handbook of Shakespeare's Queens*, 395–412; and Brown, 'The Princess's Political Mission', 324–6.

the sixteenth century. It alternated and reverted between them, including England and Navarre, a province in northern Spain later claimed by the independent Basque state. *Love's Labour's Lost* is so full of military terms that they colour the romantic affairs: words like armada, armipotent, battle-axe, corporal of [the] field, ensign, falchion, imperator, man-at-arms, mark, pell-mell, battle-axe, and others.[5] It is never explained why Don Armado, 'fashion's own knight' (1.1.176) and a traveller 'from tawny Spain', is in Navarre's court, but he seems to be the stock kind of soldier stereotyped by Character Writers as 'Braggart'. In the play-let 'The Nine Worthies' he plays Hector, 'The worthy knight of Troy' (5.2.869), who is to reappear in *Troilus and Cressida*.

One would be hard-pressed to mount an argument that a likelihood of armed confrontation is ever a serious issue in *Love's Labour's Lost*, but the fact that the international disagreement is not formally resolved within the play is one of several, unstated reasons behind the unusual ending. It also subtly confirms the gender politics of the play, insofar as it is the women who are keen for a rational and peaceful settlement to the dispute, while the men generally show themselves to be evasive, oath-breaking, and emotionally changeable, thus needing their commitments to be tested personally in something like 'community service' before they can be trusted. Kenneth Branagh's film version of *Love's Labour's Lost* (2000) accentuates the disruptions wrought by war to lovers, by setting the play during the years leading up to and including World War Two, and his ending fast forwards to newsreel of post-war celebrations and marriage. This Shakespeare does not do – 'That's too long for a play' (5.2.866). For all we know (which is next to nothing) the 'lost' sequel *Love's Labour's Won* may have continued the amatory and political issues left in abeyance.[6]

Branagh set his movie *Much Ado About Nothing* (1993) at the end of the Anglo-French wars culminating at Waterloo, beginning with the stirring sight of glamorous, uniformed English soldiers returning triumphantly on horseback from war, much to the excitement of the young women. In *Much Ado* the actual war plays little direct part in the plot, but as a prevailing metaphor it points towards a new set of emotional wars about to unfold. In the context of *Much Ado* which is a romantic comedy with a happy ending ('the world must be peopled'), the reminder of war renders ambiguous some aspects of the love-plots. The two love

---

5. Edelman in *Shakespeare's Military Language*, 413, lists ten such terms in the play.
6. David McInnis in *Shakespeare and Lost Plays: Reimagining Drama in Early Modern England* (Cambridge University Press, 2021), 11–14, 78–80, is the most recent critic to summarise the few known facts about this intriguing work.

relationships depicted are, on close examination, neither ideal nor idealised. The glamorous returning soldier described sarcastically as 'the
exquisite Claudio . . . a proper squire', has covered himself with glory
on the battlefield, 'doing, in the figure of a lamb, the feats of a lion' (1.1
passim). For this he attracts not only love-interest from Hero, but also
unwittingly makes himself a target for revenge by Don John, because
Claudio has usurped the affections of his own half-brother, Don Pedro:
'That young start-up hath all the glory of my overthrow: if I can cross
him any way, I bless myself every way.' Indirectly, then, success in war
initiates a chain of consequences leading to a violent climax at the altar
in Claudio's rejection of Hero. The situation is saved only by evidence of
the plot unearthed by a kind of civilian equivalent to 'Dad's Army' under
the command of Dogberry, and by the resuscitation from feigned death
of Hero as a casualty. The actual liaison between Claudio and Hero
is disturbing for its lack of communication between man and woman.
In amatory affairs Claudio's image is the timid reversal of his warlike
conduct in war. Without even speaking to Hero he asks Don Pedro to
woo her on his behalf, in a mask which further emphasises the absence
of emotional contact or communication between the lovers. Claudio's
violent language at the broken wedding ceremony shows him as a prototype of Othello, preferring to believe in a false slander than trust a truth
based on love: 'Give not this rotten orange to your friend / She's but
the sign and semblance of her honour.' 'Honour', as both Hotspur and
Falstaff in *1 Henry IV* confirm, can hold different meanings in war and
in peace. In this instance military prowess is to the fore: 'Don Pedro hath
bestowed much honour on a young Florentine called Claudio' (1.1.9).
But when the issue of Hero's 'honour' in chastity is thrown into doubt,
the *machismo* returning soldiers are quick to believe the slander since it
relates directly to the reputation of their brother-in-arms Claudio and the
ranks close. The implication is that their attitudes are fashioned through
the soldier's crude stereotype of female untrustworthiness and fickleness,
and male trust among soldiers. These attitudes are to be instrumental in
the tragedy of jealousy, *Othello*.

Meanwhile, in the other love-plot between Beatrice and Benedick,
there is from the start 'a kind of merry war' (1.1.159). A harmonious
resolution is the result of first a trick played on them, and secondly an
armistice between the gender representatives who have entered a state
of hostile segregation, if not open warfare, over the issue of Hero's innocence. It comes to a head in Beatrice's command to 'Kill Claudio':

BEATRICE
You dare easier be friends with me than fight with mine enemy.

BENEDICK
Is Claudio thine enemy?
BEATRICE
Is a not approved in the height a villain, that hath slandered, scorned, dishonoured my kinswoman? O that I were a man! O God, that I were a man! I would eat his heart in the market-place.

(4.2.285–307 *passim*)

Beatrice's violent words echo her earlier, jocular but premonitory preoccupation with Benedick's conduct in war: 'I pray you, how many hath he killed and eaten in these wars? But how many hath he killed? for indeed I promised to eat all of his killing' (1.1.40–1). Delivered in jest at this stage, the phrase is a premonition of Beatrice's more chilling outburst later. The Messenger responds to her jests, saying that Benedick had 'done good service, lady, in these wars' and he is 'a good soldier too', to which she quibbles, 'And a good soldier to a lady' (1.1.52). Leonato diplomatically intervenes, speaking of 'a kind of merry war betwixt Signior Benedick and her: they never meet but there's a skirmish of wit between them' (1.1.59–60). The words in the play unmistakably link conflict in war with 'skirmishes' of love and their near-disastrous consequences. More generally in *Much Ado*, issues of conflict, slander, entrapment, and male domination carry over into love relationships, developing from the apparently insignificant context of soldiers returning victorious from war. In civilian life, war as a dominant metaphor is internalised in affairs of the heart.

Some support for this way of reading comedies comes unexpectedly from a literary scholar trained also as a Jungian philosopher. Carl Jung, a proclaimed public pacifist, was writing in a period of history when world wars were endemic and could not have failed to have effects on personal relationships. Susan Rowland in 'Shakespeare and the Jungian Symbol: A Case of War and Marriage' proposes to link Shakespeare and Jung through their shared concern with 'the importance of symbols to collective culture and the horror of war', arguing that 'Shakespeare and Jung intuited that the social breakdown caused by war is directly connected to a problem with the relationships between men and women':

Both Shakespeare and Jung sensed that a patriarchal inheritance had failed. Those collective ritual practices, such as marriage, meant to maintain collective psychic health, had become dangerously empty of numinous energy . . . It is in the unlikely guise of Shakespeare's comedies, such as *A Midsummer Night's Dream* and *Much Ado About Nothing*, that we are brought squarely face to face with the loss of marriage's symbolic value and the resulting consequences for a culture of war.[7]

We could just as easily reverse the equation and conclude that the 'culture of war' has been internalised in love relationships, with destructive consequences. Both plays are considered by Rowland as depicting 'a period of crisis in a male-oriented society' in which marriage becomes 'an empty transaction of power'. Rites of connection between each partner with the Other are lost and there is a disjunction between feminine and masculine values: 'In play after play, Shakespeare associates this crisis in the marriage symbol with war'. In *A Midsummer Night's Dream*, the play begins with Theseus' linking of war and marriage, and proceeds to challenge it as a sterile male obsession, through Hermia's disobedience and through the wild transformations in the forest. Although male supremacy in marriage is not fundamentally challenged, love must incorporate the female Other, and Rowlands concludes, 'The play wants to end at an imaginary place where there is no more war' (42). In *Much Ado* the clash between war and love is not so peacefully resolved, since there remain intimations, anticipated in the cruel and slanderous denunciation of Hero at the wedding ceremony, that the war between the sexes will go on: 'So, framed by war, social fragmentation is most horrifically enacted'. Both plays, like Jung's philosophy itself, are regarded as deeply concerned with healing the trauma of war. Rowlands looks also at other plays, in particular *Hamlet* and *Richard II*, and if her association between Jungian thought and repeated Shakespearean practice is taken seriously, it points to what I consider a temperamentally attuned sensibility in the dramatist, enacted in the plays as a continuing, anxious search for peaceful resolutions to conflict, a tendency explored by Garrison and Pivetti in *Shakespeare at Peace*.

Likewise, the explanatory backdrop of 'brawls' amounting to civil war in Verona in *Romeo and Juliet* is essential to the love story, and the military settings in *Othello*, *Antony and Cleopatra* (as we shall see) and *Troilus and Cressida* provide bellicose framings for the love plots. In the History plays, which are invariably focused on war, inset scenes demonstrate the different ways in which public conflict eats into private, marital relationships. Shakespeare's Dido-like 'war wives', some destined to become widows, represent in different ways the many innocents who are briefly but memorably spotlighted in their respective plays who, as

---

7. Susan Rowland, 'Shakespeare and the Jungian Symbol: A Case of War and Marriage', *Jung Journal: Culture & Psyche*, 5 (2011), 31–46, 34–5, 37.

Ruth Morse points out, suffer as 'social costs' of war.[8] Portia's poignant recrimination to Brutus as he contemplates igniting civil war could be echoed by the others: 'Dwell I but in the suburbs / Of your good pleasure?' (2.1.285–6).

To this group of women eventually left grieving we may add Shakespeare's 'last words' in the theatre, in his presentation of the three Theban queens who open *The Two Noble Kinsmen* in a scene now accepted as written by Shakespeare. Widowed in civil war by the tyrant Creon, they plead with Theseus, himself newly returned victorious from the war against the Amazons and sporting his own bride-to-be Hippolyta, to make war against Creon and recover the bodies of their husbands to give them burial rites. Significantly, the queens appeal to the feminine empathy of Hippolyta and her sister Emilia to intercede with Theseus, lamenting the graphically described bodies of their husbands on the battlefield: 'Tell him, if he i'th'blood-sized field lay swollen, / Showing the sun his teeth, grinning at the moon, / What you would do' (1.1.99–101). The play draws a contrast between Athens, in which a war has ended with a conciliatory marriage between the victor and vanquished, and fratricidal Thebes which has generated grief-stricken widows, and the glimpse of war's destructiveness is presented from the female point of view. Hippolyta and Emilia later perform the same function by persuading Theseus not to execute the Theban prisoners of war, Palamon and Arcite.

It is a commonplace that war separates families, most poignantly young wives from their husbands, first by military service and then for some by death. Such fates are movingly expressed by Vera Brittan in her autobiographical *Testament of Youth*. In these and other ways, women are indirect, disproportional casualties of war, bearing its human cost. They could be forgiven for sharing the opinion of Anna Plavovna in *War and Peace*: 'I can't make out why he wants to go to the war . . . I simply do not understand why men cannot get on without war. Why is it we women want nothing of the kind. We don't care for it'.[9]

8. Ruth Morse discusses the semantics of terms such as 'civilian' and 'casualty' in her fine essay, 'Some Social Costs of War', in *Shakespeare and War*, ed. Ros King and Paul J. C. M. Franssen, 56–68, 60–1.

9. Leo Tolstoy, *War and Peace*, transl. Rosemary Edmonds (Harmondsworth: Penguin Classics, 1957), 28.

Lady Percy and Lady Mortimer

In *Henry IV Part 1* Shakespeare presents in microcosmic scenes two war wives trying to prevent their husbands from going to war, one successfully, thus saving his life, the other unsuccessfully and to be finally widowed. In arguing for their importance, Kelsey Ridge points out that 'There has been a long history of ignoring, excising, and trivializing Lady Mortimer and Lady Percy. The scenes in which these women appear are usually shortened or deleted entirely.' Even some feminist critics, Ridge argues, have contributed inadvertently to their neglect and marginalisation.[10] However, 'a production can choose to make the women stronger forces'.[11] The account offered here differs slightly from that of Ridge who focuses on the effect the women have on their husbands and on their insight into their husbands' condition. Most of Ridge's references are on masculinity and gender roles rather than war itself. Speaking of Shakespeare's History plays, she writes that 'These plays do not, as a whole, produce an aggregate response either in favor of or opposed to war, nor will this text. Indeed, in the world of these plays, pacifism is an almost untenable position'.[12] However, her explanation indicates that she means this conclusion pertains to the characters within their plays, and who with rare exceptions have no choice but to accept the prevalence of war – pacifism to them is not an option. However, I argue that this is not necessarily true for plays as a whole, since directors, actors, readers and critics may give a variety of interpretive choices to their audiences and readers by selective emphases.

Lady Percy recognises the symptoms that Hotspur's mentality bears striking resemblance to the condition now recognised as post traumatic disorder caused by battle fatigue:[13]

> Kate's disenchantment with the martial ethos seems based not on inherent pacifism but on her husband's changed behaviour since his return from the last war and an augmented fear that he will not survive the next one . . . Concern about that trauma explains readily why she has come to question her husband's continued combat participation.[14]

10. Especially singled out are Phyllis Rackin, 'Anti-Historians: Women's Roles in Shakespeare's Histories', *Theatre Journal*, 37 (1985), 329–344, and Jean E. Howard and Phyllis Rackin, *Engendering a Nation* (London: Routledge, 1997); Ridge, *Shakespeare's Military Spouses*, 60.
11. Ridge, *Shakespeare's Military Spouses*, 60; 58–68 *passim*.
12. Ridge, *Shakespeare's Military Spouses*, 20.
13. Ridge, *Shakespeare's Military Spouses*, 70 ff.
14. Ridge, *Shakespeare's Military Spouses*, 72.

I present Lady Percy and Lady Mortimer as both expressing pacifist perspectives, and their scenes more generally as implicitly commenting on war itself, as the play's counterpoint to the masculine pursuit of glory in battle. As Dorothy Kehler in *Shakespeare's Widows* puts it, 'the war widows in the History plays fight calamity with words, not actions and that from this place they establish a pacifist ethos countering that of the play's dominant warrior ideology'.[15] In these plays, words are the only resources available to the women, while the men fight.

Sir Henry Percy (Harry Hotspur), described derisively as 'Mars in swaddling clothes' (*1 Henry IV*, 3.2.112) and 'gunpowder Percy' (*1 Henry IV*, 5.4.121), personifies single-minded commitment to war. He manages the moment of separation from his wife with characteristically abrupt bluntness: 'How now, Kate! I must leave you within these two hours' (2.4.36). Lady Percy, having seen the moment coming, is more fully conscious than he is of the divided claims war has made on the emotional lives of both. Her harrowed description, longer than it needs to be for its narrative function, powerfully evokes the heavy toll taken on married life by war even before death itself strikes, and her recrimination is a circumstantial amplification of Portia's complaint:

LADY PERCY
O my good lord, why are you thus alone?
For what offence have I this fortnight been
A banished woman from my Harry's bed?
Tell me, sweet lord, what is't that takes from thee
Thy stomach, pleasure and thy golden sleep?
Why dost thou bend thine eyes upon the earth,
And start so often when thou sit'st alone?
Why hast thou lost the fresh blood in thy cheeks,
And given my treasures and my rights of thee
To thick-eyed musing and curst melancholy?
In thy faint slumbers I by thee have watched,
And heard thee murmur tales of iron wars,
Speak terms of manège to thy bounding steed,
Cry 'Courage! To the field!' And thou hast talked
Of sallies and retires, of trenches, tents,
Of palisadoes, frontiers, parapets,
Of basilisks, of cannon, culverin,
Of prisoners ransomed, and of soldiers slain,
And all the currents of a heady fight.
Thy spirit within thee hath been so at war,
And thus hath so bestirred thee in thy sleep,

---

15. Dorothy Kehler, *Shakespeare's Widows* (NY: Palgrave Macmillan, 2009), 94.

That beads of sweat have stood upon thy brow
Like bubbles in a late-disturbèd stream;
And in thy face strange motions have appeared,
Such as we see when men restrain their breath
On some great sudden hest. O, what portents are these?
Some heavy business hath my lord in hand,
And I must know it, else he loves me not.

(2.4.37–64)

Lady Percy's cataloguing of her husband's behavior when awake and asleep, marks her out as one already widowed to war, which is internalised as a 'third presence' in the marriage. Andrew Hiscock has pointed out that her imagery suggests that although 'determined not to submit to the prevailing *zeitgeist* of warfare' yet this stance is itself expressed in terms that cannot avoid war:

> If she repeatedly attempts to challenge with unfailing eloquence the military ambitions of her husband, it is revealing that even she is unable to purge her language of the lexis of the battlefield. Hotspur's night-time catechism 'of sallies and retires, of trenches, tents / Of palisadoes, frontiers, parapets' is clearly deeply engraved in her consciousness and remains her only means of mental navigation through the war-torn landscape.[16]

Hotspur is unresponsive to his wife's anxious pleas, calling instead 'What ho!' to summon a servant with whom he discusses no more than the breed of his horse. To Kate's persistent, 'But hear you, my lord', he is distracted, and callously facetious:

HOTSPUR
What sayst thou, my lady?
LADY PERCY
What is it carries you away?
HOTSPUR
Why, my horse,
My love, my horse.

(2.4.73–5)

Reproving him for levity, she responds, 'In faith, I'll break thy little finger, Harry, / An if thou wilt not tell me all things true,' a line delivered (I feel mistakenly) in Welles's in *Chimes at Midnight* as a playful joke, confirming her ineffectuality but missing the note of distress. Hotspur's

---

16. Andrew Hiscock, 'Shakespeare and the Fortunes of War and Memory', *Société Française Shakespeare*, 30 (2013), 11–26, at para. 12.

reply is even more brutally final, delivered in a tone which is hard to interpret as softened by any genuine hint of domestic affection:

> Away, away, you trifler! Love? I love thee not,
> I care not for thee, Kate. This is no world
> To play with maumets and to tilt with lips.
> We must have bloody noses and cracked crowns,
> And pass them current, too. God's me, my horse! –
> What sayst thou, Kate? what wouldst thou have with me?
>
> (2.4.87–91)

Love and marriage are central to the woman's world, an integral part of her identity:

> Do you not love me? Do you not, indeed?
> Well, do not, then, for since you love me not,
> I will not love myself. Do you not love me?
> Nay, tell me if you speak in jest or no.
>
> (2.4.92–6)

Hotspur evades her question, downgrading love to a status below horse riding:

> Come, wilt thou see me ride?
> And when I am a-horseback, I will swear
> I love thee infinitely.
>
> (2.4.97–9)

In the gentlest tone he can muster, he belittlingly qualifies that no matter how 'wise' his wife is, 'constant you are, / But yet a woman', and therefore (in his view) not to be involved in wartime planning. His promise that she will follow him meets with a resigned fatalism: 'Today will I set forth, tomorrow you. / Will this content you, Kate? / LADY PERCY It must of force. / *Exeunt*' (2.4.112–14).

We see the couple once more (3.1) in Wales, and this time Hotspur is ill-at-ease and contemptuous in the company of Lady Percy's brother Mortimer and her uncle Glendower, whose daughter sings and plays the harp. Theatrically, the music sets up a strong contrast to the tumult of war raging elsewhere, but Hotspur is as unable to appreciate the moment of musical harmony and stasis which he ridicules: 'I had rather hear Lady my brach howl in Irish' (3.1.223–32). The moment provides an emotional context for Lady Mortimer to persuade her own husband not to fight, even though the war is over his own right to become king. Ridge describes Lady Mortimer as 'the closest [her] book may come to including a pacifist',[17] though Ridge takes her to be 'a kind of siren' distracting her husband from his 'performance of martial masculinity', rather than presenting a more generalised implicit rejection of war. Hotspur in the scene continues to verge on psychological abuse in taunting his wife for her feminine inability to deliver a 'good mouth-filling oath' instead of the weak expletive 'in sooth'. In callous provocation he jokes about going 'To the Welsh lady's bed' (3.1.238), and impatiently urges the men to leave for battle. Hotspur himself later wins a grudging eulogy from the victorious Hal, but his wife is left to suffer in silence, unregarded in this play but to return as widow in its sequel. In *2 Henry IV* she supports Northumberland's wife in pleading with the new Lord Percy not to engage in war, just as she had pleaded with her husband in the previous play: 'O yet, for God's sake, go not to these wars' (2.3.9). Although yet again many productions omit her two lengthy and impassioned speeches, the dramatist draws attention to them. Kate first reminds Northumberland that he has lost his son to war and that it was partly his own fault for not accompanying him into battle, but then gives way to grief for her own loss;

> so came I a widow,
> And never shall have length of life enough
> To rain upon remembrance with mine eyes,
> That it may grow and sprout as high as heaven
> For recordation to my noble husband.
>
> (2.3.)

Lady Percy's presence in *1 Henry IV* makes clear that the loss of emotional intimacy with her husband happens long before his death in battle, and as a direct consequence of his compulsive identification with his profession to the extent that his emotional life is stunted and his marriage abandoned. Shakespeare need not have given any attention to the domestic situation since it adds little to the plot, but in choosing to do so he gives a haunting insight into the fate of war wife and future war widow alike.

Spoils of war: Princess Katherine Valois

A future wife may also be among the expected spoils of war, as Theseus triumphantly acknowledges in *A Midsummer Night's Dream*: 'Hippolyta, I wooed thee with my sword, / And won thy love, doing thee injuries'

---

17. Ridge, *Shakespeare's Military Spouses*, 59–60.

(1.1.16–19). One character who could make Theseus's claim is the victorious Henry V in his robustly jocund courtship of Princess Katherine of France, his former enemy. Ringing still in the audience's ears is Henry's brutally worded demand conveyed by Exeter to Katherine's father to give up his throne to the invader who knows full well how victory in war can be used to turn the destruction of families onto the 'head' of a vanquished power:

> Deliver up the crown, and . . . take mercy
> On the poor souls for whom this hungry war
> Opens his vasty jaws; and on your head
> Turns he the widows' tears, the orphans' cries,
> The dead men's blood, the pining maidens groans,
> For husbands, fathers and betrothed lovers,
> That shall be swallowed in this controversy.
>
> (2.4.103–9)

Shakespeare leaves little doubt in the 'wooing scene' (5.2) that love is subsidiary to affairs of state. The crowded *personae* of power brokers mentioned in the initial stage direction tells us as much:

> *Enter, at one door King Harry, the Dukes of Exeter and 'Clarence', the Earl of Warwick, and other lords; at another, the King Charles the Sixth of France, Queen Isabel; the Duke of Burgundy, and other French, among them Princess Katherine and Alice.*

Queen Isabel is under no illusions that Henry may demand what he wishes, and she is aware that these include an enforced, political wedding between the King and her daughter Katherine, a situation in which she must tread carefully, hiding resentment behind unctuous flattery:

> QUEEN ISABEL
> So happy be the issue, brother England,
> Of this good day and of this gracious meeting,
> As we are now glad to behold your eyes –
> Your eyes, which hitherto have borne in them,
> Against the French that met them in their bent,
> The fatal balls of murdering basilisks.
> The venom of such looks we fairly hope,
> Have lost their quality, and that this day
> Shall change all griefs and quarrels into love.
>
> (5.2.12–20)

Burgundy's equally diplomatically couched speech emphasises the sheer waste of war in every sense, in its destructive effects on the agricultural seasons, its distractions from the occupations of a population normally in tune with the diurnal course of civil society in a state of 'gentle peace.' Out of context it can be read as pacifism, but in context as fatalistic defeatism. Henry, to drive home his advantage, relentlessly blames France for the war, and in his curt reply to Burgundy insists that,

> you must buy that peace
> With full accord to all our just demands,
> Whose tenors and particular effects
> You have enscheduled briefly in your hands.
>
> (5.2.70–3)

It is already a 'done deal' in writing, with limited opportunities for the French to do no more than 'augment, or alter' the schedule, an exercise which Isabel hopes will benefit from the woman's touch:

> Our gracious brother, I will go with them.
> Haply a woman's voice may do some good
> When articles too nicely urged be stood on.
>
> (5.2.92–4)

However, despite her hint, Henry's legalistic vocabulary and tone do not waver from what Shelley in 'Ozymandias' described as 'the sneer of cold command', using the formal royal plural:

> Yet leave our cousin Katherine here with us.
> She is our capital demand, comprised
> Within the fore-rank of our articles.
>
> (5.2.95–7)

On this somewhat unpromising note of imperial acquisition and possession, one of the best known wooing scenes in literature proceeds. As Barber and Wheeler note, it comes only after the exclusively 'all-male solidarity' of a 'band of brothers' have finished fighting at Agincourt, and in it 'Henry's battlefield logic is simply domesticated for use in the peaceful field of courtship . . . The wooing of Katherine is completed by an elaborate, displaced threat of violence', as he speaks in 'soldier terms'[18]

> Fair Katherine, and most fair,
> Will you vouchsafe to teach a soldier terms
> Such as will enter at a lady's ear
> And plead his love-suit to her gentle heart?

18. Barber and Wheeler, *The Whole Journey*, 236.

KATHERINE
Your majesty shall mock at me. I cannot speak your England.
(5.2.97–101)

Despite the almost universal rendition of this scene as charming and romantic, and the language puns as harmlessly comic, Katherine's reply suggests something more problematical. In emotional terms as well as linguistic, for much of the time she simply does not understand what Henry is talking about, and she is manoeuvred into being the target of patronising English jokes. At no stage does Katherine either acknowledge or return Henry's protestations of love, and while with dignity insisting on her '*sage*' command of her own language, she realises full well that Henry is taking advantage of her lack of English as an exercise of deception: 'Your majesty 'ave *fausse* French enough to deceive de most *sage demoiselle* dat is *en France*' (5.2.216–17). Henry speaks down to her as to a child rather than a Princess, and he presumes uninvited to use the diminutive familiar 'Kate'. As his mock-modest pitch he makes the most of his plain, rough self-image as a soldier, asking her if she can love this coarse and violent persona. His own capacity to love a woman is offered only as a brief, casual afterthought:

> If I could win a lady at leapfrog, or by vaulting into my saddle with my armour on my back, under the correction of bragging be it spoken, I should quickly leap into a wife. Or if I might buffet for my love or bound my horse for her favours, I could lay on like a butcher, and sit like a jackanapes, never off. But, before God, Kate, I cannot look greenly nor gasp out my eloquence, nor I have no cunning in protestation, only downright oaths, which I never use till urged, nor never break for urging. If thou canst love a fellow of this temper, Kate, whose face is not worth sunburning, that never looks in his glass for love of anything he sees there, let thine eye be thy cook. I speak to thee plain soldier. If thou canst love me for this, take me; if not, to say to thee that I shall die is true; but for thy love, by the Lord, no; yet I love thee too.
>
> (5.2.137–53)

One hundred lines later he still harps on 'the poor and untempering effect of [his] visage' as the birthmark of a soldier:

> Now beshrew my father's ambition! He was thinking of civil wars when he got me; therefore was a I created with a stubborn outside, with an aspect of iron, that when I come to woo ladies, I fright them.
>
> (5.2.222–31)

His curious vow to love Katherine 'cruelly' (200), his stated preference in love to 'lay on like a butcher' (142), and his hope that she will prove 'a good soldier-breeder' (203), come as words spoken in the language of 'plain soldier': 'If thou would have such a one, take me; and take me, take a soldier; take a soldier, take a king' (166–7). Jordi Coral describes his approach as a mixture of 'latent violence' and 'crude sexuality'.[19] To his persistent questions as to whether she can love – or even like – him, Katherine replies first by non-committally acknowledging his meaning ('Sauf votre honneur, me understand vell' [132]), and later with stunning frankness: 'Is it possible dat I sould love de enemy of France?' (170). Henry predictably uses this to stake his proprietary claim as conqueror with a black joke: 'for I love France so well that I will not part with a village of it; I will have it all mine' (173–5). His insensitive and offensive attempt at humour no doubt amuses him but is lost on Kate, who replies, 'I cannot tell vat is dat' (177). He will not leave her alone in attempting to extract her agreement – 'But, Kate, dost thou understand thus much English, canst thou love me?' – but she will not give him the satisfaction of a straight answer, responding only 'I cannot tell' (192–3). The only concession Katherine allows is to say that she will be 'content' to do what pleases her own father ('Dat is as it sall please *de roi mon père*'). This patriarchal reliance is enough for Henry: 'Nay, it will please him well, Kate; it shall please him Kate' (245–7). Actual consent on her own behalf is not given by her, and his offer to kiss her hand is met with polite but firm refusal: '*Laissez, mon seigneur, laissez, laissez*' (250). Whether it occurred to Shakespeare or not, in Henry's insistent 'Then I will kiss your lips, Kate' is almost exactly reminiscent of his most coercive and bullying relationship in *The Taming of the Shrew*: 'Why, there's a wench! Come on and kiss me Kate' (5.2.196; 343). Kate does in fact kiss Petruchio (5.1.151), but there is no certainty in *Henry V* whether or not the kiss offered by Henry is received with any reciprocated warmth. It is up to actors to decide whether his comment that there is 'witchcraft' in her lips (275) suggests a kiss in return, or whether it is a self-satisfied smirk of triumph as he forces it on her against her stated wishes. The other political figures bustle back onstage and Kate says not one more word in the play. Instead, we hear a lengthy, misogynistic exchange between Henry, Burgundy, and the King of France, in which women are likened to summer flies, until the negotiations are finally clinched by the now deposed Queen Isabel.

As one might expect, Olivier and Branagh in their filmed productions do everything possible to mute or eliminate the notes of reluctant

19. Jordi Coral, '"Maiden Walls That War Hath Never Entered": Rape and Post-Chivalric Military Culture in Shakespeare's *Henry V*', *College Literature*, 44 (2017), 404–35, 429.

capitulation, political bargaining, and subtly menacing threats which I have chosen to emphasise, and to present the scene instead as full of charm and reciprocated love. Olivier turns it into a kind of 1950s' style *Carry On Wooing a Frenchwoman*, playing up the English anti-foreign prejudices and sexual innuendos in the language of body parts. The comic interpretation is all but universal, as William B. Robison shows in canvassing nine different filmed performances. One of these, Michael Bogdanov's in the BBC's *The Wars of the Roses*, 1990, presents Katherine as ambiguously sullen.[20] Robison does not mention Hytner's controversial, satirical and ostentatiously anti-heroic stage production referencing the invasion of Iraq (2003), which set the 'wooing' scene amidst body-bags of dead soldiers. One reviewer wrote at the time, '[Katherine] reacts with stiff, stricken distaste, clearly regarding this heavy artillery chat-up as just the continuation of the rape of her country by more courtly and cringe-making means'.[21] Otherwise, directorial lurches into romantic comedy in this scene are surprising in the light of heightened sensitivity to gender issues, especially since Shakespeare's non-judgemental and arguably less sentimental presentation suggests that, as certainly as Lady Percy is a war widow, so Katherine of France is a reluctant war bride, worn down by beguiling words, threats and emotional duress, all based on a military victor's complacent sense of entitlement after winning his war of invasion.

Cressida

Katherine's experience of an arguably enforced marriage as the result of conquest by an enemy is but one example from many in Shakespeare's plays of how women become tangled up in war whether they wish it or not. Lady Macduff, murdered with her children on suspicion of her husband's treachery in a civil war, is an openly shocking and tragic victim. Women's experiences in times of war can be maddeningly arbitrary and contingent, at the mercy of chance encounters precipitated by an existential crisis not of their making, driven by a sense of urgency that would not operate in peace time, and seeing their families destroyed in needless tragedy. Several times in the *Iliad* violent deaths in battle are presented in the context of wives and children:

20. William B. Robison, 'The Bard, the Bride and the Muse Bemused: Katherine of Valois on Film in Shakespeare's *Henry V*', *The Palgrave Handbook of Shakespeare's Queens*, 475–501, 482.
21. Review by Paul Taylor in *The Independent* 19 October 2013 [sic] at https://www.in dependent.co.uk/arts-entertainment/theatre-dance/reviews/henry-v-olivier-national -theatre-london-104805.html accessed 12 January 2021.

In all ignorance she had asked her ladies-in-waiting to set a great caul-
dron on the fire so that Hector would have hot water for a bath, when
he returned ... She ran through the halls, her heart pounding, beside
herself, and her ladies followed. When they came to the wall, where the
men were thronging, she rushed to the battlements and gazing out saw
Hector's corpse being hauled from the city, the powerful horses dragging
it savagely towards the hollow ships ... Now you are gone to the House
of Hades under the earth, but I remain cold with grief, a widow in your
halls. And your son, the child of doomed parents, our child, a mere babe,
can no longer give you joy, dead Hector: nor can you give joy to him.[22]

Emotional lives become playthings of historical circumstances, and
unfettered free choice cannot operate in private life when armies clash.

Cressida, in love and against her wishes, is caught up in a hostage
exchange between warring nations. *Troilus and Cressida* has been
seen as one of the great anti-war works, puncturing with withering
frequency the myth of the most iconic war from ancient times. While
to the men who willingly engage, war is like a game, 'good sport' in
Troilus's phrase, the competitive metaphor applies also to their attitudes to women. The fundamental and squalid cause of the war is the
Trojan abduction of Helen, who is regarded as a symbolic prize. Despite
the war's manifest unjustifiability, many die and will be mourned as
Cassandra prophesies, speaking as much for future generations as her
own, in protest at the 'mass of moan to come' (2.2.107). She is dismissed
as 'our mad sister' with 'brain-sick raptures' (2.2.122) by Troilus, the
youthfully impetuous apologist for war. The play's emotional range has
been identified as generally negative – satirical, bitter, angry are words
frequently used by critics – stemming from the relentless undercutting
of rhetoric espousing militaristic values such as national pride, honour,
just war, courage, military glory, masculine stereotypes, and Ulysses'
advocacy of 'order' in the state based on social hierarchy. In linking
war with sexuality, Shakespeare is radically revising the dominant view
of preceding writers who had dealt with the Trojan War.[23] Montaigne
also expressed a sceptical judgement, building first on a line in Horace's
Epistles:

It was because of the lechery of Paris that all Asia was ruined and
destroyed: one man's desires, the annoyance and pleasure of one man,
one single family quarrel – causes which ought not to set two fishwives

22. *Iliad*, 461–2.
23. See the various accounts covered in Piero Boitano (ed.), *The European Tragedy of
Troilus* (Oxford: Clarendon Press, 1989).

clawing at each other's throats – were the soul, the motive-force, of that great discord [war].[24]

This harshly judgemental tone is not much different from the play's own from its very start. The cause of the war between Troy and Greece, in the most reductively jaundiced view, is inherently related to sexuality:

> The ravished Helen, Menelaus' queen,
> With wanton Paris sleeps – and that's the quarrel.
>   . . .
> Now, good or bad, 'tis but the chance of war.
>
> (Prologue, 9–10, 31)

According to the play's most cynical commentator, Thersites, the consequence of war as a form of legitimised rape is venereal disease: 'After this, the vengeance on the whole camp – or rather, the Neapolitan bone-ache, for that methinks is the curse dependent on those that war for a placket' (2.3.17–19).

Embedded in the account that follows of Cressida's role, lies a century-long debate about how we are to evaluate her actions. Sharon M. Harris has economically summarised the character's critical fortunes,[25] from multiple readings of her as flirtatious, promiscuous and unfaithful, contrasting with more recent feminist readings from the 1980s which see her as a victim of masculine prejudices.[26] Claire M. Tylee has also traced how the character has been regularly re-constructed and re-evaluated in radically different ways by performers and critics, and by characters within the play.[27] Significantly, she points out that amongst her earlier admirers were some who held publicly antiwar views:

> The one Victorian critic to speak up for Cressida was G. B. Shaw, who was vilified for the stand he took against war fever during the 1914–18 War. One of the first recorded English productions was mounted by the pacifist William Poel as that fever was gathering momentum in 1912; it

24. Montaigne, 'An apology for Raymond Sebond, *The Complete Essays*, 529.

25. Sharon M. Harris, 'Feminism and Shakespeare's Cressida: "*If* I be false . . ."', *Women's Studies: An Interdisciplinary Journal*, 18 (1990): 65–82.

26. The first seems to have been Gayle Greene, 'Shakespeare's Cressida: "A kind of self"', in *The Woman's Part: Feminist Criticism of Shakespeare*, eds Carolyn Ruth Swift Lenz, Gayle Greene and Carol Thomas Neely (Urbana: University of Illinois Press, 1980), 133–49.

27. Claire M. Tylee, 'The Text of Cressida and Every Ticklish Reader: *Troilus and Cressida Act Four Scene 5*', *Atlantis*, 11 (1989), 53–69. https://www.jstor.org/stable /pdf/41055418.pdf

was not a success, and the play only gained appreciative audiences from among the war-weary in 1920.[28]

Later, writing in the shadow of World War Two, Jan Kott, who had seen more of war close up than most critics, drew attention to her as an 'amazing and modern' character responding to situations over which she has little control.[29] However, earlier attitudes sometimes recur, and even some feminist critics seem tacitly to equate the Grecian's (hostile and derisive) attitudes to Cressida with both the male dramatist's intentions and potential, patriarchal audience responses. Like Desdemona ('Was this fair paper, this most goodly book / Made to write 'whore' upon?' [4.1.72–3]), she continues to be a 'text' 'written upon' by male assumptions and discourse. Like Desdemona, she is trapped within a military context, in her case without a female confidante. Cressida is a woman whose destiny is unfairly shaped by the war in which she finds herself swept up.

Even before she appears onstage, Cressida is unwittingly enmeshed in the sexualised context of this dubious war. She is first set up by her uncle Pandarus as the target of Troilus' attentions, which, despite his protestations of love, can be described as infatuation and a desire for personal conquest. It is clear from Cressida's soliloquies that she understands the fickleness of men if they are 'led on', but such knowledge is not evidence of a sexual knowingness or to replicate their behaviour, but the caution of one drawn by men into this process. Moreover, she is herself aware of how easily and unfairly women can be typed as flirtatious or promiscuous if they readily confess love, and she consciously pre-empts this: 'Then though my heart's content firm love doth bear, / Nothing of that shall from mine eyes appear' (1.2.207–8). However, she is effectively manipulated by her uncle and Troilus into confessing her love. René Girard has shown how, after their single night of lovemaking, almost instantly she is treated with 'callous indifference' by Troilus, who is eager to be off to his soldier companions and determined not to be found with her.[30] Jill Mann notes that after his wooing of Cressida he drops 'his flights of rhetoric, [and] takes on the brusque laconicism of the club or locker-room'.[31] He later asserts that it is 'womanish' to be away from

28. Tylee, 'The text of Cressida', 65.
29. Jan Kott, *Shakespeare Our Contemporary* (London: Methuen 1965), 61–7.
30. René Girard, 'The Politics of Desire in *Troilus and Cressida*', in *Shakespeare and the Question of Theory*, ed. Patricia Parker and Geoffrey Hartman (New York: Methuen, 1985), 188–209, 190–1.
31. Jill Mann, 'Shakespeare and Chaucer: "What is Criseyde worth"', in Boitano, *The European Tragedy of Troilus*, 219–42, 236.

the battlefield (1.1.106–7). Then, like the abducted Helen, she becomes a pawn in the game of war fought between Troy and Greece. Evidently even from the very beginning of the play (1.1.109–12) there are discussions that she will follow her father 'to the Greeks' in a prisoner swap for Antenor and as a kind of token exchange for Helen, the fate which does overtake her (4.3). Neither Pandarus nor Troilus is sympathetic to her refusal, or her vehemently expressed wish to stay with Troilus even at the cost of renouncing her father:

CRESSIDA
O you immortal gods! I will not go.
PANDARUS
Thou must.
CRESSIDA
I will not, uncle: I have forgot my father.
I know no touch of consanguinity,
No kin, no love, no blood, no soul, so near me
As the sweet Troilus. O you gods divine,
Make Cressid's name the very crown of falsehood
If ever she leave Troilus. Time, force, and death
Do to this body what extremity you can,
But the strong base and building of my love
Is as the very centre of the earth,
Drawing all things to it. I'll go in and weep –
PANDARUS
Do, do.
CRESSIDA
Tear my bright hair, and scratch my praised cheeks,
Crack my clear voice with sobs and break my heart
With sounding 'Troilus.' I will not go from Troy.

(4.3.20–35)

She could not be more emphatic and her prediction that, no matter what she does, her name will become 'the very crown of falsehood' is to come disastrously true. There follows a grief-stricken outburst, leaving no doubt that she is not complying with the plan which turns her into a commodity of political 'value' rather than a loving woman (4.5.1–10).

It is Troilus himself who is delegated to break the news to Cressida and escort her to the enemy side, and he does so with an impersonal fatalism that does not demur at the policy of 'the rude brevity and discharge of one' (4.4.40), even if that 'one' loves him. Despite protesting his own undying love, his commercial imagery is revealing: 'We two, that with so many thousand sighs / Did buy each other, must poorly sell ourselves' (4.4.38–9). His predominant mood is also expressed in sexual terms as 'a kind of godly jealousy' that the 'Grecian youths . . . flowing and swelling o'er with arts and exercise' (4.4.76–7) will tempt her to break her vow. He is the one who introduces the subject of infidelity, and he harps on it at length, almost consciously willing into being the proverbial valuation of a 'false Cressida': '. . . But be not tempted', to which she replies spiritedly, 'Do you think I will?' (4.5.92–3). Although, as he claims, he may have little choice in the political matter himself, his rhetoric does reveal one who is both complicit in the exchange and harbouring a mistrusting compulsion, amounting to a prophecy, to insist that Cressida reiterate her vow of constancy. He makes no attempt to protest his own love with as much passion as she does hers, and one can interpret his actions here as the very 'infidelity' he fears in Cressida. Her immediate response signals just this conclusion – 'O heavens, you love me not!' (4.4.81). Clearly uncomfortable in the situation rather than sharing her grief, Troilus tries to hasten the departure: 'Come kiss, and let us part' (4.5.98). He himself delivers her to Diomedes and the finality of this gesture in itself must reawaken Cressida's earlier fear that 'Things won are done' (1.2.283) – that possession kills male desire – and that her time with Troilus is effectively ended.

Now perilously vulnerable and lonely in the enemy camp, Cressida is paraded before the Greek soldiers who aggressively compete with each other over turns in trying to kiss her. She is given no chance to speak, and when she does it is the resistant 'Therefore no kiss' (4.5.40). Her silence may be glossed over by readers and interpreted as willing participation, but in the theatre it can easily be shown instead as reluctance and brittly concealed fear, in a situation both humiliating and dangerous for the woman surrounded by enemy soldiers in battle array. After initial, frozen passivity, she is increasingly coerced to join the banter simply because she has no choice. Nestor makes it clear that Agamemnon takes the initiative without invitation or consent from Cressida: 'Our general doth salute you with a kiss' (4.5.20), and Ulysses makes the suggestion that ''twere better she were kissed in general' with a deliberate pun on 'general'. His arrogantly dismissive and harshly judgemental speech has the force of the rapist blaming the victim for 'leading them on', without justification and with the indignant pique of one rejected:

> Fie, fie upon her!
> There's language in her eye, her cheek, her lip,
> Nay, her foot speaks; her wanton spirits look out
> At every joint and motive of her body.
> O, these encounterers, so glib of tongue,
> That give accosting welcome ere it comes,
> And wide unclasp the tables of their thoughts

> To every ticklish reader! Set them down
> For sluttish spoils of opportunity
> And daughters of the game.

> (4.6.55–64)

There is no reason to regard this as the author's view, when it clearly is the Greek leader's outburst in a war situation. He has encouraged, at least metaphorically, a gang rape of an enemy alien in the context of a war, and the scene in its way is as violent as the rape of Lavinia in *Titus Andronicus*.

Perhaps reflecting male anxieties at the time, some critics writing in the aftermath to both World Wars in the twentieth century judged Cressida as an exemplar of the faithless and weak-willed woman who does not wait for her lover to return from the war.[32] The scene in which Diomedes seduces and emotionally blackmails her is framed by Thersites' warning to the audience: 'That same Diomed's a false-hearted rogue, a most unjust knave . . . Nothing but lechery! All incontinent varlets!' (5.1.85–6, 94–5), and it is overseen by the jealously voyeuristic Troilus whose bullying premonitions become a self-fulfilling prophecy in front of his eyes. Troilus had promised Cressida that Diomedes is a trustworthy 'guardian' in a situation where there is no hope of returning to Troy on offer, willing to trust an enemy soldier but not his lover. Diomedes is placed in a position of power over Cressida, and he betrays this with crafty manoeuvring, using a mixture of cajoling, threats of abandonment, and bullying, until again she is left helplessly with little choice: 'what would you have me do?' (5.2.24). Troilus leaps to the conclusion that she is the one who is untrustworthy and 'false', not conceding that he has willingly and without demur colluded in her exchange with the Greeks, and has put her into the hands of the very man whom he watches seducing her. Instead of recriminating, she blames herself for the 'error' of her sex, but there is ample cause for mitigation which can be realised theatrically in the actor's performance and directorial control. Separated from her lover by war, exchanged, pawed over and discussed like a public object, and coerced into submission by her wartime 'protector' as she is, Cressida's fate is just as surely that of a helpless consequence of war, as those of Lady Percy and Princess Katherine of France.

---

32. For examples see Harris, 'Feminism and Shakespeare's Cressida', 65.

Virgilia

Virgilia had only once been named by Plutarch in the source for *Coriolanus*, where she plays a wordless and insignificant part as 'wife', so her emotional life is entirely Shakespeare's creation. However, he seems to have transferred to her the spirit of Plutarch's Valeria, whose idea it is that the women should approach Coriolanus as peacemakers, likening their task to that of the Sabine sisters 'when they procured loving peace, instead of hateful war, between their fathers and their sisters'.[33] Shakespeare makes his Valeria closer in attitudes to Coriolanus's mother Volumnia. Virgilia is greeted by her husband back from battle against the Corioli as his 'gracious silence', and her mood is signalled initially by weeping, a response upbraided as perverse by her husband:

CORIOLANUS
                My gracious silence, hail!
Wouldst thou have laugh'd had I come coffin'd home,
That weep'st to see me triumph? Ah, my dear,
Such eyes the widows in Corioles wear,
And mothers that lack sons.

                              (2.1.175–9)

But far from remaining in 'silence', her speech and gestures make clear her consistent attitude, which is not submissive but assertive of peaceful values. She is on each occasion accompanied by the contrasting Volumnia, a mother who would rather 'lack' her son through his death as a hero than see him as less than committed to warfare on behalf of 'honour'. Showing that not all women in Shakespeare are peace-loving, Volumnia boasts of having 'pleased to let him seek danger where he was like to find fame', ridiculing her daughter-in-law's timorousness:

VOLUMNIA . . . To a cruel war I sent him, from whence he returned, his brows bound with oak. I tell thee, daughter, I sprang not more in joy at first hearing he was a man-child, than now in first seeing he had proved himself a man.
VIRGILIA
But had he died in the business, madam; how then?
VOLUMNIA
Then his good report should have been my son. I therein would have found issue. Hear me profess sincerely: had I a dozen sons, each in my love alike, and none less dear than thine and my good Marcius, I had

33. *Shakespeare's Plutarch*, ed. T. J. Spencer (Harmondsworth: Penguin Books, 1964), 351.

rather had eleven die nobly for their country, than one voluptuously sur-
feit out of action.

. . .

VIRGILIA
His bloody brow? O Jupiter, no blood!
VOLUMNIA
Away, you fool!
(1.3.13–40 *passim*)

She scorns Virgilia as a killjoy who isolates herself from the other woman
present, Valeria: 'VOLUMNIA Let her alone, lady: as she is now, she
will but disease our better mirth. / VALERIA In troth, I think she would'
(1.3.105–6). Volumnia's stance is aligned with the masculine glorification of war, while Virgilia recoils from reports of violence:

MENENIUS
Is he not wounded? he was wont to come home wounded.
VIRGILIA
Oh no, no, no.
VOLUMNIA
Oh he is wounded; I thank the gods for't.
(2.1.118–20)

In this scene Virgilia does not speak again, though her continued presence acts as a quiet, visual rebuke to the prevailing celebrations over the
soldier's wounds. When he refuses to show these wounds publicly to
gain a consulship and is exiled from Rome, he seems as irritated with his
wife as Hotspur, replying to her anxious 'O heavens! O heavens!' with a
curt 'Nay, prithee woman' (4.1.11–12). He turns instead to reassure his
mother, who shows more fury against the citizens than reluctance to part
with her son. Just as Virgilia is ill-suited to the life of a soldier's wife, so
Coriolanus has no place in his life for a wife – Plutarch had said that he
took a wife to please his mother. Virgilia has been described by Michael
Goldman as 'a significantly shadowy and melancholy figure' whose husband 'seems bound to others only by the relations of the battlefield . . .
The language of affection in the play is reserved for descriptions of war
and enemies'.[34] The male figures Cominius, Aufidius and the paternalis-
tic but hero-worshipping Menenius who drools admiringly over the soldier's 'twenty-seven wounds' (2.1.150), stir Coriolanus's most intimate
feelings. They display the mutual attraction of male comradeship likened
to marriage:

34. Michael Goldman, *Shakespeare and the Energies of Drama* (New Jersey: Princeton
University Press, 1972), 118.

MARCIUS

O! let me clip ye
In arms as sound as when I woo'd; in heart
As merry as when our nuptial day was done,
And tapers burn'd to bedward.
COMINIUS

Flower of warriors.
(1.6.29–32)

Volumnia has been the subject of much commentary, but Virgilia has attracted virtually no critical attention, except for Kelsey Ridge who laments the 'bluntly dismissive' and 'utterly forgettable' neglect of Virgilia by other characters in the 'fiercely masculine' world of *Coriolanus*. She quotes another of the very few exceptions, Unhae Langis, who has written, '[Virgilia's] insistent femininity and protection of the domestic sphere represent Shakespeare's particular critique against Rome's hyper masculine ideology'.[35] Meanwhile, some feminist critics make the point that Volumnia is a victim of false consciousness in sharing and shaping her son's overtly masculine attitudes, while either ignoring Virgilia or adjudging her weak and unassertive.[36] Virgilia does have her rare moments of defending her husband to others (4.2.23–8), but more characteristically she expresses accessible emotions of fear and sympathy, providing a more humanly centred touchstone. Ridge's own analysis is rather different, comparing both the women with civilian '(in)dependents', relatives of soldiers in American army life today.[37] On Volumnia, Ridge seeks to move beyond 'blaming the mother' for her son's violence, instead seeking understanding for the complex and contradictory experiences of 'Military Mums', expected simultaneously to support their children in the army and to conceal or override their own worries. But what seems somewhat pessimistic in Ridge's analysis of Virgilia is her hypothesis that the inexperienced novitiate, mentored by Volumnia, in time 'will learn' and internalise the culture she is entering as a soldier's wife. Although untested in the play, if this is so in 'real life', then army life is a culture that can eventually be normalised by cauterizing resistant

35. Unhae Langis, 'Coriolanus: Inordinate Passions and Powers in Personal and Political Governance', *Comparative Drama*, 44 (2010): 1–27, 19. www.jstor. org/stable/23238673.

36. Ridge mentions in particular Janet Adelman, *Suffocating Mothers: Fantasies of Maternal Origin in Shakespeare's Plays, Hamlet to the Tempest* (Florence, KY: Routledge, 2012), 147; Coppélia Khan, *Man's Estate: Masculine Identity in Shakespeare* (University of California Press, 1981) 155–6 and *Roman Shakespeare: Warriors, Wounds and Women* (London: Routledge, 1997), 147.

37. Ridge, *Shakespeare's Military Spouses*, 173.

emotions, and upturning assumptions of peaceful civilian life and familial roles. In the play, however, Virgilia is constructed on an aesthetics
of sympathy with potential emotionally to guide audience response.
She is a conspicuous stage presence whose weeping can be an affective
response to the prevailing military ethos, contrasted with Volumnia's
approval of violent masculinity. When asked by Sicinius 'Are you man-
kind?' she answers, 'Ay, fool, is that a shame? Was not a man my father?'
(4.2.16–20). We might deduce that her own father was a soldier, and
that she has shaped her son's attitudes from birth. Continuing the line of
family conditioning, she proudly condones the upbringing of her grand-
son, young Martius (also Shakespeare's creation):

VOLUMNIA
He had rather see the swords and hear a drum, than look upon his
schoolmaster.
VALERIA
O' my word, the father's son! . . . has such a confirmed countenance.
I saw him run after a gilded butterfly, and when he caught it, he let it go
again; and after it again, and over and over he comes, and again, catched
it again; or whether his fall enraged him, or how 'twas, he did so set his
teeth and tear it; Oh, I warrant it, how he mammocked it!
VOLUMNIA
One on 's father's moods.

(1.3.56–67)

In the tight circuitry of Shakespeare's imagery, a comparison is drawn
with Coriolanus's followers who are unsympathetically likened by
Cominius to 'boys pursuing summer butterflies / Or butchers killing
flies' (4.6.95–6). Volumnia's advice to her daughter-in-law is to value her
husband's 'absence' at war, more 'than in the embracements of his bed
where he should show most love' (1.3.1–5). Coriolanus himself concedes
in soliloquy his literally 'unkind' refusal to follow human 'instinct' and
remain individualistic, 'like to a lonely dragon': 'But out affection! / All
bond of privilege and nature, break! / Let it be virtuous to be obstinate'
(5.3.26–7).

                                        I'll never
    Be such a gosling to obey instinct, but stand,
    As if a man were author of himself
    And knew no other kin.

(5.3.34–7)

He is seen by denigrators as more 'like a thing' than a man, and one
'Made by some other deity than nature' (4.6.92). To admirers he is an

efficient war machine, one who 'moves like an engine ... and his hum is a battery' (5.4.19). The scene in which Virgilia, Volumnia and his son '*Enter in mourning habits*' to persuade Coriolanus not to wreak vengeance on Rome shows he is not incapable of human affections. He can melt in memory of his wife's love, which almost sways him from the dramatically apportioned 'part' he plays as a soldier (5.3.38–48). However, it is not love for her but subservience to his mother that stirs him most, when she invokes notions of 'duty' and military obedience to persuade him to give up his vendetta against Rome (5.3.62–3). Chastened, Coriolanus speaks as her 'corrected son' as though taking orders from a superior officer. In doing so, he effectively signs his death warrant.

Judging by the frequency of Shakespeare's interventions throughout his canon, it seems that war is dramatically purposeful and symptomatic rather than gratuitous, when he deals with relations between men and women. Since war is omnipresent in national and social lives, it comes to be internalised into the emotional lives of citizens. War becomes a metaphor for other, conflicting emotional encounters, implying that for the soldiers themselves, love involves some level of latent violence. Shakespeare's cameos of female suffering in war are glimpses of a large and menacing truth, the intertwining of war and love relationships. The situations are perennial and representative so long as war persists as a norm. Paul Fussell, in his classic study *The Great War and Modern Memory*, speaks of war as an 'experience' which has enough similarities from age to age to confer some kind of continuity through each occurrence in its human significance.[38] One way or another, Shakespeare shows that war touches the emotional lives of each and every person living under its shadow. War is a situation in which all 'serve' in some way, and all suffer, and in which any expectation of stable emotional relationships is necessarily suspended. Shakespeare's female lovers, at least, are likely to agree with a character exceptional in Marlowe's *Tamburlaine*, 'Accurs'd be he that first invented war!'[39]

38. Paul Fussell, *The Great War and Modern Memory* (Oxford University Press, 1975) *passim*.
39. *The First Part of Tamburlaine the Great* (2.4.1), in *Marlowe: Plays and Poems,* ed. M. Ridley (London: J. M. Dent, 1955).

Chapter 7

All's Well in Love and War – or Is it?

The seed of *All's Well That Ends Well* (1601–5) may have been planted in Shakespeare's mind some years earlier, when he wrote his best-selling erotic epyllion, *Venus and Adonis*. In it the goddess of love in vain pursues a reluctant young man dedicated to hunting, while Helena, more successfully in the long run, pursues Bertram who runs away from her to war. In both, violent male pursuits are directly pitted against female love.

There had been two related themes in the poem, both relevant to the later play. The first, as Garrison and Pivetti succinctly phrase it, is that traditionally 'the goddess of love tames the god of war', in reference to Venus's plaintive boast of seducing Mars, which fails to convince Adonis:[1]

'I have been wooed, as I entreat thee now,
Even by the stern and direful god of war,
Whose sinewy neck in battle ne'er did bow,
Who conquers where he comes in every jar;
      Yet hath he been my captive and my slave,
      And begged for that which thou unasked shalt have.

'Over my altars hath he hung his lance,
His battered shield, his uncontrolled crest,
And for my sake hath learned to sport and dance,
To toy, to wanton, dally, smile and jest,
Scorning his churlish drum and ensign red,
Making my arms his field, his tent my bed.

'Thus he that overruled I overswayed,
Leading him prisoner in a red-rose chain;
Strong-tempered steel his stronger strength obeyed,
Yet was he servile to my coy disdain.

1. Garrison and Pivetti, *Shakespeare at Peace*, 76–9.

O, be not proud, nor brag not of thy might,
For mast'ring her that foiled the god of fight!'

(97–114)

On this account, at least in the pecking order among gods and goddesses, love is stronger than brute force. Venus subdues Mars, peace brings closure to war. Conventions of comedy, with their invitation 'To toy, to wanton, dally, smile and jest', avert tragedy signalled by the 'churlish drum' of battle with its endgame of likely death in the mortal world too foolish to acknowledge love. The drum recurs as a prominent symbol of army life in *All's Well* – Bertram addresses 'Great Mars' as 'A lover of thy drum' (3.3.8–11), and Parolles' loss of the drum is his comic downfall. But although this principle may operate in the faraway world of the immortals (and in literature), it does not work in *Venus and Adonis*, because a mortal like Adonis is destined to die in his own favourite but dangerous occupation of hunting. Dympna Callaghan and Catherine Bates remind us that in Renaissance mythography, hunting (venery) was 'an intensively masculine venture understood as the ritual rehearsal of warfare', which suggestively may open up a reading that makes Adonis's heavily eroticised death by the boar he hunts into an allegory of death in war.[2] As the fable unfolds it is shown that the one thing love cannot conquer is death. This enforces the second moral of the poem, as the bereft and lonely Venus predicts – and in doing so proleptically causes – human love to exist forever under the shadow of an imminent ending, in which conflict is inescapably internalised:

'It shall be cause of war and dire events,
And set dissension 'twixt the son and sire;
. . .
Sith in his prime death doth my love destroy,
They that love best their loves shall not enjoy.'

(1158–64)

The dramatist adapting a story of a loving woman in pursuit of a coy and resistant man, then, could have chosen either of the themes from *Venus and Adonis*. Bertram could have been killed in the war he so assiduously joins to achieve fame and avoid marriage, or death can be circumvented through a consummated marriage, so that metaphorically Venus as goddess of love can be left to conquer Mars. Shakespeare flirts

2. Dympna Callaghan, *Reading Shakespeare's Poetry* (Hoboken, NJ: Wiley Blackwell, 2023), 63; Catherine Bates, *Masculinity and the Hunt: Wyatt to Spenser* (Oxford University Press, 2013), 16, 61.

with the former, since it is Helena's faked death which eventually helps to shift Bertram's feelings, but true to his source he chose the latter, leaving love improbably victorious over the soldier who survives war, so that all (it seems) 'ends well'.

Generally speaking, critics have regarded the war in *All's Well That Ends Well* as amusing diversion, and the soldiers' roles played by Bertram and Parolles simply as comic variants on the New Comedy *miles gloriosus* figure, and 'butts' of jokes.[3] What has not often been recognised is the centrality of war as both narrative device and as sustained metaphor. War is seen by Bertram as a masculine escape-hatch from Helena's love, but ironically he is trapped – while at war – by infatuation with Diana.

One staged version by Sport for Jove at Sydney's Seymour Centre (2014) at least took this line seriously (perhaps to excess), judging from a review:

> Love is a battlefield . . . In Shakespeare's *All's Well That Ends Well*, love and war collide . . . At one point, Helena places her bare feet in a pool of blood left by a soldier Bertram has slaughtered . . . Director Damien Ryan captures this tension between romance and warfare beautifully. The play-world is a military one, and Ryan never lets us forget this . . . The gunfire and flickering light of his game will later be actualised in the lights and noise and blood of battle in Italy . . . The set design complements the escalating militarisation of the play-world as the men move from intensive training sequences to the battlefield . . . There is also immediate relevancy in the slow turn from trust to suspicion of military authority.[4]

The production was staged in a period dominated internationally by protests against military invasions of Afghanistan and Iraq, conflicts which brought to shocked public attention atrocities like torture (Abu Ghraib) and war crimes. Productions of *All's Well* in the period directly following World War Two had reflected the prevailing context of realities of civilian life in a wartime setting. Gary Waller describes performances that 'conveyed a sense of military authenticity and saw Parolles's betrayal of his companions as reprehensible and an affront to traditional masculinity'.[5] Arguably, in such historical periods theatrical representations of

3. Robert S. Miola, 'New Comedy in *All's Well That Ends Well*', *Renaissance Quarterly*, 46 (1993), 23–43, 34.
4. Review by Claire Hansen, *The Conversation*, 1 April 2014: https://theconversation.com/review-love-and-war-in-alls-well-that-ends-well-25014
5. Gary Waller, 'From "The Unfortunate Comedy" to "This infinitely Fascinating Play": The Critical and Theatrical Emergence of *All's Well That Ends Well*', in *All's Well That Ends Well: New Critical Essays*, ed. Gary Waller (New York: Routledge, 2007), 23.

love in the midst of war were less easily evaded in popular consciousness than at other times. During the 1980s and '90s a more indirect but
powerful influence came from feminist critiques of traditional masculine
constructs of military heroism.[6]

Some critics have at least noticed the presence of war in the play,
drawing different conclusions. David Bergeron perhaps over-schematises
the connection: 'Life and love, epitomised in Venus and Helena, triumph over death and war, symbolised in Mars and Bertram; out of the
struggle comes a peaceful union ... Military might (Mars), which is
bent largely on destruction, is set in opposition to the spiritual force
of life represented by Helena'.[7] This seems to echo (though without
citing) G. Wilson Knight's equally 'mythical' reading in *The Sovereign
Flower*, but both seem too neat for such a raw and morally knotty play.[8]
R. B. Parker in 'War and Sex in *All's Well that Ends Well*' notes the prevalence of military imagery, finding an uneasy 'irascible-concupiscible'
'accommodation' between sex and love, which informs the play's 'moral'
that 'The web of our life is of a mingled yarn, good and ill together'
(4.3.68–9).[9] But even this may be too 'accommodating' in smoothing
over the play's 'problems', especially those of genre. For all its dark cor-
ners, the play ends as a romantic comedy, though comedy is stretched to
a limit and is more formulaic than felt. Andrew Hiscock argues that the
unsettled genre erodes 'the audience's confidence in the honour of soldiers, lovers and leaders, rather than monopolizing the dramatic intrigue
with a concern for "military advantage"'.[10] In Helen Wilcox's reading,
the comedy carries 'unflinching mockery' of the 'whole world of war',
heavily dependent on the interconnected 'languages of war and sexual
desire'.[11] As G. K. Hunter puts it, 'The pride, pomp, and circumstance

6. Janet Adelman, 'Bed Tricks: On Marriage as the End of Comedy in *All's Well That
    Ends Well* and *Measure for Measure*', in *Shakespeare's Personality*, ed. Norman N.
    Holland, Sidney Homan, Bernard J. Paris (Berkeley: University of California Press,
    1989), 151–74.
7. David Bergeron, 'The Mythical Structure of *All's Well That Ends Well*', *Texas
    Studies in Literature and Language*, 14 (1973), 559–68, 559, 560.
8. G. Wilson Knight, 'The Triple Eye' in *The Sovereign Flower* (London: Methuen,
    1958), 93–160.
9. R. B. Parker, 'War and Sex in *All's Well that Ends Well*', *Shakespeare Survey*, 37
    (1984), 99–113.
10. Hiscock, '"More warlike than politique"', 229, referring to Wilcox, 'Drums and
    Roses?'
11. Wilcox, 'Drums and Roses? The Tragicomedy of War in *All's Well That Ends Well*,'
    in R. King and P. J. C. M. Franssen (eds.), *Shakespeare and War*, (London: Palgrave
    Macmillan, 2008), 84–95, 88–9.

of glorious war is exposed to . . . withering realism'.[12] We are reminded that throughout the centuries, anti-war attitudes have been expressed in savage comedy – *vide* Swift, Voltaire, Waugh, Hašek, Heller, and many more. As Bernard Shaw wrote, 'war cannot bear the terrible castigation of comedy, the ruthless light of laughter',[13] and Daniel Derrin reminds us that satirical comedy in Shakespeare's practice can be a potent form of protest against war.[14]

The prominence of war in the play was Shakespeare's own decision, in contradistinction to his likely immediate source, William Painter's translation in *The Palace of Pleasure* of Boccaccio's tale 'Giletta of Narbonne' in *Decameron* (day 3, story 9), where the war is not so prominent. There, Beltramo (Bertram) merely wanders into Italy when he leaves the French court, 'where understanding that the *Florentines* and *Sennois* were at warres, he determined to take the *Florentines* parte'.[15] He is welcomed into the army, 'continuing in their service a long time', but there is little thematic integration of war.

Right from the start, Shakespeare weaves together sex and war. Helena in her frank wish to lose her virginity 'to her own liking' (1.1.147) converses with Parolles at his most cynical:

PAROLLES
Are you meditating on virginity?
HELENA
Ay. You have some stain of soldier in you let me ask you a question. Man is enemy to virginity; how may we barricado it against him?
PAROLLES
Keep him out.
HELENA
But he assails; and our virginity, though valiant, in the defence yet is weak. Unfold to us some warlike resistance.
PAROLLES
There is none. Man setting down before you will undermine you and blow you up.
HELENA
Bless our poor virginity from underminers and blowers up! Is there no military policy, how virgins might blow up men?

---

12. Hunter (ed.), *All's Well That Ends Well*, xxxiii.
13. Preface to *Heartbreak House*, quoted (without reference) in Melvin Maddocks, 'Comedy and War', *Sewanee Review*, 112 (2004), 22–34, 27.
14. Daniel Derrin, '*Sine dolore*', 81–97.
15. Quoted G. K. Hunter (ed.) *All's Well That Ends Well* (London: The Arden Shakespeare, Methuen, 1967), xxviii.

PAROLLES
Virginity being blown down man will quicklier be blown up: marry, in blowing him down again, with the breach yourselves made, you lose your city. It is not politic in the commonwealth of nature to preserve virginity. Loss of virginity is rational increase, and there was never virgin got till virginity was first lost. That you were made of is mettle to make virgins. Virginity, by being once lost, may be ten times found; by being ever kept, it is ever lost. 'Tis too cold a companion. Away with 't!
HELENA
I will stand for 't a little, though therefore I die a virgin.

(1.1.108–31)

The exchange is marked by insistent, unrelenting imagery of siege warfare and military campaigning, incongruously linked with sexuality: 'some stain of soldier', 'enemy', 'barricado', 'assails', 'valiant in the defence', 'warlike resistance', 'undermine you and blow you up', 'is there no military policy, how virgins might blow up men?', and 'with the breach yourselves made, you lose your city'. Like a fixation, it does not let up.[16] Helena gradually turns the argument full circle, beginning with how women can preserve their virginity against male assaults, to how they 'might blow up [impregnate] men' themselves. Parolles makes no pretence that for a man virginity is anything less than an intact hymen, 'a commodity ... Off with't while 'tis vendible' (1.1.150), ''tis a wither'd pear' (1.1.158). If her open desire is considered transgressive in a woman, its expression plays to the male arena of warfare as though it is likely to be the specialist province of a man with 'some stain of soldier' in an advisory role.[17] With a quibble, Helena draws towards its close a conversation in whose distasteful content she has been complicit: 'The wars hath so kept you under that you must needs be born under Mars' (1.1.191). In order to effect her own plan, she must herself come literally to be 'born [borne] under Mars' in an act of sex with a soldier. She is anticipating the play's proffered conclusion in which these two female impulses – defence and offence – are embodied in two different women. The virginity of Diana (named for the goddess of chastity) is preserved by the bed-trick substitution, while Helena more assertively loses her virginity to the man she loves and has lawfully married, though he does not know her true identity.

16. Parker, in 'War and Sex in *All's Well that Ends Well*', 99–113, 108, points out the train of imagery, without following up its critical significance in any detail.
17. On Helena's 'transgressive overtones' see Julia Briggs in 'Shakespeare's Bed-Tricks', *Essays in Criticism*, 44 (1994), 293–314, 302, though Briggs's attention is on social and class grounds rather than gender: 'she has broken at least three unspoken social rules' in loving a man socially above her.

Bertram's motivation to go to the wars is to abandon his enforced marriage before it is consummated: 'Although before the solemn priest I have sworn ... I'll to the Tuscan wars and never bed her' (2.3.265–9 *passim*). We are presented with various masculine attitudes that to some extent are shared by other soldiers in Shakespeare's works. The men are itching for battle to prove their 'gentlemen' class: 'It well may serve / A nursery to our gentry, who are sick / For breathing and exploit' (1.2.15–17), while civilian life and marriage amount to 'the dark house and the detested wife'. War represents freedom and adventure:

PAROLLES
       To th' wars, my boy, to the wars!
He wears his honour in a box unseen
That hugs his kicky-wicky here at home,
Spending his manly marrow in her arms,
Which should sustain the bound and high curvet
Of Mars's fiery steed. To other regions!
France is a stable; we that dwell in't jades;
Therefore, to th' war!

                              (2.3.277–84)

Given the sexual *doubles entendres* here, Parolles sees war as an enticement towards promiscuity and flight from the dull monogamy that Bertram thinks he faces. It is also regarded by other men in *All's Well* and other plays as a noble cause in itself, designed to enhance a man's 'honourable' breeding, and Bertram's enlistment as a soldier is applauded by the Duke as a 'noble purpose' which will bring Bertram 'all the honour' (3.2.70–2). The King of France waves off the young nobles with a curiously revealing phrase, suggesting that honour and fame achieved in war will amount to a kind of marriage: 'see that you come / Not to woo honour, but to wed it' (2.1.14–15), repeated by the Duke: Then go thou forth; / And fortune play upon thy prosperous helm / As thy auspicious mistress! (3.3.6–8). War is now perversely seen as a 'mistress' worthy of an officer. Equally telling is the King's warning to them to avoid 'Those girls of Italy, take heed of them ... beware of being captives / Before you serve' (2.1.19–21), as though he also regards women as entrapping and distracting men from their proper mission. Bertram himself, upon being promoted to officer class as 'general of the horse', understands the 'hazard' of his grim mission, and also seeks to prove himself in battle as a devotee:

BERTRAM
               This very day,
Great Mars, I put myself into thy file;

Make me but like my thoughts and I shall prove
A lover of thy drum, hater of love.

(3.3.8–11)

There are discrepant reports of Bertram's exploits in war. The Widow
has overheard that, 'It is reported that he has taken their great'st commander, and that with his own hand he slew the duke's brother' (3.5.5–
7). However, the Countess's Clown (Lavatch) 'has heard' differently,
quibbling on the sexual innuendo of dying as 'standing to't' which again
associates battle with sex:

1 CLOWN
Nay, there is some comfort in the news, some comfort; your son will not
be kill'd so soon as I thought he would.
COUNTESS
Why should he be kill'd?
CLOWN
So say I, madam – if he run away, as I hear he does: the danger is in
standing to't; that's the loss of men, though it be the getting of children.
Here they come will tell you more. For my part, I only hear your son was
run away.

(3.2.33–43)

Bertram on his return sports a 'patch' of velvet on his cheek which excites
debate over whether it is (or is not, as the cynical Clown suspects) band-
aging a wound or 'scar nobly got, a noble scar' (4.5.90–7).[18]

The hints of Bertram's undistinguished record, alongside the open
farce of Parolles' loss of his drum, cowardice, and readiness to betray his
fellow-soldiers, mean the war itself is presented in a comic light. Wilcox
describes the war as an event safely mocked and at a distance from dangerous realities:

The play's main characters are French but the wars are in Italy; there is
hardly any danger involved on the battlefield, precious little anxiety, and
a complete absence of identification with any cause or principle. These
wars are a sort of boys' game, taking place outside France and safely
off-stage – a knowing parallel, perhaps, with the wars of Shakespeare's
own lifetime, fought not on English soil but in Ireland and the United
Provinces. *All's Well* supplies its audience with minimal information

18. On this teasing detail which although usually ignored in stage performances has
    excited colourful critical debate, see the discussion by Michael W. Shurgot, 'Bertram's
    Scar and Courts of Healing', *Shakespeare Bulletin*, 37 (2019), 391–407. Shurgot
    likens the emblem to Helena's curing of the King's fistula and therefore of 'symbolic
    importance' to the play.

about the nature of the conflict that is being fought; we simply hear that it is a 'braving war' (1.2.3) between the armies of the Tuscan city states of Florence and Siena.[19]

In short, the presence of the war in the 'problem' comedy is generically consistent with Sidney's 'mongrel tragi-comedy',[20] invoking what Guarini had described as 'the danger not the death'.[21]

But although the outcome is benign, Shakespeare provides sufficient evidence of 'the danger' that war poses. As in the source, the combatants are mercenaries who can 'freely' choose whether they join the French army or the Tuscan (1.2.13–14), as though the outcome either way is inconsequential. However, the historical circumstances and conduct of these particular wars provided a context that Elizabethans would have been aware of. The Italian Wars (1449–1559, also known as the Habsburg-Valois Wars), which were known to Erasmus, were certainly not remembered as harmless. They were waged with a brutality that became reputed internationally as harbinger of modern warfare, described in this way by Robert Apelbaum in *The Renaissance Discovery of Violence*:

> These were wars such as had not been seen before. Because of innovations in the use of infantry and artillery, they were more rapidly destructive. For a variety of reasons, including the recruitment of mercenaries to do the fighting, combat became more ruthless, focused on killing and despoiling, the more victims the better … [quoting J. R. Hale]. Now the wars were international, and wholesale destruction was on offer. Armies grew in size, swollen with mercenaries and conscripts. Siege warfare became more lethal, and combat was aimed not toward hostage-taking and intimidation, those rites of chivalric warfare, but toward killing—followed up by pillage.[22]

Shakespeare's version may not fully reflect this reality, but the fact that he chose this specific war as his setting would have carried to audiences some of its well-known reputation for extreme violence. The involvement in this war of hapless mercenaries like Bertram and Parolles would

---

19. Helen Wilcox, 'Drums and Roses?, 84–95, 85.
20. Sidney, *Defence of Poetry*, in *Miscellaneous Prose of Sir Philip Sidney*, ed. Katherine Duncan-Jones and Jan van Dorsten (Oxford: Clarendon Press, 1973), 114.
21. Giambattista Guarini, *Compendium of Tragicomic Poetry* (1601), in Allan H. Gilbert, *Literary Criticism Plato to Dryden* (New York: American Book Co., 1940), 505–33, 511.
22. Robert Apelbaum, *The Renaissance Discovery of Violence* from Boccaccio to Shakespeare (New York: Anthem Press, 2021), 105.

have carried more of a *frisson* to Elizabethan audiences than modern, and as the Sport for Jove's production evidently showed, the sense of 'danger' can be restored in performance.

The likelihood of danger is emphasised several times in the play. The Duke reminds the soldiers of 'The fundamental reasons of this war, / Whose great decision hath much blood let forth, / And more thirsts after' (3.1.1–4). The King at first tries to deter Bertram from risking his life in a spirit of rash bravado and 'warlike principles' (2.1.1–3), underlining the gravity as *'divers young lords take leave for the Florentine war'* (stage direction). His 'Farewell, young lords' (2.1.1) may be their last farewell. The likelihood of danger and death is most powerfully expressed in Helena's sense of remorse for being the cause of Bertram's flight from marriage to war. As the play's central consciousness, she muses soulfully on the dreadful irony that she is herself to blame for his likely death in battle:

HELENA
                           Poor lord, is't I
That chase thee from thy country, and expose
Those tender limbs of thine to the event
Of the none-sparing war? And is it I
That drive thee from the sportive court, where thou
Wast shot at with fair eyes, to be the mark
Of smoky muskets? O you leaden messengers,
That ride upon the violent speed of fire,
Fly with false aim; move the still-piecing air,
That sings with piercing; do not touch my lord.
Whoever shoots at him, I set him there;
Whoever charges on his forward breast,
I am the caitiff that do hold him to't;
And, though I kill him not, I am the cause
His death was so effected. Better 'twere
I met the ravin lion when he roar'd
With sharp constraint of hunger; better 'twere
That all the miseries which nature owes
Were mine at once. No; come thou home, Rousillion,
Whence honour but of danger wins a scar,
As oft it loses all; I will be gone;
My being here it is that holds thee hence.
Shall I stay here to do't? No, no, although
The air of paradise did fan the house
And angels offic'd all. I will be gone,
That pitiful rumour may report my flight
To consolate thine ear. Come, night; end, day;

For with the dark, poor thief, I'll steal away.
Exit

(3.2.102–29)

The grim speech visualises the physical destructiveness of a war in which gunpowder is the main weapon and danger. Helena fully articulates the likelihood that although war may inflict an honourable scar, yet it could just as likely cause death, for which she feels personally guilty. Helena repeats her anguish in the letter to the Countess, pleading to have Bertram extricated from 'the bloody course of war' (3.4.8):

His taken labours bid him me forgive;
I, his despiteful Juno, sent him forth
From courtly friends, with camping foes to live,
Where death and danger dogs the heels of worth:
He is too good and fair for death and me;
Whom I myself embrace, to set him free.

(3.4.12–17)

Both these moving speeches are more detailed and clearly heartfelt than would be delivered if the war were nothing more than a dramatic pre-text or comic backdrop. They trace in visceral detail 'the bloody course of war' (3.4.8). There are enough signs in *All's Well* to indicate that Shakespeare is using war as a reference point for a multitude of 'dangers', subjective and objective, and not as an inconsequential diversion.

In Shakespeare's richly interpenetrating dramaturgy, nothing is wasted. Some critics suggest it is notions of courtly 'honour' and its betrayal which operate in both the amatory and military contexts and link them,[23] but the connections go further. As in his other comedies, the two locations of the play represent contrasting values. The court is linked with magical healing, Helena's desire, the gentle clowning of Lavatch, elderly nostalgia for the good old days in the autumnal note struck by the Countess, Lafew and the King. These are juxtaposed with the feckless youthfulness, sordid practical jokes, pranks, betrayals and desertions operating in the Florentine army camp, as the blind-folded, literally 'hood-winked' Parolles informs on the state of the rag-tag Florentine army, not realising his interlocuters are his own officers:

23. Derrin, '*Sine Dolore*' 93–4; Broomhall, '"The ambition in my love"': The Theater of Courtly Conduct in *All's Well That Ends Well*' in *The Palgrave Handbook of Shakespeare's Queens*, 367–8; Patrick Gray, *Critical Survey* 30 (2018), 1–25, 10, mentioning the dishonouring of Parolles in his 'betrayal of his comrades in arms' and Bertram's 'infidelity to his wife'.

PAROLLES
The troops are all scattered and the commanders are very poor rogues . . .
a truth's a truth; the rogues are marvellous poor.
FIRST SOLDIER
[*Reads*] *Demand of him, of what strength they are a-foot.* What say you
to that?
PAROLLES
By my troth, sir, if I were to live this present hour, I will tell true . . . so
that the muster-file, rotten and sound, upon my life, amounts not to fifteen thousand poll; half of the which dare not shake the snow from off
their cassocks lest they shake themselves to pieces.

(4.3.127–8; 156–65)

Bertram must swallow his previous 'warranted testimony' to Parolles'
valour and 'expertness in war' when he hears himself betrayed, much to
the amused sarcasm of the Second Lord:

BERTRAM
He shall be whipp'd through the army, with this rhyme in's forehead.
SECOND LORD
This is your devoted friend, sir, the manifold linguist and the armipotent
soldier.

(4.3.225–6)

It may all be comic in tone, but there are more sinister implications when
the play moves forward to the off-stage turning-point of the love-plot.

Curiously, it is the bed-trick which epitomises the 'rotten and sound'
army ethos in this play. For all its expedience in effecting a union which
in a utilitarian way 'ends well' for Helena, it is sordid and humiliating
for the woman. Sincere in her love, she is reduced to performing a clandestine sexual congress in the darkness in which her identity is a secret
as she acts as a 'dark, poor thief'. The 'hood-winked' trickery involved is
as shabby as the ridiculed deception of the blindfolded Parolles. The circumstances of the bed-trick return us disconcertingly to Helena's initial
aspiration, to lose her virginity to her own liking, whatever the means.

Shakespeare rarely (if ever) uses even the most unlikely and artificial
convention without investing it with some symbolic or psychological res-
onance, and the two occurrences of the bed-trick in his plays in *Measure
for Measure* and *All's Well* are no exceptions.[24] In both cases the event itself

24. Although there were two pre-Shakespearean plays using the bed-trick, *All's Well*
    seems to have been the one to 'bring the device into dramatic currency', according
    to Briggs in 'Shakespeare's Bed-Tricks', 1. But it was used earlier in prose romances,
    especially in the highly influential Sidney's *Arcadia* (Briggs 298–301). Here a
    psychological dimension is present in that it reunites the married couple who have

is a kind of 'revenge of the repressed', bringing back to consciousness an experience which each man would prefer to leave behind and forgotten – his marriage to Helena in Bertram's case, and the existence of Mariana in Angelo's. On both occasions the man literally does not know whom he is sleeping with. Analogously, in *Much Ado About Nothing* Claudio may not 'bed' Hero in darkness, yet he is prepared at the end of the play to marry a woman whom he has never seen, Hero's fictional 'sister', who is in reality Hero herself who is presumed dead. What links the cases is that both Claudio and Bertram are soldiers, and more importantly they have had virtually no meaningful or personal communication with the women who love them. Claudio's tongue-tied shyness is explicitly linked to his male, military company – a lion in war but a lamb in company. Bertram's case may be different in that he joins the army to escape a woman who has chosen him, but similar to Claudio's in that meaningful communication between them has been minimal.[25] Shakespeare emphasises that in one sense they have known each other since childhood and have even shared the same mother figure, the Countess,[26] but in another sense Bertram has never really known her as more than an inferior social type: 'A poor physician's daughter my wife? Disdain / Rather than corrupt me ever!' (2.3.115–16). His distaste and inability to appreciate her personal qualities are as superficial as Claudio's attraction to Hero's appearance. Like Claudio, Bertram has chosen as his congenial cohorts Parolles and the male company of an army camp. John C. Bean sees *All's Well* as a play which combines 'old tales and humanized women': 'What shocks us is not the bed-trick itself or any subtle problem of ethics, but the collusion of the human and the mechanical'.[27] In the military world Bertram has adopted, there is little room for 'humanized' women like Helena and Diana, and the only way he can relate to them is in a perfunctory, 'mechanical' act, a travesty of love.

For him, both Helena and Diana may just as well be interchangeable. Diana is the woman he thought he was fornicating with, professing his

---

both strayed into potentially adulterous relationships, desiring the same androgynous figure, a man disguised as a woman. Sidney seems to imply that since they have been driven by 'blind' sexual desire, coupling with each other is eventually the glue that holds them together and prevents adultery as in Marston's play *The Insatiate Countess* (1607).

25. Waller, 'Critical and Theatrical Emergence', 24.
26. For Adelman this raises the issue of incest: 'Bed Tricks', 154–6.
27. John C. Bean, 'Comic Structure and the Humanizing of Kate in *The Taming of the Shrew*', *The Woman's Part: Feminist Criticism of Shakespeare*, ed. Carolyn Ruth Swift Lenz, Gayle Greene, Carol Thomas Neely (Urbana: University of Illinois Press, 1980), 65–76, 75.

love and desire, but he can afterwards deny this and dismiss her as a prostitute who hangs around soldiers, 'a common gamester to the camp' (5.3.87) and the kind of 'Italian girl' the King had warned him against. By vigorously protesting, Diana joins the list of women in Shakespeare's 'army' plays accused of being 'common' camp-followers – Joan of Arc in *1 Henry VI* (at least in the eyes of English soldiers), Bianca in *Othello*, Cressida (and even Helen) in *Troilus and Cressida*. In different senses, they are as much victims of wartime circumstances and casual male assumptions, as the neglected wives, lovers and widows found elsewhere in Shakespeare.

The final *anagnorisis* or 'discovery' is revealed first by Helena's ostentatiously pregnant belly which solves one of the two 'riddles', proving visibly that 'one that's dead is quick' (5.3.297) as evidence of consummation. It also 'blows up' Bertram in more senses than one. The other apparently impossible condition set by Bertram is the exchange of the ring, a more material 'thing' exchanged by Diana and Helena as evidence of sexual union. As in *The Merchant of Venice*, the ring signifies a commodification symbolising marriage, and here it carries an explicit sexual reference betraying the 'wicked meaning in a lawful deed / And lawful meaning in a lawful act / Where both not sin, and yet a sinful act' (3.7.46–8). The depersonalised 'thing', to be made 'use' of (Parolles' word, 'use him as he uses thee' [1.1.210], and also Helena's 'But, O strange men! / That can such sweet use make of what they hate ...' [4.4.20–1]), is as much a material spoil of war as token of love. As in the ultimately successful, quasi-military campaign initiated by Helena with her battlefield imagery, the means of conquest justify the ends, and in the King's hesitantly qualified conclusion, 'All *yet seems* well, and if it end so sweet, / The bitter past, more welcome is the sweet' (5.3.327–8, my italics). The platitudinous sentiment is dangerously close to the other common adage that 'all's fair in love and war', or as Cervantes' Don Quixote amplified:

> observe that love and war are all one: and as in war it is lawful to use sleights and stratagems to overcome the enemy: So in amorous strifes and competencies, impostures and juggling tricks are held for good, to attain to the wished end.[28]

The sentiment can act as an ominous drum-roll to usher in the next of Shakespeare's soldiers, though in the minds of Iago and Othello the 'wished end' is not 'sweet', but murderous.

28. Miguel de Cervantes, *The History of Don Quixote of the Mancha*, transl. Thomas Shelton (London: 1620), Vol. 3, Second Part, ch. 21, 163 (modernised spelling).

Chapter 8

Make War, not Love: Othello's 'Occupation'

'The trade of war'

Othello is Shakespeare's most thoroughgoing anatomy of military life in its public and private facets. Prompted by bare hints in his source, he built upon them a disturbingly intimate vision of army relationships. However, he chooses to depict the ethos not in combat but while soldiers are 'at ease', highlighting not so much the violence of war but simmering professional rivalries, attitudes to women, and pressures on army marriages.

The protagonist's critical fortunes have swung more widely than those of other Shakespearean heroes, between admiration for a naïve but 'Noble Moor' and contempt for a 'braggart' whose 'self-pride becomes stupidity, ferocious stupidity, an insane and self-deceiving passion'.[1] Quite apart from the much debated subject of race and the disturbing focus on domestic violence, I suggest that this variability also partly stems from an ambivalence concerning the army context as depicted by the writer, particularly through its male protagonists. The perspective of critical distancing from the military ethos, implicit in *Othello*, *All's Well*, and *Antony and Cleopatra*, is made even more explicit in *Troilus and Cressida* and *Coriolanus*, forming a series of 'war plays'. An ever-growing mountain of criticism explores race and ethnicity in *Othello*, but the significance of the setting in an exclusively military environment, analysing characters as products of their ingrained professional training and standing, has attracted little sustained commentary.

1. Helen Gardner, 'The Noble Moor', *Proceedings of the British Academy*, 41 (1955); F. R. Leavis, 'Diabolic Intellect and the Noble Hero', *Scrutiny* 6 (1937), repr. In *The Common Pursuit* (London: Chatto and Windus, 1952), 146–7. See also Barbara Everett, 'Reflections on the Sentimentalist's Othello', *Critical Quarterly* 3 (1961), 127–39.

As with *All's Well* so with *Othello*, an arresting production can visually suggest an interpretation which sidesteps mainstream critical discourse and opens up new readings. Nicholas Hytner's acclaimed National Theatre production (2013), as one reviewer put it, 'pulls off, almost casually, a major reinterpretation, batting away the notion that Shakespeare's drama is dominated by racism', in favour of foregrounding the army setting:

> So central did Hytner consider the military context that he hired as an adviser Jonathan Shaw, who served in the army for more than 30 years. The appointment paid dividends. The sense of dependency between Othello and Iago which Shaw traces in an illuminating programme note is apparent in the production. 'Betrayal is the most heinous of military sins,' he writes, 'so it is the last to be suspected.' For once, Othello's credulity is convincing and Iago's hatred has not justification but cause.[2]

In Hytner's own words, 'the army is absolutely central to this play, [what] a life spent devoted to violence has done to the men who are at the centre of the play'.[3] According to another reviewer at the time, '. . . once the action shifts to Cyprus, we are in a modern military encampment, all wire fences, concrete bunkers and towering lights resembling erect cobras.[4]

The distinctiveness of this conception can be illustrated graphically by contrasting Olivier's version filmed from the stage (1965), where military visual imagery and costuming are erased from view, and the setting seems more like the court in Venice than army barracks in Cyprus.[5] The same is true of Orson Welles's movie, though its atmosphere is different again, and in *Othello* offshoots like *Jubal* (1956), *All Night Long* (1962) and *O* (2001) the army setting is completely removed as though it is not relevant to the play. The latest National Theatre production (2022) directed by Clint Dyer reduces the military imagery to minor status with Cassio wearing a kind of 'wing commander' badge, Emilia (presumably) an army number on her shoulder, and Othello practising martial arts and boxing. In contrast to Hytner's production, Dyer's is focused on the theme of race, though the last scenes show the influence of contemporary feminism, with Emilia being visually branded a victim of domes-

2. https://www.theguardian.com/culture/2013/apr/28/othello-adrian-lester-national-re view
3. https://www.youtube.com/watch?v=qHsaO2IpTYg
4. https://www.theguardian.com/culture/2013/apr/23/othello-iago-adrian-lester
5. See Honigmann's Arden edition (series 3) under 'Costume', 17. Like the other accounts to which he refers, this editor never addresses as important Othello's primarily, indeed sole 'occupation' as a military officer.

tic violence by a bruise under her eye. But the production does not tie the play directly to the army setting which, I shall argue, has profound repercussions for the three women in the play and their relationships with army officers.

I do not wish to minimise the important issue of race in the play which has fuelled an ever-growing and highly contested area of scholarship,[6] but will instead concentrate on the ubiquitous military setting. It is through and through an 'army play', turning on issues of military hierarchy, discipline, and 'the bubble reputation'. This will in its turn illuminate the issue of race in the play, since the construction of an alien, 'enemy other' lies at the heart of war strategy, here and more generally. Iago is the vehicle carrying this theme, from his early, prejudiced invective delivered to Brabantio, to his clinical undermining of Othello's initial confidence and self-assurance, forcing the general into social isolation, mental insecurity, paranoid jealousy, and finally murder. By internalising Iago's view, Othello creates in his own mind a fatal self-division that turns him, in effect, into his own enemy, the Other he should be fighting against, convinced that 'the devil hath ensnar'd his soul and body' (5.2.299), which in a secular sense is true. By the end, as Jonathan Burton suggests, in his act of killing himself, Othello himself becomes the 'malignant' Turk' that his profession in a Christian society dictates he must oppose.[7] Misogyny, racism, and xenophobia are identified as interrelated habits of mind, conditioned within the overarching, mascu-

6. Eldred Jones, *Othello's Countrymen: The African in English Renaissance Drama* (Oxford University Press, 1965); G. K. Hunter, 'Othello and Colour Prejudice', *Dramatic Identities and Cultural Tradition* (Liverpool University Press, 1978), 31–59 remains authoritative but there have been many more recent explorations of the subject. More recently, Patricia Akhimie, *Shakespeare and the Cultivation of Difference: Race and Conduct in the Early Modern World* (London: Routledge, 2018); Ania Loomba, *Shakespeare, Race, and Colonialism* (Oxford, 2002); Mary Floyd-Wilson, *English Ethnicity and Race* (Cambridge University Press, 2003); Stephen Cohen, 'I am what I am not: identifying with the other in Othello', *Shakespeare Survey* 64 (Cambridge, 2011); Ayanna Thompson, *Passing Strange: Shakespeare, Race, and Contemporary America* (Oxford, 2011); Carol Mejia LaPerle, 'Race in Shakespeare's tragedies', in *The Cambridge Companion to Shakespeare and Race*, ed. Ayanna Thompson (Cambridge University Press, 2021); Ayanna Thompson, *Colorblind Shakespeare: New Perspectives on Race and Performance* (London: Routledge, 2006), Ian Smith, *Black Shakespeare: Reading and Misreading Race* (Cambridge University Press, 2009). These are just the tip of a scholarly iceberg which includes many articles. A useful and thorough account of criticism generated by the play can be found in the resources of The Internet Shakespeare, accessed 1 April, 2023: https://internetshakespeare.uvic.ca/doc/Oth_CriticalSurvey/complete/index.html%3Fview=print.html

7. Jonathan Burton, '"A most wily bird": Leo Africanus, *Othello* and the trafficking

line context of a military worldview. They are both causes and effects of a profession dedicated to waging war against a clearly defined enemy.

Iago's self-definition is exclusively that of a professional soldier whose mindset is shaped by military matters. So much is clear from the opening exchange between Iago and Roderigo, which is significantly cut from Dyer's stage version. Iago's apoplectic rage, conveyed through incomplete lines and splenetic outbursts ('I know my price') and sarcasm, is entirely preoccupied with his general's decision to overlook him for promotion to lieutenant, in favour of Cassio:

IAGO   Three great ones of the city,
In personal suit to make me his lieutenant,
Off-capped to him, and, by the faith of man
I know my price, I am worth no worse a place.
But he, as loving his own pride and purposes,
Evades them, with a bombast circumstance
Horribly stuffed with epithets of war,
And in conclusion
Nonsuits my mediators. For 'Certes,' says he,
'I have already chose my officer.'
And what was he?
Forsooth, a great arithmetician,
One Michael Cassio, a Florentine,
A fellow almost damned in a fair wife,
That never set a squadron in the field
Nor the division of a battle knows
More than a spinster – unless the bookish theoric,
Wherein the toged consuls can propose
As masterly as he. Mere prattle without practice
Is all his soldiership – but he, sir, had th'election
And I, of whom his eyes had seen the proof
At Rhodes, at Cyprus and on other grounds,
Christian and heathen, must be be-leed and calmed
By debitor and creditor. This counter-caster,
He, in good time, must his lieutenant be
And I, God bless the mark, his Moorship's ancient!

               . . .
. . . 'tis the curse of service:
Preferment goes by letter and affection
And not by old gradation, where each second
Stood heir to th' first.

                             (1.1.7–37)

in difference', in Ania Loomba and Martin Orkin (eds), *Post-Colonial Shakespeares* (London: Routledge, 1998), 43–64, 58.

Here is 'engendered' the true 'monstrous birth' which the play must bring 'to the world's light' (1.3.403). Iago's professional jealousy towards Cassio, his hatred for the general who made the decision, and the slight to his own professional reputation, are what drive Iago towards the play's tragic 'foregone conclusion' (3.3.430). The toxic combination of competitiveness and jealousy mark also the Greek and Trojan armies in *Troilus and Cressida*, especially in attitudes towards Achilles and Nestor and existing in the mind of Troilus. As if confirming the continuing way in which professional norms infiltrate personal relationships, it is noteworthy how frequently jealousy based on rigid army expectations these days become a central issue in defamation cases concerning accusations of abusive relationships, and domestic violence, brought by and against army personnel.

There have been occasional critics who write with insider knowledge of army life from a Military Institute, seeing their own first-hand observations reflected in the plays. One such is a serving soldier (presumably male), writing anonymously and anecdotally in a 'blog' titled '"Tis the Curse of Service" ...'. The writer finds painfully recognisable the fierce competitiveness in the army ethos, emerging in the first scene and reflected in the play as a whole:

> My question is when did Shakespeare serve in the military? And I don't mean the 16th century English army or navy, but the 21st century US armed forces. I grew up in the Air Force and was married to the Air Force 20-plus years, and, as a journalist, worked for or with every branch of the US military. To me, Iago's actions and Othello's reactions are integral to the play's military context. Maybe Iago takes his being passed over for promotion to extremes – but maybe not.[8]

He sees the action that follows as unfolding inexorably from the first statements by Iago expressing a subaltern's resentment at being passed over for promotion. Iago is recognisable as an 'old school' career-soldier who believes promotion should be based on 'service', merit, experience, and order of ranking (the phrase 'Buggins' turn' originated in the British armed forces), and that criteria of class, academic qualifications and book-learning may be contemptuously disparaged as capricious favouritism. Jealousy is fashioned within an institution where competitiveness

---

8. '"Tis the Curse of Service": Iago is the Soldier's Soldier, That's Motivation Enough': http://www.shakespeareances.com/dialogues/commentary/Iago_Soldier-130517.html

   See also the article by another self-professed soldier-academic, C. F. Burgess, 'Othello's Occupation', *Shakespeare Quarterly* 26 (1975), 208–13, 210.

is the norm, and commonly encouraged to enhance individual efforts. Far from exhibiting the 'motiveless malignity' mooted by Coleridge,[9] Iago acts from a cluster of motives all leading back to his perception of professional humiliation in Othello's promotion of Cassio which activates his congenital proneness to jealousy.

From the outset, then, the three main male characters are defined in terms of their place within the professional hierarchy. There are different, carefully differentiated ranks of army officers in the play, as James Siemon points out, taking his lead from Michael Neill's words: 'The displaced Venetians of the Cypriot garrison are solidly located solely by virtue of the "place" they bring with them, above all their rank in the state's military hierarchy'.[10] Othello in his descriptions of his exotic past exploits seems to embody old-fashioned chivalric idealism and 'service' to the state, relying on his reputation and martial lineage (despite a period of enslavement). He asserts in his first words, 'My services which I have done the signiory ... I fetch my life and being / From men of royal siege' (1.2.18), and in his last, 'I have done the state some service, and they know't' (5.2.337). Others confirm this, including grudgingly even the one who hates him: 'Another of his fathom they have not / To lead their business' (1.1.152–3). Iago as ensign or 'ancient' (etymological variants in army terminology),[11] is a non-commissioned officer, and he exudes a time-serving and cynical attitude to his own place in the profession. He regards his lot as wearing out time, much like 'his master's ass, / For nought but provender, and when he's old, cashier'd' (1.1.43–7). He sees Cassio as a book-trained 'arithmetician' (1.1.18). 'Arithmetic' in the early modern period was regarded as an esoteric field of study, confined to the highly educated, and used especially by trained mariners in finding directions through the stars.[12] Accordingly, Iago regards Cassio as an arm-chair soldier, full of 'Mere prattle, without practice'. 'Toged consuls' has puzzled scholars, who sometimes propose it is a misprint for 'tongued', but I suggest it may indicate Iago's sneering

9. *Coleridge on Shakespeare*, ed. Terence Hawkes (Harmondsworth: Penguin Shakespeare Library, 1959).

10. Michael Neill, 'Changing Places in *Othello*', *Shakespeare Survey*, 37 (1984), 115–31, 116. The essay is reprinted in Michael Neill, *Putting History to the Question: Power, Politics and Society in English Renaissance Drama* (New York: Columbia University Press, 2000), 207–37, 118; James Siemon, 'Making Ambition Virtue? *Othello*, Small Wars, and Martial Profession' in Lena Cowen Orlin (ed.), *Othello: The State of Play* (London: Bloomsbury, 2014), 177–202, esp. 181–3.

11. Edelman, *Shakespeare's Military Language*, 124.

12. R. S. White, 'Making Something out of "Nothing"', *Shakespeare Survey*, 66, (2013): 232–45, 236–7.

contempt for university academics who wear robes and claim the superiority of intellectual 'consuls'. It may even obliquely reveal Shakespeare's own attitude towards the 'university wits' among his fellow playwrights. Given his educational attainments and his father's status in the community, Shakespeare could himself have attended university, but that he precluded himself from the obligatory bachelordom of a student by his pre-nuptial impregnation of Anne Hathaway. If he harboured any Iago-like resentment, it may have been shared by Ben Jonson, who was destined for Cambridge but was, instead, unwillingly apprenticed to his stepfather as a bricklayer. If so, the auto-didact Jonson's posthumous judgement of Shakespeare's 'small Latin and less Greek' may be more sympathetic and ironic than it seems.

Shakespeare is almost certainly tapping into an emerging, fashionable Elizabethan genre which has been analysed in some detail by Elizabeth Heale: 'The vivid expression of the experience of the soldier in war characterises what might be described as a new form of soldiers' writing that emerges in the 1570s'.[13] Heale does not mention *Othello* in her analysis of Gascoigne's *The Fruites of Warre*, Rich's *A Right Excelent and Pleasant Dialogue*, and *Churchyardes Chippes*, but these can be seen as indicating conceptual reference points for the play, familiar to audiences. In particular, Gascoigne's work turns on an implicit debate between a 'moralist', who is generally anti-war, and a journeyman soldier who claims authority from personal experience. The latter presents his testimony on behalf of war, but his point of view is also marked by exactly the complaining spirit voiced by Iago, as one who feels 'despised and abject'.[14] At the same time paradoxically, in Heale's words,

> solidarity, plainness and straightforwardness, rather than courtly eloquence and appearance, are the defining characteristics of these soldiers and their speech ... [presenting] the soldiers as simple and unpretentious, without 'any curiouse philed (filed) phrace' (para. 8).

Iago's public pose of 'honest' plain-speaker artfully distances him equally from what he represents as Othello's inflated 'bombast' and Cassio's 'learned lore' (Rich's phrase) drawn from book-learning. Iago defines himself as a soldier who, in Gascoigne's words, 'trudges' and 'toils' in service, with unrewarded humility.[15] With disastrous results, Othello trusts at face value his ensign's 'honest' service and his worldly knowledge, both of marriage and military life:

13. Heale, 'The Fruits of war', para. 3.
14. Heale, 'The Fruits of War', para. 10.
15. Gascoigne, quoted Heale, 'The Fruits of War', para. 36.

The fellow's of exceeding honesty
And knows all qualities, with a learned spirit,
Of human dealings.

$$(3.3.262\text{--}4)$$

In Iago's mind, hierarchy should also operate in marriage, as the man should rule his wife. However, even in this sphere he dreads the sexual anarchy of male competitiveness and female rebellion resulting in cuckolding. He advises Roderigo that the high-born and beautiful young woman who accompanies his general to war has married him only from 'a lust of the blood' and that 'she must change for youth' (1.3.335, 350). The marriage highlights emotional deficiencies in Iago's own, evidently jaded conjugal situation. His congenital jealousy extends to his own wife, having implausibly suspected Emilia of adultery with Othello (2.1.289–300). At the same time, he envies Othello's happiness in marriage, while acting as pimp for Roderigo's obsession with Desdemona, and even lusts after her himself. Iago is virtually a one-man embodiment of the evil proscribed by the Christian tenth commandment, 'Thou shall not covet . . .', admitting that his own jealousy affects him 'like a poisonous mineral' (2.1.296). He goes about transmitting the 'poison' of jealousy and envy, first to Brabantio and then to his general, determined to be 'evened with him, wife to wife'.[16] The cluster of emotions, emphasised by the dramatist at the outset but no more than hinted in his source, is located primarily in the professional sphere of army hierarchy, rank, obedience and reputation, and by analogy transposed by the men into marriage. This context provides webbing for 'The 'net / That shall enmesh them all' (2.3.368).

Circumstances fortuitously lead Iago towards his twin vengeances, to have Cassio disgraced and demoted, and to destroy his general's composure and marriage. His immediate act of revenge is against Othello, in his obscenity-laden outcry to inform Brabantio of his daughter's marriage. The animalistic imagery introduces the theme of dehumanising racial prejudice, as he warns the father that his new son-in-law is an 'old black ram' at that moment 'tupping' a 'white ewe', a 'Barbary horse' (with its calculated linguistic proximity to 'barbarian') with 'sooty bosom', and that the lovers are at that moment 'making the beast with two backs' (1.1.81–115 *passim*). It is arguably not clear from the text whether in fact Brabantio responds primarily to Iago's racial slurs, or instead is preoccupied with the secretiveness of the elopement and his daughter's

16. Meek, 'Othello's Sympathies: Emotion, Agency and Identification', *Shakespeare Survey* 74 (2022), 194–207, 200.

perceived betrayal: 'O, she deceives me / Past thought! ... O treason of the blood!' (1.1.166–7). His daughter's 'deception' is his first and primary concern. It is only later, prompted by Iago, that he mentions the issue of miscegenation in one speech (1.3.95–107). The power of Iago's imaginative projection is infectious. His value system is swallowed uncritically by Roderigo as the gull from whom Iago is extracting money to buy Desdemona, and it is imprinted on Brabantio who, it seems, has never had cause to see Othello in this way during a lengthy, hospitality-based friendship. Iago is seen as driven by an indoctrinated, guiding metaphor of readiness for war, valuing the dominance and aggression towards alien others that go with this, a mindset that permeates and explains his more general attitudes and actions. To explore the military context is to explain much else in the play, including racial and sexual stereotyping of an enemy as weapons of war.

If jealousy fanned by competition is one mainspring motivation in the Shakespearean army ethos here, so is the division of the world into opposed forces of 'us and them'. It is the inherently divisive logic of war itself, with its starkly binary definition of allies and enemies. Iago is locked into an indoctrinated mentality of conflict at every level, between a self and de-individualised 'other'.[17] Movies made during World War Two amply demonstrate that whole populations can be persuaded to identify an 'enemy' by cues based on crude stereotypes of language (in the case of Germans) and visible racial markers (Japanese), just as Iago defines Othello by his language ('horribly stuffed with epithets of war'), and his appearance as 'the Moor'. During the Gulf Wars between Anglo-American alliances and Muslim countries, language, religion and national or gendered clothing were used to differentiate enemy populations. In *Othello*, 'turban'd' Turks and the Ottoman empire in general are similarly demonised.

In a speech in which he gives the first of his many lies (in this case lying that he defended Othello's reputation against Roderigo's slights), Iago speaks with almost casual candour of the soldier's training to kill without compunction or 'iniquity' as part of his 'service' in 'the trade of war', when he deems moral or legal constraints to be lifted:

> Though in the trade of war I have slain men
> Yet do I hold it very stuff o' th' conscience
> To do no contrived murder: I lack iniquity
> Sometimes to do me service.

> (1.2.1–4)

---

17. See Dympna Callaghan, *Woman and Gender in Renaissance Tragedy* (Hemel Hempstead: Harvester Wheatsheaf, 1989), 129–30.

Even today, a defence against committing war crimes exists in Iago's distinction as killing in 'the heat of battle'. Like most of what Iago says, this must be addressed with suspicion. Although he claims to abide by a distinction of 'conscience' between what is appropriate in war but barred in civilian life, yet this is given the lie by his actions. His amoral understanding of 'service' in the military spills over into domestic life. By extension, marriage is seen by Iago as conflictual, amounting to enmity between man and woman. The central strategy used in his various vendettas equates to a habit of waging guerrilla warfare in the same way as actual war is, separating relationships by pitting man against man (Othello against Cassio), father against daughter (Brabantio and Desdemona), husband against wife (Othello and Desdemona, himself and Emilia), rank against rank (his own and Cassio's), and in racial terms white against black. Until he infects Brabantio, Iago is the only character who harps upon Othello's ethnicity, whereas the universally accepted identity of the general in the play is as a soldier and military hero. Iago systematically prises apart trust and intimacy by using his own obsessions with differences of skin colour (black and white), race (Venetian and Moorish), and gender (man and woman) to undermine Othello's initially secure and integrated sense of identity in his love relationship. Othello's later recognition when driven by Iago's insinuations, that 'Haply for I am black' (3.3.268), seems almost to come as a surprise to himself, just as when he surmises his age might be a problem in the marriage, seeing himself as 'declined / Into the vale of years – yet that's not much'. (3.3.269–70). By this stage he has become 'enmeshed' in Iago's binary way of thinking. In all these divisions, oppositions, and dislocations, Iago is working from two ingrained constructions integral to his own training as a soldier: hierarchical ordering of rank, and war's opposition between ally and enemy pitched in murderous conflict. The third military assumption, absolute obedience in following orders even in army marriage, will become relevant in the second half of the play in determining the tragic fate of Desdemona.

The source and the play

The story is told by Cinthio (nickname for Giovanni Battista Giraldi), in his prose work *Gli Hecathommithi* (1565), which Shakespeare also used in writing *Measure for Measure*.[18] Since the 'novella' is very short and

18. https://www.bl.uk/collection-items/cinthios-gli-hecatommithi-an-italian-source-for
    -othello-and-measure-for-measure

gave him little to work with, the dramatist needed to flesh out a lot of detail to turn it into his psychologically pitched play. In Cinthio the only name given is 'Disdemona' ('unfortunate') while the others are mere generic descriptors. 'Un capitano moro' is personalised in the play as Othello but referred to as much by his role as 'general' or his ethnicity as 'the Moor'. Conspicuously in Shakespeare's version, the wife is the only character who consistently refers to her husband by name, and she never sees his race or colour as an issue in their relationship: 'I saw Othello's visage in his mind' (1.3.253). Cinthio's unnamed 'ensign' becomes Iago, a near anagram for Spenser's villain in *The Faerie Queene*, Imago, as arch-magician or false image-maker. Allegorically, Iago also resembles 'Rumour' in *2 Henry IV* and Spenser's Blatant Beast of slander, spreading scandalous rumours about courtiers with its hundred biting dog-heads.[19] It insidiously infects everybody with whom it comes into contact. Spenser's Beast can be periodically imprisoned but always escapes and can never be killed, just as rumours of scandal cannot be finally extinguished, and Iago's final words seem to carry a similar sense of the indestructibility of slander: 'Demand me nothing, what you know, you know. / From this time forth I never will speak word' (5.2.300–1). In Shakespeare's adaptation the ensign's wife becomes Emilia ('industrious worker'). Cinthio describes her as 'young' but in the play she is a mature and experienced army wife. Her role is crucial as female confidante for the newly wed Desdemona, who (so far as we know) is motherless, abandoned by her father, jettisoned into a war zone with her officer husband, and in Kelsey Ridge's words, she has 'attached herself to his military life, military values, and military standards'.[20] Cinthio's 'captain' becomes Cassio, perhaps because he comes to be 'cashiered' for drunkenly assaulting Montano the governor of Cyprus. Others, such as Brabantio, the aristocratic gull Roderigo, Montana, Lodovico, and Bianca are Shakespeare's additions.

Another original creation is the marginalised 'Clown', Shakespeare's least relevant 'sad clown'. Although invariably cut in performance, in Shakespeare's text he is unobtrusively entrusted with the important function of punning on the significance for a soldier of the word 'lie':

DESDEMONA
Do you know, sirrah, where Lieutenant Cassio lies?
CLOWN
I dare not say he lies anywhere.

19. I suggested this in R. S. White, *Innocent Victims* (London: Athlone Press, 1986), 94, but it seems relevant here as well, given the strategy of 'false flags' in war.
20. Ridge, *Military Wives*, 35–6.

DESDEMONA
Why, man?
CLOWN
He's a soldier, and for one to say a soldier lies, 'tis stabbing.
(3.4.1–5)

The fatal ambiguity of lying is central to the main plot. Iago persistently lies. Desdemona is accused of lying to her father and husband, and later induced to tell her own 'white lie' about the handkerchief – 'It is not lost, but what an if it were?' (3.4.85). But it is the Fool's last line which stands out. It points towards the fatal mistake made by Othello, to trust implicitly as truth the lies told by his ensign, confident that a soldier would never lie since punishment would be death – ''tis stabbing'. The element of professional trust within military ranks is a key issue. Hemingway, who authored a short story collection significantly called *Men Without Women*, wrote in his memoir of wartime Paris, *A Moveable Feast*, 'In those days we did not trust anyone who had not been in the war, but we did not completely trust anyone'.[21] Any woman in the '*Othello* world' is presumed to be potentially less trustworthy than an army officer, as Jonathan Shaw sums up:

> this trust is why Othello believes Iago more than his wife. He has known him far longer. He thinks he understands him far better and he trusts him far more profoundly. Poor Desdemona doesn't stand a chance.[22]

One major area of dramaturgical amplification by Shakespeare of his source is the way he foregrounds the setting of Cyprus as an army camp. Described by Othello as 'a town of war', its inhabitants 'Yet wild, the people's hearts brimful of fear' (2.3.209–10) under occupation by troops from Venice. Awareness of disrupting such a community demonstrates Othello's sensitivity to the surrounding social context as the prime reason for condemning Cassio's disorderliness in a 'private and domestic quarrel' as a particularly 'monstrous' (2.3.211–13) breach of civil order in a foreign country. Toria Johnson sees the characterisation of Cyprus as suggestive of the 'affective community' of Cyprus apprehensively expecting Ottomite invasion.[23]

21. Ernest Hemingway, *A Moveable Feast* (New York: Charles Scribner's Sons, 1964), 41.
22. Jonathan Shaw, '"Mere prattle without Practice is all his Soldiership", Shaping the Soldier in Nicholas Hytner's *Othello*', Lidster and Massai, *Shakespeare at War*, 243.
23. Toria Johnson, 'Fear: Macbeth, Othello', in *Shakespeare and Emotion*, ed. Katharine Craik (Cambridge University Press, 2021), 199–210, 201.

Even though the play's Folio title is 'Othello, the Moore of Venice', it is not Venice but Cyprus which after the first Act becomes the dominant setting, and here the characters from Venice are foreigners or 'strangers'. This is an important counter to one critical tradition (stemming from the devious Iago himself) that Venice is traditionally a site associated with sexual intrigue, and that in this sense *Othello* is a 'Venetian' play.[24] Iago creates an imagined concept of now-distant Venice, as a kind of fusion between Nicolas Roeg's horror movie *Don't Look Now* (1973) and Casanova's obscene autobiography. He plays upon Othello's ignorance of 'super-subtle Venetian' aristocrats (1.3.357), secretive 'chamberers' with their 'soft parts of conversation' (3.3.269). In fact, however, even in Venice the soldiers are aliens. Othello is an indeterminate 'Moor', whose unknown provenance has generated much scholarly enquiry. Michael Cassio is variously and confusingly described as a Florentine (1.1.19) and a 'stranger' (3.3.204–5), from Verona (in the Folio with its ambiguous punctuation [2.1.26]).[25] Iago is also described as a 'Florentine' by Cassio (3.1.41), whose praise – 'I never knew / A Florentine more kind and honest' – is somewhat backhanded since in English propaganda Florentines were regarded as notorious masters of dissimulation and haters of 'virtue', hailing from the birthplace of Machiavelli.[26] Cassio may mean, 'If only my own [Florentine] compatriots were as kind and honest as this [non-Florentine] man'. Iago's name, it has been suggested, may indicate Spanish extraction,[27] but he projects himself as a man-of-the world, claiming to know from his travels the drinking habits of Danes, the 'swag-bellied Hollander', Germans, and English.[28] What the general, the ensign ('ancient') and lieutenant do have in common is not a common nationality but that they are all bound in the command structure of military service.

The circumstances drawing the characters to Cyprus is quite different in Cinthio's account from Shakespeare's. In the source the couple has been happily married for some time, against her family's wishes

---

24. Even Siemon in 'Making Ambition Virtue?' seems repeatedly to locate the events as primarily Venetian.

25. Both the Arden and Cambridge editors suggest the ship's provenance is Veronese, not Cassio, presumably because of the discrepancy with the reference to Cassio being a Florentine.

26. Honigmann (Arden ed.) *Othello*, 207; see also Susan Broomhall, '"The ambition in my love"', 360.

27. See Barbara Everett, 'Spanish Othello', *Shakespeare Survey*, 35 (1982), 101–112, repr. in *Young Hamlet*: 'Roderigo has a Spanish name, in short, because Iago has' (190).

28. Honigmann, *Othello*, 334; Everett, 'Spanish Othello'.

but without much apparent drama, and without the whirlwind speed of Shakespeare's opening scenes. In the source, Cyprus does not face a crisis, and the Moor is despatched routinely as the new chief in command:

> It happened at this time that the Venetian lords made a change in the forces they used to maintain in Cyprus; and they chose the Moor commandant of the soldiers whom they sent there. Although he was pleased by the honor offered him, (for such high rank and dignity is given only to noble and loyal men who have proved themselves most valiant), yet his happiness was lessened when he considered the length and dangers of the voyage, thinking that Disdemona would be much troubled by it.[29]

'Disdemona', however, like her namesake in *Othello*, proclaims her willingness to accompany her husband to war. She longs to be 'crossing the water with [him] in a safe, well-furnished galley' (272). This settled, they sail in the same boat on 'a sea of the utmost tranquillity' (373), and 'arrive safely' in Cyprus. It is all quite leisurely and untroubled. The presence of the Iago and Emilia figures is explained by Cinthio, leaving no doubt about the former's proclivity to evil and deception:

> The Moor had in his company an Ensign, of handsome presence, but of the most scoundrelly nature in the world. He was in high favour with the Moor, who had no suspiciousness of his wickedness; for, although he had the basest of minds, he so cloaked the vileness hidden in his heart with high sounding and noble words, and by his manner, that he showed himself in the likeness of a Hector or an Achilles. This false man had likewise taken to Cyprus his wife, a fair, and honest young woman. Being an Italian she was much loved by the Moor's wife, and spent the greater part of the day with her. (p. 373)

There is little sign of Shakespeare's astonishingly complex character, except in Cinthio's remark that he 'cloaked the vileness hidden in his heart'.

In Shakespeare's adaptation, Venice is buzzing with news that Othello is chosen to lead an immediate embarkation of troops to Cyprus, as Iago informs Brabantio even before Othello himself knows it (1.1.147–52). Cassio brings the 'news' to his general as a matter of 'post-haste' urgency, 'even on the instant':

> It is a business of some heat. The galleys
> Have sent a dozen sequent messengers

---

29. Quotation from Honigmann, *Othello*, Appendix 3, 371–2.

> This very night, at one another's heels,
> And many of the consuls, raised and met,
> Are at the duke's already. You have been hotly call'd for.
>
> (1.2.36–44)

Shakespeare provides considerable detail about the war which is considered the main business of the day by all except Brabantio. In the council-chamber, the Duke of Venice and senators discuss the report that a 'disproportion'd' Turkish fleet, rumoured to estimate between 107, 140 and 200 galleys, is preparing to invade Cyprus which is governed by Venice (1.3.5–8). A 'Sailor' enters as 'A messenger from the galleys', confirming that 'The Turkish preparation makes for Rhodes' (1.3.15), which the Duke and Senators sceptically think is a diversionary ruse, 'a pageant / To keep us in false gaze' (1.3.19–20), believing the Turks are heading to Cyprus: 'Nay, in all confidence, he's not for Rhodes' (1.3.32). News now comes that the Ottomites' fleet is indeed 'Steering with due course towards the isle of Rhodes' but that they will there be 'injointed with an after fleet' of thirty ships, 'bearing with frank appearance / Their purposes toward Cyprus' (1.3.39–40). The Duke concludes, ''Tis certain, then, for Cyprus'. Othello is rapidly given his orders: 'Valiant Othello, we must straight employ you / Against the general enemy Ottoman' (1.3.49–50). Compared with his source, Shakespeare's account is more circumstantially focused on military details, and far more precipitate.

Brabantio enters, and brushes off the 'affairs of state' since he is personally distraught by the news that his daughter has apparently been seduced by the Moor. His outburst comes as a distraction from state affairs, and after hearing from Othello and Desdemona, the Duke overrules him, choosing to base his judgement on moral grounds: 'If virtue no delighted beauty lack, / Your son-in-law is far more fair than black' (1.2.331). He returns to the main task of briefing Othello as a soldier: 'you must therefore be content to slubber the gloss of your new fortunes with this more stubborn and boisterous expedition' (1.3.227–9). Othello accepts his orders as a welcome change from peaceful 'custom' which he regards as lazy self-indulgence, in contrast to his mission as soldier:

> The tyrant custom, most grave senators,
> Hath made the flinty and steel couch of war
> My thrice-driven bed of down. I do agnize
> A natural and prompt alacrity
> I find in hardness, and do undertake
> These present wars against the Ottomites.
>
> (1.3.230–5)

Still unwilling to accept the marriage, Brabantio refuses to take his daughter into his house while Othello is absent, and Desdemona herself rejects this possibility, strongly voicing her determination to accompany her new husband: 'That I did love the Moor to live with him / My downright violence and storm of fortunes / May trumpet to the world' (1.3.249–51), forthrightly swearing that she will not 'be left behind, / A moth of peace, and he go to the war' (1.3.248–67). She is herself elevating her husband's priority and the vocabulary of war over love, declaring herself an 'army wife'. Undoubtedly it had been Othello's life of 'battles, sieges, fortunes' which had awakened her love. For his part, Othello reassures the Duke he will not let marital desire interfere with military duties, considering the 'serious and great business' of soldiering in the service of the state as more important than 'light-wing'd toys / Of feather'd Cupid' (1.3.266–75). Here is at least a faint foreboding that in the circumstances of potential war he may come to face an inner conflict between his roles as lover and soldier. A psychologically inclined critic, Joanna Byles (at that time working on-the-spot at the University of Cyprus and therefore alert to the importance of the setting), has described Othello's attitude as the soldier's 'denial of eros, and the displacement of the erotic energy' into the needs of warfare.[30] Preoccupied by the military situation, the Duke leaves it up to the couple to decide, so long as they are quick: 'Be it as you shall privately determine, / Either for her stay or going: th'affair cries haste / And speed must answer it' (276–8). Shakespeare has changed his source, using the urgency of an impending military encounter to explain an immediate change of location, and to contrast love and war as though they are alternatives. Othello's ingrained priority is for military service, and in this Desdemona supports him.

Shakespeare makes another, complementary change to his source, which will also have symbolic and narrative reverberations. Desdemona is to sail with Emilia and Iago, while Othello travels on a different boat. The latter's journey is far from Cinthio's 'safe' transition on 'a sea of the utmost tranquillity', since Shakespeare invents a massive storm at sea which risks shipwrecks (2.1.11–17). Michael Neill interprets this in a psychological and allegorical sense: 'the sea-voyage amounts to a rite of passage; it is as though some fatal boundary had been crossed – from where this bourne no traveller returns'.[31] Neill also sees the significance

---

30. Joanna Montgomery Byles, 1989, 1995. Quoted also in '"The Cyprus Wars": Psychoanalysis and Race in Shakespeare's *Othello*', *Actes du colloque tenu à Lyon*, 1997, Université Lumière-Lyon 2, Université de Chypre, 139–46, 142. Repr. online at https://www.persee.fr/doc/mom_1274-6525_2000_act_31_1_1852.
31. Neill, 'Changing Places in *Othello*', 116.

of the changed geographical location as 'a movement to a narrower, more enclosed world, a place of colonial exile – a movement from city to garrison town'.[32] The Venetian convoy does arrive safely, one ship at a time, the first carrying Cassio. He greets the governor of 'this warlike isle' Montano, who emphasises the military context by commenting that Othello 'commands / Like a full soldier' (2.1.35–6). Then comes the ship bearing Desdemona, Iago, Emilia and Roderigo, and finally, after some suspense, Othello's, vessel. His greeting to his wife maintains the martial note: 'O my fair warrior' (2.1.180). C. F. Burgess sees the exclamation as not just an extravagant 'random term of endearment', but a reflection of Othello's satisfaction at Desdemona's 'passing her first test as a soldier's wife', tying her in to the army environment.[33] Her more personal response, 'My dear Othello', is subtly inauspicious in that she is looking forward to loving companionship while her husband is focused on the war.[34] In a kind of verbal embrace, she has been drawn into the mental world of her husband's past: 'Of moving accidents by flood and field, / Of hair-breadth scapes i'th' imminent deadly breach' (1.3.6–7). Desdemona has been inducted into Othello's familiar territory of army ranks as his 'fair warrior', and the marital is already in the process of being infiltrated by the martial.

Something disturbingly similar had already happened for Desdemona while waiting anxiously on the beach for her husband. Iago's misogynistic contempt for his wife and his sexualised banter verbally coerce Desdemona into simply tolerating and responding in kind: 'I am not merry, but I do beguile / The thing I am by seeming otherwise' (2.1.121–2). It is a Freudian theory that 'tendentious' jokes are a sexually charged ploy, and that if a woman can be lured into such repartee it is taken as a sign that she shares its assumptions and 'enjoys' the innuendos.[35] The note struck by Iago is a part of what Lynda E. Boose has described as a 'pornographic aesthetic' running through the play, in which men – or at least these particular men who are comfortable in their masculine professional and social culture – routinely adopt a 'defensive fantasy that all women are insatiably carnal', and see them as '"fair papers" and "goodly books" that are made to write "whore" upon'.[36] In a play which deals with deeply unpleasant subjects including racism, domestic vio-

32. Neill, 'Changing Places in *Othello*', 115.
33. C. F. Burgess, 'Othello's Occupation', *Shakespeare Quarterly* 26 (1975), 208–13, 210.
34. Martin Elliott, *Shakespeare's Invention of Othello* (London: Macmillan, 1988), 19.
35. Sigmund Freud, *The Joke and its Relation to the Unconscious* (1905), trans. Joyce Crick (London: Penguin Classics, 2003).
36. Lynda E. Boose, '"Let it be hid": The Pornographic Aesthetic of Shakespeare's

lence, murder, and suicide, the age-old and multi-faceted nexus between war and sex is continually activated through unrestrained language of prejudice in its various guises.[37] It is the ethos in which Iago thrives, and which from now on owns, as his special zone of social operation.

Cyprus

In an anticlimax, the enemy vessels are all shipwrecked. War itself is no longer an issue and the Venetian army finds itself unexpectedly idle.

This is not a genuine moment of peace in the play, but merely a temporary and uneasy cessation of arms in an ongoing war against the Turks, which is the only reason the Venetian army is occupying Cyprus. Since war is the ultimate forum of validation for armed forces, their own *raison d'être*, an imminent conflict which never takes place or is at most deferred, can be perceived as within military operations. However, the decimation of the Turkish threat is cause for overnight festivity, to which is added the occasion for celebrating the general's nuptials, as twin excuses for 'sport and revels':

> HERALD
> *It is Othello's pleasure, our noble and valiant general, that, upon certain tidings now arrived, importing the mere perdition of the Turkish fleet, every man put himself into triumph; some to dance, some to make bonfires, each man to what sport and revels his addiction leads him. For besides these beneficial news, it is the celebration of his nuptial.* – So much was his pleasure should be proclaimed. All offices are open, and there is full liberty of feasting from this present hour of five till the bell have told eleven. Heaven bless the isle of Cyprus and our noble general Othello!
>
> (2.1.1–12)

Even at leisure the military culture prevails in a spirit of camaraderie and indulgence. The women, Desdemona, Emilia and later the Cypriot Bianca now face an all-male domain of idle soldiers on 'rest and recreation'

Othello', *New Casebooks Othello*, ed. Lena Cowen Orlin (London: Palgrave Macmillan, 2004), 22–48, 29.

37. For research on modern manifestations, see Daniel M. Clayton, 'Whitewashing WWII Sexual Memory', *War, Literature and the Arts: An International Journal of the Humanities*, 27 (2015), online journal (accessed 28 April 2021): https://www.wlajournal.com/wlaarchive/27/Clayton.pdf. See also Joshua S. Goldstein, *War and Gender* (Cambridge University Press, 2001), esp. ch. 6, 'Conquests: sex, rape, and exploitation in wartime'.

in foreign parts. An emotional equivalent might be the phenomenon in Australian football known as 'Mad Monday' after the season ends. Players are let off the leash of discipline, on a day marked all too often by charges of intoxicated carousing and disruptions to civilian life, a microcosm of every V-Day after war as triumphant soldiers return to civilian life. The new context is explained by Hytner's military adviser in this way:

> I described how it is easier to command on operations than in peace-time. Operations give an urgency, a motivation, an overriding reason for orders and obedience; having an enemy disciplines the troops . . . In a peacetime garrison, your enemy is boredom, particularly in the heat of Cyprus. Command involves that fine judgement of working the troops just hard enough to keep them occupied but not too hard to provoke a revolt.[38]

At such times, alcohol is the danger, leading to 'loose tongues' and worse.

Iago describes the fraternising of Cypriots and Venetian soldiers as a 'flock of drunkards' (2.3.56), as he jokingly sings a soldier's *epileny* for 'boys', accompanied by the clanking of (no doubt) army-ration metal cups:

> IAGO
>   A soldier's a man,
>   O, life's but a span,
> Why, then, let a soldier drink!
> Some wine, boys!
>
> (2.3.68–70)

In the unrestrained revelry Iago cajoles Cassio into unaccustomed drunkenness, and the night degenerates into bar-room arguments leading to the inflammatory violence of a 'barbarous brawl' (2.3.168) between Cassio and Montano. The noisy mêlée disturbs the marital 'rites' of Othello and Desdemona, who never seem to have an opportunity to consummate their marriage, and leads to the next stage of the play.

Some cultural historians analyse the attitudes lying behind such 'misrule' as psychologically driven and an inverted product of the soldiers' ethos:

> Basic training, from the donning of a uniform to being subjected to a relentless series of drills and chants, induces a lessening of self-awareness.

38. Shaw, 'Shaping the Soldier', *Shakespeare at War*, 240.

Such a process of de-individuation can lead to the weakening of restraints against prohibited forms of behaviour. This is coupled with the fact that positive military values include aggression, dominance and overt displays of physical prowess. Sensitivity, understanding and compassion are routinely derided.[39]

Joanna Byles's reading runs along the same lines:

Within this military-garrison setting, Shakespeare is possibly adopting an anti-war view, or at any rate a critical view of military life and the uncontrolled male violence it allows as it 'carves' for itself its 'own rage'.[40]

To support this view, some additional details might be offered. First, the setting illuminates male bonding in military life as evidenced not in war but in recreation linked with peace regarded as 'wanton dullness'. Secondly, it unleashes a set of disparaging, fantasy views of women. Thirdly, it liberates latent aggression and jealousy now unlicensed by strict regulations, orderly regimentation, and parade ground orders, signifying the breach of the third pillar of army life beside competition and hierarchy – discipline. Barbara Everett puts the same point in a different way:

The Venetians' staying on in Cyprus without the rationalization of military activity generates an energy of anxiety exacerbated by Cassio's loss of control – an action which implies a threat to Othello's control over his men. Desdemona's own headstrong if generous support of Cassio extends that male threat to the General's dignity by something new: the much larger if sweeter challenge given to male superiority and status by the undermining, unhierarchical directness of the female, unimpressed by male ranking.[41]

It is Cassio's insubordination which especially arouses Othello's anger:[42]

Now, by heaven,
My blood begins my safer guides to rule,

39. Joanna Bourke, 'From Surrey to Basra, abuse is a fact of British army life', 26 February 2005 (accessed 24 August 2022). https://www.theguardian.com/uk/2005/feb/26/military.iraq
    Bourke is the writer of *Fear: A Cultural History* (Avalen: Shoemaker & Hoard, 2006).
40. Byles, 'The Problem of the Self', 144.
41. Barbara Everett, *Young Hamlet: Essays on Shakespeare's Tragedies* (Oxford: Clarendon Press, 1989), 55.
42. Richard Meek, 'Othello's Sympathies', 198.

And passion, having my best judgement collied,
Assays to lead the way.

(2.3.197–200)

In the second half of the play it is discipline, seen as sacrosanct in any armed forces, which will become a major issue.

As part of the male environment, the 'general camp' in Cyprus is represented as a culture where men sleep in close proximity. Iago, who seems not to sleep with his wife, takes advantage of this understanding in his voyeuristic and salacious description of sleeping with Cassio. It is a typically concocted lie which Iago knows Cassio can hardly refute, and certainly part of Iago's revenge against the now ex-lieutenant, but it adds substance to the impression of the garrison's overwhelmingly masculine *milieu*:

> There are a kind of men
> So loose of soul that in their sleeps will mutter
> Their affairs – one of this kind is Cassio.
> In sleep I heard him say 'Sweet Desdemona,
> Let us be wary, let us hide our loves'
> And then, sir, would he gripe and wring my hand,
> Cry 'O sweet creature!' and then kiss me hard
> As if he plucked up kisses by the roots
> That grew upon my lips, then laid his leg o'er my thigh,
> And sigh, and kiss, and then cry 'Cursed fate
> That gave thee to the Moor!'

(3.3.418–28)

The general air of intimate masculinity dominates how the soldiers talk, behave, and think. Women are regarded as a distraction (as Cassio comes to regard Bianca), a nuisance (as Iago regards Emilia), targets for sexist jokes from Iago, or as a cause of divided attention (as Othello finds when their marital privacy is constantly disrupted). The basis of the prevailing misogyny seems normative and unchallenged amongst soldiers, mirroring the preference for war expressed by the Servingmen in *Coriolanus*, that 'peace is a great maker of cuckolds' (4.5.237).

Army Parlance

Despite its anticlimactic deferral of war itself, *Othello* is built upon a foundation of army protocol, signalled in insistent rhetoric, preoccupations, and codes of conduct. In repenting of his public loss of self-control which turns him into a 'night brawler', Cassio acknowledges remorsefully that his 'reputation' as a soldier is the only thing that concerns him:

> CASSIO
> Reputation, reputation, reputation! O, I have lost my reputation, I have lost the immortal part of myself – and what remains is bestial. My reputation, Iago, my reputation!
>
> (2.3.258–61)

Montano too has 'unlaced' his public 'reputation' in fighting with Cassio. All four army officers regard the 'immortal part' of individual selfhood is reputation in the eyes of their professional peer group, while Desdemona loses her life because of a false and fabricated 'reputation' as promiscuous. Cassio's outburst is scorned by Iago, punning on the word 'repute' and reinterpreting reputation as something just as easily retrieved as lost (as easily as a handkerchief, it transpires):

> Reputation is an idle and most false imposition, oft got without merit and lost without deserving. You have lost no reputation at all, unless you repute yourself such a loser.
>
> (2.3.264–7)

Iago's riposte has a touch of barely concealed bitterness, in the light of his opinions that Cassio's promotion was 'got without merit' and his own deserved status 'lost' – or at least overlooked – 'without deserving'. However, his cynically lighthearted tone is explained by the fact that he has just proved his own adage, by successfully plotting to reinstate himself into his general's favour and regain the office of lieutenant. Othello equally regards his good name in the eyes of his superiors as all-important, and when he is wrongly convinced of his wife's infidelity his main worry is that his 'occupation's gone' (3.3.360). In two senses this word invokes army status. Regarding himself as a cuckolded husband whose possession of a wife has been taken over by another, the word is a reference to an army 'occupying' a piece of land, akin to the Venetian troops 'occupying' Cyprus. But more simply, Othello is referring to losing his 'job' or career, as the commanding general in an army on a state mission, since being an army officer is the main marker of his identity. To neutral onstage observers, the change that comes over Othello's equanimity and competence is mystifying. Lodovico asks incredulously, 'Is this the noble Moor, whom our full senate / Call all-in-all sufficient? This the nature / Whom passion could not shake?' (4.1.264–5). His military control and command over his men is lost and he is stripped of his rank in disgrace and 'commanded' back to Venice. In Iago's word he is a 'loser' (2.3.267) who has forfeited the army's most important male aspiration, a reputation based on meritorious praise. The anguish Othello is misguidedly made to feel about his marriage and his wife, resulting in all-consuming jealousy, is the feeling he has betrayed his military 'occupation' and has threatened his identification with its code of conduct and its culture measured – precisely the shame, indeed, that Cassio feels after being disgraced in the public eye.

Accustomed to issuing clear, irresistible orders that must be obeyed, and relying absolutely on the integrity of the men under his command,[43] the general succumbs to 'doubt' his military judgement. 'Doubt' is not a word with substantive meaning in the soldier's lexicon: 'No: to be once in doubt / Is once to be resolved' (3.3.182–3). Gayle Greene points out that we hear from Othello's lips 'words like "never", "all", "forever", in a tendency to absolutes which points to an inability to tolerate ambiguity or uncertainty, a failure of irony'.[44] But Greene sees this trait as that of a generalised male personality rather than an occupational hazard of the army's relentless training in decisive action. Derek Cohen notes that Othello's mission as a soldier signifies that 'he cannot be allowed, as perhaps Hamlet can, to take two sides at once', in the light of a militia's totalist identification with the aims of nationhood and nationalism.[45] We might ask why the arch-ironist Iago does not suffer from the same 'failure'. The answer seems to lie partly in his capacity to convince himself of certitudes even when they are not true, substituting judgemental certainty for all grey areas of ambiguity, and partly because as part of his binary thinking he has identified a new set of enemies in Cassio and Othello. All his generalised opinions are categorical prejudices: that academically trained officers are not as qualified for promotion as soldiers trained in the field, that black men are barbarians, foreigners are cheap (Cyprians), enemies are heathen (Turks), women are fickle and lustful, and so on. His way of coping with uncertainty, ambiguity and complex reality is to adopt such rigid and divisive assumptions. Othello reacts to 'doubt' with confusion, mental disintegration, and radical mistrust of evidence. In many ways his marital behaviour is more like that of the stereotyped returned serviceman who suspects his wife of having affairs in 'stolen hours of lust' (3.3.341) in his absence, frustrated because he can never be given 'ocular proof' (3.3.363) because clandestine episodes

43. Burgess, 'Othello's Occupation', 211.
44. Gayle Greene, '"This that you call love": Sexual and Social Tragedy in *Othello*', in *Shakespeare And Gender: A History*, ed. Deborah E. Barker and Ivo Kamps (London: Verso, 1995), 47–62, 49.
45. Derek Cohen, 'Tragedy and the Nation: *Othello*', *Searching Shakespeare: Studies in Culture and Authority* (University of Toronto Press, 2003), 3–18, 11.

are by definition kept secret. 'Perplexed in the extreme' (5.2.346), past, present and future become jumbled in his mind, as psychological time displaces the evidence and logic of chronological time under the pressure of jealousy. The 'doubt' sowed by Iago and the temporal anomalies of a 'double time scheme' operating in the play as a whole have upended Othello's mind.[46]

Language provides the sharpest insight into the internalisation of military values in the play. Othello's own distinctive poetic utterance has always aroused hotly debated critical responses. It was Iago, using a contrasting prose designed to forward the image of himself as an 'honest', sceptical truth-teller, who set the critical debate going, in skewering his general's habit of speaking poetry laced 'with a bombast circumstance / Horribly stuff'd with epithets of war' (1.1.10–13), motivating his own determination to 'set down the pegs that make this music' (2.1.199). He is right, insofar as simultaneously Othello's poetry is initially 'well tuned' (2.1.198) music[47] used in the service of 'epithets of war'. Even in his early self-confidence, he confesses he has no experience of anything beyond the military life:

> Rude am I in my speech,
> And little blest with the soft phrase of peace,
> For since these arms of mine had seven years' pith,
> Till now some nine moons wasted, they have used
> Their dearest action in the tented field,
> And little of this great world can I speak
> More than pertains to feats of broil and battle,
> And therefore little shall I grace my cause
> In speaking for myself.
>
> (1.3.82–90)

His excuse for not speaking with 'the soft phrase of peace' is that he is more accustomed to barking orders to men in the 'tented field' than whispering pleasantries to a wife. In initially dazzling Desdemona, Othello has recounted mainly battle stories: 'From year to year – the battles, sieges, fortunes / That I have passed . . .' (1.3.130–2). 'Tyrant custom' has made the 'flinty and steel couch of war' his accustomed bed. Language is the instrument of his leadership, able to quell a brawl

---

46. For evidence of the double time scheme and its importance to the play, see Steve Sohmer, 'The "Double Time" Crux in *Othello* Solved', *English Literary Renaissance*, 32 (2002), 214–38, and references. However, Sohmer's 'solution' based on the differences between the Gregorian and Julian calendars seems over-ingenious.
47. G. Wilson Knight, *The Wheel of Fire* (Oxford University Press, 1930), 106.

with a sentence mingling command and 'a kind of soldierly simplicity' as Burgess describes it[48] – 'Keep up your bright swords, for the dew will rust them' (1.2.59). His later, tormented moments of self-denigrating abjection return to war as his prime frame of reference, a world he is losing in what he describes in child-like terms as 'the big wars' and 'glorious war':

> Farewell the neighing steed and the shrill trump,
> The spirit-stirring drum, th'ear-piercing fife,
> The royal banner, and all quality,
> Pride, pomp and circumstance of glorious war!
>
>   (3.3.354 –357)

It is quite a peculiar and revealing train of thought, since he does not 'farewell' the wife whom he is deluded has been unfaithful, nor his marriage, but the pageantry of war. He reveals his priorities in lamenting the loss of 'content' provided by male companionship in 'the general camp' as the congenial source for his 'tranquil mind'. What he now thinks of his wife is also obscenely linked with his troops:

> I had been happy if the general camp,
> Pioneers and all, had tasted her sweet body,
> So I had nothing known.
>
>   (3.3.348–50)

'Pioneer' is a silent and unnecessary emendation from the text's 'pioner', which was a specific noun denoting a '(military) Digger, miner, one employed in minor engineering works', the lowly soldier who goes ahead of the army to dig trenches and is thus placed vulnerably in the vanguard, like the proverbial canary sent down a mine to test its safety.[49] Edelman adds that he is one who needs 'no skill other than the ability to do hard labour . . . Such dangerous or unpleasant tasks could be assigned as punishment duty'.[50] It is, then, a class reference and a specialised military term, and would occur only to one whose world revolves exclusively around the clear definition of ranks and duties in the army. Such knowledge is Othello's *modus operandi* in the 'hard wiring' of his mind. He stands alongside Coriolanus as an example of Shakespeare's observation of the military mind, reliant on the certainties of a professional hierarchy.

48. Burgess, 'Othello's Occupation', 211.
49. C. T. Onions, rev. Robert D. Eagleson, *A Shakespeare Glossary* (Oxford University Press, 1986), 201.
50. Charles Edelman, *Shakespeare's Military Language: A Dictionary* (London: Athlone Press, 2000), 256.

In such a world, as Burgess puts it, 'Othello has been conditioned to expect absolute loyalty and honesty from his subordinates', so why would he mistrust Iago or suspect duplicity and dissembling? He works within parameters which are 'regimented, disciplined and, above all, unequivocal'.[51] This philosophy is understood only too well by Iago, who swears 'service' to his superior in his most blood-curdling affirmation:

> IAGO   Let him *command*
> And to *obey* shall be in me remorse[52]
> What bloody business ever.
>
>   (3.3.470–3, my italics)

Iago concludes chillingly, 'I am your own forever' (482), confirming the relationship is based on a reassuring certainty of issuing and obeying commands. A psychologist who has worked with army veterans suffering combat trauma has observed how important is trust in the armed forces, and how its breakdown is a threat to self-trust and identity itself, a fact which Iago, even as an underling in the hierarchy, knows full well and exploits to the full:

> Lies and euphemisms by the soldier's own military superiors and civilian leaders of course undermine social trust by destroying confidence in language ... The enemy [strikes] not only at the body but also at the most basic functions of the soldier's mind, attacking his perceptions by concealment; his cognitions by camouflage and deception; his intentions by surprise, anticipation, and ambush. These mind games have been part of war since time immemorial.[53]

To the very end Othello is incapable of relinquishing habits of thought about military obligations revealed in the specialist vocabulary, imagery and assumptions of a concealed enemy. The habits persist to his dying words, as 'weapon'd' he refers to his 'soldier's thigh' holding a 'good sword', and claiming once again that he has obediently 'done the state some service and they know't', (5.2.256–337 *passim*). In speaking his

---

51. Burgess, 'Othello's Occupation', 211.
52. 'Remorse' is puzzling, but modern editors accept its meaning as 'pity' for the 'wronged Othello', but at the cost of disrupting the scansion, 'in me ^*no*^ remorse' [regret] seems to make better sense and is a more normal sense of the word as contrition or repentance.
53. Whalen, 'A Hell of One's Own', 6–7, paraphrasing Jonathan Shay, *Achilles in Vietnam: Combat Trauma and the Undoing of Character* (New York: Touchstone, 1995), 34.

own obituary he emphasises the dictates of his military service, and in doing so reverts to professional type. His fatal mistake has been to trust his army training and his ingratiating colleague-in-arms Iago, and gullibly allowed himself to turn marriage into a misplaced battlefield.

Military wives and lovers

In this play, Shakespeare foregrounds the company of men in arms whose collective attitudes exclude, distort, misjudge, or at least marginalise women. They see three dehumanised categories of women, angels, whores (fallen angels), and 'housewives' (2.1.112 and 4.1.95) who are destined, in Iago's dismissive phrase, 'To suckle fools, and chronicle small beer' (2.1.160). As in the case of racial slurs in the play, Iago is again the initiator, turning his 'slanderous' invective on his wife, despite her protests and Desdemona's disapproval:

> IAGO
> Come on, come on, you are pictures out of doors,
> Bells in your parlours, wild-cats in your kitchens,
> Saints in your injuries, devils being offended,
> Players in your housewifery, and housewives in . . .
> Your beds!
> DESDEMONA
>   O, fie upon thee, slanderer!
>
>   (2.1.109–13)

In contrast, Cassio's hyperboles are an opposite but equally stereotyped and almost laughable idealisation of 'the divine Desdemona' (2.1.73):

>   O, behold,
> The riches of the ship is come on shore:
> You men of Cyprus, let her have your knees!
> Hail to thee, lady, and the grace of heaven,
> Before, behind thee, and on every hand,
> Enwheel thee round!
>
>   (2.1.82–7)

The women all resist the reductive valuations imposed upon them.

Bianca is a social casualty of what is sometimes indulgently described as harmless male 'locker room banter'. Iago, casual visitor to Cyprus as he is, speaks knowingly of her as a prostitute suffering 'the strumpet's plague' (4.1.97.120) of falling in love with a 'customer', Cassio. In the First Folio, an anonymous editorial hand (probably not the author's) has

appended a list of 'The Names of the Actors', which repeats Iago's judgement by describing Bianca as 'a curtezan'. Though nobody in the play
actually uses this word, Iago is once again the carrier of its substance. He
seems to have persuaded at least his wife, since Emilia repeats the charge
to Bianca herself, only to be indignantly rebuffed: 'I am no strumpet /
But of life as honest as you, that thus / Abuse me' (5.1.121–4). The manifestly wrongful accusation of 'strumpet' is to be hurled at Desdemona by
Othello and denied with the same vehemence. In a play so full of ironic
references to 'honesty' and 'lying', Bianca's resounding assertion strikes
us as trustworthy a note as Desdemona's, especially since the demeaning
opinion of her can be traced directly back to the deeply untrustworthy
arch-liar in his defamatory contempt for women in general:

> Now will I question Cassio of Bianca,
> A housewife that by selling her desires
> Buys herself bread and clothes: it is a creature
> That dotes on Cassio – as 'tis the strumpet's plague
> To beguile many and be beguiled by one.
>
> (4.1.91–5)

Jane Adamson, makes the obvious point, that given his track record
we should not believe him,[54] though many critics have done so, from
Thomas Rymer in the eighteenth century onwards. The easy acceptance
of Bianca as prostitute is another example of Iago's insidious capacity
for linguistic infection, spreading 'poison' through words even to readers
of the play. In an incisive essay, Edward Pechter challenges demeaning
views of Bianca, arguing that 'in a play whose final action is driven by
the projection of men's guilt onto the women who arouse sexual interest,
Iago's substitution of desire for desirability should be worth at least a
passing nod'.[55] For Iago, all women are potentially promiscuous.

What we do know of Bianca is that she is not Venetian but a local
Cypriot, evidently a 'housewife' (4.1.95), a description which need not
imply Iago's derogatory tone. She is vulnerable also to ethnic stereotyping of Cypriots. Generally speaking they hold the soldiers at a 'wary
distance' (3.3.51–7) but she has had the misfortune to fall in love with
Cassio, evidently a glamorous soldier who has encouraged her attentions
or seduced her. She charges him with abandoning her after a week's
absence (a part of the play's general puzzle of a 'double time scheme' since

---

54. Jane Adamson, *'Othello' as Tragedy: Some Problems of Judgement and Feeling*
    (Cambridge University Press, 1980), 242.
55. Edward Pechter, 'Why Should We Call her Whore?', 366–7.

a week in Cyprus cannot have passed).[56] We know that she is caught up in Iago's web of plotting, as the hapless recipient of Desdemona's incriminating handkerchief, and she is genuinely spurned by Cassio when he comes to view her as a stalker 'haunting' him. She shows genuine grief on hearing of the wounding of Cassio: 'O my dear Cassio! my sweet Cassio! O Cassio, / Cassio, Cassio!'. Jyotsna Singh draws attention to her much overlooked loyalty to Cassio,[57] and notes that her forgiving nature persists even when she is abused by him, mirroring Desdemona's steadfastness when acting with 'the authority of her merit' (2.1.145). From the admittedly fragmentary details, it is possible to see Bianca is a victim of army gossip and disdainfully dismissed as a camp follower by the soldiers in occupation of the island. Her voice of protest is silenced, and in this sense her situation is a cameo version of Desdemona's.

Shakespeare's Emilia is an experienced but downtrodden wife to an army officer, and any vestige of resistance to her husband has been worn down over years into accepting her lot. She exercises a tone of truculent hostility to Iago but does not actually disobey him, at best tolerating Iago's general abuse of her sex, and doing his bidding. In a play full of lying, she herself errs into 'filching' for him the controversial handkerchief 'dropped by negligence', with disastrous consequences for her mistress. Her compliance is explained in a revealing soliloquy, confiding that she will 'please his fantasy' by giving him the lost-and-found handkerchief. After being first berated as 'a foolish wife' she is rewarded with no more than a phrase, 'a good wench, give it me' and cursorily dismissed when, too late, she questions his motives:

EMILIA
What will you do with 't, that you have been so earnest
To have me filch it?
IAGO
                                        Why, what's that to you?
EMILIA
If it be not for some purpose of import
Give't me again. Poor lady, she'll run mad
When she shall lack it.
IAGO
                    Be not acknown on 't,
I have use for it. Go, leave me.

(3.3.318–23)

---

56. See Honigmann (ed.), *Othello*, 68–72.
57. Jyotsna Singh, 'The Interventions of History: Narratives of Sexuality' in *The Weyward Sisters: Shakespeare and Feminist Politics*, ed. Dympna Callaghan et al (Oxford: Blackwell, 1994), 50.

Despite harbouring suspicions, her abjectness is illustrated in her desire to 'please his fantasy' at the cost of betraying her mistress.[58] Kelsey Ridge's present-day analysis goes so far as to diagnose Emilia's behaviour as evidence of medically defined 'battered person syndrome' familiar in military marriages, observing that Emilia and Desdemona 'both face from their different vantages, the issues of jealousy and domestic abuse, reflections of toxic masculinity'.[59] Emilia clearly speaks cynically from experience in referring to 'the abuses men can direct at women', mentioning in particular what has just happened to the younger woman – 'or say they strike us' (4.3.89) – implying that this is the lot to which the army wife must simply grow accustomed.

Later in the 'willow song' scene (4.3), Emilia shows that she has over years internalised her husband's attitude to love and marriage, accepting a masculine construction of sexual promiscuity while also realising the double standard for women. Her speech is sometimes read as a feminist demand for the same sexual freedom enjoyed by men, but it is just as convincingly seen as colluding with male values rather than challenging them. Desdemona cannot 'in conscience' believe in female promiscuity, 'That there be women do abuse their husbands / In such gross kind', but Emilia jokes that 'for all the world' some women will: 'The world's a huge thing: it is a great price / For a small vice'. She jokingly adds she would not do it 'by this heavenly light' but 'I might do't as well I'th'dark', inadvertently echoing her husband's insistence to Othello that adultery is by its nature always hidden from sight.

> But I do think it is their husbands' faults
> If wives do fall. Say that they slack their duties
> And pour our treasures into foreign laps;
> Or else break out in peevish jealousies,
> Throwing restraint upon us; or say they strike us,
> Or scant our former having in despite.
> Why, we have galls: and though we have some grace
> Yet have we some revenge.
>   . . . .
>   And have not we affections?
> Desires for sport? and frailty, as men have?
> Then let them use us well: else let them know,
> The ills we do, their ills instruct us so.
>
>   (4.3.59–102 *passim*)

---

58. Irene Dash, *Women's Worlds in Shakespeare's Plays* (London: Associated Presses 1997), 123.
59. Ridge, *Military Wives*, 32.

It is men who set the rules, and a canny woman of the world will, she asserts, emulate them rather than change those rules. However, notwithstanding Emilia's hard-edged sharpness, the dominant tone of the scene in its hushed intimacy, is captured in Weil's reading of the *Iliad*:

> Still more poignant — so painful is the contrast — is the sudden evocation, as quickly rubbed out, of another world: the faraway, precarious, touching world of peace, of the family, the world in which each man counts more than anything else to those about him.

Only at the end does Emilia find her own voice, as Byles points out: 'Although Emilia is a submissive wife to Iago for most of the play, in the last Act it is she who represents feminine outrage and outspokenness; this courage with the spoken word costs her life'.[60] After her husband's guilt has become clear she says ''Tis proper I obey him – but not now' (5.2.195), adding 'Perchance, Iago, I will ne'er go home' (5.2.193–4) in response to Iago's order, 'Be wise, and get you home' (5.2.221). Where is 'home', one wonders – the temporary lodging in Cyprus? Her marriage? Or is she remembering Venice, a quieter world where women can escape harassment, orders, and threats from male soldiers in a brutalising foreign garrison?

Desdemona is assertive from the start. She defies her father, speaks unhesitatingly and eloquently before the whole senate, shows no sign of racial prejudice in valuing her husband, and she is frank in her admission of sexual desire for him. She refuses to be pigeon-holed as a 'moth of peace', instead insisting on accompanying her husband into a battle zone. She stands up to him him by continuing to supplicate for Cassio's reinstatement, even in the face of his increasingly baffling anger. The contemporary eye-witness reporter of the play, Henry Jackson, praised her sustained, eloquent resistance:

> But that Desdemona, murdered by her husband in our presence, although she always plead her case excellently, yet when killed moved us more, while stretched out on her bed she begged the spectators' pity with her very facial expression.[61]

---

60. Byles, 'The Problem of the Self', 51.
61. Folger Library accessed 6 August 2023: https://shakespearedocumented.folger.edu/resource/document/excerpts-henry-jacksons-letter-recording-performance-othello-oxford
   Noted by Edward Pechter, 'Why Should We Call her Whore? Bianca in *Othello*', *Shakespeare and the Twentieth Century: The Selected Proceedings of the International Shakespeare Association World Congress Los Angeles, 1996*, ed. Jonathan Bate, Jill Levenson, Dieter Mehl (Newark: University of Delaware Press,

Responding to his false accusations, she forthrightly proclaims 'By heaven, you do me wrong' (4.2.83), and when he strikes her before company, she retorts with ringing dignity, 'I have not deserved this' (4.1.240). Desdemona continues to maintain her innocence, until she realises she has no realistic choice in the face of Othello's violent and bewildering verbal onslaught in 4.2 when he hurls insults: 'as false as hell', 'a whore', a 'public commoner' and an 'impudent strumpet'. To her, these come as not only false but inexplicable, since she has no way of knowing that her continued intercessions on behalf of Cassio are feeding his jealousy. Even to onlookers his actions raise questions about his sanity – Lodovico asks, "Are his wits safe?" (4.1.269). As her protestations are met with further accusations of lying, she is charged with lying if she speaks and of betraying a guilty conscience if she does not, placed in an impossible catch-22, Joseph Heller's ironic formulation of army logic.

Increasingly out of her depth, Desdemona is given no choice but to accept the rules of this military world she is now inhabiting through marriage, however crazy these appear. She seeks to excuse her husband's erratic mood as a product of professional commitment to stressful affairs of state which have muddied his insight:

> Something, sure, of state,
> Either from Venice, or some unhatch'd practice
> Made demonstrable here in Cyprus to him,
> Hath puddled his clear spirit: and in such cases
> Men's natures wrangle with inferior things,
> Though great ones are their object.
>
> (3.4.154–9)

Being unaware of the importance of the lost handkerchief ('inferior things') and innocent of the charge of adultery, she realises she must have offended in some other way by being dragged in to the 'great' and weighty military matters which concern her husband in his public capacity. Thanks to Iago's artful choreography, she is unaware that she is violating two fixed assumptions of army life. First, as the Clown had warned, the punishment for lying is 'stabbing', and secondly defying orders from a superior officer is mutiny. These are the two charges on which Desdemona is impaled.

Othello's agitation is exacerbated by his perception that she is presuming to usurp a position in the military hierarchy. She persists in

1998), 364–77. Pechter extended this essay to cover other issues in the play, in his book *'Othello' and Interpretive Traditions*, (Iowa City: University of Iowa Press, 1999), esp. ch. 5, 'The Pity Act'.

ordering the general on a matter of military protocol, to reinstate Cassio as lieutenant, something that no male officer would dare to do. This understood army protocol is exploited by Iago in his darkly insinuating 'Our general's wife is now the general' (2.3.310), calculated to encourage Cassio to solicit Desdemona's petitioning. Othello's diagnosis of her moist palm is that it indicates she is prone to insubordination, in need of avoiding 'liberty' and practising self-discipline:

> This hand of yours requires
> A sequester from liberty, fasting and prayer,
> Much castigation, exercise devout;
> For here's a young and sweating devil here
> That commonly rebels.
>
> (3.4.45–9)

Desdemona learns too late that becoming a military wife entails unquestioning capitulation to dictates of her husband's 'occupation', in which hierarchy, rank, 'honesty' and unfailing discipline prevail. Once again, language is important in the context. Desdemona's use of the word 'commanded' takes on special force since it is used in relation to a man who is not only her husband but a commander of men, and Othello's order to 'dismiss' Emilia is equally associated with military discipline and terminology:

> He hath *commanded* me to go to bed
> And bade me to *dismiss* you.
> EMILIA
>   *Dismiss* me?
> DESDEMONA
> It was his *bidding*.
>
> (4.3.11–13, my italics)

His 'bidding' is his command and 'dismiss' has a specific meaning in the soldier's lexicon. Ordered to go to bed, and with no inkling of how she has offended nor that her life is in danger, Desdemona's parting words to Othello imply a sarcastic edge, given that 'fancies' can mean 'fantasies' (the word used by Emilia to describe Iago's wish to have Desdemona's handkerchief [3.3.303]) – 'Be as your fancies teach you: / Whate'er you be, I am obedient' (3.3.88–9) – 'however mad you are, you're the boss'. Obedience – 'obeying orders' – is the bottom-line and *sine qua non* of strict army discipline and cannot be breached without punishment. Desdemona finds herself caught in the painful new reality in which the normative language code depends upon issuing orders to subordinates. Choosing her own words to Othello with diplomacy and circumstantial precision, combining a mixture of characteristic defiance and politeness, her resistance is yet interpreted as disobedience. As the tragic ending comes into sight, Desdemona's growing fatalism marks her incipient understanding of what Emilia has learned from her own years of experience as an army wife, that unquestioning obedience is the safest course.

The 'willow song' scene (4.3) is the only one in which the women can be alone together and share intimacies, such as Desdemona's lamentation (or angry outburst in Dyer's National Theatre production), 'O, these men, these men!' (4.3.59). Eamon Grennan speaks of 'the atmosphere of private freedom within this protected feminine enclosure which the men (Othello, Lodovico and attendants) have just left . . . [an] interlude suggesting peace and freedom, within the clamorous procession of violent acts and urgent voices'.[62] Their conversation while Desdemona is 'unpinned' from her dress and clad in her wedding gown soon to be her shroud, is the authorial sounding of a moral tuning fork, establishing a harmony that indicates 'what should be' rather than the discord of 'what is'. It provides a longed-for, poignant respite from conflict. But what ensues between Othello and Desdemona re-introduces the intrusion of a military command structure transferred into marriage. The fusion of martial and marital is complete, as the command-and-obey injunctions invade the bedchamber, a place meant for privacy and love. Desdemona's initial desire to share Othello's world and accompany him into dangerous enterprises, along with his acceptance of her as 'fair warrior', have led her unwittingly into the full and terrible consequences of what transpires. In the words of Ridge, Desdemona learns, as many young wives still do:

> Part of this self-perpetuating culture is that military spouses must make a commitment to the military, often at a young age, just as their service-member does, and marriages can become inextricably tied to their shared military identity. Pushing away from the military, then, would undermine the marriage itself.[63]

Shakespeare changes the *modus operandi* of Desdemona's murder from Cinthio's gratuitously brutal and arbitrary account in which the Ensign comes out of a closet and gives her 'a frightful blow in the small of her back' with a stocking filled with sand. After then breaking her skull, the two men 'made the ceiling fall as they had previously planned',

62. Eamon Grennan, 'The Women's Voices in *Othello*: Speech, Song, Silence', *Shakespeare Quarterly*, 38 (1987), 275–292, 277.
63. Ridge, 15.

in order to make it seem like an accident.[64] Instead, in Shakespeare's version, Iago restrains Othello from his gruesome urge to 'chop her into messes' (4.1.190) (''tis stabbing') or to poison her, and persuades him to do the deed, in a way that strikes them both as holding a perversely aesthetic decorum and misplaced poetic 'justice':

IAGO
Do it not with poison, strangle her in her bed – even the bed she hath contaminated.
OTHELLO
Good, good, the justice of it pleases; very good!
IAGO
And for Cassio, let me be his undertaker. You shall hear more by midnight.

(4.1.201–9)

Piotr Sadowski has argued that Iago is indifferent to Desdemona's consequential fate so long as Othello will be punished as the murderer. His own desire to become Cassio's 'undertaker' returns us to his first and primary motive, to take his own private revenge on Cassio.[65] However, Othello does not strangle Desdemona but chooses another method which is metaphorically even more grimly appropriate, silencing her by suffocation with a pillow. The stage direction '*Smothers her*' is printed in the Folio text, while '*He stifles her*' appears in the 1622 Quarto. Both amount to depriving her of breath and a voice to call for help, and just as pertinently to prevent her from more 'lies' and indiscipline. However, she is not yet dead for we hear her voice twice more:

DESDEMONA
O, falsely, falsely murdered!
EMILIA
O lord, what cry is that?
OTHELLO
That? what?
EMILIA
Out and alas, that was my lady's voice:
        [*She draws the bed-curtains*]
Help, help, ho, help! O lady, speak again,
Sweet Desdemona, O sweet mistress, speak!
DESDEMONA

64. Cinthio, 385.
65. Piotr Sadowski, '"Do it not with poison": Iago and the Killing of Desdemona', *Shakespeare Quarterly*, 71 (2020), 242–57.

A guiltless death I die.
EMILIA
                    O, who hath done
This deed?
DESDEMONA
                    Nobody. I myself. Farewell.
Commend me to my kind lord – O, farewell!

(5.2.–123)

Her multiply riddling 'guiltless death' followed by an apparently apologetic 'Nobody. I myself' and 'kind lord' act to excuse her husband and recriminate herself for inadequacy in playing the role of a general's wife. This time the stage direction follows, '*She dies*', but this occurs only in the Quarto, leaving the reader of the Folio and audiences in the theatre in some doubt as to whether she will 'speak again' as Emilia pleads. The fluttering hope is doomed to disappointment and her 'O, farewell' is final.

By concentrating on the garrison setting in Cyprus and the army rules of conduct, we see that the world of *Othello* is one where masculine, military attitudes are pervasive in an increasingly 'stifling' way leading to the claustrophobic 'tragic loading of this bed' (5.2.454). Iago's desire for revenge (the major cause of war, as we have seen in Chapter 4) has precipitated and manipulated domestic events in a mixture of calculated 'tactics' and seizing on opportunities. Love in marriage is first infiltrated from without by his lies, then besieged as effectively as an invading army subjugating a city in 'the cause' of duty (a word repeated fifteen times in the play, triggering thoughts of 'just war' theory). Up to his miserable end, Othello chooses military discipline and 'service' to the state to live and die by. Mark Antony, an even more historically illustrious commander, makes a different choice.

Chapter 9

Farewell to Arms:
Antony and Cleopatra

Love and empire

War and conflict, or peace and love? In *Antony and Cleopatra* Shakespeare chooses to enact the debate openly as one waged between two contrasting ideologies, and the male protagonist faces a choice between starkly opposed value systems. As a variation on the theme of a love relationship complicated by the soldier's past, Antony is shown in the throes of attempting to escape his reputation as 'the greatest soldier of the world' (1.3.58), and instead choosing love.

Linda Charnes sees both Antony and Cleopatra as examples of 'notorious' figures bearing the weight of fame while at personal crossroads attempting to fashion new identities.[1] Cleopatra gives signs she is living down her previous liaison with Julius Caesar when she was 'green in judgement' (1.5.758), but the process applies more especially to Antony. Yet again he is a high-ranking military officer whose past exploits have become the stuff of legends. Despite his assertion, 'Things that are past are done, with me' (1.1.108), Antony is dogged by the inescapable reputation of his public 'occupation', shuttling compulsively back and forth between Rome and Egypt, war and love, to and from Cleopatra. However, in death, his lover (or rather, her scriptwriter) so eloquently magnifies his memory beyond professional boundaries that military reputation becomes too limited and confining to capture the truth of his identity. Glory in war has become of little significance in how he will be remembered and at last he makes his desired 'farewell to arms'.

In this case, just as the soldier's background conflicts with his present emotions, so the psychological confusions are externalised and writ large

---

1. Linda, Charnes, 'Spies and Whispers: Exceeding Reputation in *Antony and Cleopatra*', *Notorious Identity: Materializing the Subject in Shakespeare* (Cambridge, MA: Harvard University Press, 1993), 103–47.

on an international stage, because of his political and military status in the crucial historical period when the Roman Republic was transformed into the autocratic Roman Empire under a victorious Octavius. Although it is not an antiwar play in the spirit of *Troilus and Cressida*, and nor is there any sign that Antony has chosen consistent pacifism, yet there are suggestions that the dramatist represents war and military heroism by turns as unnecessary, degrading, contradictory, petty, and self-defeating, in the face of a compelling, emotionally complex love in an alluring and peaceful emotional environment that owes more to comedy than tragedy.

If Antony finds himself caught between his past and present, so Shakespeare also seems to be tracing a moment of authorial transition. Fresh from the unremitting tragedies *Macbeth* and *King Lear*, he returns to his favourite genres in the 1590s, namely chronicle history replete with wars, love tragedy in *Romeo and Juliet*, and romantic comedy which he had left behind with *Twelfth Night* some five or six years before. In *Antony and Cleopatra*, as Robert Wilcher points out, 'the genres of tragedy, comedy and history contrast and fuse with each other in a complex design'.[2] The blended genres denote something new and experimental, 'a tragic experience embedded in a comic structure', as Janet Adelman describes it,[3] and in this sense, *Antony and Cleopatra* preludes the final phase of Shakespeare's writing career in the tragi-comic mode of romance, based on attempts to transcend conflict in an ennobling vision of reconciliation and love. Donald A. Stauffer, drawing on the genre theory of G. Wilson Knight and Northrop Frye, argued that *Antony and Cleopatra* is 'the first and greatest of the dramatic romances'.[4] Coincidentally (and in a different way), Octavius Caesar's military conquest of Egypt ('Afric') at the end of the play anticipates *The Tempest* as a paradigm of imperial colonisation,[5] and also as a study of the power and limitations of poetic drama. Just as Antony appears at a turning point in his career, so it seems is the playwright.

Despite its historical source, the play is not unfiltered history, though it has itself shaped Western preconceptions concerning Cleopatra.

2. Robert Wilcher, 'Antony and Cleopatra and Genre Criticism' in Nigel Wood (ed.), *Antony and Cleopatra: Theory in Practice* (Buckingham: Open University Press, 1996), 92–124, 109.

3. Janet Adelman, *The Common Liar: An Essay on 'Antony and Cleopatra'* (New Haven, Yale University Press, 1973), 52.

4. Donald A. Stauffer, *Shakespeare's World of Images: The Development of his Moral Ideas* (Bloomington: Indiana University Press, 1949), 247.

5. The suggestion is made by Christopher J. Kane in *Shadows of Empire: The Displaced New World of 'Antony and Cleopatra'*, unpubl. dissertation, John Carroll University, 2016).

Egyptian historians see the historical figure in terms of her status as the last Pharaoh descended from the line of Greek Macedonian Ptolemies, a strong reformist ruler and political figure. She spoke nine languages fluently and was highly educated in all fields of learning including medicine. Her domain in Alexandria was not so much a place of leisure and pleasure as Shakespeare paints it, but internationally famous as a centre of learning with a huge library.[6] This record is largely effaced by Plutarch in *Lives of the Noble Grecians and Romans* translated by Thomas North (1579). The Graeco-Roman historian gives a selective and partisan view, since his real interest lies in decisive political events in the history of the Roman republic. Shakespeare in turn modifies this bias in his adaptation, selectively reshaping the record into dramatic form and turning it into a western myth of the Queen for a Jacobean audience and modern times. Michael Neill describes the Romans' attitude to Cleopatra's world as 'the orientalist fantasy of an all-consuming sensuality'.[7] In Edward Said's post-colonial view, orientalism is perceived primarily as an ideological construction on grounds of race, class and gender imposed on non-Western, exotic societies, thus making them a frequent target for wars of imperial conquest.[8] Ania Loomba, deals with 'issues of imperial expansion, political power, and sexual domination' in the play.[9] Dympna Callaghan has applied to *Antony and Cleopatra* Gayatri Chakravorty Spivak's notions that the orient is an 'ideologically excluded other' from Rome, and that 'West and East are rather more states of mind than geographical locations'.[10] However, in applying orientalism as an interpretive lens, some crucial distinctions need to be made. First, a stereotypical emphasis on her exoticism and sexuality is only a partial view of Shakespeare's complex creation. Jyotsna Singh quotes actors playing the role who have found that 'this woman has a mind' and is a 'multi-dimensional' character.[11] Secondly, there is in the

6. For a convenient Egyptian overview based on historical sources, see the film documentary 'Cleopatra', dir. Curtis Ryan Woodside (2023), based on Western movies, including adaptations of Shakespeare's play.

7. Michael Neill (ed.), *Anthony and Cleopatra* (Oxford University Press, 1994), 46. For a brief reading of the play as an 'orientalist text' in terms of race and gender, see MacDonald, *Women and Race*, 52ff, though this account makes no reference to war as an outcome.

8. Edward W. Said, *Orientalism* (New York: Pantheon Books, 1978).

9. Ania Loomba, *Shakespeare, Race, and Colonialism* (Oxford University Press, 2002); see also Singh, *Shakespeare and Postcolonial Theory*, 109–18.

10. See especially Dympna Callaghan, 'Representing Cleopatra in the Post-colonial Moment', in Wood (ed.) *Antony and Cleopatra. Theory in Practice*, 41–65, 41.

11. Jyotsna Singh, *Shakespeare and Postcolonial Theory* (London: Routledge, 2019), 112, quoting Josette Simon.

play a radical difference between the respective attitudes to Egypt, each illuminating different aspects of how orientalism can operate. Motives of extending empire through war certainly applies in the case of Octavius, but not so for Antony, whose attitude to Egypt is more emotional than proprietorial.

Shakespeare's Antony nowhere shows an impulse to control or dominate Egypt, despite his administrative appointment to Egypt as Rome's client state with its own ruler, Cleopatra. Instead, he retreats to Alexandria as a congenial refuge from his duties in the triumvirate and the ever-grinding Roman military machine. He continually finds himself controlled, helplessly in 'thrall' to its Queen, and he is emotionally subjugated by her aura without a will to conquer. Shakespeare's own evident fascination is in the same vein, signalled in the eloquent poetry the heroine and her setting inspires. It seems that the poet-author, like Pygmalion, has fallen in love with his own creation and is in the process of bringing her to life on stage, as a mortal equivalent of the goddess of love. As a result, his play may be an act of literary and cultural appropriation of Egypt, but without aggrandising the Roman military colonisation. Octavius Caesar, on the contrary, is coldly impervious to the glamour of the oriental, and instead he comes to regard Egypt exclusively as a decadent society and a potential territorial acquisition by force, and Cleopatra as a prize trophy of war. Late in the play he seizes the opportunity offered by his war against Antony at Actium to invade the nation and gain mastery over its Queen in the name of Rome. This has the added benefit of finally ridding himself of his main political antagonist, leaving himself as sole emperor, to be renamed historically as Augustus Caesar. He invites upon himself the reputation of a pragmatic and mercenary-minded 'universal landlord' (3.13.87) – 'Caesar gets money / Where he loses hearts' (2.1.16–17). Cleopatra is fully aware of Caesar's plans and takes steps to outfox him in small ways by planning to conceal the bulk of her treasures as 'some lady trifles' (5.2.198), only to be betrayed by her over-honest treasurer Seleucus. More existentially, she thwarts Caesar's possessive plan to include her own self in 'the roll of conquest' (5.2.217) to be displayed in Rome, by committing suicide in her own chosen fashion.

Joyce Green MacDonald in *Women and Race in Early Modern Texts* discusses the links between desire, race and empire in the play, but neglects the overarching contrast between Roman commitment to politics and warfare and Egypt's dedication to peaceful pursuits.[12]

---

12. Joyce Green MacDonald in *Women and Race in Early Modern Texts* (Cambridge University Press, 2004), esp. ch. 2.

Shakespeare's Cleopatra shows no aptitude or serious desire to conquer or control others by military means, she repeatedly mocks the masculine, Roman preoccupation with conflict, and monitors Antony's moods: 'He was disposed to mirth, but on the sudden / A Roman thought hath struck him' (1.2.87–8). Addressed as 'Royal Egypt, Empress', Cleopatra asserts the primacy of her femininity over imperial power by replying, 'No more but e'en a woman, and commanded / By such poor passion as the maid that milks / And does the meanest chares' (4.15.75, 77–9). Whether spoken purely for effect or fully felt, she locates herself exclusively in feminine and non-violent terms. Her later implication in the disastrous international war is directly precipitated by her association with Antony and by Octavius's ambitions.

'Behold and see'

With dramatic economy in a mere fifty-five lines, Shakespeare sets up the central polarity of attitudes towards war and love. The concision may owe something to the fact that he had already in *Othello* worked through in painful, psychological detail the dilemmas of the trained army commander in love. The plays are rarely compared, and vastly different in atmosphere, but they mine essentially similar materials, with both male protagonists committing suicide in a spirit of 'self-betrayal and self-division', as if dislocated and destroyed by the internalised clash of values.[13]

Dramaturgically, both plays in their opening scenes challenge the audience to make a premature, adverse judgement on the central characters.[14] Iago's late-night, racist-laden arousal of Brabantio parallels the Roman Philo's unsympathetic judgement on the discrepancy between Antony's past military prowess and his present infatuation:

PHILO
Nay, but this dotage of our general's
O'erflows the measure. Those his goodly eyes,
That o'er the files and muster of the war
Have glowed like plated Mars, now bend, now turn
The office and devotion of their view
Upon a tawny front. His captain's heart,
Which in the scuffles of great fights hath burst

---

13. Rowland Wymer, *Suicide and Despair in the Jacobean Drama* (Brighton: The Harvester Press, 1986), 129.
14. See John Danby, 'The Shakespearian Dialectic' in *Scrutiny*, xvi (1949), 196–213.

The buckles on his breast, reneges all temper,
And is become the bellow and the fan
To cool a gipsy's lust.

(1.1.1–10)

As in *Othello*, ethnicity and skin colour are used as insulting markers
of the cultural 'other', and therefore a threat, as Farah Karim-Cooper
notes in *The Great White Bard*.[15] Ania Loomba has explored phrases
like 'tawny front' and Cleopatra's own description of herself as pinched
'black' by amorous Apollo (1.5.29). 'Gypsy' is linked etymologically
with 'Egypt', but it has always carried disreputable connotations, and is
used by Philo to demean pejoratively the Queen of the Ptolemaic state,
But Loomba argues that Shakespeare is reversing the colonial presumption, since the black Egyptian woman is seen to be conquering the white
male general.[16] Philo continues:

Look where they come!

Take but good note, and you shall see in him
The triple pillar of the world transformed
Into a strumpet's fool. Behold and see.

(1.1.11–13)

'Strumpet' adds another demeaning layer of sexist prejudice to the racial
innuendos, as though any woman (like Desdemona and Bianca) is vulnerable to the male accusation. Meanwhile, the phrase 'the triple pillar
of the world' celebrates Roman hegemony built upon military conquest
as touchstone of observation. Philo's injunctions to 'Look', 'Take but
good note' and 'Behold and see' are addressed as much to the off-stage
audience as onstage onlookers, functioning like Iago's 'You shall mark'
(1.1.44) to Roderigo, and his 'Look to your house, your daughter'
(1.1.81) to Brabantio. In each case the initial, predisposing judgement is
soon to be tested against the evidence of our own eyes and ears. James
Shapiro argues that the negative evaluations of war-weary Antony (and
possibly also of the black Othello) could well have catered to Elizabethan
audiences' presuppositions, and that Shakespeare is taking on a difficult
task in the rest of the play in strenuously qualifying the prejudiced judgements.[17] Karim-Cooper is also inclined to believe that 'Shakespeare is

15. Farah Karim-Cooper, *The Great White Bard: Shakespeare, Race and the Future*
(London: Oneworld Publications, 2023).
16. Loomba, *Shakespeare, Race, and Colonialism*, 116. Historians disagree on the
colour of Cleopatra's skin.
17. James Shapiro, *1606: Shakespeare and the Year of Lear* (London: Faber and Faber,
2015), 268–9.

critiquing the limiting, harmful symbolism and racist stereotypes of his day'.

The main point of Philo's speech, however, is his invitation to onlookers to share his contempt for Antony's 'transformation' from a great soldier to a 'strumpet's fool'. Like a *tableau vivant* the objects of discussion are immediately revealed to our eyes and ears:

> *Flourish. Enter* ANTONY, CLEOPATRA, *her ladies* CHARMIAN *and* IRAS, *the train, with eunuchs fanning her.*
> CLEOPATRA
> If it be love indeed, tell me how much.
> ANTONY
> There's beggary in the love that can be reckoned.
> CLEOPATRA
> I'll set a bourn how far to be beloved.
> ANTONY
> Then must thou needs find out new heaven new earth.
>
> (I.1.14–17)

The medium of drama allows Shakespeare to present Antony's 'vices' in his own words, as a gesture of withdrawing from a constricted set of values to break boundaries where he experiences and can express a fuller emotional range. Absent without leave, he disregards 'conference harsh' in Rome in favour of 'the love of Love and her soft hours' (1.1.45). Cleopatra taunts him with his vestigial sense of professional duty when the 'scarce-bearded Caesar' issues imperial edicts: 'Do this, or this; / Take in that kingdom and enfranchise that' 1.1.23–4), but at least in Cleopatra's presence Antony is emboldened to spurn Roman expectations in favour of 'new heaven new earth': 'Let Rome in Tiber melt, and the wide arch / Of the ranged empire fall! Here is my space! / The nobleness of life / Is to do thus (1.1.34–41). It is yet to be tested how substantial is Antony's transformation from soldier *manqué* to a lover's new-found freedom, but at least for the time being he is in a *carpe diem* mood: 'There's not a minute of our lives should stretch / Without some pleasure now. What sport tonight?' (1.1.47–8). If anything, such uninhibited expressiveness licenses audiences to recall the *datum* of Shakespearean comedy, that love is a healthy and necessary rebellion against social conventions and patriarchal restrictions.

Plutarch versus Shakespeare, history versus drama

The play begins at a critical historical moment when, after the Roman army suffered a disastrous defeat by Parthian forces, Antony's wife

Fulvia and his brother Lucius had joined forces against Octavius. This marks the moment of Antony's perceived reputational decline since he was absent in Egypt, and Octavius uses as propaganda the accusation of Antony's dereliction of duty to strengthen his own position in the triumvirate. Plutarch's account of these events broadly aligns with the dominant Roman perspective of Philo, but as Vivian Thomas and Geoffrey Bullough suggest, 'Plutarch was one of the few Roman historians to treat the lovers with any sympathy', though in the attempt his cultural limitations are exposed.[18] Plutarch does try hard to understand Cleopatra and Antony's feelings,[19] but he generally accepts Rome's moralistic condemnation of Antony's betrayal of his military past. He describes battles and army deployments in greater detail than Shakespeare, since his main priority lies in documenting war and empire over distractions of love. Plutarch regards Cleopatra's beauty as a conscious ploy to ensnare and degrade men, among whom Antony is the greatest catch of all:

> [She] did waken and stir up many vices yet hidden in him, and were never seen to any: and if any spark of goodness or hope of rising were left him, Cleopatra quenched it straight and made it worse than before.[20]

Antony's love is deprecated by Plutarch as a 'pestilent plague and mischief' (222) and a fatal diversion from his martial duties. He 'had not only lost the courage and heart of an Emperor, but also of a valiant man ... he was so carried away with the vain love of this woman, as if he had been glued unto her'. Shakespeare, as Thomas points out, goes much further in softening the harsher judgements of the characters, suppressing some aspects critical of Antony and Cleopatra in the source, exaggerating Octavius Caesar's 'calculating and manipulative character', and rendering poetically the pleasures of Egypt.[21] Using the heightened emotions of poetic drama, Shakespeare tugs away from the historian's bloodless and prosaic chronicling of a world in which war is priority and love a regrettable distraction. He foregrounds Antony's quandary as a genuine, emotional upheaval, and enhances Egypt's imaginative appeal. Perhaps recalling the compelling charms of his own 'woman coloured ill' in the Sonnets, Shakespeare the poet extends the degree of emotional understanding in portraying a 'well divided' Antony (1.5.56) caught in a *psychomachia* or 'soul war' between war and love.

18. Vivian Thomas, *Shakespeare's Roman Worlds* (London: Routledge, 1989), 93.
19. See Lucy Hughes-Hallett, *Cleopatra: Histories, Dreams, Distortions* (London: HarperCollins, 1990), chs. 1–3.
20. *Shakespeare's Plutarch*, ed. Spencer, 199.
21. See also Shapiro, *1606*, 271–2.

Shakespeare paints the Romans themselves, led by Octavius Caesar, as censorious, unimaginative, and above all military-minded politicians who keep feelings severely controlled. The arranged marriage between Antony and Octavia (approved by Plutarch) is a loveless, political arrangement, using the woman as little more than a commodity and a means to formalise the two brothers-in-law in a newly united front against the threat posed by Pompey. Through no fault of her own, she is forced to be a passive and ineffectual 'reconciler' in the men's political world, in order to prevent 'slain men' in war:

> The Jove of power make me, most weak, most weak,
> Your reconciler! Wars 'twixt you twain would be
> As if the world should cleave, and that slain men
> Should solder up the rift.

(3.4.29–32)

Critical dialectic

Over the centuries many commentators have accepted at face value Philo's scathing judgement. Samuel Johnson thundered, 'The woman's a whore, and there's an end to it', and Bernard Shaw's Antony is a 'soldier broken down by debauchery'.[22] Emrys Jones harshly judges Antony and qualifies even his own qualification:

> a great man certainly ruined by his sexual passion as well as – possibly exalted by it. However against the view that he is finally exalted by love must be set the play's insistence on his humiliation, dejection, and appalling sense of personal deliquescence.[23]

Anthony Miller judges him primarily in terms of his failures in war: 'Antony's generalship proves increasingly irresponsible'.[24] His challenge later to meet Caesar in single combat at Pharsalia (3.8) is brushed aside as foolhardy bravado, demonstrating declining judgement rather than resurgent militarism, exactly as Caesar observes. Antony himself, in his recurrent moments of waning conviction, is well aware of such negative valuations. When told of Fulvia's death he greets the news not so much

---

22. Quoted David Bevington, *Antony and Cleopatra*, The New Cambridge Shakespeare, (Cambridge University Press, 2005), 13.
23. Emrys Jones (ed.), *Antony and Cleopatra* (Harmondsworth: New Penguin Shakespeare), 40.
24. Anthony Miller, 'Varieties of Power in *Antony and Cleopatra*', *Sydney Studies in English*, 30 (2004), 42–59, 46.

as an emotional blow as a reproof for neglecting a military vocation that has led to 'Ten thousand harms' for others:

> I must from this enchanting queen break off.
> Ten thousand harms, more than the ills I know,
> My idleness doth hatch.

> (1.3.133–5)

If Shakespeare had chosen to underwrite such a parable of the soldier ruined by sexual passion for a temptress, he could have finished at the end of Act 4 without adding the whole fifth Act, his most substantial embroidering of the source. The banal 'moral' of the play would then be that famous soldiers should not fall in love for fear of losing their reputations (a conclusion with which military theorists of the time would likely have agreed). In opposition, Dryden entitled his revision of the play *All for Love, or The World Well Lost* (1677), and concentrated on the last few hours of the lovers' lives in Alexandria, and on Cleopatra's grief, 'A tale / As sad as Dido's' (Prologue).[25]

More recent critics have avoided such polarised attitudes. Sidney Homan argues that Shakespeare is generating a dialectic which 'allows for no clear choice between them'.[26] But almost inadvertently he reveals a bias in concluding that Cleopatra is a mere 'victim of her own escapism', and that 'Rome, however degenerate and unimaginative represents the one hope for the future, Octavius himself the master bringing in "a time of universal peace"' (4.6.5), the *pax Romana* based on military victory and coercive repression. This formulation tacitly ignores a different kind of 'peace' prevailing in Egypt before being disrupted by the Roman presence. Maynard Mack's influential study proposed a principle of 'defiant pluralism' through a fluctuating ambiguity of 'mutability and mobility' which resists unitary judgement,[27] pointing to the spatial and geographic shifts and emotional reversals. A leading image is the ebb and flow of the tides describing the lovers' temperamental shifts – Caesar refers disparagingly to Antony as an 'ebbed man' who 'Like to a vagabond flag upon the stream, / Goes to and back, lackeying the varying tide / To rot itself with motion' (1.4.42–6), while Antony uses the

25. See D. R. C. Marsh, 'The Conflict of Love and Responsibility in *Antony and Cleopatra*', *Theoria: A Journal of Social and Political Theory*, 15 (1960), 1–27, 2.
26. Sidney R. Homan, 'Divided Response in *Antony and Cleopatra*', *Philological Quarterly* 49 (1970), 460–8, 460, 468.
27. Maynard Mack, '*Antony and Cleopatra*: The Stillness and the Dance. in *Shakespeare's Art: Seven Essays,* ed. Milton Crane, (Chicago: University of Chicago Press, 1973) 79–113.

trope more lyrically when he likens the disjunctions between Cleopatra's 'tongue' and her 'heart' to 'the swan's-down feather / That stands upon the swell at the full of tide / And neither way inclines' (3.2.54–6). Embracing the ambiguities, Janet Adelman in *The Common Liar: An Essay on 'Antony and Cleopatra'* pleads for a suspension of judgement, arguing that the conflict between opposite viewpoints does not enforce the need for a settled choice between measure or excess, conflict or love. The play, Adelman argues, presents a 'contrariety' which demands 'that the extreme of skepticism must be balanced by an extreme of assent' when evaluating its hyperboles and paradoxes.[28] This she calls the play's inbuilt 'structure of belief and unbelief'. But in performance it may be impossible to maintain such a balance between points of view, and directors and actors also play their part in steering our sympathies in the theatre. It may be more fruitful to see *Antony and Cleopatra* not as a play requiring us to make a choice, but as a play *about* making a choice in a narrative of personal and political transition. In this sense, Shakespeare provides his own reliable critical commentator and guide to audience responses within the play.

Enobarbus, a character considerably amplified by Shakespeare from a very minor role in Plutarch, is both observer of and participant in the action, and an emblematic casualty of Antony's internal transition. His dramatic role is to mirror and redefine the kind of inner conflict undergone by Antony, caught between a code of military honour and emotional attachment. He follows the Roman creed of loyalty in staying with his military master despite recognising Antony's failures as a general, but eventually loses patience and leaves, retreating to ingrained allegiance to Rome's values. His personal bonding with Antony is closer to love than obedience. He recognises that Antony's inspirational quality as a leader amounts to more than simple valour in battle, and closer to a personal capacity for human empathy and fellow-feeling in his general's capacity 'to make his followers weep' and 'onion-eyed' (4.2.8–20), a characteristic acknowledged by Plutarch.[29] The Egyptian soothsayer puts this allegorically, saying that Antony's superior 'daemon' or 'spirit' is 'Noble, courageous, high, unmatchable' (2.3.18–21), but eclipsed in worldly terms by Caesar's 'power'.[30] Enobarbus feels shamed by Antony's generosity in sending largesse after him with the words, ' gentle adieus and greetings. / Say that I wish he never find more cause / To change a master'

28. Janet Adelman, *The Common Liar*, 110.
29. Thomas, *Shakespeare's Roman Worlds*, 114–15.
30. The Soothsayer's speech is very close to the words of the source: *Shakespeare's Plutarch*, 216.

(4.5.12–16). Antony himself displays a largeness of spirit capable, even in military failure, of inspiring such personal sacrifices as the suicides of Enobarbus and Eros (neither in Plutarch). In theatrical terms, the emotional pathos supersedes stereotypes of military decorum and heroism, and such personal qualities are more suggestive of love than of leading men into war.

Enobarbus also has the pivotal mediating function of responding appreciatively to the qualities of Egyptian life which transfix Antony, as a Roman capable of relishing the seductive ambience of Alexandria. In a spirit of a tourist's orientalism, he speaks some of the most imaginative and least 'Roman' poetry in his description, 'The barge she sat in, like a burnish'd throne / Burned on the water':

> The silken tackle
> Swell with the touches of those flower-soft hands
> That yarely frame the office. From the barge
> A strange invisible perfume hits the sense
> Of the adjacent wharfs . . .

(2.2.219–123)

Even his language here takes on an Egyptian hue. The lengthy passage has some precedent in the source, where Plutarch briefly itemises an inventory of Cleopatra's environment,[31] but Shakespeare's goes much further, evoking the mesmerising appeal of the world in which Cleopatra exists and which she epitomises. It is an exercise in hyperbole, which Madeline Doran claimed is the distinctive rhetorical figure dominating the play and culminating in Cleopatra's eulogy for Antony.[32] Enobarbus's pivotal speech confirms the persuasiveness of the ethos which compels Antony in the way that Hazlitt described: 'The rich and poetical description . . . seems to prepare the way for, and almost to justify the subsequent infatuation of Antony when in the sea-fight at Actium, he leaves the battle and 'like a doating mallard follows her flying sails'.[33] Livia Sacchetti argues that the speech is the play's turning point towards the redemption of Cleopatra in the audience's eyes, leading away from the negative judgements voiced by unsympathetic observers.[34] She is a force-field, the

31. See Shapiro, *1606*, 177–8.
32. Madeleine Doran, '"High Events as These": The Language of Hyperbole in *Antony and Cleopatra*', in *Shakespeare's Dramatic Language,* (Madison: University of Wisconsin Press, 1976), 154–81.
33. *Hazlitt's Criticism of Shakespeare*, 119.
34. Livia Sacchetti, '"A Gap in Nature": Rewriting Cleopatra Through *Antony and Cleopatra*'s Cosmology' in *The Palgrave Handbook of Shakespeare's Queens* 413–30.

centrepiece of an alluring, art-inspired environment, capable of making 'defect perfection' (2.2.241) through sheer charisma, adding weight to the emotional validity of choosing love over war as a 'world well lost'.

The ethos of comedy

Samuel Johnson, noting (and deploring) the generic hybridity of Shakespearean drama, asserted that the dramatist generally 'indulged his natural disposition' through an instinctive preference for comedy:

> In tragedy he is always struggling after some occasion to be comick; but in comedy he seems to repose, or to luxuriate, as in a mode of thinking congenial to his nature ... His tragedy seems to be skill, his comedy to be instinct.[35]

Ever alert to literary indecorum, Johnson clearly has in mind this very play when he reproaches Shakespeare for his punning and metaphorical style: 'A quibble was to him the fatal Cleopatra for which he lost the world, and was content to lose it'.

It may have been a single sentence in Plutarch which gave Shakespeare a clue for experimenting with an audacious genre-bending structure in *Antony and Cleopatra*. Plutarch is intellectually aware of the differences between Rome and Egypt, remarking that to the Alexandrians Antony showed 'a comical face, to wit a merry countenance; and the Romans a tragical face, to say a grim look'.[36] The wholly Roman, masculine-dominated *Coriolanus* and *Julius Caesar* depict a world in which Cassius seems representative as one who 'loves no plays ... he hears no music. Seldom he smiles' (1.2.202). In Rome the only music comes from trumpets and drums of war, recalling the education of Coriolanus' son (1.3.56). In stark contrast, Cleopatra and her retinue occupy their time in 'moody' music, 'sport', eating and drinking, amplifying through poetry the rich sounds, sights and even perfumes of Alexandria, indulgence in the senses, and 'the pleasure principle'. Where Rome represents 'work and war', Egypt is 'play and love' and for the battle-weary Antony, 'recreation and re-creation'. Barbara Everett pointed out that 'Cleopatra's world is essentially a world of play',[37] and as a playwright himself Shakespeare would likely see this as no reason for condemnation,

35. Johnson, 'Preface to Shakespeare', *Dr Johnson on Shakespeare*, ed. W. K Wimsatt (Harmondsworth: Penguin Shakespeare Library, 1960), 64.
36. *Shakespeare's Plutarch*, ed. Spencer, 206.
37. Barbara Everett (ed.), *Antony and Cleopatra* (New York: Signet, 1963), xxxvi.

especially if the play is a comedy. He puns several times on the ambiguity of actors whose 'work' is to 'play' on the stage: 'Good now, play one scene / Of excellent dissembling' (1.3.94–5). The debate between duty and apparent idleness is one which Shakespeare had been considering ever since Henry V's 'St Crispin's Day' speech, the companionship between Falstaff and the future King in the Eastcheap tavern, and the contrast between Sir Toby's 'cakes and ale' and Malvolio's 'austere regard of control' (2.5.65). Furthermore, *Antony and Cleopatra*'s juxtaposition of environments as opposing value systems is almost absent in Shakespearean tragedy but definitional of his comedies.[38] His other tragedies generate a sense of increasing claustrophobia by being set predominantly in one place with a constricting atmosphere, while comedies such as *A Midsummer Night's Dream*, *As You Like It* and *The Merchant of Venice* move between contrasting settings, one of which represents conflict and legalism, the other a 'green world' allowing love to flourish. In this sense, the structure of *Antony and Cleopatra*, established in the opening scene, raises more expectations of comedy than tragedy.[39]

The contrasts are not only generic but also gendered. Apart from this play and *Romeo and Juliet*, Shakespearean tragedy is dominated by men while his comedy allows free play to feminine consciousness.[40] Plutarch speaks of Antony's 'effeminate mind' when in Egypt,[41] with the same negativity as later Francis Bacon wrote that '. . . a just and honourable war is the true exercise . . . for in a slothful peace, both courages will effeminate and manners corrupt'.[42] The Romans see Antony as emasculated in Egypt, Octavius describing him as 'not more manlike / Than Cleopatra, nor the queen of Ptolemy / More womanly than he' (1.4.5–7). A cautionary example lingers in the memory of the Romans, that their all-conquering military leader Julius Caesar had also been literally disarmed by Cleopatra, as Agrippa recalls: 'She made great Caesar lay his sword to bed' (2.2.35), and they had borne offspring: 'He ploughed

38. Janet Adelman is one critic who in *The Common Liar* finds comedy important in the play.
39. Comic structure in the play is examined by J. L. Simmons, '*Antony and Cleopatra*: New Heaven, New Earth', in *Shakespeare's Pagan World: The Roman Tragedies* (Charlottesville: University Press of Virginia, 1973), 109–63.
40. Adelman's second chapter in *The Common Liar*, 'Tradition as Source in *Antony and Cleopatra*' deals with the dichotomy between god and goddess, and also between Aeneas and Dido in the *Aeneid*.
41. *Shakespeare's Plutarch*, ed. Spencer, 241.
42. Bacon, 'Of the True Greatness of Kingdoms and Estates'. For other examples, see Eugene Giddens, 'Honourable Men: Militancy and Masculinity in *Julius Caesar*', *Renaissance Forum*, 5.2 (2001), para 13.

her, and she cropped'. But Octavius's cold circumspection renders him immune to Cleopatra's charms. In Rome, women are either like Fulvia – warlike, political, and aligned with masculine Roman values (Enobarbus wryly observes, 'Would we have all such wives, that the men might go to wars with the women' [2.2.80]) – or like Octavia, who is allowed to be little more than 'of a holy, cold and still conversation' (2.6.122).

Alexandria is dominated by women who are as indifferent to war as Rome is to love. Female sexuality is a prime topic of conversation, as Charmian and Iras spend their time bawdily joking about their future husbands and love lives (1.2.33). Asking how many children Charmian will have, the Soothsayer's answer comes, 'If every of your wishes had a womb / And fertile every wish, a million' (1.2.38–9). Love is likened to 'angling', recalling the imagery of hooking fish with 'false sweet bait' in *Much Ado About Nothing* (3.1.26–33). Conflict is banished, apart from eruptions of jealousy and petulance over trivial issues. Cleopatra's refusal to accept bad news from the hapless messenger delivering news of Antony's marriage invariably arouses laughter in the theatre, despite her threat to kill him. In female-centred Egypt, the males include emasculated eunuchs who can only 'think' 'What Venus did with Mars' (1.5.19), an elderly soothsayer, and 'a rural fellow' exhibiting a sardonic, cryptic humour: 'I wish you joy of the worm' (5.2.227). The contrasting environments represent a larger clash between male aspirations for conquest and female consciousness based on passion between presiding deities – Antony's past is associated with 'Plated Mars' and Cleopatra is described as 'o'erpicturing that Venus where we see / The fancy outwork nature' (2.3.210–11). Johnson's judgement on Shakespeare can be extended: if comedy is 'congenial to his nature', then so are love and peace which belong to the genre.

Questioning heroism

Behind the Roman reproofs of Antony lies an assumption that there is something so self-evidently appealing about the life of a Roman general in war that only a besotted and morally crippled man would relinquish his military reputation. He is said no longer to have any enthusiasm for 'the scuffles of great fights' (1.1.7), nor for observing with triumph 'the files and muster of the war' (1.1.3–4). But the play itself questions the attraction of this heroic life.

Caesar's adverse judgement of the present Antony is based on firm presumptions about masculinity: 'he fishes, drinks, and wastes / The lamps of night in revel', having become 'womanly' and 'A man who is the abstract of all faults / That all men follow' (1.4.1–10 *passim*). He reveals a snobbish and fastidious distaste for any physical contact that is not based on achieving 'kingdom' by winning wars:

> To give a kingdom for a mirth, to sit
> And keep the turn of tippling with a slave,
> To reel the streets at noon, and stand the buffet
> With knaves that smell of sweat: say this
> Becomes him.
>
> (1.4.18–21)

Caesar's early complaint is the self-interested one, that Antony is no longer prepared to fight their common enemy, Pompey, at a moment when 'we do bear / So great weight in his lightness' (1.4.24–5). His 'we' refers as much to himself as Rome. Antony's absence has created what Caesar sees as a 'vacancy with his voluptuousness, / Full surfeits ...' (1.4.26–7), leaving a gaping hole in the Roman army and revealing a lack of responsibility by valuing 'present pleasure' over commitment to war. More personally, his grievances include Antony's desertion of his sister Octavia, which he uses as part pretext for war against Egypt. Octavius's sense of betrayal is couched in both personal and imperial terms, as though the two are conflated in his mind.

In his moment of genuine affection after Antony dies, Caesar's thoughts nostalgically return to former times when Antony was his 'mate in empire, / Friend and companion in the front of war' (5.2.52–3). However, his own description of the life that Antony has relinquished is hardly an appealing advertisement for the career of a soldier. Heroism is reduced to tolerating disgusting conditions, and described as though these are evidence of admirable qualities in enduring more hardships 'Than savages could suffer':

> Thou didst drink
> The stale of horses and the gilded puddle
> Which beasts would cough at. Thy palate then did deign
> The roughest berry on the rudest hedge.
> Yea, like the stag, when snow the pasture sheets,
> The barks of trees thou browsed. On the Alps,
> It is reported, thou didst eat strange flesh
> Which some did die to look on. And all this –
> It wounds thine honour that I speak it now –
> Was borne so like a soldier that thy cheek
> So much as lanked not.
>
> (1.4.61–72)

All these repulsive, near-bestial privations 'borne so like a soldier' may be lauded by the Roman as the stuff of a war hero, but are hardly intrinsically appealing, especially when suffered in the doubtful service of defending territories acquired violently by an imperial power. One does not need to adopt a pacifist point of view to find a compelling validity in Antony's choice when faced with the contrast offered in Alexandria by the Queen of Egypt. Whether we see Antony's transition from warrior to lover as what we now call a midlife crisis or an honest choice, there seems an element of aversion therapy involved – if this is what war entails, who would willingly choose it?

The symbols and trappings of war are comically debunked in the scene of Antony's arming before battle (4.4.), which is Shakespeare's invention. The gesture should be a heroic arming of Mars as a convention of the epic genre, but it here descends into domestic farce as Cleopatra demonstrates her ignorance of military clothing. Her clumsiness diminishes the heroic body and accentuates the literal and metaphorical hollowness of armour and its absurdity in any field other than war. The scene starts at a high rhetorical pitch only to be immediately undercut by Cleopatra's incompetent playfulness, and it is always milked for laughter and sexual suggestiveness in the theatre, evidenced in Shakespeare's choice of the incongruously named 'Eros':

> MARK ANTONY
> Eros! Mine armour Eros!
> > *Enter* EROS *with armour.*
> Come, good fellow, put thine iron on.
> If fortune be not ours to-day, it is
> Because we brave her. Come!
> CLEOPATRA
> > Nay, I'll help too.
>
> What's this for?
> MARK ANTONY
> Ah, let be, let be! Thou art
> The armourer of my heart. False, false! This, this!
> CLEOPATRA
> Sooth, la, I'll help. Thus it must be.
>
> (4.3.3–8)

The ritual of protecting the hero's 'militant masculine body' as Susan Harlan describes it,[43] is disrupted in open mockery, and even Antony's

43. Susan Harlan, *Memories of War in Early Modern England: Armour and Militant Nostalgia in Marlowe, Sidney, and Shakespeare* (London: Palgrave Macmillan, 2016), 8. See also Laura Levine, 'Strange Flesh: *Antony and Cleopatra* and the story

description of himself when armed as a 'man of steel' (4.4.33) has a mechanical ring. Cross-dressing – once again common in comedy but absent from tragedy – had been earlier recalled as 'merry' cause for laughter between the women and as a subversive reversal of gender roles, when Cleopatra boasts that she, 'Then put my tires and mantles on him, whilst / I wore his sword Philippan' (2.5.15–23). Shakespeare seems here to be alluding to Spenser's description of the Amazon Radigund when she subdues the knight of Justice in *The Faerie Queene*. Artegall 'at first or last was trapt in womens snare' (Book V, Canto VI) by being dressed 'in womens weedes' and forced to undertake feminine chores, 'To spin, to card, to sew, to wash, to wring', all to the embarrassment of Britomart, Artegall's female rescuer. While a tone of amused conde-scension plays through Spenser's account, Shakespeare's intention seems more consistently comic, down to the phallic connotations of the man's 'sword Philippan'.[44] Here the trappings of war are innocuously neutral-ised as anti-heroic, and the nature of masculinity defining the soldier's identity is disabled.

Although Antony's change of priorities is not traced in the same ago-nising, moment-by moment detail as Othello's mental disintegration, yet Shakespeare would not be Shakespeare without at least suggesting psy-chological signs of the process. The nature of Antony's transition is a central issue in the play, leaving open radically different evaluations and appropriations. The naval battle between Roman and Egyptian forces is waged on the broadest political canvas of international war, but more personally it is waged over Antony himself. First one side then the other claims him for its own, and he tries to break shackles from one, then from the other. Pompey's phrase, 'Looking for Antony' (2.1.20) encapsulates the quest of many people in the play, including the protagonist himself. Many claim to know his essential identity, who he 'really is'. Cleopatra's relief that 'Antony will be himself' (I.i.42) when he reverts from anger to affability is followed a few lines later by the Roman spokesman who uses a similar phrase with opposite import:

of the dissolving warrior', in *Men in Women's Clothing: Anti-Theatricality and Effeminization, 1579–1642*, (Cambridge University Press, 1994), 44–72.

44. Michael Neill cites the Artegall episode as a source without amplifying (114). For other accounts of the Spenserian incident without citing *Antony and Cleopatra*, see Joan Curbet, 'Repressing the Amazon: Cross-Dressing and Militarism in Edmund Spenser's *The Faerie Queene*', in *Dressing Up For War: Transformations of Gender and Genre in the Discourse and Literature of War*, ed. by Aránzazu Usandizaga and Andrew Monnickendam (Amsterdam: Rodopi B.V., 2001), 157–72; and John Henry Adams, 'Assembling Radigund and Artegall: Gender Identities in Spenser's *Faerie Queene*', *Early Modern Literary Studies*, 18 (2015), issue 1–2.

PHILO
Sir, sometimes when he is not Antony,
He comes too short of that great property
Which still should go with Antony.

(1.1. 57–9)

Even Antony himself becomes confused and uncertain about his identity, as he sheds the conditioning of his military 'occupation' of general, and sees himself as like a shifting cloud: 'Here I am Antony, / Yet cannot hold this visible shape . . .' (4.14.2–14). Speaking haltingly as if groping for clarity through an internal crisis, this speech is among the rare moments of introspection by a character who otherwise exists exclusively in action rather than interior self-analysis. Fluctuating in moods, Antony himself is struck from time to time by a self-reflective 'Roman thought': 'These strong Egyptian fetters I must break / Or lose myself in dotage' (1.2.120–1); 'And then when poisoned hours had bound me up / From mine own knowledge' (2.2.95–6); 'If I lose mine honour, / I lose myself' (3.4.22–3). When his orders are no longer obeyed he angrily complains, 'I am Antony yet' (3.13.97–8). Such moments mark his reversion to a Roman 'disposition', but at other moments his 'self' has a rival allegiance: 'And though I make this marriage for my peace / I'th'East my pleasure lies' (2.3.38–9). Cleopatra for one takes this as his more authentic emotional identity:

It is my birthday.
I had thought t'have held it poor; but since my lord
Is Antony again, I will be Cleopatra.

(2.13.190–2)

Cleopatra perceives an Antony who is not necessarily 'in decline' but rejuvenant and in the process of making a positive choice of a new 'self', by emotionally opting for love and against war.

Questioning war

Like heroism, war itself is presented in the play in ways that make Antony's reluctance to do battle even more understandable. Depending on how we count them, there are anywhere between five and seven wars fought or threatened in the play (the conflict between Rome and Egypt alone amounts to three wars). The resultant confusion is no doubt an inevitable consequence of covering a lengthy period of history, but the effect is to present war as the constant norm for Romans, a never-ending, humanly destructive treadmill necessitated by consolidating an empire. The first battle, without Antony, is lost disastrously to the Parthians under Labienus, wresting Asia from Roman hegemony (1.1.109). The second is a civil war led by Fulvia and Antony's brother, Lucius, against Octavius, again in Antony's absence, but his name alone becomes the cause to expand his share of the Roman empire, earning Caesar's recrimination:

> CAESAR   Your wife and brother
> Made wars upon me, and their contestation
> Was theme for you; you were the word of war.
>
> (2.2.46–8)

Antony replies to Caesar that this war was nothing to do with him: 'against my stomach / Having alike your cause'. The next potential war is threatened by Pompey as a challenge to the triumvirate of Caesar, Antony and Lepidus who rule the Roman empire. What Caesar sees as Antony's 'idleness' in Egypt is this time a positive disinclination to fight, as Pompey had foreseen:

>   I did not think
> This amorous surfeiter would have donned his helm
> For such a petty war. His soldiership
> Is twice the other twain.
>
> (2.1.33–6)

This war is averted in the shipboard negotiations, in which Pompey is bought off with promise of controlling Sardinia and Sicily (2.6). Lepidus, like Antony and Pompey, sees this conflict as based on 'trivial difference' (2.2.22) which can be 'gently heard' and settled by 'soft and gentle speech' (2.2.3) rather than arms. But Lepidus becomes the loser in a ruthless competition. The next war is fought in revenge against Parthia, yet again in Antony's absence, and his replacement Ventidius is careful not to claim too much credit for himself:

> I'll humbly signify what in [Antony's] name,
> That magical word of war, we have effected;
> How, with his banners and his well-paid ranks,
> The ne'er-yet-beaten horse of Parthia
> We have jaded out o' th' field.
>
> (3.1.34–9)

Linda McJannet summarises that the wars 'consist almost exclusively of political and diplomatic negotiation aimed at avoiding military action

. . . it suggests that the "deeds" required of an emperor are as likely to be political as martial'.[45] What this underplays, however, is that Antony is the one who in every case is clearly reluctant to fight and eager to negotiate peace, even if it requires marriage to his rival's sister. He makes a serious attempt to avert the crucial Actium battle by offering intercession. War is always in the offing as the threat behind Roman strategy, and the one who repeatedly tries to 'patch a quarrel' and go to war, is Caesar. He breaks the truce between both Pompey and Lepidus, and finally gets his way against Antony.

The war(s) against Egypt climaxing at Actium is where Antony is drawn, and he fights to protect Cleopatra's Ptolemaic empire against Roman invasion. It is described by Enobarbus as also being fought over Antony, this time with his actions being a direct justification: '. . . at such a point, / When half to half the world oppos'd, he being / The mered question' (3.13. 8–10). Antony's political marriage to Octavius's sister has failed to cement their unity, since Antony returns to Egypt. Apparently secure in not expecting war, he devolves his share of Roman colonies to Cleopatra and her children in Alexandria, among whom is Octavius's own half-sibling (3.6.1–11) sired by Julius Caesar. In initiating this war Octavius uses his personal grievances opportunistically to justify war and further his political aim to add Egypt to the Roman empire. Responding to what he construes as insulting provocations, Octavius precipitates the major war as an invasion, his act of 'orientalist' colonisation, intending also to disarm the Queen of Egypt as the spoils of war. Meanwhile, Antony's demeanour, mingling tactical carelessness and reckless bravado, suggests he underestimates Caesar's serious, deadly intentions and does not foresee the massacre which his soldiers warn him of, an air supported dramatically by the evident humour of the mock-epic arming and his surprise when informed of Caesar's seizure of Tyrone. Whether the actor playing Antony chooses to interpret his behaviour here as irresponsible capriciousness, genuine disbelief of Octavius's military determination, amatory distraction, or a trust that once again a diplomatic agreement will emerge as previously, before damage is done, at the least we may see Antony as a man disinclined to engage seriously with the war situation facing him.

Driven reluctantly to enter combat, Antony commits a series of strategical errors. Instead of trusting to his Roman military training he follows Cleopatra's flawed judgement in fighting by sea instead of land. Using another emasculating image, he realises his mistake: 'She has

---

45. Linda McJannet, 'Gesta Romanorum: Heroic Action and Stage Imagery in *Antony and Cleopatra*', *Shakespeare Bulletin* 11 (1993), 5–9, 5.

robbed me of my sword' (4.14.23). The defeat and ignominious retreat of Cleopatra's navy, however much wrath it provokes in the 'valiant and dejected' Antony, is treated by the playwright as another general note of comic belittlement of the military enterprise: 'Swallows have built / In Cleopatra's sails their nests' (4.12.3–4). This is followed by Antony's own helpless lament:

> My fleet hath yielded to the foe, and yonder
> They cast their caps up and carouse together
> Like friends long lost.
>
> (4.12.10–12)

At such points, even if the play is not overtly anti-war, there is a satirical edge, as the war is built on murky foundations and is lost in openly risible fashion. Octavius Caesar achieves the exclusive governing power he seeks, but the final scenes reduce this to a pyrrhic victory, showing him unable to secure the body and spirit of the Queen of Egypt, while she scathingly regards him as one 'rendered ass / Unpolicied' (5.2.306–7). His political machinations are thwarted and exposed as paltry and cynically expedient. The pacifist Shelley, when challenged to write a sonnet on Egypt ('Ozymandias'), skewered the futile pretensions of all empires, led by commanders whose 'frown, / And wrinkled lip, and sneer of cold command' recall (and may refer to) Shakespeare's prototype, Octavius Caesar.

Even the Roman power-brokers are subjected to the scorning perspective of comedy when they are away from their homeland and inclemently afloat on the sea. The scene on the galley in which the triumvirate meet with Pompey for serious negotiations is intended as a kind of summit conference between 'these three world-sharers, these competitors' (2.7.70), but it descends into a comical shambles. While Antony in social command boasts anecdotally of Egypt's exotic sights like the crocodile, the stiffly inhibited Octavius becomes uncomfortably tipsy – 'It's monstrous labour when I wash my brain / And it grows fouler' – at a time when 'our graver business / Frowns at this levity'. In his inebriation he likens the bacchic scene to a comedy in which his 'own tongue / Splits what it speaks': 'The wild disguise hath almost / Antick'd us all' (2.7.123–4), where 'antick'd' refers to playing the part of stage jester. Antony, in his element, responds expansively, 'Be a child o'th' time' (2.7.97–9). Lepidus is carried off drunk, and Enobarbus leads them all into a ridiculous 'Egyptian bacchanals' dance. The momentous meeting intended to divide up the Roman empire belongs in a comedy and not a heroic tragedy. The only touch of serious business comes at the end, when the sober Menas takes Pompey aside to ask if he wants the rest of the triumvirate assassinated here and now, only to be told that he should have done the deed without asking. The 'grim look' of war has re-asserted itself.

The Roman view of war is that it is the main forum where masculinity is displayed as a mark of personal valour and heroism, but as in his other plays, Shakespeare casts a cold eye on these values. Kirby Farrell in *Play, Death, and Heroism in Shakespeare* spends little time on Antony's reputation as a soldier and more on viewpoints that challenge military values, citing especially Cleopatra's transformative and revisionary rhetoric of 'mystic rebirth', drawing in turn on her female roles of 'queen, lover, priestess, wife, mother, and more'.[46] After Antony's death in Act 4, the alternative values she represents take over the play.

'Past the size of dreaming'

After the play's 'dizzying speed'[47] and rapid changes of location, the last Act changes gears and radically slows down the action. The triumphant closure is given to Cleopatra and her poetically elevated declarations of a love which reduces military might to transience. She orchestrates her suicide, not with the sword in the 'high Roman fashion' as an act of ritual violence, but in an altogether more peaceful manner of her own choosing. In so doing, she exercises qualities that link her with the playwright's own 'plotting' control. In an audacious metatheatrical moment, delivered as it is by a 'squeaking' boy-actor addressed directly to the 'mechanic slaves' at the Globe, Cleopatra predicts the women's fate if they are taken to Rome:

> CLEOPATRA
> 	Now, Iras, what think'st thou?
> Thou, an Egyptian puppet, shalt be shown
> In Rome as well as I. Mechanic slaves
> With greasy aprons, rules, and hammers shall
> Uplift us to the view. In their thick breaths,
> Rank of gross diet, shall be enclouded
> And forced to drink their vapour.
> IRAS
> 	The gods forbid!
> CLEOPATRA
> Nay, 'tis most certain, Iras. Saucy lictors
> Will catch at us like strumpets, and scald rhymers

---

46. Kirby Farrell, *Play, Dearth, and Heroism in Shakespeare*, 43.
47. William D. Wolf, '"New Heaven, New Earth": The Escape from Mutability in *Antony and Cleopatra*'. *Shakespeare Quarterly*, 33 (1982), 328–35, 328.

Ballad us out o' tune. The quick comedians
Extemporally will stage us and present
Our Alexandrian revels; Antony
Shall be brought drunken forth, and I shall see
Some squeaking Cleopatra boy my greatness
I' th' posture of a whore.

                                                    (5.2.216–19)

What she is describing is a parody version of the very play the Elizabethan audience is witnessing, but she determines to preside over the ending.

The play's design has developed towards the full revelation that Cleopatra is close to a Shakespearean comic heroine, with her commitment to love and a mercurial capacity like Falstaff's to draw many laughs, both 'at' and 'with' her. Her request, 'Give me some music – music, moody food / Of us that trade in love' (2.5.1–2) revives Duke Orsino's opening lines in *Twelfth Night*, 'If music be the food of love, play on . . .' (1.1.1). In the play's generic hybridity, Cleopatra's Egypt resembles Illyria or the 'green world' of Shakespearean comedy more closely than a tragic setting. It is created as a space where the imagination prevails, and as a place for playing roles and games. In Alexandria characters trade witticisms, mock Roman messengers, drink wine and carouse, play billiards, ride down the Nile on decorated barges, call for hallucinogenic mandragora, as each denizen 'fishes, drinks, and wastes / The lamps of night in revel' (1.4.4–5). In plot-function Cleopatra resembles Rosalind, the irrepressible heroine of her own romantic comedy, determined to steer the action towards a peaceful resolution where love triumphs against all worldly odds. She is conceived as a stage personage who is endlessly fluctuating, adaptive and situational in her role-playing, and like Rosalind it is hers, 'to chide, to laugh, / To weep; whose every passion fully strives / To make itself' in her fashion (1.1.50–2). Antony under her influence has been willing to indulge the spirit of make-believe, willingly accepting the part of a hero like Orlando in a female dominated comedy: 'Now, for the love of Love and her soft hours, / Let's not confound the time with conference harsh' (1.1.45–6). Such *carpe diem* hedonism is associated with the festive 'cakes and ale' of comedy.

Antony's much-vaunted magnanimity was a quality praised by Aristotle as a prime mark of honour, and traditionally regarded as a military virtue instilled in officers, and therefore consistent with Antony's conditioning.[48] However, Shakespeare's word for it is 'bounty', placing it connotatively beyond war. It is what predisposes Antony to break 'bourns' and seek to

---

48. See Paul Robinson, 'Magnanimity and Integrity as Military Virtues', *Journal of Military Ethics*, 6 (2007), 259–69.

evade masculine, narrowly military expectations that have been imposed upon him by Rome. Adelman suggests that it is a gendered quality, linked with the bountifulness of a child-bearing female, and therefore more associated with comedy.[49] Enobarbus, shamed by his master's generosity, addresses him as 'Thou mine of bounty' (4.6.33), and Antony himself had used the word when treating his servants ('Let's tonight be bounteous at our meal' [4.2.88]). So will Cleopatra, in describing him: 'For his bounty / There was no winter in't: an autumn 'twas / That grew the more by reaping' (5.2.85–7). Antony's 'bounty' is the quality which posthumously redeems his reputation, not as a soldier but as a full human being. The bias of the imagination establishes that *Antony and Cleopatra* is not so centrally about politics as are the other three Graeco-Roman plays, but a play about love intruded upon by public events and war. It embraces comedy's unifying force of the lover's metamorphosing perception of the beloved, creating a 'bounty' that is 'past the size of dreaming' (5.2.96) which exists in relationship and is expressed through poetry.

Of course, it cannot be claimed that *Antony and Cleopatra* is a comedy in any singular, generic sense ending in betrothal on earth, but it is a tragedy of a uniquely celebratory kind, mingling the comic with an elegiac sense of profound loss and a vision of reconciliation beyond the grave. Cleopatra invokes the presiding spirit of Shakespearean romantic comedy, ultimately derived from Ovid,[50] a metamorphic capacity 't'imagine', which leads characters towards making dreams come true:

CLEOPATRA
Think you there was or might be such a man
As this I dreamt of?
DOLABELLA
                    Gentle madam, no.
CLEOPATRA
You lie up to the hearing of the gods!
But, if there be nor ever were one such,
It's past the size of dreaming. Nature wants stuff
To vie strange forms with fancy; yet, t'imagine
An Antony were nature's piece 'gainst fancy,
Condemning shadows quite.

                                                 (5.2.92–9)

49. Janet Adelman, *Suffocating Mothers: Fantasies of Maternal Origin in Shakespeare's Plays* (New York and London: Routledge, 1992), 176–7.
50. Heather James finds in Shakespeare's Roman plays an ongoing debate between influences of Ovid and Virgil: *Shakespeare's Troy: Drama, Politics, and the Translation of Empire* (Cambridge University Press, 2007).

The ending resoundingly reverses the play's opening, as Cleopatra reveals that Philo's judgement of Antony as a great Roman soldier undone by love, is just as much a 'lie' – or at most a partial and partisan truth – as Dolabella's general Roman incapacity 't'imagine'. Writing of the scene, Cynthia Marshall concludes,

> Reassuringly familiar as the terms of Octavius' moral opprobrium and Dolabella's realism may be, the play offers pleasures beyond them. Neither love nor imagination will square with Roman virtue, and in pursuing these two themes Shakespeare subverts a victory of Roman over Egyptian values. Perhaps he was appealing to an English audience aware that their country was once a colonial 'other' to Rome.[51]

While the other Graeco-Roman plays by Shakespeare are firmly placed in the political realm with love reduced to insets, Cleopatra's intervention is used by the dramatist to turn *Antony and Cleopatra* into a play about love, where war is reduced to the inset.

Cleopatra's eulogy is not only a hyperbolic funeral oration but also Shakespeare's most ambitious defence of his own art and craft, and distancing his play from his source's account of historical 'facts'. It also constitutes a deflation of 'the god Hercules', war's destructiveness, and military heroism, and instead invests poetic art as key to achieving lasting fame. By raising the issue of 'lies' and truth in poetry, Shakespeare is explicitly reaching back to Plato's ringing onslaught in Book X of *The Republic* on writers and artists as 'liars', who simply give representations of reality, opposed to the kind of 'truth' written by historians like Plutarch. Shakespeare had earlier put Plato's condemnation into the words of Theseus in *A Midsummer Night's Dream* as he deplores the tendency of 'the lunatic, the lover and the poet' who 'Are of imagination all compact', indulging in mistruths and inflated exaggerations. This view was triumphantly challenged in the forest in the *Dream*, as theatregoers witness a confirmed 'truth' happening before their eyes. Shakespeare had also rehearsed the argument between historian and poet when Prince Hal in exasperation berates Falstaff for his 'lies . . . gross as a mountain, open, palpable', to be answered with the retort, 'What, art thou mad? Is not the truth the truth?' (*1 Henry IV*, 2.4.235–40).[52] Sir Philip Sidney in his own *Defence of Poesie* (written in 1579), which Shakespeare had

---

51. Cynthia Marshall, 'A Modern Perspective: *Antony and Cleopatra*', Folger Shakespeare Library, accessed 4 April 2023: https://www.folger.edu/explore/shakespeares-works/antony-and-cleopatra/antony-and-cleopatra-a-modern-perspective/

52. Wilcher draws attention to similarities between Cleopatra and Falstaff in 'Genre Criticism', 110.

likely read in the posthumously published 'Ponsonby' edition (1595), provides an Elizabethan refutation of Plato, structured like a law case. Sidney maintains that poets deliver moral truths through emotionally moving, fictional *exempla*, trumping both abstract lessons taught by didactic philosophers, and the 'bare *was*' of historians like Plutarch whose words are 'captived to the truth of a foolish world' (90). The poet shows 'what should be, and not stories what have bin'. Shakespeare's 'green world' is Sidney's 'golden world' of poets, more 'true' than nature itself:

> Only the poet ... lifted up with the vigour of his own invention, doth grow in effect another nature, in making things either better than nature bringeth forth, or quite anew ... Nature never set forth the earth in so rich tapestry as divers poets have done; neither with so pleasant rivers, fruitful trees, sweet-smelling flowers, nor whatsoever else may make the too much loved earth more lovely. Her world is brazen, the poets only deliver a golden.[53]

Cleopatra sets up the image of Antony as the 'true' creation of a poet and not of a 'lying' historian. She also uses Sidney's reasoning, that poets speak in metaphors and figurative language, rather than making affirmative statements that can be 'fact checked'. Even children, Sidney writes, 'will never give the lie to things not affirmatively but allegorically and figuratively written' (103). Cleopatra's universalising vision of Antony is unrepentantly pitched as non-literal, metaphorical language spoken 'figuratively' by a poet claiming the high ground of moral truth.

The contrast with Plutarch could not be more stark. The historian gives little scope for Cleopatra's claims for sublimity in Shakespeare's version, by allotting her a brief 'doleful plaint' bewailing her loss. In his words, she 'crowned the tomb with garlands and sundry nosegays, and marvellous lovingly embraced the same', but then deflatingly 'commanded they should prepare her bath' and 'fell to her meat, and was sumptuously served'.[54] In Shakespeare's prolonged ending, Cleopatra's poetic vision of Antony changes the mode of discourse away from the historical record and the crude military judgement of Antony as a soldier in decline, obliterating from the record his military defeat and marginalising his exploits in war:

---

53. Sir Philip Sidney, *A Defence of Poetry*, 78. See Alwin Thaler, *Shakespeare and Sir Philip Sidney: The Influence of 'The Defence of Poetry'* (Harvard University Press, 1947).
54. *Shakespeare's Plutarch*, 290–1.

His legs bestrid the ocean; his reared arm
Crested the world; his voice was propertied
As all the tuned spheres, and that to friends;
But when he meant to quail and shake the orb,
He was as rattling thunder. For his bounty,
There was no winter in't; an autumn it was
That grew the more by reaping. His delights
Were dolphin-like: they showed his back above
The element they lived in. In his livery
Walked crowns and crownets; realms and islands were
As plates dropp'd from his pocket.
(5.2.81–91)

Only a poet or artist would claim imaginative 'truth' for such a meta-phorical canonization, except by relying on 'figurative and allegorical' utterances to 'grow in effect another nature'. Susan Harlan likens the speech to a gigantic trophy like the Colossus of Rhodes, a work of art which depicted the god Apollo:

> Her own speech is an act of memorializing and an act of spoiling, for Cleopatra re-envisions, or reconstitutes, Antony as an object of wonder, an aesthetic object to be admired. Antony's monument derives its power as a token of identity and as a reminder, or memorial, from its massive-ness and its supposed permanence.[55]

In her myth-making, Cleopatra answers Philo's criticisms with an asser-tive '*you* lie!', ensuring that for the playgoer the lasting image of Antony is neither limited nor swayed by ephemeral political and battlefield events.[56]

Peace

To deprive Octavius of claiming herself as his own war trophy, Cleopatra sets about orchestrating her own death. Her eye had been fixed on love as immortality from early in the play: 'Eternity was in our lips and eyes' (1.3.36) and 'my oblivion is a very Antony' (1.3.91). Antony had also

---

55. Harlan, *Memories of War in Early Modern*, 228.
56. For more discussion of Cleopatra's 'universal terms' see Ekbert Faas, *Shakespeare's Poetics* (Cambridge University Press, 1986), 111 and elsewhere; and for wider dis-cussion of some issues (without reference to *Antony and Cleopatra*) see Diana Akers Rhoads, *Shakespeare's Defense of Poetry: 'A Midsummer Night's Dream' and 'The Tempest'* (Lanham: University Press of America, 1979).

invoked the fictional afterlife of Dido and Aeneas, envisaging a union of souls in posterity: 'Where souls do couch on flowers, we'll hand in hand, / And with our sprightly port make the ghosts gaze' (4.14.52–3). She choreographs her own final moments with a majestic calm, seeking 'easeful death', determined to affirm a consummation rather than regret defeat and grieve for a death, as if celebrating a marriage concluding a comedy. Her willed vision of unity in death recalls the paradoxes of Shakespeare's teasing poem, 'The Phoenix and the Turtle', in which 'reason' is 'confounded', and logic, corporeality, division, and death are sublimated into 'concordant one': 'Love has reason, reason none, / If what parts can so remain'. The lovers are 'Co-supremes and stars of love, / As chorus to their tragic scene'.[57] Antony dies seeing himself as a 'bridegroom' and Cleopatra echoes, 'Husband, I come'.

Unlike all the other tragedies (except for *Timon of Athens*), *Antony and Cleopatra*'s ending is devoid of violence, and marked instead by a spirit of willed serenity signalled by the manner of Cleopatra's leavetaking, mingling comedy and tragedy. To introduce a 'Clown' at this stage of a tragedy is a daring dramatic stroke, and this 'rural fellow' bearing figs and deadly serpents lives up to the comic, quibbling legacy of his role as fool:

> Give it nothing, I pray you, for it is not worth the feeding.
> CLEOPATRA
> Will it eat me?
> CLOWN
> You must not think I am so simple but I know the devil himself will not eat a woman. I know that a woman is a dish for the gods, if the devil dress her not.
> (5.2.266–73)

When asked 'Remember'st thou any that have died on't?', he replies with garrulous illogic by claiming to quote a dead woman's words, and concluding 'The worm's an odd worm' (5.2.248–56). His paradoxical description of 'a very honest woman, but something given to lie as a woman should not do, but in the way of honesty', shows Shakespeare picking up again the poet's theme of lying 'in the way of honesty'.

In order to establish final sympathy for Cleopatra, Shakespeare erases Plutarch's sceptical innuendo that she had experimented on prisoners to find the most painless way to die.[58] He milks the image of the serpent with its traditional sexual associations, by having the 'pretty worm of

57. 'The Phoenix and the Turtle'.
58. Shapiro, *1606*, 272.

Nilus' applied to Cleopatra's breast, rather than her arm as Plutarch less suggestively recounts, claiming as his source Cleopatra's physician. The open eroticism and metrical rhythm of the heartbeat continue in Cleopatra's 'If thou and nature can so gently part, / The stroke of death is as a lover's pinch, / Which hurts, and is desired' (5.2.293–5), and Charmian's 'Now boast thee, death, in thy possession lies / A lass unparallel'd' (5.2.375).

As the play transitions to its ending, the mood changes again from celebration to quietus, with Iras's gently doom-laden words, 'Finish, good lady. The bright day is done / And we are for the dark' (5.2.232–3). Charmian's 'Peace, peace Iras' strikes the dominant tone, and the phrase is repeated by her mistress as she applies the asp: 'Peace, peace! / Dost thou not see my baby at my breast / That sucks the nurse asleep?' (5.2.307–9). The gesture mingles sexuality with the innocent pathos of a madonna and child. Kenneth Burke describes it as 'the imagery of a simple, irreducibly natural person whose death is presented without "ostentation" in terms of a woman nursing a child, facing death defined euphemistically in terms of sleep'.[59] The scene is marked by an air of quietude, prompted again by Charmian, 'Speak softly, wake her not', and by Cleopatra herself: 'As sweet as balm, as soft as air, as gentle' (371). 'Dost thou lie still?' is her response to Iras's parting from life. 'Stillness' reigns, alongside Charmian's almost housewifely attentiveness to tidying and chores, mingled with a child-like innocence of 'play': 'Your crown's awry. / I'll mend it, and then play' (378–9). There is poignancy in the regal reference since Cleopatra has evaded Caesar's attempt to dethrone her, and she dies in her queen's robes, orientalist mystique intact. Charmian, herself another victim of the asp, guides audience responses in the scene: 'Dissolve, thick cloud, and rain / That I may say the gods themselves do weep' (5.2.354–5), 'Downy windows, close, / And golden Phoebus never be beheld / Of eyes again so royal'.

1 GUARD
Where's the Queen?
CHARMIAN
          Speak softly. Wake her not.
1 GUARD
Caesar hath sent–
CHARMIAN
          Too slow a messenger.

                                      (5.2.316–8)

59. Burke, *Kenneth Burke on Shakespeare*, ed. Scott L. Newstok (West Lafayette: Parlor Press, 2008), 117.

The hushed atmosphere, oddly closer to the sleepy ending of *A Midsummer Night's Dream* than to that of any of the tragedies, is fundamentally different from Octavius's self-satisfied political claim to usher in a 'universal peace', which is no more than a temporary lull between wars past and to come, and delivered in words 'self-aggrandizing, full of imperialist triumph':[60]

> The time of universal peace is near:
> Prove this a prosperous day, the three-nook'd world
> Shall bear the olive freely.
>
> (4.6.4–6)

Caesar is still incapable of revising his adverse, settled judgement that Cleopatra with her wiles and 'weakness' have robbed Rome of its famous soldier:

> O noble weakness!
> If they had swallowed poison, 'twould appear
> By external swelling; but she looks like sleep,
> As she would catch another Antony
> In her strong toil of grace.
>
> (5.2.342–6)

His command to give the lovers a military farewell seems insulting and dismissive, reflecting his own priorities: 'Our army shall / In solemn show attend this funeral, /And then to Rome' (5.2.361–2).

There are episodes in *Antony and Cleopatra* where authorial shifts of perspective between Shakespeare's own past and present compositions are mirrored in his protagonist's oscillations, and at times metatheatrically evoked in the play. The strange '*Music of the hautboys as under a stage*' is interpreted by a witnessing Soldier as ''Tis the god Hercules whom Antony loved / Now leaves him' (4.3.21–2), a signal of Antony's own, albeit fitful retreat from full allegiance to his reputed ancestor in arms, showing more of Antony's withdrawal from Hercules than vice versa. Shakespeare was gifted this symbolic episode by Plutarch, who explains that Hercules is 'the God unto whom Antonius bare singular devotion to counterfeit and resemble him, that did forsake them'. But its effect in the theatre is suggestive of something more symbolic than a matter of historical record, pointing towards the playwright's choice of subject-matter here – relinquishing war, embracing love and peace. This orphic, supernatural moment anticipates the romances with their

---

60. Callaghan, 'Representing Cleopatra', 64.

apparently miraculous use of mysterious music. In *Cymbeline* a similar moment of '*Solemn music*' heralds '*an apparition . . . attired like a warrior*'. It is the ghost of Posthumus's father, ',along with his dead mother, and his brothers '*with wounds as they died in the wars*' (5.4. stage direction). Pericles hears 'the music of the spheres' when reunited with his daughter Marina. In *The Winter's Tale* a statue proves to be Leontes' living wife presumed sixteen years dead, her revival being accompanied by '*Music*'. *Antony and Cleopatra* points towards such a vision, in which recuperation can be effected, at least imaginatively, in the word-music of Cleopatra's eulogy over Antony, as an intersection of end-stopped time and timeless eternity. The scene crystallises Shakespeare's own career choice, along the lines of Antony's life-choice in the play. Shakespeare, like his Antony and Cleopatra, is turning away from tragedy and wars, towards romance and reconciliation.

Chapter 10

Beyond War:
'"If" is your only peacemaker'

Beyond revenge

What, then, is the antidote to the self-annihilating pattern of revenge that causes conflict and war and prevents the achievement of Kantian perpetual peace? What can close the yawning jaws of incessant revenge and turn conflict into concord and war into peace? Again, Bacon provides in epigrammatic directness the solution:

> the first wrong, it doth but offend the law; but the revenge of that wrong, putteth the Law out of Office. Certainly, in taking revenge, a man is but even with his Enemy. But in passing it over, he is Superior: For it is a princes part to Pardon.[1]

Shakespeare, as well as demonstrating in his tragedies the self-destructive futility of revenge, follows Bacon's advice 'to Pardon' with dramatic examples, most explicitly in his distinctive deployment of comedy, the genre whose destination is community harmony.

Shakespeare has been credited with creating a type of drama in its own right, called by R. G Hunter comedy of forgiveness, as an alternative to tragedy of blood.[2] His plays focus on love as one potential route to peacemaking and resolution of conflict, and equally fundamentally they demonstrate the way to break the circuit of revenge once and for all, by activating the powerful, and in some ways psychologically more difficult, emotional state of forgiveness. The word 'forgive' itself is used in thirty-one of his thirty-eight plays, suggesting its importance. In the comedies, characters choose forgiveness as a way to arrest the tendency to serial recriminations, by overcoming emotions of even justified anger.

1. Francis Bacon, 'Of Revenge'.
2. Robert Grams Hunter, *Shakespeare and the Comedy of Forgiveness* (New York: Columbia University Press, 1965).

From the early comedies to the final romances, the rankling sense of having been wronged, felt by jilted, betrayed, slandered or thwarted lovers, is defused by forgiveness. And if it seems anomalous to read comedies as microcosms of war and peace, Shakespeare's words themselves frequently draw attention to the metaphorical analogy: 'this civil war of wits' (*Love's Labour's Lost*) and the 'merry war' between Beatrice and Benedick in *Much Ado* are examples from many, where love is said at times to resemble a battlefield. Not for nothing does Cupid carry a bow.

It is another fairly remarkable statistic to find also that so many occurrences of the word 'pardon' appear in the final Acts of comedies, as though it is central to love's final liberation from the impulse to revenge, and a formal declaration of forgiveness. We find it in *Measure for Measure* (11 times), *All's Well That Ends Well* (8), *The Tempest* (5), *The Winter's Tale* (4), *The Merchant of Venice* (4), *The Taming of the Shrew* (3), *The Merry Wives of Windsor* (2), *Love's Labour's Lost* (2); and once each in the final Acts of *A Midsummer Night's Dream*, *Much Ado About Nothing*, *Twelfth Night*, and *The Two Gentlemen of Verona*. *All's Well* is in form a comedy, no matter how 'problematic' it has been considered, and acts of both pardon and forgiveness are required to bring about the ending. An exchange between the Countess and the King sums up the logic of reconciliation running through the comedies. Bertram begs 'pardon' from Helena when confronted with evidence that he has slept with her (5.3.298) assuming it is another woman, and the Countess begs the King to overlook Bertram's low 'estimation' of Helena and the wrongs done to her, as 'Natural rebellion, done i' the blaze of youth'. The King obligingly replies in terms that clearly define forgiveness as the remedy for thoughts of revenge:

> My honoured lady, I have forgiven and forgotten all,
> Though my revenges were high bent upon him,
> And watched the time to shoot.
>
> (5.3.8–11)

In *A Midsummer Night's Dream*, if true peace is to prevail by the end without further retaliations, some characters must forgive their occasional victimisers to achieve a state of 'gentle concord in the world' (4.1.148). Hermia must forgive Lysander, Helena Demetrius, Titania Oberon, Oberon Puck. In the Epilogue Puck craves indulgent 'pardon' from the audience for any 'offence' the players may have given. The Duke 'overbears' Egeus's will so we do not know if father and daughter are reconciled (his tragic counterpart, Brabantio in *Othello*, dies of grief). In the first words of the play we had heard an initial sign that we are in a forgiving world, on hearing that Hippolyta, having been 'won' by Theseus 'doing [her] injuries', seems to have forgiven him enough to consent to marriage. The final phrase from Oberon, 'sweet peace', encapsulates the general harmony of the play's ending.[3] Keyishian also mentions in passing revenge plots in *The Winter's Tale* and *The Tempest*, and it seems significant that, while in the earlier tragedies all members in families involved in revenge are dead, in the last romances families are reconciled. Although there is ample reason for Leontes to be left unrewarded for his injustice against Hermione (the penance is the death of their son Mamillius), and for Prospero to exact full revenge as he fleetingly considers, yet Leontes is forgiven by his wife, and Prospero forgives his long-standing political enemies. As Garrison and Pivetti point out, the last word in *Cymbeline*, is 'peace':[4] 'Never was a war did cease / Ere bloody hands were wash'd, with such a peace' (5.5.485–6). The one exception of a comedy without the words 'forgiveness' and 'pardon', *As You Like It*, does still enact several acts of forgiveness for wrongs, though they are rendered superfluous because Oliver and Duke Frederick are 'converted' from conflict to love in the forest. Though forgiveness is not a serious issue in the play, the destination is still the same, signalled in Hymen's words, 'Peace ho, I bar confusion / 'Tis I must make conclusion / Of these most strange events'. And as we shall see, without using the words, Touchstone gives Shakespeare's most sustained description of conflict resolution as a peacemaking formula that by extension can end war.

Exceptions in the comedies prove the necessity of forgiveness to avoid further conflict and achieve peace. Those who cannot forgive may not be forgiven, and pardon may be withheld from those who will not pardon. Some figures are left conspicuously angry and vengeful as exceptions that prove the rule, and accordingly they are excluded from the comic resolution in which forgiveness governs. These include Don John in *Much Ado*, Malvolio in *Twelfth Night*, Shylock in *The Merchant of Venice*, and Caliban in *The Tempest*. Malvolio's final threat, 'I'll be reveng'd on the whole pack of you!' (5.1.370), is the ominous note sounded by the vanquished at the end of a war, presaging the next. Although Olivia at least concedes apologetically that he has been 'most notoriously abus'd' (5.1.371) and Orsino urges that he be followed to 'entreat him to a peace' (5.1.372), yet his final exit signals an unresolved revenge plot since the perpetrators of his humiliation have not apologised. In Shylock's case, the lesson is not learned in the courtroom, despite Portia's eloquent but

3. For a consistently 'peace-centred' analysis of *a Midsummer Night's Dream*, see Garrison and Pivetti, *Shakespeare at Peace*, 95–108.
4. Garrison and Pivetti, *Shakespeare at Peace*, 136.

unsuccessful appeal to an ethic of 'mercy' which is an adjunct to forgiveness for mutual wrongs. The Duke offers pardon to Shylock for his attempt on Antonio's life – 'I pardon thee thy life before thou ask it' – but it is spurned:

> SHYLOCK
> Nay, take my life and all, pardon not that, –
> You take my house, when you do take the prop
> That doth sustain my house: you take my life
> When you do take the means whereby I live.
> PORTIA
> What mercy can you render him, Antonio?
> GRATIANO
> A halter gratis; nothing else, for Godsake!

> (4.1.367, 372–7)

As actors discover (following Charles Lamb's lead in finding 'tragic interest' in Malvolio)[5] there is a serious moral point behind his words, since Portia's repeated appeals to 'mercy' are so abruptly and vindictively rejected by Gratiano, proving that the Christians themselves are untrue to Christ's teaching. Forgiveness comes neither from Shylock nor from the Christians who are intent on continuing the spirit of revenge, and as in *Twelfth Night* the sequence of vendettas is left unresolved for lack of acts of mutual forgiveness. The full social harmony is withheld in the muted ending of *The Merchant*, even to the extent of the marital bickering over the ring given by Portia to Bassanio, who breaks his promise in giving it to her when she is disguised as lawyer, a betrayal which in itself requires forgiveness from Portia. In Shakespeare's plays and poems the related, more religiously inflected word 'repent' occurs 176 times spread over thirty-four different works. Before mutual forgiveness can reconcile foes and end conflict definitively, there must come recognition and admission of wrongdoing or guilt. When repentance – taking responsibility for wrongdoing – is not offered, so the basis for forgiveness is not laid, another confirmation that Shakespeare's idealism is grounded in realism.

To forgiveness, pardon and repentance must be added one more ingredient to achieve peace in the Shakespearean world – 'the whirligig of time'. The most extreme cases where the passing of time is required come in the final group of plays, and each spans the time it takes for a daughter to grow up. Time appears as a character in *The Winter's Tale*, announcing an interim sixteen years for Perdita to reach womanhood.

---

5. *Charles Lamb on Shakespeare*, ed. Joan Coldwell (Buckinghamshire: Colin Smythe Ltd., 1978), 52–6.

Marina in *Pericles* declares, 'time hath rooted out my parentage' (5.1.103) in her fourteen years of living; and it takes twelve years for Miranda to grow up and Prospero to achieve a forgiving distance from the time he was usurped as Duke of Milan.

The reasoning extends beyond the world of Shakespearean drama and into our own world. The terms nowadays used for forgiveness and pardon are restorative or reparative justice, contrasted with the punitive and vengeful justice inflicted by unforgiving victors.[6] Three very different but indisputably major examples chosen from many, demonstrate the paradigmatic effectiveness, in spite of the apparent impracticality of a theory derived from Shakespearean comedy. First, formal apology for wrongdoing (repentance) with offer of reparations from oppressors, accompanied by their victims' forgiveness, provide the fundamental basis of formal Reconciliation agreements between indigenous populations and their historical invaders. A second, war-related example was the near-catastrophic Cuba missile crisis in 1962:

> the leaders of both superpowers recognized the devastating possibility of a nuclear war and publicly agreed to a deal in which the Soviets would dismantle the weapon sites [on Cuba] in exchange for a pledge from the United States not to invade Cuba. In a separate deal, which remained secret for more than twenty-five years, the United States also agreed to remove its nuclear missiles from Turkey.[7]

The 'separate deal' was kept secret no doubt because it would have been opposed politically by many Americans as not bellicose and confrontational enough, but it was decisive in averting a world war. In abstract terms, Kennedy's gesture can be construed as admission of an initial provocation by NATO in placing nuclear weapons as close as possible to the Soviet Union, and Kruschev's reciprocation as forgiveness or pardon. A third, closely related example refers back to René Girard writing on *Hamlet* in the Cold War shadow of Mutual Assured Destruction as a strategy of 'deterrence:

> The only way out of the logic, without causing the humiliation of defeat which will simply defer the destruction, is for one side to forgive the other and resolve not to retaliate.[8]

6. Jean Axelrad Cahan, 'Reconciliation or Reconstruction? Further Thoughts on Political Forgiveness', *Polity*, 45 (2013), No. 2, 'Forgotten Virtues', 174–197, 175ff. Cahan's footnote lists many important works on political forgiveness.
7. John F. Kennedy Presidential Library and Museum, accessed 28 July 2022: https://www.jfklibrary.org/learn/about-jfk/jfk-in-history/cuban-missile-crisis
8. Girard, 'Hamlet's Dull Revenge', 294.

He adds, 'This is no utopian scheme, no folksy anarchism dreamed up by a romantic reformer', but a lesson taught by Shakespeare. Archbishop Tutu, for one, has repeatedly asserted forgiveness as the only lasting form of reconciliation in all contexts, international and personal:

> Let us hope that those whom we have wronged, defeated, subjugated and humiliated can find their way to forgive, and if not then we must plead for pardon and reconciliation, hoping that the world can be as it should be, 'If' we can imagine this, not how it is. Otherwise, the pattern of revenge will repeat until there is nobody left to sustain the vendetta. Then a higher justice – called history – will judge us all.[9]

His 'If' is highly significant in this context, as we shall see. The Archbishop, like Dietrich Bonhoeffer before him,[10] works within a Christian framework (as did the Elizabethan Shakespeare), though others like Hannah Arendt have provided secular equivalents.[11] On psychological, personal and domestic levels, The 'Forgiveness Project' builds upon this philosophical procedure in helping to resolve grievances between perpetrators and victims in virtually any context.[12]

Diplomacy and negotiation: '"If" is your only peacemaker'

The pattern of repentance and forgiveness is in essence a method of conflict resolution through diplomatic negotiation, and once again Shakespeare reveals understanding of the process. We are reminded of Timothy Hampton writing on *Hamlet*, describing the 'development of diplomatic culture in the fifteenth and early sixteenth centuries' refined during the Religious Wars, which 'stressed the role of the ambassador as an agent of international concord, as a promoter of peace among nations ...'.[13] There are several chapters on Shakespeare in Nathalie Rivère de Carles's *Early Modern Diplomacy, Theatre and Soft Power: The Making of Peace*, based on the premise that 'as a place of entertainment for ambassadors, theatre is the most appropriate genre to examine diplomacy', and this is especially true of Shakespeare's theatre.[14]

9. Desmond Mpilo Tutu, *No Future Without Forgiveness* (New York: Doubleday, 1997), 272.
10. Dietrich Bonhoeffer, *The Cost of Discipleship* (London: Macmillan, 1963).
11. Hannah Arendt, *The Human Condition* (The University of Chicago Press, 1958).
12. Accessed 27 July 22: https://www.theforgivenessproject.com/our-purpose/
13. Hampton, 'Hamlet's Diplomacy', 138.
14. Nathalie Rivère de Carles, *Early Modern Diplomacy, Theatre and Soft Power: The Making of Peace* (London: Palgrave Macmillan, 2016), 4.

Although not cited in that book, *As You Like It* could be read in this light as *par excellence* a play about diplomatic negotiation as the art of peacemaking through diplomacy, an art demonstrated in action by both Rosalind and Duke Senior. Touchstone, in a 'very swift and sententious' monologue (again significantly in the final Act, as the betrothals are about to take place) traces the stages of a hypothetical 'quarrel' from its eruption to resolution, claiming to speak from his own experience (5.4.43–100): 'I have been politic with my friend, smooth with mine enemy ... I have had four quarrels, and like to have fought one'. He goes on to cite an example of finding 'the quarrel was upon the seventh cause', which was based 'upon a lie seven times removed', and he itemises the series of trivial issues which, if unchecked, can eventually lead to the mortal risk of duelling, or worse still war:

> I did dislike the cut of a certain courtier's beard; he sent me word, if I said his beard was not cut well, he was in the mind it was; this is called the Retort Courteous. If I sent him word again, it was not well cut, he would send me word he cut it to please himself; this is called the Quip Modest. If again it was not well cut, he disabled my judgement; this is called the Reply Churlish. If again it was not well cut, he would answer I spake not true; this is called the Reproof Valiant. If again it was not well cut, he would say, I lie; this is called the Countercheck Quarrelsome. And so to the Lie Circumstantial and the Lie Direct.
>
> (5.4.68–80)

The sequence from 'dislike' to 'Retort' to 'quip' to 'Reply churlish' to 'Reproof Valiant' to 'Countercheck Quarrelsome' to 'lie', however light-heartedly offered, charts a series of retaliations which become increasingly acrimonious. The hypothetical parties avoid the last two outright 'lies' because they realise they would lead directly to violence: 'I durst go no further than the Lie Circumstantial, nor he durst not give me the Lie Direct; and so we measured swords and parted'. In the passage, which is often dropped in performance for its digressiveness (though it does give time for 'Ganymede' to dress as Rosalind), Touchstone then repeats in summary form 'the degrees of the lie', ending again with 'the seventh, the Lie Direct' which teeters on the brink of an outright fight:

> All these you may avoid but the Lie Direct; and you may avoid that too, with an If. I knew when seven justices could not take up a quarrel, but when the parties were met themselves, one of them thought but of an

If, as, 'If you said so, then I said so'. And they shook hands and swore brothers. Your If is the only peacemaker: much virtue in If.

(5.4.94–101)

What Touchstone is describing is a negotiated settlement to avoid a duel, by reshaping the terms of the conflict to statements which both can agree to. That the disputing parties 'durst not' go further indicates an instinctual wish to avoid violence, as well as a degree of bluff behind the altercation in tune with the character's comic role. There is a structural significance for *As You Like It* as a whole, whose title indirectly points to what the audience 'likes' as a comic resolution. What was initially set up as a revenge play stemming from the respective wrongs committed, brothers against brothers, by Oliver against Orlando and Duke Frederick against Duke Senior, evaporates when all the characters enter the 'as if' world of the forest and are 'converted' to peaceful coexistence. Revenges by the wronged Orlando and Rosalind are avoided by Oliver's love for Celia and by Duke Senior's pardon of Frederick who is now a contrite 'convertite'.

The stakes are much higher in political and international disputes, but Touchstone's analysis has more general application even here. It provides an apt illustration of what Stuart Rees calls 'negotiation in multi-dimensional form', opening up possibilities for resolving disputes by redefining propositions and transforming conflict into eventual agreement.[15] It depends on shifting the disagreement away from categorical and conflicting statements, which increasingly give offence and heighten the likelihood of violence, to a mutual compromise based on each party understanding the other's conditions. This change of direction disables differences and turns them into little more than misunderstandings. Understanding is a necessary prelude to forgiving. As one peace psychologist advocates, to avoid escalating disagreements into violence it is critical 'for one to consider multiple sides of a conflict situation':

> Considering one's own point of view is easy but to be nonviolent one must consider the side of one's opponent as well. Nonviolent thinking requires one to consider the varying viewpoints in a conflict in a calm and peaceful manner . . . Being nonviolent therefore requires that everyone understand how others interpret their actions in their lives.[16]

15. Stuart Rees, *Passion for Peace Exercising Power Creatively* (Sydney: NewSouth Publishing, 2003), 129–31.
16. Daniel M. Mayton, *Nonviolence and Peace Psychology*, 34.

The corollary applies, that understanding the other's point of view, which is central to Touchstone's formulation, entails critiquing one's own, as the biblical admonition advocates: 'judge not lest ye be judged . . . And why beholdest thou the mote that is in thy brother's eye, but considerest not the beam that is in thine own eye?' (Matthew 7. 13). In more secular terms, the process turns on exercising empathy. A practical equivalent of Touchstone's 'if you said so . . .' is the magic phrase when it is delivered in good faith – 'I see what you mean'. Garrison and Pivetti draw a close modern equivalent in popular song to Touchstone's reasoning when extended to consideration of war:

> The solution functions in the same way as the continually postponed utopia of Lennon's 'Imagine'. The song does not demand that society must be religionless and warless immediately. Rather, it asks us to accept the possibility of such harmonious living.[17]

To this we might add that in the song itself come the lines 'Imagine there's no heaven / It's easy IF you try' and 'Imagine no possessions / I wonder IF you can'. Lennon with insistent repetition uses Touchstone's specific syntax in another song written in protest against the Vietnam war:

> And so this is Christmas (War is over)
> For weak and for strong (IF you want it)
>   . . . .
> And so happy Christmas (War is over)
> For black and for white (IF you want it)
>   . . . .
> And so this is Christmas (War is over)
> And what have we done? (IF you want it)
>   . . .
> And so happy Christmas (War is over)
> We hope you had fun (IF you want it)

It is unlikely that Lennon had Touchstone in mind, but the reasoning is analogous. Elise Boulding, a writer on peace negotiations, uses the suggestive phrases 'utopian imagery' and 'peaceful futurism' to describe the 'as if' process of imagining peaceful scenarios.[18] More generally, a strategy of 'just imagine', like the metaphor 'just a dream', is the fulcrum

---

17. Garrison and Pivetti, *Shakespeare at Peace*, 49.
18. Elise Boulding, 'Can Peace be Imagined?', in *Peace: Meanings, Politics, Strategies*, ed. Linda Rennie Forcey (Westport CT: Praeger, 1989); repr. Fahey and Armstrong, *Peace Reader*, 377–90.

on which Shakespearean comedy turns, achieving fulfilled love from chaos, conflict, and impending tragedy. The Epilogue to *A Midsummer Night's Dream* incorporates the spectrum of 'If' reasoning and language – imagining, dreaming, repentance, forgiveness, pardon, and mercy – as the keys to conflict resolution and 'mending' offences to create sustained, collaborative peace. The actor playing Puck in *A Midsummer Night's Dream* turns to the audience asking for 'pardon' 'if' the play has offended:

> If we shadows have offended,
> Think but this, and all is mended,
> That you have but slumber'd here
> While these visions did appear.
> And this weak and idle theme,
> No more yielding but a dream,
> Gentles, do not reprehend:
> If you pardon, we will mend:
>
>   . . .
>
> Give me your hands, if we be friends,
> And Robin shall restore amends.
>
> (Epilogue)

Almost immediately after Touchstone's speech in *As You Like It*, a volley of 'If's clinch the untangling of the romantic knots in the play:

> ROSALIND
> [*to the Duke.*] To you I give myself, for I am yours.
> [*To Orlando*] To you I give myself, for I am yours.
> DUKE SENIOR
> If there be truth in sight, you are my daughter.
> ORLANDO
> If there be truth in sight, you are my Rosalind.
> PHEBE
> If sight and shape be true,
> Why then my love adieu!
> ROSALIND
> I'll have no father, if you be not he.
> I'll have no husband, if you be not he:
> Nor ne'er wed woman, if you be not she.
>
> (5.4.115–23)

Touchstone's realm of 'If' – hypothesising 'what *should be*' applying within a fiction – reinforces the notion that Shakespeare knew of Sidney's claim in his *Defence of Poetry* for the poet's figurative truth in its fictional context:

the Poet is the least liar: and though he would, as a Poet can scarcely be a liar . . . Now for the Poet, he nothing affirmeth, and therefore never lieth: for as I take it, to lie, is to affirm that to be true, which is false.[19]

Touchstone had already made reference to such paradoxes when he earlier proclaimed that 'the truest poetry is the most feigning . . . and lovers are given to poetry' (3.3.18–19) – lovers like Cleopatra, for example. Sidney asserts 'that a feigned example hath as much force to teach as a true example (for as to move, it is clear, since the feigned may be tuned to the highest key of passion)'.[20] The imaginative writer gives us not an 'affirmation' with a claim to be true in the workaday world, but an imagined world which *might* exist *if* its fictional situations are accepted as 'conjectured likelihoods'[21] It is the basis of the disguised Rosalind's feigned wooing of Orlando by pretending to be Rosalind which becomes a game too much for the man who yearns for the fiction to become true in the diurnal world: 'I can live no longer by thinking' (5.2.53). Another glance towards Sidney comes in the 'Epilogue' spoken by the actor playing Rosalind, in which 'she' (or rather 'he') speaks for the dramatist – 'My way is to conjure you' (5.4.206) – slyly reversing Sidney's reasoning while making the same point: 'The poet never maketh circles about your imagination, to conjure you to believe for true what he writes', because 'the poet never affirmeth'.[22]

Nowadays, 'Much virtue in "If"' informs the Harvard Negotiation Project's emphasis on role-playing and searching for face-saving, 'win-win' resolutions to civil conflict, through processes of arbitration and negotiation. Even in the face of potential war almost anything can be resolved through skilful diplomacy, especially if (a big 'if', this one) it is exercised by a scrupulously impartial, supra-national agency with enforceable legal powers, and no compromising ties with the belligerents.

Forgiveness and tragedy

Forgiveness as countermeasure to revenge may be built into the structure of romantic comedy and romance, but it is not confined to these genres, since it can be relevant also in Shakespearean tragedy. *King Lear*

19. Sidney, *The Defence of Poetry*, 102.
20. Sidney, *The Defence of Poetry*, 89.
21. Itself a conscious nod to Aristotle's 'For poetic effect a convincing impossibility is preferable to that which is unconvincing though possible', *Poetics* 1461(b).
22. Sidney, *The Defence of Poetry*, 102.

provides an example of a moving, successfully negotiated reunion based on mutual forgiveness, between Lear and his youngest daughter in their eventual reconciliation. In the first scene of the play, Lear's impetuous rage in disinheriting and banishing his daughter precipitates civil war in England and international war against France, leading to multiple deaths. Both father and daughter can bear some blame for the ruptured relationship by initially withholding empathy, each with a brutally categorical affirmation of their different understandings of 'love'. Kent's vehement 'See better, Lear' (1.1.180) implicitly begs for such empathy. In Lear's later awakening, both literal and spiritual, he admits his mistake and asks for forgiveness: 'Pray you now, forget and forgive: I am old and foolish' (4.7.60).[23] The crucial section is all the more moving for its brevity, since so much of its eloquence is inferred from bodily responses as much as expressed in words. Cordelia seems to smile as Lear wakes, which he misinterprets as laughing at him, but then realises she has been crying:

>   Do not laugh at me,
> For, as I am a man, I think this lady
> To be my child Cordelia.
> CORDELIA
> And so I am, I am.
> LEAR
> Be your tears wet? Yes, 'faith. I pray; weep not.

He raises the issue of revenge:

> If you have poison for me, I will drink it.
> I know you do not love me, for your sisters
> Have, as I do remember, done me wrong:
> You have some cause, they have not.
> CORDELIA
>   No cause, no cause.

>   (4.7.68–75)

Much hangs on this last line, and in some ways it is as enigmatic as Cordelia's earlier 'Nothing' when refusing to speak her love – 'I cannot heave / My heart into my mouth' (1.1.91–2). Without trying ponderously to apply all seven stages in Touchstone's model, in the reconciliation scene Cordelia does have options, and she could respond with a range

---

23. In the Folio *Tragedy* this line comes at the end of the scene, as though definitively to clinch the reconciliation on both sides, while in the Quarto *History* it introduces the exchange.

of 'retorts' depending on which part of Lear's speech she is addressing. First, she could respond, 'No, I have no cause to forgive you since I refused to say "how much" I loved you, choosing not to express my love with "the glib and oily art" of my sisters'. The audience knew this to be true, having had the benefit of her asides, and the Latin etymology of her name suggests she spoke with 'heart' instead of her sisters' 'art'. But this response, however well intentioned, is pitched as a negative and leaves open the risk of further misunderstandings. The second option is to admit, 'yes, I have "cause" to resent you but I now relinquish such feelings'. Again, this 'retort courteous' would leave something of the conflict still in play, as it continues to cast blame on the father. Thirdly, an admission from Cordelia that she herself had been obstinately responsible for angering her father, followed by an apology, would also tacitly continue the 'blame game', which could lead back into reliving or even replaying the violent altercation. It could be seen as the kind of 'lie circumstantial' practised by Desdemona in her death scene in answer to Emilia's 'O, who hath done this deed?': 'Nobody. I myself. Farewell / Commend me to my kind lord – O, farewell', followed by Othello's brutal 'She's like a liar, gone to burning hell: / 'Twas I that kill'd her' (5.2.123–9). Fourth, Cordelia's actual response – 'No cause, no cause' – could have acted as a trigger recalling her cryptic 'Nothing' which had unleashed Lear's tirade in the first place. But it is effective as a circuit breaker of conflict since, like Touchstone's seventh 'lie', it is calculated to move outside the terms of disagreement altogether, and thus avoid further recriminations on either side. Its power in fully defusing conflict lies in its removal of the concept of blame, wiping the slate clean with 'pardons' on which full reconciliation can be built.[24] Cordelia has already recognised this by kneeling and asking her father to bless her:

> O, look upon me, sir,
> And hold your hands in benediction o'er me!
> No, sir, you must not kneel.

(4.7.58–60)

In the moment of mutual forgiveness and mutual pardoning, there is simply 'no cause' for sustaining any 'quarrel'. The father and daughter can now turn attention towards their true persecutors, who are far from forgiving types. The witnessing Gentleman's ominous prediction, 'The arbitrement is like to be bloody' (4.7.95) does not portend a comparable arbitration.

24. See the discussion by Sarah Beckwith, *Shakespeare and the Grammar of Forgiveness* (Ithaca: Cornell University Press, 2011), 36.

Psychoanalysts have shown interest in Cordelia's phrase. Reading 'as clinician', Roy Schafer in his essay 'Cordelia, Lear, and Forgiveness' reads the initial 'quarrel' scene in *King Lear* alongside the later reconciliation, paying attention to the psychological and emotional needs of the daughter in her 'transition to adulthood'. He is sceptical that full forgiveness operates in the later scene, arguing that Cordelia retains a degree of 'unforgiveness' as a residual legacy of the earlier altercation. He sees Lear's 'forgive and forget' as weak and platitudinous, and Cordelia's 'no cause' as evasive and ambiguous. The premise is that after such traumatic events, 'completely transcending forgiveness' may not actually be possible for a person with Cordelia's 'ego strength' who is notably 'true to herself': 'she could consciously say 'no cause' wholeheartedly and yet unconsciously remain disappointed, hurt, angry, and unforgiving . . . she has never healed completely'. Schafer lays his cards on the table in generalising from his own experience:

> I believe that in clinical and theoretical psychoanalysis of unconscious mental processes in relation to serious abuse, it is not possible to waive forgiveness totally or to be entirely forgiving. Unconsciously, the talion law prevails; violence breeds violence; revenge is sweet; memory is long; and reflex-like retaliation needs no justification.[25]

This view of 'human nature', I have argued, is highly contentious, but at least Schafer goes on to suggest that, although forgiveness may not be possible at the level of Freudian 'unconscious mental processes', yet it may be possible to choose a 'conscious' rejection of feelings of anger, and simply override them. It is making the choice which matters:

> Either explicitly or implicitly, Freudian psychoanalysts view the forgiveness we achieve or waive as triumphant advances in ego functioning. On this basis, we are able to see ourselves through the eyes of others . . . Cordelia shines in these respects.

Touchstone, without drawing on terminology like 'ego functioning', implies that forgiveness is a positive choice, based on exercising the moral imagination to avoid further 'quarrels', and as we shall see, Prospero's forgiveness of his enemies is such a conscious decision rather than a spontaneous reaction. As a Christian analogy, Christ on the cross could still harbour hostile feelings but choose to overrule these in his 'Forgive them for they know not what they do' (Luke 23:34). Shakespeare understood

---

25. Roy Schafer, 'Cordelia, Lear, and Forgiveness', *Journal of the American Psychoanalytic Association*, 53 (2005), 389–409, 406.

the discrepancy between warring feelings and moral action, and his conclusion is firmly in favour of choosing rational forgiveness as an end to
conflict and a way of healing wounds.

The last plays

Schafer's interesting argument stimulated a 'Response' by Madelon
Sprengnether, who 'muses' on the nature of forgiveness in ruptured
family relationships. She argues that Shakespeare's last four plays are
preoccupied with 'disruptions of families and how to repair them' by
'reconstituting family ties' (420). These plays, she says, 'absorb and move
past the tragic emotions which precipitate civil and domestic chaos', by
including 'forgiving older women (such as Paulina and Hermione in *The
Winter's Tale*)' who redeem family ties, maternal figures absent from the
Lear and Gloucester families:

> the world of mixed emotions of mature women, in which they may expe-
> rience varying degrees of ambivalence, yet remain capable of knowing
> – and choosing – what and whom to forgive.[26]

Whether or not there is such a maternal figure in attendance (*The
Tempest* depicts a single parent family while *Pericles* and *The Winter's
Tale* include mothers who 'die' but return), the drive towards mutual
forgiveness as a permanent solution to violence becomes more insistent and thematically central in Shakespeare's last four tragi-comedies or
romances. These plays return to the earlier, forgiving ethos of comedy,
now enacted not in romantic relationships but within families.

Sarah Beckwith in *Shakespeare and the Grammar of Forgiveness*,
describes these plays as 'post-tragic', and explains their focus on forgiveness by recalling Reformation religious rituals. But the more immediate
sources are Shakespeare's plays which develop his own characteristic
'grammar of forgiveness'. Leontes in *The Winter's Tale* after sixteen
years of penitence can be forgiven by his wronged wife, in order to have
a second chance in the marriage which he had destroyed. Imogen in
Cymbeline must forgive Posthumus for his morally reprehensible challenge to Iachimo and his own jealousy. Prospero in *The Tempest* struggles consciously to overcome a desire for revenge against his wrongdoers,

26. Madelon Sprengnether, 'Musing on Forgiveness: A Response to Roy Schafer',
Journal of the American Psychoanalytic Association, 53 (2005), 389–409. See also
Schafer, 'Reply to Madelon Sprengnether', *Journal of the American Psychoanalytic
Association*, 53, (2005), 425–426.

and instead chooses to forgive them. He spends much of his time in the play addressing knowingly his angry and vengeful thoughts towards his usurpers, and finally choosing to forgive them. We cannot tell whether Caliban, now restored to post-colonial rule in his island, can manage a similar feat of forgiving his oppressor Prospero, but at least he is left to his longed-for freedom.[27]

At the heart of forgiveness is an affective appeal to the sympathetic imagination able to feel and suffer with others' misery. Eric Langley has drawn attention to the ways in which this concentration weaves through *The Tempest*, from its early vignette of Miranda's reaction to the tempest spirited up by her father onwards:

> Looking out to sea at the 'direful spectacle of the wreck' in the opening scene of Shakespeare's *The Tempest*, Miranda's 'piteous heart' is 'touch'd [with] / The very virtue of compassion' (1.2.14ff). As the 'mounting' sea mingles with the 'pour[ing]' skies, she suffers in sympathetic synergy with the 'poor' souls who perish in its wild waters: 'O! I have suffered', she exclaims, 'With those that I saw suffer'. Allowing herself empathetic engagement with the drowning sailors, Miranda is an involved and vulnerable spectator, alive to the invasive haptic 'touch' of sensitive contact as the mariners' cries that 'knock / Against [her] very heart'.[28]

In Prospero's case, by contrast, forgiveness springs not from a spontaneous empathy like Miranda's, but an intellectually reasoned choice to overcome vengeful feelings. He is prompted by Ariel the spirit, who paradoxically has no human feelings but does have a clear perception that pity for those suffering is a natural 'human' response:

ARIEL
        Your charm so strongly works 'em
That, if you now beheld them, your affections
Would become tender.
PROSPERO
                Dost thou think so, spirit?
ARIEL
Mine would, sir, were I human.
PROSPERO
               And mine shall!

---

27. Post-colonial readings of *The Tempest* are legion, most referring to Ania Loomba's pioneering *Shakespeare, Race, and Colonialism*.
28. Eric Langley, 'Standing on a Beach: Shakespeare and the Sympathetic Imagination', in Steenberg and Ibbett (eds), *Compassion in Early Modern Literature and Culture*, 197–215, 201.

Hast thou, which art but air, a touch, a feeling
Of their afflictions, and shall not myself,
(One of their kind, that relish all as sharply,
Passion as they) be kindlier moved than thou art?
Though with their high wrongs I am struck to th'quick,
Yet with my nobler reason 'gainst my fury
Do I take part. The rarer action is
In virtue than in vengeance.

(5.1.17–28)

Ariel's appeal to 'tender' feelings towards enemies is Biblical in reference: 'And be ye kind one to another, tenderhearted, forgiving one another, even as God for Christ's sake hath forgiven you' (Ephesians 4: 32). Prospero's final nine lines, delivered in the tone of drawing attention to a didactic 'moral' of the play, explicate some major themes in this book. They acknowledge that the law of 'kind' in human beings should preclude revenge as the unnatural path perpetuating war. Garrison and Pivetti point out that Ariel's phrase 'were I human' which stimulates Prospero to this decision, is another 'If' grammatical construction, and that 'In fact, as the play winds to its conclusions, we see that literal "if" appear over and over again' (126), listing several of the conditionals that make peaceful resolution possible: 'The "if" works its own kind of magic by revealing multiple possibilities'.[29] For Prospero, forgiveness is not easy, and it requires that he must assert 'nobler reason' over feelings of vengeful 'fury'. But he is also, somewhat abstractly, aware of the operation of sympathetic emotions as well as reason – 'a touch, a feeling / Of their afflictions', if reconciliation and peace are to be attained.

The Epilogue spoken by Prospero (or more properly by the actor playing Prospero and speaking for all the players and the playwright), is an appeal to the audience to exercise the kind of universal 'pardoning' carried out by the character Prospero:

> Now, 'tis true
> I must be here confined by you,
> Or sent to Naples. Let me not,
> Since I have my dukedom got
> And pardoned the deceiver, dwell
> In this bare island by your spell;
> But release me from my bands
> With the help of your good hands.
> Gentle breath of yours my sails

---

29. Garrison and Pivetti, *Shakespeare at Peace*, 126–7, and more generally 125–31.

Must fill, or else my project fails,
Which was to please. Now I want
Spirits to enforce, art to enchant,
And my ending is despair,
Unless I be relieved by prayer,
Which pierces so that it assaults
Mercy itself, and frees all faults.
    As you from crimes would pardon'd be,
      Let your indulgence set me free.

(Epilogue)

Among Shakespeare's last words in his final, single-authored play, 'mercy' and the repeated 'pardon' are Prospero's farewell, and 'indulgence' in technical Church language meant a formal remission of sin. The audience has the power to 'confine' the actors onstage, but the 'mercy' of forgiving their 'faults' and allowing them to escape into 'freedom' lies literally in their hands, if they should simply use their 'hands' to applaud and depart the theatre. The final sentence in the Epilogue amounts to yet another 'If' construction, since we could substitute this word for 'As'. The Epilogue is a reminder of the shared, participatory contract between players and audience which Beckwith associates with the theatre's 'grammar of forgiveness'.[30]

'All is True, Henry VIII' and 'the merry songs of peace'

Henry VIII or *All is True* is the last play in which Shakespeare had a major authorial role, signalled by its inclusion in the First Folio. Although marking his return to the war-torn Chronicle sources, it comes emphatically to rest upon peace as its centre of gravity. David McInnis has described the play as one which 'revisits historical material through the lens of romance and thus marks a turn in Shakespeare's handling of history away from the *Henry V* model'.[31] It contains none of the endless wars which had marked the earlier works in this genre, but instead is devoted to an achieved state of peace, as if this is Shakespeare's preferred destination for history itself. The Prologue announces the absence of both a bawdy, comic fool in motley and 'A noise of targets', warning audiences not to expect 'such a show / As fool and fight is' (Prologue.14, 18). It ends with a prediction that the birth of the infant Elizabeth presages 'Peace, plenty, love, truth', though adding 'terror' as the state's

30. Beckwith, ch. 3, 'Rites of Forgiveness', 34.
31. David McInnis, *Shakespeare and Lost Plays*, 158.

guarantee of civil order (5.5.47). An unabashed admirer of the play, G. Wilson Knight, writing immediately after World War Two, described *Henry VIII* as among Shakespeare's greatest achievements. He placed it, thematically, structurally and chronologically among Shakespeare's last plays, the romances, in emphasising 'peace-making' and 'unity', and enacting a 'universal forgiveness' to wash away conflict: 'the key-thought binding them being "peace"'.[32] Knight continues,

> Peace dominates our ritual and our thought . . . both social warmth and community unity receive an emphasis directly contrasted with war, as in the interruption of the feast by cannon and the light comment thereon (I.iv. 44–52); the contrast of Anne's coronation with "the old time of war" (IV.i.78); and the burlesque war-imagery in the crowd speech of the Porter's man (V.iv). Peace itself is a recurring concept. . . .[33]

The otherwise lukewarm modern critical reception of the play (despite its theatrical success) may be, as the Prologue anticipates, connected with the very absence of war which may have been expected from memories of the playwright's earlier History plays. Could it be that the play is *too* lacking in 'normalised' armed conflict to please?

Some major editors have taken their lead from Knight's positive assessment, placing *Henry VIII* among the romances and defining its unifying theme as peace. R. A. Foakes as the Arden editor writes:

> This careful organization goes to shape a play radically different from Shakespeare's earlier histories in dealing with peace, and in having for its general theme the promise of a golden future, after trials and sufferings terminating in the attainment of self-knowledge forgiveness, and reconciliation.[34]

John Margeson in the New Cambridge edition argues it is an 'experimental' work in adapting history sources to the fashionable mode in the Jacobean theatre, romance:

> What is lacking is the momentum given to the narrative line in earlier plays by powerful motives like ambition or revenge . . . Hence there are no armed insurrections, no rival armies, no ultimate decisions by means of murder or battle. *Henry VIII* is remarkable in being a history play without corpses.[35]

32. G. Wilson Knight, *The Crown of Life* (Methuen: London, 1947), 319–20.
33. Knight, *The Crown of Life*, 329.
34. R. A. Foakes (ed.) *King Henry VIII*, The Arden Shakespeare (London: Methuen, 1964), lviii.
35. John Margeson (ed.) *Henry VIII*, New Cambridge Shakespeare (Cambridge University Press, 2012), Introduction.

Another renaissance in the play's critical fortunes has been led recently by commentators interested in Shakespeare's female characters.[36] They take their cue from the Epilogue in which the centrality of female consciousness is underlined in reference to Queen Katherine of Aragon, Anne Bullen, and their respective female attendants:

> I fear,
> All the expected good we're like to hear
> For this play at this time, is only in
> The merciful construction of good women.
>
> (Epilogue 8–10)

This is an exaggeration, since by common critical consent the characters of Buckingham and Wolsey (the latter part probably written by Fletcher) are important as dramatic personages, but it signals an authorial emphasis in dramatised history, away from masculine power struggles and conflict, to 'The merciful construction of good women'. Hero Chalmers examines 'the way in which the playwrights' deployment of the possibilities of female performance as a focus of pity serves to heighten awareness of the plight of subjects in the face of the abuse of regal power',[37] again an emphasis leading away from war.

Even the play's title may be symptomatic. The famous eyewitness account by Sir Henry Wotton on the day the first Globe Theatre burned down in the masque scene, significantly names the play: 'The King Players had a new Play called *All is True*, representing some principal pieces of the Reign of *Henry 8*'.[38] By relegating to the status of subtitle the patriarchally weighted *King Henry VIII*, the title *All is True* undermines expectations of a male-dominated focus and also stresses an 'up-to-date' topicality finishing with not only a prophecy of the birth

---

36. See especially Rebecca M. Quoss-Moore, 'The Political Aesthetics of Boleyn's Queenship in *Henry VIII*', and 'The Fortification of Elizabeth I's Rhetoric and Performance in Shakespeare and Fletcher's *Henry VII*', both in Kavita Mudan Finn and Valerie Schutt (eds), *The Palgrave Handbook of Shakespeare's Queens* (London: Palgrave Macmillan, 2018) respectively 271–94 and 295–309. The bibliographies to these essays give further evidence of feminist interest in the play.

37. Hero Chalmers, '"Break up the court": Power, Female Performance and Courtly Ceremony in *Henry VIII*', *Shakespeare* 7 (2011), 257–68. Chalmers acknowledges Donna Hamilton, *Shakespeare and the Politics of Protestant England*, New York: Harvester Wheatsheaf, 1992); and Annabel Patterson, '"All is True": Negotiating the Past in *Henry VIII*', *Elizabethan Theater: Essays in Honor of S. Schoenbaum*, ed. R. B. Parker and S. P. Zitner (Newark, NJ: University of Delaware Press, 1996), 147–66.

38. Foakes (ed.), *King Henry VIII*, xxviii.

of Elizabeth but also a compliment to her successor James, the monarch who by this time was Shakespeare's company's patron:

> good grows with her:
> In her days every man shall eat in safety,
> Under his own vine, what he plants; and sing
> The merry songs of peace to all his neighbours.
> Nor shall this peace sleep with her . . .

(5.5.35–39)

'Peace' could not be more emphatic. Gonzalo's blueprint in *The Tempest* for the ideal republic in which 'Sword, pike, knife, gun, or need of any engine / Would I not have' is now no idle utopian dream, but instituted in Shakespeare's 'present' time. King James's reputation lay in the judgement that he 'lived in peace, dyed in peace, and left all his kingdoms in a peaceable condition, with his owne Motto: *Beata Pacifici*'.[39] Such a description also fits a dramatist who wished to conclude the crafted 'kingdoms' of his works 'in a peaceable condition'.

Forgiveness and war

Words like 'forgiveness', 'pardon', 'mercy' and certainly 'if', sound tepid and ineffectual in the face of the terrifying realities of war in any historical period, not to mention the vast and all-powerful financial and political might of the weapons industry today. It would be naïve to expect any time soon a spontaneous laying down of arms and universal 'tender-hearted' forgiveness breaking out on all sides when international disputes portend war. However, even allowing for the extreme difference in weaponry between long bows, pistols and cannons in one era, drones and nuclear bombs in another, the Shakespearean examples in History plays suggest that war nowadays is exactly as it was then, primitive, barbaric, vengeful and ultimately futile. It continues to inflict torture, kill young conscripts, wreak havoc upon civilian families, and unleash destruction. In Shakespeare's histories and tragedies, any world views that valorise revenge, selfish ambition and heroism in war, and in which 'strength' is defined as military might, are proved to be self-defeating, and even victory is invariably reversible. There must be a more civilised answer.

The sheer range of examples in Shakespeare across all his plays suggests that 'forgiveness', 'pardon' and 'peace' are catch-all terms connot-

---

39. Sir Anthony Weldon, *The Court and Character of King James* (1650), cited Foakes, xlv.

ing general concepts, transferable on a transhistorical scale. As shown elsewhere in this book, particular and individualised instances reveal processes and patterns underlying recurrent conditions of war and peace. In this case, the pacifying terms encapsulate an affective and ethical model standing in opposition to belligerent and dehumanising institutions and structures of thought. Opposed to the wasteful and never-ending sequences of wars is a moral insistence on preservation of life, encoded in diverse systems of religious and secular thought from the medical Hippocratic Oath, classical Natural Law, and tolerant humanitarianism. Appeals to such emotions as pity for war's casualties, mercy extended to wrongdoers, repentant admission of wrongdoing, fulfilled love in romantic comedies and family reconciliations in romances, all cohere as an interconnected Shakespearean philosophy based on mutual 'forgiveness'. The practical outcome of reconciliation requires the diplomat's art of reframing points of conflict to reveal grounds for potential agreement on the shared need for preserving life. In this way, Shakespeare's example summed up in Touchstone's formulation shows the way. To counter the ugly nightmare scenarios facing the world, it is worth considering that concepts of mutual forgiveness have political equivalents of diplomacy, negotiation, law and mediation, capable of uniting non-violent revolutions and holding a mighty capacity for Kant's vision of 'perpetual peace'. The necessary, voluntary choices and actions, based on altruism, sympathy and imagination, are found in abundance in Shakespeare, if we care to look for them.

Bibliography

Adams, John Henry. 'Assembling Radigund and Artegall: Gender Identities in Spenser's *Faerie Queene'. Early Modern Literary Studies*, 18 (2015):1–2.

Adamson, Jane. *'Othello' as Tragedy: Some Problems of Judgement and Feeling.* Cambridge University Press, 1980.

Adelman, Janet. 'Bed Tricks: On Marriage as the End of Comedy in *All's Well That Ends Well* and *Measure for Measure'. Shakespeare's Personality.* Eds. Norman N. Holland, Sidney Homan, Bernard J. Paris. Berkeley: University of California Press, 1989: 151–74.

Adelman, Janet. *The Common Liar: An Essay on 'Antony and Cleopatra'.* New Haven: Yale University Press, 1973.

Adelman, Janet. *Suffocating Mothers: Fantasies of Maternal Origin in Shakespeare's Plays, Hamlet to the Tempest.* Florence, KY: Routledge, 2012.

Akhimie, Patricia. *Shakespeare and the Cultivation of Difference: Race and Conduct in the Early Modern World.* London: Routledge, 2018.

Allman, Eileen. *Jacobean Revenge Tragedy and the Politics of Virtue.* Newark: University of Delaware Press, 1999.

Altman, Joel B. '"Vile Participation": The Amplification of Violence in the Theater of *Henry V'. Shakespeare Quarterly*, 42 (1991): 1–32.

Anderson, Linda. *A Kind of Wild Justice: Revenge in Shakespeare's Comedies.* Newark: University of Delaware Press, 1987.

Apelbaum, Robert. *The Renaissance Discovery of Violence.* Bristol University Press, 2021.

Arendt, Hannah. *The Human Condition.* The University of Chicago Press, 1958.

Augustine. *Concerning the City of God against the Pagans.* Trans. Henry Bettinson. Harmondsworth: Penguin Books, 1972.

Bacon, Francis. *Essays.* London: 1625.

Baker, David J. '"Wildehirissheman": Colonialist Representation in Shakespeare's *Henry V'. Shakespeare's History Plays.* Ed. R. J. C. Watt. London: Longman and Pearson Education, 2002: 193–203.

Barber C. L. and Richard Wheeler. *The Whole Journey: Shakespeare's Power of Development.* Berkeley: University of California Press, 1986.

Barker, Juliet. *Henry V and the Battle that Made England: Agincourt. War, Literature and the Arts*, 18 (review) (2006).

Barker, Simon. *'Like a soldier to the stage': Field Commander Hamlet and the Ends of Tragedy.* Cheltenham: Cyder Press, University of Gloucestershire, 2009.

Barker, Simon. *War and Nation in the Theatre of Shakespeare and his Contemporaries.* Edinburgh University Press, 2021.

Bate, Jonathan. *The Genius of Shakespeare.* London: Picador, 1997.

Bates, Catherine. *Masculinity and the Hunt: Wyatt to Spenser.* Oxford University Press, 2013.

Baxter, Archibald. *We Will Not Cease: The Autobiography of a Conscientious Objector.* Christchurch, New Zealand: The Caxton Press, 1939.

Beckwith, Sarah. *Shakespeare and the Grammar of Forgiveness.* Ithaca: Cornell University Press, 2011.

Bergeron, David. 'The Mythical Structure of *All's Well That Ends Well*'. *Texas Studies in Literature and Language*, 14 (1973): 559–68.

Bevington, David. *Antony and Cleopatra.* The New Cambridge Shakespeare. Cambridge University Press, 2005.

Black, Ernest G. 'Torture Under English Law'. *University of Pennsylvania Law Review*, 75 (1927): 344–8.

Boitano, Piero, ed. *The European Tragedy of Troilus.* Oxford: Clarendon Press, 1989.

Bonadeo, Alfredo. 'Montaigne on War'. *Journal of the History of Ideas*, 46 (1985): 417–26.

Bonhoeffer, Dietrich. *The Cost of Discipleship.* London: Macmillan, 1963.

Boose, Lynda E. '"Let it be hid": The Pornographic Aesthetic of Shakespeare's *Othello*'. *New Casebooks Othello.* Ed. Lena Cowen Orlin. London: Palgrave Macmillan, 2004: 22–48.

Boulding, Elise. 'Can Peace be Imagined?'. *Peace: Meanings, Politics, Strategies.* Ed. Linda Rennie Forcey. Westport, CT: Praeger, 1989.

Bourke, Joanna. *Fear: A Cultural History.* Avalen: Shoemaker & Hoard, 2006.

Bowers, Fredson. *Elizabethan Revenge Tragedy.* Princeton University Press, 1940.

Boyajian, Zabelle C. 'War and Peace in Shakespeare'. *The Contemporary Review* 114 (1918): 569–77.

Boynton, L. *The Elizabethan Militia 1558–1638.* London: Routledge & Kegan Paul, 1967.

Braden, Gordon. *Renaissance Tragedy and the Senecan Tradition: An Anger's Privilege.* New Haven: Yale University Press, 1985.

Bregman, Rutger. *Humankind: A Hopeful History.* London: Bloomsbury, 2020.

Breight, Curtis. *Surveillance, Militarism and Drama in the Elizabethan Era.* Basingstoke: Macmillan, 1996.

Briggs, Julia. 'Shakespeare's Bed-Tricks'. *Essays in Criticism*, 44 (1994): 293–314.

Broomhall, Susan. '"The ambition in my love": The Theater of Courtly Conduct in *All's Well That Ends Well*'. *The Palgrave Handbook of Shakespeare's*

Queens. Eds. Kavita Mudan Finn and Valerie Schutte. London: Palgrave Macmillan, 2018: 367–8.

Broude, Ronald. 'Revenge and Revenge Tragedy in Renaissance England'. *Renaissance Quarterly*, 28 (1975).

Brown, Carolyn E. 'The Princess's Political Mission in *Love's Labour's Lost*: The Embassy to get Aquitaine and "All that is" Navarre's'. *The Palgrave Handbook of Shakespeare's Queens*. Eds. Kavita Mudan Finn and Valerie Schutte. London: Palgrave Macmillan, 2018: 313–29.

Bruckner, Lynne and Dan Brayton, eds. *Ecocritical Shakespeare*. Burlington VT: Ashgate, 2011.

Bulman, James. *Heroic Idiom of Shakespearean Tragedy*. University of Delaware Press, 2003.

Burgess, C. F. 'Othello's Occupation'. *Shakespeare Quarterly*, 26 (1975): 208–13, 210.

Burke, Kenneth. *Kenneth Burke on Shakespeare*. Ed. Scott L. Newstok. West Lafayette: Parlor Press, 2008.

Burton, Jonathan, '"A most wily bird": Leo Africanus, *Othello* and the trafficking in difference'. *Post-Colonial Shakespeares*. Eds. Ania Loomba and Martin Orkin. London: Routledge, 1998.

Butler, Judith. *The Force of Nonviolence: An Ethico-Political Bind*. London: Verso, 2020.

Byles, Joanna Montgomery. '"The Cyprus Wars": Psychoanalysis and Race in Shakespeare's *Othello*'. *Actes du coloque tenu à Lyon*, 1997, Université Lumière-Lyon 2, Université de Chypre, 139–46, 142.

Cahan, Jean Axelrad. 'Reconciliation or Reconstruction? Further Thoughts on Political Forgiveness' *Polity*, 45, no. 2 (2013), 'Forgotten Virtues': 174–197.

Cahill, Patricia A. *Unto the Breach: Martial Formations, Historical Trauma, and the Early Modern Stage*. Oxford University Press, 2008.

Callaghan, Dympna. *Reading Shakespeare's Poetry*. Hoboken, NJ: Wiley Blackwell, 2023.

Callaghan, Dympna. 'Representing Cleopatra in the Post-colonial Moment'. *Antony and Cleopatra. Theory in Practice*. Ed. Nigel Wood. Buckingham: Open University Press, 1996: 41–65.

Callaghan, Dympna. *Woman and Gender in Renaissance Tragedy*. Hemel Hempstead: Harvester Wheatsheaf, 1989.

Campbell, Lily B. 'Theories of Revenge in Renaissance England'. *Modern Philology*, 38 (1931): 281–96.

Carles, Nathalie Rivère de. *Early Modern Diplomacy, Theatre and Soft Power: The Making of Peace*. London: Palgrave Macmillan, 2016.

Cavell, Stanley, 'The avoidance of love: A reading of *King Lear*'. *Must We Mean What We Say?* Cambridge University Press, 1976.

Cervantes, Miguel. *The History of Don Quixote of the Mancha*. Trans. Thomas Shelton. London: Edward Blount, 1620.

Chalmers, Hero, '"Break up the court": Power, Female Performance and Courtly Ceremony in *Henry VIII*'. *Shakespeare*, 7 (2011): 257–68.

Charnes, Linda. 'Spies and Whispers: Exceeding Reputation in *Antony and Cleopatra*'. *Notorious Identity: Materializing the Subject in Shakespeare.* Cambridge, MA: Harvard University Press, 1993.

Charney, Maurice. 'The Voice of Marlowe's Tamburlaine in Early Shakespeare'. *Comparative Drama*, 31 (1997): 213–222.

Cheng, Elyssa Y. 'Moral Economy and the Politics of Food Riots in *Coriolanus*'. *Concentric: Literature and Cultural Studies*, 36 (2010): 17–31.

Chickera, Ernst de. 'Divine Justice and Private Revenge in *The Spanish Tragedy*'. *Modern Language Review*, 57, no. 2 (1962): 38–58, 228–32.

Clare, Janet. *Revenge Tragedies of the Renaissance.* Liverpool University Press, 2003.

Clayton, Daniel M. 'Whitewashing WWII Sexual Memory'. *War, Literature and the Arts: An International Journal of the Humanities*, 27 (2015).

Cohen, Derek. *Shakespeare's Culture of Violence.* London: Palgrave, 1993.

Cohen, Derek. 'Tragedy and the Nation: *Othello*'. *Searching Shakespeare: Studies in Culture and Authority.* University of Toronto Press, 2003: 3–18.

Coleridge, S. T. *Coleridge on Shakespeare.* Ed. Terence Hawkes. Harmondsworth: Penguin Shakespeare Library, 1959.

Cookson, J. E. *The Friends of Peace; Anti-war liberation in England 1793–1815.* Cambridge University Press, 1982.

Cooper, Helen. 'Speaking for the Victim'. *Writing War: Medieval Responses to Warfare.* Eds. Corinne Saunders, Francoise le Saux, and Neil Thomas. Cambridge: D. S. Brewer, 2004: 213–31.

Coral, Jordi. '"Maiden Walls That War Hath Never Entered": Rape and Post-Chivalric Military Culture in Shakespeare's *Henry V*'. *College Literature*, 44 (2017): 404–435.

Corbin, Peter and Douglas Sedge, eds. *The Oldcastle Controversy.* Manchester University Press, 1991.

Cowie, Peter. *The Cinema of Orson Welles.* New York: Da Capo Press, 1983.

Crawford, Emily, *Identifying the Enemy: Civilian Participation in Hostilities* (Oxford University Press, 2015).

Crawford, Emily. *The Treatment of Combatants and Insurgents Under the Law of Armed Conflict.* Oxford University Press, 2010.

Crawford, Emily and Aaron Fellmeth. '"Reason to know" in the international law of command responsibility'. *International Review of the Red Cross*,184 (2022): 1223–1266.

Cruickshank, C. G. *Elizabeth's Army.* London, 1946.

Curbet, Joan. 'Repressing the Amazon: Cross-Dressing and Militarism in Edmund Spenser's *The Faerie Queene*'. *Dressing Up For War: Transformations of Gender and Genre in the Discourse and Literature of War.* Ed. Aránzazu Usandizaga and Andrew Monnickendam. Amsterdam: Rodopi B.V., 2001: 157–72.

Cutrofellow, Andrew. *All for Nothing: Hamlet's Negativity.* Cambridge MA: MIT Press, 2014.

Cutrofellow, Andrew. 'Kant's Debate with Herder About the Significance of the Genius of Shakespeare'. *Philosophy Compass*, 3 (2008): 66–82.

Danby, John. 'The Shakespearian Dialectic'. *Scrutiny*, xvi (1949): 196–213.

Daniel, Samuel. *The Complete Works of Samuel Daniel*. Ed. Alexander Grosart. London: Spenser Society, 1885.

Dante Alighieri. *The Divine Comedy*. Trans. John D. Sinclair. Oxford University Press, 1948.

Dash, Irene. *Women's Worlds in Shakespeare's Plays*, London: Associated Presses 1997.

Dawson, Anthony B. and Gretchen E. Minton. *Timon of Athens*. Ed. Anthony B. Dawson, Arden Shakespeare Third Series. London: Cengage Learning, 2008.

Deagon, Donald David. *Pacifism in Greek and Modern Drama*. Unpub. PhD Tulane University: ProQuest Dissertations Publishing, 1969, 7006391.

Dekker, Thomas. *A larum for London*. Ed. W. W. Greg. Malone Society Reprints, Oxford University Press, 1913.

Derrin, Daniel. '*Sine dolore*: Relative Painlessness in Shakespeare's Laughter at War'. *Critical Survey*, 29 (2018): 81–97.

Dollimore, Jonathan. '*King Lear*: A Materialist Reading'. *Radical Tragedy*. Hemel Hempstead: The Harvester Press, 1984.

Donne, John. *John Donne: The Complete English Poems*. Rev. edn. Ed. A. J. Smith. Harmondsworth: Penguin English Poets, 1977.

Donne, John. *No Man is an Island: A Selection from the prose of John Donne*, ed. Rivers Scott (London: The Folio Society 1997).

Doran, Madeline, '"High Events as These": The Language of Hyperbole in *Antony and Cleopatra*', in *Shakespeare's Dramatic Language*, (Madison: University of Wisconsin Press, 1976).

Dunant, J. Henri. *A Memory of Solferino*. Geneva: Imprémerie Jules-Guillaume Fick, 1862.

Dunne, Derek, '"Superfluous Death" and the Mathematics of Revenge', *Journal of the Northern Renaissance*, 6 (2014).

Edelman, Charles, *Brawl Ridiculous: Swordfighting in Shakespeare's Plays* (Manchester University Press, Revels Plays Companion Library, 1992).

Edelman, Charles, *Shakespeare's Military Language: A Dictionary*. (London: Athlone Press, 2000).

Edelman, Charles, '"Then Every Soldier Kill His Prisoners": Shakespeare at the Battle of Agincourt', *Parergon*, n.s. 16 (1998), 31–45.

Edsforth, Ronald, ed. *A Cultural History of Peace*, 6 vols. London: Bloomsbury, 2020.

Elliott, Martin, *Shakespeare's Invention of Othello* (London: Macmillan, 1988).

Elton, William, *King Lear and the Gods* (San Marino: Huntington Library, 1966).

Erasmus, Desiderius. *The Collected Works of Erasmus: Literary and Educational Writings* in sundry volumes. Toronto University Press, 1986.

Erasmus, Desiderius. *Complaint of Peace*. English edition 1795; quoted from first American edition. Boston and New Jersey: Charles Williams and D. Allinson, 1813.

Everett, Barbara, ed. *Antony and Cleopatra*. New York: Signet, 1963.

Everett, Barbara. 'Reflections on the Sentimentalist's Othello'. *Critical Quarterly*, 3 (1961): 127–39.

Everett, Barbara. 'Spanish Othello'. *Shakespeare Survey*, 35 (1982): 101–112

Everett, Barbara. *Young Hamlet: Essays on Shakespeare's Tragedies*. Oxford: Clarendon Press, 1989.

Faas, Ekbart, *Shakespeare's Poetics* (Cambridge University Press, 1986).

Farrell, Kirby. *Play, Death and Heroism in Shakespeare*. Chapel Hill: University of South Carolina Press, 1989.

Fissel, Mark Charles in *English Warfare 1511–1642* (London: Routledge 2001).

Floyd-Wilson, Mary, *English Ethnicity and Race* (Cambridge University Press, 2003); Cohen, Stephen, 'I am what I am not: identifying with the other in Othello', *Shakespeare Survey* 64 (Cambridge, 2011).

Fly, Richard D.. 'The Ending of *Timon of Athens*'. *Criticism*, 15 (1973): 242–52.

Foakes, R. A. *Hamlet versus Lear* (Cambridge University Press, 1993).

Foakes, R. A., ed. *King Henry VIII*. The Arden Shakespeare. London: Methuen, 1964.

Friedman, Alan Warren. *Shakespeare's Returning Warriors – and Ours*. New York: Routledge, 2021.

Freeman, Sonya Loftis. *Shakespeare and Disability Studies*. Oxford University Press, 2021.

Freud, Sigmund. *The Joke and its Relation to the Unconscious* (1905). Trans. Joyce Crick. London: Penguin Classics, 2003.

Fuller, David. 'The Bogdanov Version: The English Shakespeare Company "Wars of the Roses"'. *Literature/Film Quarterly*, 33 (2005): 118–141, 119.

Fussell, Paul. *The Great War and Modern Memory*. Oxford University Press, 1975.

Gandhi. *Collected Works of Mahatma Gandhi*. 16 (1960–1999).

Gardner, Helen. 'The Noble Moor'. *Proceedings of the British Academy*, 41 (1955).

Garrison, John S. and Kyle Pivetti. *Shakespeare at Peace*. London: Routledge, 2019.

Ghervas, Stella and David Armitage, eds. *A Cultural History of Peace in the Age of Enlightenment*. London: Bloomsbury, 2020.

Giddens, Eugene. 'Honourable Men: Militancy and Masculinity in Julius Caesar'. *Renaissance Forum*, 5.2 (2001).

Girard, René. 'Hamlet's Dull Revenge'. *Literary Theory / Renaissance Texts*. Eds. Patricia Parker and David Quint. Baltimore: Johns Hopkins University Press, 1986: 280–302.

Girard, René. 'The Politics of Desire in *Troilus and Cressida*'. *Shakespeare and the Question of Theory*. Eds. Patricia Parker and Geoffrey Hartman. New York: Methuen, 1985: 188–209.

Gittings, John. *The Glorious Art of Peace: From the Iliad to Iraq*. Oxford University Press, 2012.

Goldman, Michael. 'Falstaff Asleep' in *Shakespeare and the Energies of Drama*. New Jersey: Princeton University Press, 1972.

Goldstein, Joshua S. *War and Gender*. Cambridge University Press, 2001.

Gower, John. *Confessio Amantis*. Trans. Terence Tiller. Harmondsworth: Penguin Books 1963.

Gray, Patrick, ed. *Shakespeare and the Ethics of War*. New York: Berghahn Books, 2019.

Gray, Patrick. 'Shakespeare and War'. *Critical Survey*, 30 (2018).

Greene, Gayle. '"This that you call love": Sexual and Social Tragedy in *Othello*'. *Shakespeare And Gender: A History*. Eds. Deborah E. Barker and Ivo Kamps. London: Verso, 1995: 47–62.

Greenslade, Mark. 'Montaigne and the Wars of Religion'. *The Oxford Handbook of Montaigne*. Ed. Philippe Desan. Oxford University Press, 2016.

Grennan, Eamon. 'The Women's Voices in *Othello*: Speech, Song, Silence'. *Shakespeare Quarterly*, 38 (1987): 275–292.

Griffin, Aurélie. 'The Princess of France: Difference and Diff(é)rance in *Love's Labour's Lost*'. *The Palgrave Handbook of Shakespeare's Queens*. Eds. Kavita Mudan Finn and Valerie Schutte. London: Palgrave Macmillan, 2018: 395–412.

Griffiths, Paul. *Lost Londons: Change, Crime, and Control in the Capital City, 1550–1660*. Cambridge University Press, 2008.

Guarini, Giambattista. *Compendium of Tragicomic Poetry* (1601). *Literary Criticism Plato to Dryden*. Ed. Allan H. Gilbert. New York: American Book Co., 1940: 505–33.

Gurr, Andrew (ed.) *Henry V*. New Cambridge Shakespeare. Cambridge University Press, 1992.

Halio, Jay L. *The Tragedy of King Lear*. The New Cambridge Shakespeare. Cambridge University Press, 1992.

Hallett, Charles A. and Elaine S. Hallett. *The Revenger's Madness: A Study of Revenge Tragedy Motifs*. Lincoln, Nebraska: University of Nebraska Press, 1980.

Hamilton, Donna. *Shakespeare and the Politics of Protestant England*. New York: Harvester Wheatsheaf, 1992.

Hampton, Timothy. *Fictions of Embassy: Literature and Diplomacy in Early Modern Europe*. New York: Cornell University Press, 2011.

Harlan, Susan. *Memories of War in Early Modern England: Armour and Militant Nostalgia in Marlowe, Sidney, and Shakespeare*. London: Palgrave Macmillan, 2016.

Harris, Sharon M. 'Feminism and Shakespeare's Cressida: "*If* I be false . . ."'. *Women's Studies: An Interdisciplinary Journal*, 18 (1990): 65–82.

Hazlitt, William, *Hazlitt's Criticism of Shakespeare, Studies in British Literature*, ed. R. S. White (Lampeter: The Edwin Mellon Press, 1996).

Heale, Elizabeth. '"The Fruits of War": The Voice of the Soldier in Gascoigne, Rich and Churchyard'. *Early Modern Literary Studies*, 14 (2008): 1–39.

Hemingway, Ernest. *A Moveable Feast*. New York: Charles Scribner's Sons, 1964.

Hiscock, Andrew. '"Man is a Battlefield Within himself": Arms and the Affections in the Counsel of More, Erasmus, Vives and their Circle'. *Emotions and War: Medieval to Romantic Literature*. Eds Stephanie Downes, Andrew Lynch and Katrina O'Loughlin. London: Palgrave, 2015: 152–68.

Hiscock, Andrew. '"More warlike than politique": Shakespeare and the theatre of war – a critical survey'. *Shakespeare*, 7 (2011): 221–247.

Hiscock, Andrew. 'Shakespeare and the Fortunes of War and Memory'. *Société Française Shakespeare*, 30 (2013).

Holderness, Graham. *Shakespeare Recycled: The Making of Historical Drama*. Brighton: Harvester Wheatsheaf, 1992.

Holland, Norman H., Sidney Homan and Bernard J. Paris, eds. *Shakespeare's Personality*. Berkeley: University of California Press, 1989.

Homan, Sidney, R. 'Divided Response in *Antony and Cleopatra*'. *Philological Quarterly*, 49 (1970): 460–8.

Homer. *Iliad*. Trans. A. S. Kline. (online, Rijksmuseum, 2009).

Honigmann, E. A. J., ed. *Othello*. Arden Shakespeare Third Series (Walton-on-Thames: Thomas Nelson, 1997.

Honigmann, E. A. J. 'Shakespeare and London's Immigrant Community circa 1600'. *Elizabethan and Modern Studies*. Ed. J. P. Vander Motten. Ghent: Seminarie voor Engelse en Amerikaanse Literatuur, R.U.G., 1985: 143–53.

Honigmann, E. A. J. 'Shakespeare, Sir Thomas More and Asylum Seekers'. *Shakespeare Survey*, 57 (2007): 225–35.

Honselaars, Tom. 'Great War Shakespeare: Somewhere in France, 1914–19'. *Actes des congrès de la Société française Shakespeare*, 33 (2015).

Hortman, Willheim. 'Shakespeare on the Political Stage in the Twentieth Century'. *The Cambridge Companion to Shakespeare on Stage*. Eds. Stanley Wells and Sarah Stanton. Cambridge University Press, 2002: 212–29.

Howard, Jean and Phyllis Rackin. *Engendering a Nation*. London: Routledge, 1997.

Hudson, Geoffrey L. 'Disabled Veterans and the State in Early Modern England'. *Disabled Veterans in History*. Ed. David Gerber. Ann Arbor: University of Michigan Press, 2000.

Hughes-Hallett, Lucy. *Cleopatra: Histories, Dreams, Distortions*. London: HarperCollins, 1990.

Huizinga, Johan. *The Waning of the Middle Ages*. London: Edward Arnold, 1924.

Hunter, G. K., ed. *All's Well That Ends Well*, Arden Shakespeare Second Series, 1967.

Hunter, G. K. 'Othello and Colour Prejudice'. *Dramatic Identities and Cultural Tradition*. Liverpool University Press, 1978.

Hunter, G. K. 'Seneca and English Tragedy'. *Dramatic Identities and Cultural*

Tradition: Studies in Shakespeare and his Contemporaries. Liverpool University Press, 1978.

Hunter, Robert Grams. *Shakespeare and the Comedy of Forgiveness.* New York: Columbia University Press, 1965.

Igarashi, Hirohisa. 'The Impossibility of Turning Rancour to Love: The Post-war Controversy over the Pacifist Constitution and Yukio Ninagawa's Construing of *Romeo and Juliet*'. *Shakespeare*, 17 (2001): 230–41.

Jackson, MacDonald P. 'The Date and Authorship of Hand D's Contribution to Sir Thomas More: Evidence from "Literature Online"'. *Shakespeare Survey*, 59 (2006): 69–78.

James, Heather. *Shakespeare's Troy: Drama, Politics, and the Translation of Empire.* Cambridge University Press, 2007.

Johnson, Samuel. 'Preface to Shakespeare'. *Dr Johnson on Shakespeare.* Ed. W. K. Wimsatt. Harmondsworth: Penguin Shakespeare Library, 1960.

Johnson, Samuel. *Samuel Johnson on Shakespeare.* Ed. W. K. Wimsatt. New York, 1960.

Johnson, Toria. 'Fear: Macbeth, Othello'. *Shakespeare and Emotion.* Ed. Katharine Craik. Cambridge University Press, 2021: 199–210.

Johnson, Toria. '"To feel what wretches feel": Reformation and the Re-naming of English Compassion'. *Compassion in Early Modern Literature and Culture.* Eds. Kristine Steenberg and Katherine Ibbett. Cambridge University Press, 2021.

Jones, Adam, ed. *Gendercide and Genocide.* Nashville: Vanderbilt University Press, 2004.

Jones, Eldred. *Othello's Countrymen: The African in English Renaissance Drama.* Oxford University Press, 1965.

Jones, Emrys, ed. *Antony and Cleopatra.* Harmondsworth: New Penguin Shakespeare.

Jorgensen, Paul A. *Shakespeare's Military World.* Los Angeles: California University Press, 1956.

Journal of the American Psychoanalytic Association, 53 (2005), 389–409.

Kane, Christopher J. *Shadows of Empire: The Displaced New World of 'Antony and Cleopatra'*, unpubl. dissertation, John Carroll University (2016).

Kant, Immanuel. *Critique of Judgment* [1790]. Trans. J. H. Bernard. New York: Hafner Publishing, 1951.

Kant, Immanuel. *Perpetual Peace: A Philosophical Essay* (1795).

Karim-Cooper, Farah. *The Great White Bard: Shakespeare, Race and the Future.* London: Oneworld Publications, 2023.

Keegan, John. *The Face of Battle.* New York: Viking Press, 1976.

Keen, Maurice. *Chivalry.* New Haven, NJ: Yale University Press, 1984.

Kehler, Dorothy. *Shakespeare's Widows.* New York: Palgrave Macmillan, 2009.

Kelly, Philippa. *The King and I.* London: Continuum, 2011.

Kelly, Philippa, ed. *King Lear: The Bell Shakespeare.* Sydney: Halstead Press, 2002.

Kerrigan, John. *Revenge Tragedy: Aeschylus to Armageddon*. Oxford University Press, 1996.

Keyishian, Harry. *The Shapes of Revenge: Victimization, Vengeance, and Vindictiveness In Shakespeare*. New Jersey: Humanities Press, 1995.

Khan, Coppélia Khan. *Man's Estate: Masculine Identity in Shakespeare*. Berkeley CA: University of California Press, 1981.

Khan, Coppélia. *Roman Shakespeare: Warriors, Wounds and Women*. London: Routledge, 1997.

King, Ros and Paul J. C. M. Franssen, eds. *Shakespeare and War*. Basingstoke: Palgrave Macmillan, 2008.

Knight, G. Wilson. *The Crown of Life*. London: Methuen, 1947.

Knight, G. Wilson. *The Sovereign Flower*. London: Methuen, 1958.

Knight, G. Wilson. *The Wheel of Fire: Interpretations of Shakespearian Tragedy*. Oxford University Press, 1930.

Knowles, Richard. 'Revision Awry in Folio *Lear* 3.1', *Shakespeare Quarterly*, 46 (1995): 32–46.

Kott, Jan. *Shakespeare Our Contemporary*. London: Methuen 1965.

Kujawińska, Krystina Courtney and Katarzna Kwapisz Williams. '"The Polish Prince": Studies in Cultural Appropriation of Shakespeare's *Hamlet* in Poland'. Poland: University of Łódz, 2001: 1–15.

Lake, Peter. *How Shakespeare Put Politics on the Stage: Power and Succession in the History Plays*. New Haven: Yale University Press, 2016.

Lamb, Charles. *Charles Lamb on Shakespeare*, ed. Joan Coldwell (Buckinghamshire: Colin Smythe Ltd., 1978).

Langis, Unhae. 'Coriolanus: Inordinate Passions and Powers in Personal and Political Governance'. *Comparative Drama*, 44 (2010): 1–27.

Langley, Eric. 'Standing on a Beach: Shakespeare and the Sympathetic Imagination'. *Compassion in Early Modern Literature and Culture*. Eds. Kristine Steenberg and Katherine Ibbett. Cambridge University Press, 2021: 197–215, 201.

LaPerle, Carol Mejia. 'Race in Shakespeare's tragedies'. *The Cambridge Companion to Shakespeare and Race*. Ed. Ayanna Thompson. Cambridge University Press, 2021.

Lawrence, David R. 'Reappraising the Elizabethan and Early Stuart Soldier: Recent Historiography on Early Modern English Military Culture', *History Compass* 9 (2011), 16–33.

Lazzarini, Isabella. *A Cultural History of Peace in the Renaissance*. London: Bloomsbury, 2020.

Leavis, F. R., 'Diabolic Intellect and the Noble Hero', *Scrutiny* 6 (1937), repr. In *The Common Pursuit* (London: Chatto and Windus, 1952), 146–7.

Lenz, Carolyn Ruth Swift, Gayle Greene, and Carol Thomas Neely (eds), *The Woman's Part: Feminist Criticism of Shakespeare*. Urbana: University of Illinois Press, 1980.

Lerner, Laurence, 'Peace Studies: A Proposal', *New Literary History*, 26 (1995), 641–65.

Levine, Laura, 'Strange Flesh: *Antony and Cleopatra* and the story of the dissolving warrior', *Men in Women's Clothing: Anti-Theatricality and Effeminization, 1579–1642,* (Cambridge University Press, 1994), 44–72.

Lidster, Amy and Sonia Massai, eds. *Shakespeare at War: A Material History.* Cambridge University Press, 2023.

Liivoja, Raine, 'Chivalry without a Horse: Military Honour and the Modern Law of Armed Conflict' in Raine Liivoja, Andres Saumets (eds), *The Law of Armed Conflict: Historical and Contemporary Perspectives* (Tartu, Estonia: Tartu University Press), 2012, 75–100.

Limon, Jerzy. 'Poland'. *The Oxford Companion to Shakespeare.* 2nd ed. Eds. Michael Dobson, Stanley Wells, Will Sharpe, Erin Sullivan. Online version. Oxford University Press, 2015: 117.

Lodge, Thomas. *A Fig for Momus.* London: 1595.

Logan, Sandra. 'Cordelia, Foreign Queenship, and the Commonweal'. *The Palgrave Handbook of Shakespeare's Queens.* Eds. Kavita Mudan Finn and Valerie Schutte. London: Palgrave Macmillan, 2018: 69–86.

Loomba, Ania and Martin Orkin, eds. *Post-Colonial Shakespeares.* London: Routledge, 1998.

Loomba, Ania. *Shakespeare, Race, and Colonialism.* Oxford University Press, 2002.

Lowe, Ben. *Imagining Peace: Imagining Peace: A History of English Pacifist Ideas.* Pennsylvania University Press, 1997.

Lynch, Andrew. 'Preface'. *Literature, Emotions, and Pre-Modern War.* Eds. Claire McIlroy and Anne M. Scott. Yorkshire: Arc Humanities Press, 2021.

MacDonald, Joyce Green. *Women and Race in Early Modern Texts.* Cambridge University Press, 2004.

Mack, Maynard. '*Antony and Cleopatra*: The Stillness and the Dance'. *Shakespeare's Art: Seven Essays.* Ed. Milton Crane. Chicago: University of Chicago Press, 1973: 79–113.

Mack, Maynard. *King Lear in Our Time.* London: Methuen, 1966.

Maddocks, Melvin, 'Comedy and War', *Sewanee Review,* 112 (2004), 22–34.

Mallin, Eric, *Inscribing the Time: Shakespeare and the End of Elizabethan England* (Berkeley, Los Angeles: University of California Press, 1995).

Mann, Jill, 'Shakespeare and Chaucer: "What is Criseyde worth"'. *The European Tragedy of Troilus.* Ed. Piero Boitano. Oxford: Clarendon Press, 1989: 219–42, 236.

Manning, R. B. *Swordsmen: The Martial Ethos in the Three Kingdoms* (Oxford University Press, 2003).

Margeson, John, ed. *Henry VIII.* New Cambridge Shakespeare. Cambridge University Press, 2012.

Marlowe, Christopher. *The Complete Plays.* Ed. J. B. Steane. London: Penguin Classics, 1969.

Marlowe, Christopher. *Plays and Poems.* Ed. M. Ridley. London: J.M. Dent, 1955.

Marsh, D. R. C., 'The Conflict of Love and Responsibility in *Antony and Cleopatra*', *Theoria: A Journal of Social and Political Theory*, 15 (1960), 1–27.

Marshall, Cynthia, 'A Modern Perspective: *Antony and Cleopatra*', Folger Shakespeare Library online.

Martin, Randall, *Shakespeare and Ecology* (Oxford University Press 2015).

Marx, Steven. 'Holy War in *Henry Fifth*'. *Shakespeare Survey*, 48 (1995): 85–99.

Marx, Steven. 'The Prophet Disarmed: Milton and the Quakers'. *Studies in English Literature 1500–1800*, (Winter, 1992): 1–26.

Marx, Steven. 'Shakespeare's Pacifism'. *Renaissance Quarterly*, 45 (1992): 49–95.

Materyk, Irena K. and Joseph G. Price, *Shakespeare in the World of Communism and Socialism* (University of Toronto Press 2006).

Mattox, John Mark. 'Henry V: Shakespeare's Just Warrior'. *War, Literature, and the Arts*, 12 (2000): 30–54.

Maxwell, J. C. 'Simple or Complex? Some Problems in the Interpretation of Shakespeare'. *Durham University Journal*, xlvi (1954): 112–15.

Maxwell, J. C. 'The Technique of Invocation in King Lear'. *Modern Language Review*, 45 (1950).

Mayton, Daniel M., *Nonviolence and Peace Psychology: Intrapersonal, Interpersonal, Societal and World Peace*. Heidelberg: Springer, 2009.

McChesney, Sam, 'The Meaning of Courage in Montaigne's *Essays*', *The European Legacy*, 26 (2020), 141–48.

McInnis, David, *Shakespeare and Lost Plays: Reimagining Drama in Early Modern England* (Cambridge University Press, 2021), 11–14.

McJannet, Linda, 'Gesta Romanorum: Heroic Action and Stage Imagery in *Antony and Cleopatra*', *Shakespeare Bulletin* 11 (1993): 5–9, 5.

McKeown, Adam, N. *English Mercuries: Soldier Poets in the Age of Shakespeare* (Vanderbilt University Press, 2009).

McLoughlin, Kate. *Authoring War: The Literary Representation of War from the 'Iliad' to Iraq*. Cambridge University Press, 2011.

McLoughlin Kate. *The Cambridge Companion to War*. Cambridge University Press, 2009.

Meek, Richard and Erin Sullivan, eds. *The Renaissance of Emotion: Understanding Affect in Shakespeare and his Contemporaries*. Manchester University Press, 2015.

Meek, Richard. 'Othello's Sympathies: Emotion, Agency and Identification'. *Shakespeare Survey* 74 (2022): 194–207.

Meek, Richard. *Sympathy in Early Modern Literature and Culture 1580–1640*. Cambridge University Press, 2023.

Meron, Theodor. *Bloody Constraint: War and Chivalry in Shakespeare*. Oxford University Press, Incorporated, 1998.

Meron, Theodor. *Henry's Wars and Shakespeare's Laws: Perspectives on the Law of War in the Later Middle Ages*. Oxford: Clarendon Press, 1993.

Meron, Theodor. 'Shakespeare: a dove, a hawk, or simply a humanist?'. *American Journal of International Law*, 111 (2017): 936–56.

Miller, Anthony, 'Varieties of Power in *Antony and Cleopatra*', *Sydney Studies in English*, 30 (2004), 4259.

Miola, Robert S. 'New Comedy in *All's Well That Ends Well*'. *Renaissance Quarterly*, 46 (1993): 23–43.

Montaigne, Michel de, *The Complete Essays*, transl. M. A. Screech (London: Penguin Books, 1987).

Morgann, Maurice, *An Essay on the Dramatic Character of Sir John Falstaff* (London: T. Boys, Ludgate Hill, 1777).

Morreall, John, 'Philosophy of Humour', *Stanford Encyclopedia of Philosophy*, (online, 2016).

Morse, Ruth, 'Some Social Costs of War', in *Shakespeare and War*, ed. Ros King and Paul J. C. M. Franssen, 56–68.

Muir, Edwin, *The Politics of King Lear* (Glasgow: Jackson, 1947).

Murrin, Michael, *History and Warfare in Renaissance Epic* (University of Chicago Press, 1997).

Neill, Michael, ed. *Anthony and Cleopatra*. Oxford University Press, 1994.

Neill, Michael. 'Changing Places in *Othello*'. *Shakespeare Survey*, 37 (1984): 115–31.

Neill, Michael. 'English Revenge Tragedy'. *A Companion to Tragedy*. Ed. Rebecca Bushnell (Oxford: Blackwell, 2005).

Neill, Michael. *Issues of Death: Mortality and Identity in Renaissance Tragedy*. Oxford: Clarendon Press, 1997.

Neill, Michael. *Putting History to the Question: Power, Politics and Society in English Renaissance Drama*. New York: Columbia University Press, 2000.

Newstrom (Newstok), Scott. 'Right Pitches Dubya as Henry V'. *AlterNet*, May 29, 2003.

O'Rourke, James. *Re-Authorizing Shakespeare Through Presentist Readings*. London: Routledge, 2012.

Onions, C. T. *A Shakespeare Glossary*. 3rd ed. rev. Robert D. Eagleson. Oxford University Press, 1986.

Oppitz-Trotman, George. *The Origins of English Revenge Tragedy*. Edinburgh University Press, 2019.

Parker, R. B. 'War and Sex in *All's Well that Ends Well*'. *Shakespeare Survey*, 37 (1984): 99–113.

Patterson, Annabel. '"All is True": Negotiating the Past in *Henry VIII*'. *Elizabethan Theater: Essays in Honor of S. Schoenbaum*. Ed. R. B. Parker and S. P. Zitner. Newark, NJ: University of Delaware Press, 1996: 147–66.

Patterson, Annabel. *Shakespeare and the Popular Voice*. Oxford: Basil Blackwell, 1989.

Patterson, David S. 'Pacifism'. *1914–1918 Online International Encyclopedia of the First World War*, 2014, accessed 18 January 2023. https://encycloped ia.1914-1918-online.net/article/pacifism

Pechter, Edward. *'Othello' and Interpretive Traditions*. University of Iowa Press, 1999.

Pechter, Edward. 'Why Should We Call her Whore? Bianca in *Othello'*. *Shakespeare and the Twentieth Century: The Selected Proceedings of the International Shakespeare Association World Congress Los Angeles, 1996*. Eds. Jonathan Bate, Jill Levenson, Dieter Mehl. Newark: University of Delaware Press, 1998: 364–77.

Peck, Russell. 'Edgar's Pilgrimage: High Comedy in *King Lear'*. *Studies in English Literature 1500–1900*, 7 (1967): 219–37.

Pierce, Robert B. *Shakespeare's History Plays: The Family and the State*. Ohio State University Press, 1971.

Plutarch. *Shakespeare's Plutarch*. Ed. T. J. Spencer. Harmondsworth: Penguin Books, 1964.

Pollard, Tanya. 'Tragedy and Revenge'. *The Cambridge Companion to English Renaissance Tragedy*. Ed. Emma Smith and Garrett A. Sullivan. Cambridge University Press, 2010: 58–72.

Prosser, Eleanor. *Hamlet and Revenge*. 2nd ed. (Stanford, 1971).

Proudfoot, Richard and Nicola Bennett. *King Edward III*. Arden Edition Third Series. London: Bloomsbury, 2017.

Pugliatti, Paola. *Shakespeare and the Just War Tradition*. Farnham: Ashgate, 2010.

Quabeck, Franzisa. *Just and Unjust Wars in Shakespeare*. Berlin: de Gruyter, 2013.

Quabeck, Franzisa. 'Shakespeare's Unjust Wars'. *Critical Survey*, 30 (2018): 67–80.

Queen Elizabeth I: Selected Works. Ed. Steven W. May. New York: Washington Square Press, 2004: 77.

Quint, David. *Montaigne and the Quality of Mercy: Ethical and Political Themes in the 'Essais'*. Princeton University Press, 1998.

Rabkin, Norman. *Shakespeare and the Common Understanding*. New York: Free Press, 1967.

Rackin, Phyllis. 'Anti-Historians: Women's Roles in Shakespeare's Histories'. *Theatre Journal*, 37 (1985): 329–344.

Raleigh, Sir Walter. *The Complete Works of Sir Walter Raleigh*, 8 vols. Oxford University Press, 1829.

Raw, Laurence. 'People's Theatre and Shakespeare in Wartime: Donald Wolfit's *King Lear* in London and Leeds, 1944–45'. *Shakespeare*, 12 (2016): 55–66.

Raw, Laurence. *Theatre of the People: Donald Wolfit's Shakespearean Productions 1937–1953*. Lanham, Maryland: Rowman and Littlefield, 2015.

Rees, Stuart. *Passion for Peace: Exercising Power Creatively*. Sydney: NewSouth Publishing, 2003.

Rhoads, Diana Akers. *Shakespeare's Defense of Poetry: 'A Midsummer Night's Dream' and 'The Tempest'*. Lanham: University Press of America, 1979.

Ribner, Irving. *The English History Play in the Age of Shakespeare*. London: Routledge, 1965.

Ribner, Irving. *Patterns in Shakespearean Tragedy*. London: Methuen, 1960.

Richter, Jeffrey P. 'Japan's "Reinterpretation" of Article 9: A Pyrrhic Victory for American Foreign Policy?'. *Iowa Law Review*, 101 (2016): 1223–62.

Ridge, Kelsey. *Shakespeare's Military Spouses and Twenty-First-Century Warfare*. New York: Routledge 2021.

Rigby, Andrew. *Justice and Reconciliation; After the Violence*. Boulder: Lynne Reiner Publishers, 2001.

Robinson, Paul. 'Magnanimity and Integrity as Military Virtues'. *Journal of Military Ethics*, 6 (2007): 259–69.

Robinson, Paul. *Military Honour and the Conduct of War*. London: Routledge, 2006.

Robison, William B. 'The Bard, the Bride and the Muse Bemused: Katherine of Valois on Film in Shakespeare's *Henry V*'. *The Palgrave Handbook of Shakespeare's Queens*. Eds. Kavita Mudan Finn and Valerie Schutte. London: Palgrave Macmillan, 2018: 475–501.

Rosenwald, Lawrence. 'Sketch of a Pacifist Critic'. *Raritan*, 39 (2019): 1–20.

Rossiter, A. P. *Angel With Horns*. London: Longman, 1961.

Rowland, Susan. 'Shakespeare and the Jungian Symbol: A Case of War and Marriage'. *Jung Journal: Culture & Psyche*, 5 (2011): 31–46.

Ryan, Kiernan. '*King Lear*: "men / Are as the time is"'. *Shakespeare: Harvester New Readings*. Hemel Hempstead: Harvester Wheatsheaf, 1989.

Sacchetti, Livia. '"A Gap in Nature": Rewriting Cleopatra Through *Antony and Cleopatra*'s Cosmology'. *The Palgrave Handbook of Shakespeare's Queens*. Eds. Kavita Mudan Finn and Valerie Schutte. London: Palgrave Macmillan, 2018: 413–30.

Sackville, Thomas. *The Works of Thomas Sackville*. Ed. Reginald Sackville-West. London: J. R. Smith, 1859.

Sadowski, Piotr. '"Do it not with poison": Iago and the Killing of Desdemona'. *Shakespeare Quarterly*, 71 (2020): 242–57.

Said, Edward W. *Orientalism*. New York: Pantheon Books, 1978.

Salgado, Gamini, ed. *Cony-Catchers and Bawdy Baskets*. Harmondsworth: Penguin Books, 1972.

Scannell, Paul. *Conflict and Soldiers' Literature in Early Modern Europe: The Reality of War*. London: Bloomsbury, 2015.

Schafer, Roy. 'Cordelia, Lear, and Forgiveness'. *Journal of the American Psychoanalytic Association*, 53 (2005): 389–409.

Schafer, Roy. 'Reply to Madelon Sprengnether'. *Journal of the American Psychoanalytic Association*, 53 (2005): 425–426.

Scofield, Martin. 'Drama, Politics, and the Hero: "Coriolanus", Brecht, and Grass'. *Comparative Drama*, 24 (1990–91): 322–341.

Seneca, *Letters*. Ed. and trans. Arthur Stanley. London: J. N. Dent & Sons, 1940.

Shapiro, James. *1606: Shakespeare and the Year of Lear*. London: Faber and Faber 2015.

Shay, Jonathan. *Achilles in Vietnam: Combat Trauma and the Undoing of Character*. New York: Touchstone, 1995.

Shepard, Alan. *Marlowe's Soldiers: Rhetorics of Masculinity in the Age of the Armada*. (Aldershot and Burlington, VT: Ashgate, 2002).

Shurgot, Michael W. 'Bertram's Scar and Courts of Healing'. *Shakespeare Bulletin*, 37 (2019): 391–407.

Sidney, Sir Philip. *A Defence of Poetry* in *Miscellaneous Prose of Sir Philip Sidney*. Eds. Katherine Duncan-Jones and Jan van Dorsten. Oxford: Clarendon Press, 1973.

Siemon, James. 'Making Ambition Virtue? *Othello*, Small Wars, and Martial Profession'. *Othello: The State of Play*. Ed. Lena Cowen Orlin. London: Bloomsbury, 2014: 177–202.

Simmons, J. L. '*Antony and Cleopatra*: New Heaven, New Earth'. *Shakespeare's Pagan World: The Roman Tragedies*. Charlottesville: University Press of Virginia, 1973.

Singh, Jyotsna. 'The Interventions of History: Narratives of Sexuality'. *The Weyward Sisters: Shakespeare and Feminist Politics*. Eds. Dympna Callaghan et al. Oxford: Blackwell, 1994.

Singh, Jyotsna. *Shakespeare and Postcolonial Theory*. London: Routledge, 2019.

Smith, Bruce. 'The Ethics of Compassion'. *Compassion in Early Modern Literature and Culture*. Eds. Kristine Steenberg and Katherine Ibbett. Cambridge University Press, 2021: 25–43.

Smith, David Livingston. *On Inhumanity: Dehumanization and How to Resist It*. Oxford University Press, 2020.

Smith, Ian. *Black Shakespeare: Reading and Misreading Race*. Cambridge University Press, 2009.

Sohmer, Steve. 'The "Double Time" Crux in *Othello* Solved'. *English Literary Renaissance*, 32 (2002): 214–38.

Somogyi, Nick de. *Shakespeare's Theatre of War*. Aldershot: Ashgate, 1998.

Sprengnether, Madelon. 'Musing on Forgiveness: A Response to Roy Schafer'. *Journal of the American Psychoanalytic Association*, 53 (2005): 389–409.

Stauffer, Donald A. *Shakespeare's World of Images: The Development of his Moral Ideas*. Bloomington: Indiana University Press, 1949.

Stearns, S. J. 'Military Disorder and Martial Law in Early Stuart England'. *Law and Authority in Early Modern England: Essays Presented to Thomas Garden Barnes* Eds. B. Sharp and M. C. Fissel. Newark: University of Delaware Press, 2007: 106–35.

Steenberg, Kristine and Katherine Ibbett, eds. *Compassion in Early Modern Literature and Culture*. Cambridge University Press, 2021.

Strauss, Barry. *The War that Made the Roman Empire*. New York: Simon and Schuster, 2022.

Sutherland, John. *Henry V, War Criminal? & Other Shakespeare Puzzles*. Eds. John Sutherland and Cedric Watts. Oxford University Press, 2000.

Swinden, Patrick. 'Coleridge and Kant'. *Literature and the Philosophy of Intention*. London: Palgrave Macmillan, 1999.

Taunton, Nina. *1590s Drama and Militarism: Portrayals of War in Marlowe, Chapman, and Shakespeare's Henry V.* Burlington: Ashgate, 2001.

Taylor, Gary. 'The War in *King Lear*'. *Shakespeare Survey*, 33 (1980): 27–34.

Taylor, Gary, and Michael Warren, eds. *The Division of the Kingdoms: Shakespeare's Two Versions of 'King Lear'.* Oxford: Clarendon Press, 1983.

Thaler, Alwin. *Shakespeare and Democracy.* Knoxville, Tennessee: The University of Tennessee Press, 1941.

Thaler, Alwin. *Shakespeare and Sir Philip Sidney: The Influence of 'The Defence of Poetry'.* Harvard University Press, 1947.

Thomas, Vivian. *Shakespeare's Roman Worlds.* London: Routledge, 1989.

Thompson, Ayanna, ed. *Colorblind Shakespeare: New Perspectives on Race and Performance.* London: Routledge, 2006.

Thompson, Ayanna. *Passing Strange: Shakespeare, Race, and Contemporary America.* Oxford, 2011.

Thorndike, A. H. 'The Relations of Hamlet to the Contemporary Revenge Play'. *Publications of the Modern Language Association*, 17 (1902): 125–220.

Tolstoy, Leo. *War and Peace.* Trans. Rosemary Edmonds. Harmondsworth: Penguin Classics, 1957.

Trim, David, ed. *The Chivalric Ethos and the Development of Military Professionalism.* Leiden: Brill, 2003.

Turner, Timothy Adrian. *Torture and the Drama of Emergency: Kyd, Marlowe, Shakespeare*, PhD Dissertation, The University of Texas at Austin, 2010.

Tutu, Desmond Mpilo. *No Future Without Forgiveness.* New York: Doubleday, 1997.

Tylee, Claire M. 'The Text of Cressida and Every Ticklish Reader: *Troilus and Cressida Act Four Scene 5*'. *Atlantis*, 11 (1989): 53–69.

Ullman, Harlan K. and James P. Wade. *Shock and Awe: Achieving Rapid Dominance.* Washington: National Defense University, 1996.

Virgil. *Aeneid.* Trans. John Dryden (online).

Waller, Garry, ed. *All's Well That Ends Well*: New Critical Essays. New York: Routledge, 2007.

Watt, Timothy Irish. 'The authorship of *The Raigne of Edward III*'. Eds. Hugh Craig and Arthur F. Kinney. *Shakespeare, Computers, and the Mystery of Authorship.* Cambridge University Press, 2009: 116–33.

Weil, Simone (trans. Mary McCarthy). *The Iliad*, or the Poem of Force. *Chicago Review*, 18 (1965).

West, Michael. 'Spenser's Art of War: Chivalric Allegory, Military Technology, and the Elizabethan Mock-Heroic Sensibility'. *Renaissance Quarterly*, 41 (1988): 654–704.

Whalen, Patrick. 'A Hell of One's Own': Combat Trauma in Dante's *Inferno*'. *War, Literature and the Arts*, 31 (2019): 1–10.

White, R. S. 'The Cultural Impact of the Massacre of St Bartholomew's Day in *Early Modern Civil Discourses*'. Ed. Jennifer Richards. Palgrave, 2003: 183–99.

White, R. S. *Innocent Victims.* London: Athlone Press, 1986.

White, R. S. '*King Lear* and Philosophical Anarchism'. *English*, xxxvii (1988): 181–200.

White, R. S. 'Making Something out of "Nothing"'. *Shakespeare Survey*, 66 (2013): 232–45, 236–7.

White, R. S. *Pacifism and English Literature: Minstrels of Peace*. London: Palgrave, 2008.

White, R. S. 'Pacifist Voices in Shakespeare'. *Parergon: Journal of the Australian and New Zealand Association for Medieval and Early Modern Studies*, 17 (1999): 135–62.

Wiggins, Martin. 'War'. *The Oxford Companion to Shakespeare*. 2nd ed. Eds. Michael Dobson, Stanley Wells, Will Sharpe, Erin Sullivan. Online version. Oxford University Press, 2015.

Wilcher, Robert. 'Antony and Cleopatra and Genre Criticism'. *Antony and Cleopatra: Theory in Practice*. Ed. Nigel Wood. Buckingham: Open University Press, 1996: 92–124.

Wilcox, H. 'Drums and Roses? The Tragicomedy of War in *All's Well That Ends Well.' Shakespeare and War*. Eds. R. King and P. J. C. M. Franssen. London: Palgrave Macmillan, 2008: 84–95.

Willett, John, ed. and transl. *Brecht on Theatre: The Development of an Aesthetic*. New York: Hill and Wang, 1964: 252–65.

Williams, John. *Augustus*. New York: Viking, 1972.

Wolf, William D. '"New Heaven, New Earth": The Escape from Mutability in *Antony and Cleopatra*'. *Shakespeare Quarterly*, 33 (1982): 328–35.

Wolfe, Jessica. 'Spenser, Homer, and the Mythography of Strife'. *Renaissance Quarterly*, 58 (2005): 1220–1288.

Woodbridge, Linda. *English Revenge Drama: Money, Resistance, Equality*. Cambridge University Press, 2010.

Woodcock, Matthew. '"their eyes more attentive to the show": Spectacle, Pageantry and the Structure of *All is True (Henry VIII)*'. *Shakespeare*, 7 (2011): 1–15.

Wright, Thomas. *The Passions of the Mind in General*. London, 1604.

Wymer, Roland. *Suicide and Despair in the Jacobean Drama*. Brighton: The Harvester Press, 1986.

Yeager, R. F. 'Pax Poetica: On the Pacifism of Chaucer and Gower'. *Studies in the Age of Chaucer 9* (1987): 97–121.

Yoder, J. H. *Nevertheless: Varieties of Religious Pacifism*. Scottsdale, PA: Herald Press, 1992.

Index

Note: 'n' indicates footnotes.